On Parchment

ON PARCHMENT

Animals, Archives, and the Making of Culture
from Herodotus to the Digital Age

BRUCE HOLSINGER

Yale UNIVERSITY PRESS | NEW HAVEN & LONDON

Published with assistance from the Ronald and Betty Miller Turner Publication Fund.

Yale University Press books may be purchased in quantity for educational, business, or promotional use. For information, please email sales.press@yale.edu (U.S. office) or sales@yaleup.co.uk (U.K. office).

Designed by Amber Morena.
Set in Adobe Jenson Pro type by Motto Publishing Services.
Printed in China.

Library of Congress Control Number: 2022934634
ISBN 978-0-300-26021-2 (hardcover : alk. paper)

A catalogue record for this book is available from the British Library.
This paper meets the requirements of ANSI/NISO z39.48-1992 (Permanence of Paper).
10 9 8 7 6 5 4 3 2 1

For my students

CONTENTS

Part III. The Medium and Modernity

A NOTE ON
Texts, Translations, and Terminology

The fields of book history, codicology, and diplomatics rely on an array of discipline-specific terminologies that can be confusing to the non-specialist. This holds true even for a seemingly straightforward term such as parchment (Lat. *pergamena*, Fr. *parchemin*, Hebr. *kelaf, dukhsustos, gevil*, Arab. *raqq, riqq, jild*), which refers to animal skin processed in a particular way to serve as a support for script, print, or image, though some of what passes for more ancient parchment is likely tanned leather. Parchment is often conflated with vellum, which often refers more narrowly to the processed skins of calves (from Lat. *vitulinum*, Fr. *vélin*, hence veal). Here I follow modern bibliographical practice in distinguishing the terms, though some early sources use them interchangeably—and in many writings from outside Western European or Christian contexts, the distinction is largely meaningless. More generally I have tried to keep bibliographic argot to a minimum, defining certain terms where relevant while respecting the conventions of the particular fields this study traverses. A book that draws from sources in over twenty languages across many centuries has required extensive consultation with specialists, always with an eye for philological precision in the transliteration and contextualization of key words from Greek, Arabic, Latin, Coptic, Hebrew, Aramaic, Irish, Persian, and other languages. I have generally cited existing translations where available, in some cases with silent emendations; for the most part I have embedded the originals for key phrases and terms within the translated passages.

On Parchment

PROLOGUE

For well over a thousand years, the societies of the Euro-Mediterranean world transmitted and preserved much of their written cultures on the skins of animals. A good part of what we will ever know about the premodern era we know because people wrote things down and saved them on and between the hides of slaughtered beasts. Cows and calves, rams, ewes, and lambs, camels, hyenas, deer and fawns, goats and gazelles and their kids, pigs, donkeys and horses, seals and walruses, occasionally fish and birds, and perhaps squirrels, rabbits, even cats and dogs on occasion were rendered by human animals into scrolls and codices, charters and wills, Talmuds and treatises, Qur'āns and cartularies, leases and *mezuzot*, amulets and bindings and booklets.

Other mediums for the written word were in use during this epoch, of course. Students, scholars, and merchants might record notes or transactions on wax tablets easily effaced and reused, while stone, ivory, brass, wood and bark, bone, lead sheets and gold served as popular surfaces for inscriptions of devotion and remembrance.[1] In much of the Islamic world, paper emerged as the preferred scribal medium by the late tenth century; the papal chancery still maintained certain records on papyrus until the beginning of the eleventh.[2] Nevertheless, between about the middle of the fourth century and the end of the fifteenth, between the age of St. Augustine and the advent of the Reformation, cultures of writing in this vast part of the world relied fundamentally on the rendered flesh of beasts.

Only a small fraction of this animal archive has endured the ravages of time, deliberate destruction, and disaster. Even so, the extant membrane record consists of some one to three billion discrete pieces of animal skin that together make up a large part of the surviving written inheritance of the premodern world. Medieval monks have been credited more than once with "saving civilization"—that is, with maintaining the legacy of ancient cultures through their labors of transcription and preservation.[3] Yet were it not for the countless beasts whose hides served these and other scribes and illuminators over many centuries, we might now possess only fragments of ancient written culture: the histories of Herodotus, the plays of Aristophanes and Sophocles, the epics of Homer and Virgil, the poetry of Ovid and Horace, the rhetorical and political treatises of Cicero and Marcus Aurelius, most books of the Hebrew Bible and the Christian New Testament, and, somewhat later, the Qur'ān. On whatever mediums they were first written down and remembered, the earliest surviving complete or fullest copies of nearly all these ancient writings survive on skin.[4] These membranes form but a small part of a boundless animal archive spanning three and a half millennia, from the leather rolls of Middle Kingdom Egypt to the rubles printed on walrus parchment by the Russian-America Company in the nineteenth century, from the book trade in medieval Ethiopia to the modern Acts of Parliament in the United Kingdom, written or printed on creamy vellum until a few short years ago.[5] The preservation, transcription, study, and, most recently, digitization of the animal archive have together yielded one of the great surviving records of human civilization: a material history both ecumenical and pancultural, reaching across creeds, continents, empires, and many languages, and all derived from the animals who roamed and grazed among the human creatures who consumed their flesh, boiled their bones, wore their hides, and wrote and painted and notated music on their skins.

Parchment also forms a biological record, one of immense scope and astounding variety. Every surviving piece of it is a specimen of flesh, and each specimen carries biomolecular and chemical data inherent to the structure of the membrane medium. In the course of researching and writing this book, I have collaborated with scientists, conservators, and humanities scholars in investigating the molecular content of parchment, sampling the recto of a folio, the dorse of a scroll. As this process has shown us, we are only beginning to appreciate the vast biotic record the parchment inheritance represents: countless specimens of collagen, DNA, and other proteins and molecules recoverable through non-destructive sampling protocols and ever more refined laboratory techniques just now coming on line (and perhaps superseded even by the time these words appear in print). The biomolecular data latent in the animal archive has remained largely untapped. Participating in its collection and interpretation has led me to a jarring shift of perspective on what exactly parchment *is*: its quiddity or essence, as philosophers might say.

The scientific and cultural dimensions of the parchment record do not always go hand in hand, though I have thought often about the interplay of theology and genetics, of molecules and meaning as I have approached the questions pursued in this book. As a creaturely medium invested with great imaginative energy, parchment invites speculation about the deep interconnections among nature and culture, human and animal, life and death, past and present, even as it complicates and fuses such categories at every turn. For the premodern world, parchment was a product of pastoral husbandry and urban economies, a commodity of subtle craftsmanship and ingenuity, a material of ubiquitous practical usage, a frequent object of poetic and devotional contemplation: both a measure and an agent of environmental, evolutionary, and social change.

Parchment must also be understood as an immense record of human-animal relations over millennia of civilization, though not in ways always friendly to contemporary modes of ethical reflection on the subject.[6] Here is Donna Haraway: "species of all kinds, living and not, are consequent on a subject- and object-shaping dance of encounters."[7] One such encounter, famously narrated by Jacques Derrida, occurs between the philosopher and his cat.[8] Upon stepping from the shower, Derrida finds his cat staring at his dripping body. The animal's gaze embarrasses while awakening the philosopher to a vital recognition: that the history of philosophy has failed to address the implications of the unknowable creaturely gaze, its challenges to the boundaries that Western intellectual traditions have established between the animal and human. The encounter between his own humanity and the inscrutable experience of one particular cat leads Derrida to ponder the quandaries of self-definition and subjectivity "across the abyss of the human/animal divide."[9]

Yet unlike Derrida's cat, who challenges the naked philosopher with a stare of nonhuman indifference, the parchment record confronts us with the crushing weight of all-too-human tradition, and speaks back to us mutely, in our own words. For with some occasional and short-lived exceptions, no other world cultures have deployed animals to nearly the same extent in making written records and preserving collective memory. Parchment embodies humanity's enduring and continuing dominion over the animal world. The parchment inheritance, in its immensity, longevity, and variety, might be understood as the historical and archival incarnation of this dominion, as well as a vast environmental record of its implications and effects. Perhaps the troubled intellectual legacy of the human-animal relation lies not only in our enduring philosophical entanglements with animals, but also in the peculiar and deep-seated reliance of this legacy on their inscribed physical remains.

This is not to suggest that the parchment epoch understood its animal medium in purely instrumental terms, any more than it denied agency and even emotion to the creatures whose skins made up much of its textual culture. Animals were never "simply instrumental to human economies" in the Middle Ages, Jamie Kreiner writes; rather, "they were capable of interfering with the physical and social environments through which they moved and were moved."[10] Membrane books and documents will often retain the kinetic and emotional force of the animals from which they were rendered and made, just as they preserve the shapes, fibers, odors, and blemishes of their donors' hides. In this spirit, one of my purposes here is to recover some of the many ways that the written cultures of the past conceived of themselves through those creatures whose skins would carry them into the future and to account for the wide range of reactions and emotions this awareness entailed: often indifference, yes, but also curiosity, disgust, obsession, reverence, compassion, love. The history of parchment is a diverse history of bookish emotion.

Recovering this history has led to me a wide range of sources (some relatively obscure, some canonical) from over thirty-odd centuries and across diverse genres, cultural traditions, religious creeds, and many languages. A founding narrative of Irish culture. The rabbinical disputations in the Talmud (can tefillin be written on the feather-pocked skin of a bird? on the stinky skin of a fish?). A Persian legend about a sacred text written on twelve thousand ox hides—only to be burned in its entirety by Alexander the Great. A medieval manual of ritual magic that prescribes writing a love spell on parchment made from the skin of a dog in heat. Passages from Dante's *Divine Comedy* reveal an allegorical poet's literalist fascination with the membrane page (marbled like a cut of beef), while a provocative story from Boccaccio's *Decameron* glimpses the magical properties of uterine vellum. St. Augustine of Hippo, the North African bishop, thought in arresting ways about the implications of animal skin as an emergent medium of writing. The plays of William Shakespeare imagine parchment as a totemic relay between life and death, brimming with potential both comic and tragic, political and personal. Leonora Carrington's *Samhain Skin* (1975) incarnates a late-Surrealist scene of a Celtic Harvest festival (complete with garlic-headed hybrids) on a full sheet of untrimmed vellum.

I have also drawn on recent archaeological discoveries that suggest the practice of writing on animal skin was much more widespread in the ancient epoch than we have tended to assume. If papyrus represented a dominant medium for the transmission of writing from pharaonic Egypt through the late Roman Empire, parchment had its own imaginative and material roles to play in the civilizations of the pre-Christian world.[11] Likewise, parchment coexisted with the various forms of paper manufactured at certain times and places throughout the medieval and early modern eras—before inevitably giving way to the voluminous commodity generated by the paper mills of the industrial age. The relationship between the mediums in their various forms is complex and ever changing from century to century, region to region. Adding to the confusion are terminological idiosyncrasies within particular textual communities and localities. In his *Sieta Partidas* (ca. 1270), for example, Alfonso X, king of Castile and León, legislated a distinction between those documents rendered from *pergamina de cuero* (parchment of leather) and those made of *pergamina de paño* (parchment of cloth), designating each material for specific administrative and diplomatic purposes.[12]

We might think of the long histories of papyrus, paper, and parchment as great rivers flowing in tandem, diverging for centuries at a time with the ebbs and flows of technology, while also converging in certain circumstances as textual culture allowed: among early Christian communities that transmitted codices made of papyrus or parchment alike; in royal and civic bureaucracies that discriminated among various written mediums for specific administrative needs; in medieval manuscripts that sometimes intersperse paper and parchment bifolia within a single book block; and in the archival practices of states and principalities that preserved certain records on paper made of plant or cloth and others on skin.[13] The modern world creates a depthless ocean of paper, reducing parchment to a few currents, though strong ones at times, with their own direction and pull.

In fact, parchment has proven more resilient than even its ancient proponents could have foreseen, due in part to the interplay of its physical durability and its imaginative power. My aim in what follows is to defamiliarize the animal medium in ways that allow us to examine it both up close and from a distance, and thus to avoid easy generalizations about historical conceptions of parchment that could be quite diverse in their moral, theological, and practical resonance. Many commentators outside the Christian tradition eschew the sorts of anthropocentric allegories of "body as book" that have tended to dominate the discussion of parchment's symbolic significance. Such commonplace analogies look very different when read alongside the vast parchment imaginings in the Talmud, or the more practical musings of the great traveler Abū ʿUthmān ʿAmr ibn Baḥr al-Jāḥiẓ, a ninth-century parchment hater and bibliophile who complained in eloquent detail about the weight, inconvenience, and general nastiness of the animal medium. Parchment is fetid and bulgy, al-Jāḥiẓ claimed, so heavy it breaks the backs of camels. Yet even while inveighing against the use of membrane, his writings reveal the medium's centrality to the textual culture of the Mediterranean world he and his works traversed.

A century later, Ibn al-Nadīm (ca. 935–990), a scholar, bookseller, and cataloguer working in Baghdad, imagines in his *Kitāb al-Fihrist* a history of global written culture from the beginning of the world through his own time. "It is said that first of all Adam wrote on clay," al-Nadīm avows, then the people of the earth turned to "copper and stone for the sake of durability. This was before the Flood." Afterward they wrote on wood, on leaves, on bark. Later humans "tanned hides upon which people wrote," and finally the nations of the earth each took up their own modes of written practice:

The Greeks write on white silk, parchment, and other things, as well as on Egyptian scrolls and *al-fulḥān*, which is the skin of wild asses. The Persians used to write on the skins of water buffaloes, cows, and sheep. The Arabs write on the shoulder blades of the camel and on *likḥāf*, which are thin white stones, and on *'uṣb* or palm stems; the Chinese on Chinese paper made of *ḥashish*, which is the most important product of the land; the Indians on brass and stone, also on white silk. Then there is the Khurāsānī paper made of flax . . . It is stated that craftsmen from China made it in Khurāsān like the form of Chinese paper. Its types are the Sulaymānī, the Talḥī, the Nūḥī, the Fir'awnī, the Ja'farī, and the Ṭāhirī. For a number of years the people of Baghdād wrote on erased sheets. The registers spoiled at the time of Muhammad ibn Zubaydah were parchments, which after being erased were once more written upon.[14]

Al-Nadīm's insider's account limns a bookish world of parchment and paper of every variety and texture, inscribed in every language and crafted of plant, skin, bone, stone, metal, silk. Yet persisting through it all are the myriad animal bodies rendered and inscribed, presented in exuberant zoological detail—the skins of asses, the hides of water buffaloes, cows, and sheep, the shoulder blades of camels, parchment palimpsests erased and rewritten with the full register of human culture.

Nowhere in his account of the global book trade does al-Nadīm evoke the category of sacrifice, which plays an intriguing if inconsistent role in the long history of parchment. For an urban bookseller, sheets of parchment will bear little or no ritual significance, and sacrifice is hardly the appropriate term for the workaday renderings that transform beast into book. Yet the idiom of sacrifice plays a central role in more theological strains of parchment thought, whether the beast riddling of its own sacrifice to make a holy book, or the ram slaughtered in lieu of Isaac whose skin becomes the pages of a Kabbalistic text. Hints of human sacrifice characterize the twisted history of anthropodermic bibliopegy (the making of books from human skin), though more coldly instrumental rhetorics distinguish this modern practice from premodern accounts of the human book. In what follows, I evoke the term sacrifice with some circumspection, and only when the particular context under discussion calls for its usage.

This holds less true for *archive*, a term that appears in my subtitle as convenient shorthand for diverse assemblages of membrane texts in many forms (codices, rolls, charters, maps, and so on). Literary scholars tend to use the terms archive and library interchangeably, despite the important technical and historical distinctions between these institutions of preservation.[15] In what follows, *archive* often refers narrowly to official institutional record repositories: county or parish records offices, say, or the archives of Parliament. At the same time, I hope the term retains its etymological associations as a resonant keyword for a range of simultaneously documentary and creaturely phenomena. As Sarah Novacich has shown, theologians and encyclopedists of the Middle Ages often figured Noah's ark [*arca noe*] as a kind of primordial *arca*, a term that denotes a box or container holding documents or records (as in the Ark of the Covenant). Noah was thus the first great archivist, the beasts populating his ark "the only record of a vanishing world."[16] Likewise, the panoply of animals rendered into parchment over the millennia live on in thousands of libraries and archives scattered across the earth, forming one great archive from which it is our continuing privilege to learn.

I wrote *On Parchment* in part as an attempt to explore my own enduring enchantment with a medium I have come to know through a variety of experiences over many years: as a student, seeing, touching, and studying medieval manuscripts for the first time; as a literary scholar, regularly consulting medieval books and documents as part of my research; as an occasional editor, transcribing and annotating texts in medieval Latin and Middle English from libraries in France and England; as a teacher, introducing the wonders of medieval manuscripts over many years to my students; and as a novelist attuned to the aesthetic charge of parchment in the work of poets, fiction writers, and visual artists past and present. In the course of writing this book, I have visited workshops and tanneries in New York and Morocco and practiced rudimentary parchment making at the hands of contemporary adepts of the craft. I have spent time in a bioarchaeology lab and sent samples there for proteomic extraction and analysis. I have interviewed painters and sculptors who work daily with parchment and vellum in their workshops and ateliers, and I have collaborated with a large group of scientists, archivists, conservators, and humanities scholars in researching the microbiology of the parchment record. The book thus has several readerships in mind, including those who have never touched, read from, seen, or smelled a parchment book or document in the flesh (or hair). At the same time, I hope what follows will contribute to ongoing discussions across a number of fields about the history and archaeology of the book, about human-animal relations, about emerging alliances among the humanities and the experimental sciences, and about the nature and disposition of the parchment record in an increasingly digital age.

A few words about the Common Era, a convenient index of the book's scale and scope. The phrase, long in use as an antisectarian moniker for the span of centuries since the reign of Augustus and the life of Jesus Christ, embraces an equally ecumenical history of text technologies, from the Mediterranean papyrus trade to the digital media of late capitalism. The Common Era also marks a rough beginning as well as an ever-receding terminus of the parchment epoch. The ancient world made selective use of animal skins for the transmission and preservation of writing, with scattered survivals dating all the way back to pharaonic Egypt, seventeen centuries before the Common Era. (Chapter 7 takes up this history and comments on some of its more intriguing byways.) Yet only in the two or three centuries surrounding the turn of the first millennium did membrane assume a formative role as an instrument of deliberate cultural self-fashioning, perhaps beginning with Jewish textual communities late in the Second Temple period. We get a glimpse of this process in the *Letter of Aristeas* (ca. 140–60 BCE), a pseudepigraphal work written in the voice of a pagan witness to the spread of the Jewish faith. At one point in the document, the narrator relates the arrival of a delegation from Palestine for an audience with Demetrius, the king of Egypt, at Alexandria. With them they bear a lavish gift: the Hebrew Pentateuch translated into Greek, written on rolls of parchment with their membranes artfully conjoined:

> And they came with the gifts that had been sent and the remarkable parchments [*diaphorois diphtherais*] on which the legislation had been written in golden writing in Judean characters, the parchment being worked amazingly and the common joins constructed to be imperceptible. When the king saw the men, he inquired about the books. And when they uncovered them rolled up and they unrolled the parchments, pausing for a long time and prostrating himself about seven times, the king said, "I thank you, O Men, and even more the one who sent you, but mostly the God whose utterances these are."[17]

Notable here is the aesthetic reverence accorded to the parchment medium, a secular counterpart to the more properly religious veneration of the Word of God inscribed upon the skins. The word *diphtherai* appears three times in the brief account, which delights in the lavish rolls of skin bearing the words of scripture.

The account above was written sometime in the second century BCE in Alexandria, on the African coast of the Mediterranean. Hundreds of miles to the east, along the shores of an inland sea, other scribal cultures were already at work making and copying the assemblages of texts that came to be known as the Dead Sea Scrolls, the vast majority of which consist of animal skin. These are but a few of the early textual communities that would render, craft, inscribe, and preserve the emerging parchment record, a capacious creaturely tapestry woven of Jewish and Christian scrolls, the first membrane codices, the legal parchments of Dura-

Europos documenting imperial loans and the sale of enslaved persons, the earliest copies of the written Qur'ān.

Parchment has remained in continuous use from well before the dawn of the Common Era through our own moment, a vast inheritance of culture incarnate. The deep history of parchment is an unending cycle of animal death, human craft, and cultural remembrance: the chronicle of a civilization.

PART I

>+ +<

The Medium and Its Making

→✦ ←

CHAPTER ONE

THE BOOK OF THE DUN COW

Asaint, a beast, a book.

Their story begins with an Irish legend found in the Book of Lismore, compiled in the late fifteenth century and commissioned by Fínghin Mac Carthaigh Riabhach, who was Prince of Carbery until his death in 1505. The manuscript includes, among other texts, an early life of St. Ciarán, a sixth-century saint and one of the Twelve Apostles of Ireland.[1] In 544 Ciarán founded the abbey of Clonmacnoise, which became a center of learning and worship despite his death during its initial construction.[2]

St. Ciarán, like many saints, had a way with animals.[3] He subdued a hound with his voice. He trained a fox to carry his psalter (though the fox later ate the book). He convinced a stag to allow him to use its antlers as a book stand. Ciarán even brought a calf back to life after its killing by a wolf.

When it came time for Ciarán to leave his home for schooling, he selected a cow from the herd. The animal went with him to Clonard, site of a monastery where Ciarán received his first formal education. There the cow's milk sustained the entire monastery along with the households and guests of the institution's visitors. After some years at Clonard, and with his schooling complete, Ciarán departed the monastery to begin his life of evangelizing. He left his beloved dun cow behind, though not without regret. "Ciarán later said besides, that though a multitude would be helped by her milk, there would be more to whom her hide would give help."[4] The cow's skin would remain a sacred relic at Clonmacnoise long after Ciarán's death. As it was said, if you were lucky enough to die while resting on the cow's hide, you were promised eternal life.

The story doesn't end there. Ciarán and his dun cow reappear in a text known as the *Tromdámh Guaire*, also collected in the Book of Lismore. This Middle Irish work, set in the seventh century, gives an account of a bard and his apostles setting

Figure 1.1.
A folio from *Lebor na hUidhre* (Book of the Dun Cow). Abbey of Clonmacnoise, before 1106. Dublin, Royal Irish Academy Ms. 23 E 25, p. 105.

out on a quest to find the *Táin Bó Cúailnge*, the great epic narrative of Ireland. The *Táin* had been lost, and the mission of this *tromdámh* (or company) is to recover it, record it, and thereby preserve it for posterity. After a series of adventures and mishaps, the *tromdámh* encounters Fergus mac Roich, an exiled former king of Ulster who also appears in the *Táin*, where he is killed by a jealous rival while swimming in a lake. In the *Tromdámh Guaire*, the bard's son sings over the burial place of Fergus and summons his ghost. Fergus, it turns out, knows the *Táin* like no one else. Rising up from the grave, Fergus stands before the company and intones the entire epic from memory.

But how to preserve it? The mission needs both a scribe and a means of physical preservation. So, another figure rises from the dead: none other than St. Ciarán of Clonmacnoise. And it is St. Ciarán who writes down the text of the *Táin Bó Cúailnge* as Fergus recites it—"and he wrote it down on the hide of the dun cow [*for seichid na hUidhre*]."[5]

St. Ciarán's miraculous cow provides the very parchment folios on which the text of the *Táin* is written. The book that Ciarán creates from his cow's hide will be known ever afterward as the *Lebor na hUidhre*, or Book of the Dun Cow. This same manuscript, according to legend, survives today as Royal Irish Academy MS 23 E 25—actually a twelfth-century copy of a much earlier original (see fig. 1.1). The Book of the Dun Cow is on occasional display at the Royal Irish Academy in Dublin, its sixty-seven time-darkened membrane folios all that survive of what was clearly a much larger codex rendered and compiled from the skins of multiple beasts.[6]

Like many early Irish legends, the story of St. Ciarán and his dun cow is a tangled and marvelous tale, threading through multiple writings and several manuscripts, involving numerous characters, and entailing a series of temporal leaps that bring its players together across several centuries of mythic Irish history. The story gives us a haunting founding legend for the greatest of early Irish texts, the *Táin*, as well as an apocryphal creaturely origin for one of the most important early Irish manuscripts, the *Lebor na hUidhre*. The desire that motivates the story and its characters, to fix the *Táin* in writing, entails resurrecting a long-dead saint and uniting him with a vital relic of his earthly life. The oral and the written, the human and the nonhuman, the otherworldly and the mundane: all converge here to lend an emotional immediacy to this bookish account of a saintly man and a special animal.

Yet this story is no parable for the larger ethical entailments of parchment. The relationship of man to animal and then to book imagined here is remarkable above all for its exceptionalism: the identification and celebration of a particular animal whose hide becomes the pages of a specific book. Ciarán's dun cow died a natural death at Clonmacnoise, and as any parchment maker will tell you, the hide of an old cow can make for poor product. If you're reading these legends from the folios of the Book of Lismore or, for that matter, from the Book of the Dun Cow, you are looking at and touching a manuscript made from the skins of multiple unloved beasts who probably died young and by slaughter, stillbirth, or disease, held no special place in the lives of their flayers or eaters, and yet served a crucial role in the survival of Irish literary tradition. The story of Ciarán and his dun cow is a story of mutuality, affection, and cultural survival; the history of parchment is a *longue durée* of dominion and utility.

This is the double life of parchment, defined both by the stark reality of its production from the flesh of beasts and by its intimate connection to human memory and tradition.

In parchment cultures, the animal is rarely simply the object of thought or representation but makes up the material substance of the written object—literature, law, theology, science. Writing in such cultures bears an immanent relation to the animal that modern paper and digital cultures have largely lost. Much of premodern writing is, in the most doggedly literal sense, billions of stains on animal parts. The insatiable human need for writable skin entailed the deaths of innumerable creatures and the transformation of their hides into the membrane sheets that formed the substrate and substance of the written record.

On some level these are truisms of book history, clear on a moment's reflection to anyone glancingly familiar with manuscript culture, which shares its dependence on animal hide with the history of the book more broadly construed. Books, parchment and paper alike, have been covered with tanned, tawed, boiled, or limed hides for centuries.[7] Walk through the stacks of any respectable research library and you will pass by many thousands of leather-bound volumes from the nineteenth and twentieth centuries, great bibliographic assemblages of pigskin and cowhide. "Millions of leather bindings in public and private libraries of this country are in various stages of decay," as an American report on the preservation of leather bookbindings put it in 1933.[8] The vast raw materials used over the course of book history are of no more intrinsic significance than those used over the course of shoe history.

Like the leather used for footwear and saddlery, moreover, membrane codices, scrolls, charters, and so on were frequently repurposed or discarded, sometimes in repositories designed for non-destructive preservation. Some of the earliest extant copies of the Qur'ān survive as forty-thousand-odd fragments of parchment discovered in the walls of a Yemeni mosque and dating back as far as the seventh century.[9] Medieval nuns would sometimes sew scraps of old parchment books into the linings and cuffs of their habits and dresses, recycling the written medium as a way to maintain folds and stiffen seams.[10] Incunables and later printed books were frequently rebound in parchment leaves repurposed from medieval manuscripts, membrane codices and records destroyed in the process of saving and strengthening their paper successors.[11] This was a practice bemoaned by our forebears even in the early modern period itself. As Ambrosio de Morales lamented of the monks of San Bernardo de Carracedo, "They had many books and have given them away for their old parchments [*pergamino viejo*]."[12] John Bale, the English bishop and antiquarian, famously beomoaned "the library books of monasteries . . . reserved by the purchases of those houses, to serve their jakes, to scour their candlesticks, and to rub their boots; some were sold to grocers, ropesellers, and some sent over the sea to the bookbinders, not in small number, but at times whole ships full. A merchant bought two noble libraries for 40s."[13] Parchment leaves employed as toilet paper, or pliable skin suitable for the cleaning of a shoe.

No surprise that writers will sometimes describe their preferred medium as so much waste product. Suspect papal bulls could be derided as "the skins of wethers blackened with ink and weighted with a little lump of lead," imputing their worthlessness to their creaturely materialism.[14] St. Bernard of Clairvaux, in a mournful passage on memory in one of his conversion sermons, wants to blot out the impurities of his earthly life through analogy with the whitening of parchment: "The dark ink has drenched my cheap, flimsy parchment (*membrana vilis et tenuis*): by what technique can I blot it out? It has not only stained the surface, it has soaked into the whole thing. It is useless for me to attempt to rub it out: the skin will be torn before the wretched characters have been effaced."[15] Such sentiments about parchment's inconsequence are shared by a host of jurists who denigrate membrane instruments as "mere sheepskin," a phrase with a deep lineage in legal thinking down through the modern era. "Only a blank parchment, only a white lambskin," wrote John Caven in 1899 about the original U.S. Declaration of Independence, "yet it was a sacred thing to patriot millions dead . . . Only a blank parchment, only a white lambskin, yet the grandest page the muse of history has ever read or written, or ever will."[16]

Despite its animal materiality, parchment can bear a mystical, even transcendent significance for its users, as in the many medieval allegories of the body of Christ as a parchment, his wounded flesh the flayed skin of a slaughtered beast; or in Jewish traditions such as the wearing of tefillin, pieces of parchment inscribed with Torah verses and worn bound to the arm and head with straps of ritually pure leather; or in certain medieval manuals of ritual magic that call for parchment to be worn next to the skin. "If you have a slave who is slow to learn Arabic," advises a Syriac mantle ode, "write these two verses on a piece of gazelle parchment, hang it on his arm, and he will speak Arabic in no time."[17] In a fourteenth-century fresco from the Church of St. George in Oberzell, four demons stretch out a full-hide parchment while a fifth devil inscribes the same skin with a stern warning about the fate

Figure 1.2. Demons stretching and writing on an untrimmed parchment, from a fourteenth-century fresco in the Church of St. George in Oberzell, Reichenau, north side of nave.

of the foolish and the blabbering on Judgment Day (fig. 1.2).[18] And in a Latin necromancer's manual composed in the fifteenth century, a spell requires the use of parchment rendered from a quite particular kind of animal at a certain stage of life:

> When you wish to have the love of whatever woman you wish, whether she is near or far, whether noble or common, on whatever day or night you wish, whether for the furtherance of friendship or to its hindrance, first you must have a totally white dove and a parchment made from a female dog that is in heat [*cartam factam de cane femina*

dum est in amore], from whom it is most easily to be had. And you should know that this kind of parchment is most powerful for gaining the love of a woman.[19]

Interspecies dominion and gendered coercion go hand in hand, with a dog's inscribed skin as their mutual instrument. On the one hand, impurity, lowliness, and waste; on the other, reverence, transformation, miracle, the power over life and love, death and judgment. The phenomenon of parchment can thus seem both deflatingly banal and unendingly fascinating.

A similar disparity characterizes the ethical valence of this boundless archive. Is the animality of parchment an uncomplicated fact of book production that medievalists learn on their first day of paleography, or is it a harbinger of that "eternal Treblinka" that Isaac Bashevis Singer found in the unending cycle of mass animal slaughter in the modern world?[20] Is parchment simply a useful technology in a civilization that had yet to adapt paper on a wide scale (as the Chinese had by the second century and a medium in regular use throughout the Islamic world by the eleventh), or is it an unremarked part of a long history of interspecies dominion? Do we encounter the parchment inheritance with the poet's moral shudder or the bibliographer's indifferent shrug—or with the saint's enduring intimacy with one beast, one fantastical book?

I pose these questions in a modern idiom shaped in part by a well-developed philosophical and political discourse on animals and ethics elaborated over the last thirty years. Words like "slaughter" and "butchery" carry a particular charge in our time, resonant as they are with recent work on agribusiness such as Timothy Pachirat's *Every Twelve Seconds*, David Kirby's *Animal Factory*, and Gale Eisnitz's *Slaughterhouse*, on the politics and ethics of mass animal slaughter and the global trade in meat. The parchment micro-industries of the premodern world operated on much smaller economies of scale, of course. The butchers, skinners, and parchmenters involved in the production of parchment and vellum bear only a distant resemblance to the belly rippers, bung stuffers, and ear cutters working on the (dis) assembly lines of modern slaughterhouses, where the specific practices of killing, flaying, butchering, and packaging are inseparable from the cold efficiencies of modern industrialization. Timothy Pachirat, who worked undercover in a Nebraska slaughterhouse while writing his book on the beef industry, argues for making the often invisible facts of animal suffering, death, and dismemberment a manifest part of how we comprehend the wider cultures that consume and use their flesh. In the face of federal and state laws that make it illegal to record the interior workings of slaughterhouses, Pachirat calls for a "politics of sight" aimed at "making visible a massive, routinized killing that many would prefer to keep hidden."[21] Such a politics needs modification for the study of premodern cultures, which (with some important exceptions) only rarely questioned the ethics of killing animals, almost never in the language of rights, and had few qualms about the open display of animal slaughter.[22] Killing could take place on quite large scales, as during slaughters at certain times of the year: for Christians, the "blood-months" regulated by the Julian calendar; for Jewish communities, the ritual cycles of killing and butchering governed by kashrut.[23] Though cities would eventually regulate the meat and hide trades, pushing them out to less populated areas to avoid excessive flows of blood and offal in streets and rivers, such crafts were practiced more openly and regarded less squeamishly than in most of the modern developed world.[24]

Nevertheless, writing a book about what is, after all, a massive collective repository of animal skin has meant grappling with the fibrous, gristly signs of animal death at every turn. The facts of butchery and flaying are simply there on the membrane folio and charter—or rather, they *are* the folio and charter, staring back at human readers as a constant if most often unheeded reminder of the deep and enduring dominion of one species over others. This is an archaeological as much as an ethical observation, and it helps to clarify the distinctiveness of parchment in relation to other commodities rendered from animal bodies, past and present. The function of meat is nutritional and thus ephemeral, rendered to be consumed, digested, excreted, forgotten. Likewise, the purposes of leather goods (shoes, saddlery and tack, belts, and so on) are, for the most part, transitory and utilitarian, serving everyday human needs without regard for their long-term durability (one notable exception is bookbindings, an exception that helps prove the point I am trying to make).[25] The function of parchment is eternal, or at least often imagined as such: the point of writing something down on lime-bathed and sun-dried and blade-scraped animal skin is to preserve it indefinitely, perhaps forever—unlike, say, Old Russian birchbark letters, which were "meant to be ephemeral, meant for the business of the day, and to be discarded afterwards."[26]

One of the purposes of parchment, by contrast, is to endure; its mission, which its countless creaturely donors were never asked to accept, is to outlast us, as individuals and even as cultures. Past writers who thought most deeply about the medium recognized its exceptionalism as an animal product intended to survive the lifespans of its human makers and users. The Roman historian Pliny the Elder (23–79 CE), though fascinated by the nature, quality, and manufacture of papyrus, described the medium of parchment (*membranas Pergami*) as "that commodity by which immortality is ensured to man": a small source of consolation, perhaps, for our own sad impermanence.[27] Fourteen centuries later, the Benedictine monk Johannes Trithemius (1462–1516), abbot of Sponheim, agreed, railing against paper and print by favorably comparing the durability of parchment and script: "The word written on parchment will last a thousand years. The printed word is on paper. How long will it last? The most you can expect a book of paper to survive is two hundred years."[28] A distorted view of book history, of course: paper had long been part of manuscript cultures in Europe, while printing on vellum was already a well-established niche market by the time Trithemius was writing.[29] But one lesson embedded in the story of St. Ciarán is the sheer resilience of the membrane medium, and indeed parchment is one of the few animal-derived products of human manufacture that survives in large quantities from the premodern world. We might think of it this way: one of the largest faunal records surviving from the first three-quarters of the Common Era is also a primary record of Euro-Mediterranean civilization.

Yet one of the more unexpected parts of this project has been fielding questions that reflect the inherent awkwardness of the subject with respect to other animal products. So are you implying that my shoes and my belt are the moral equivalents of a parchment codex? Can vegans be medievalists? Are you suggesting that it's unethical to read from a parchment manuscript?

I am not, nor do I wish to draw a moral equivalence between the acts of reading from the skins of long-dead animals and eating the flanks, gnawing the bones, or wearing the hides of recently living ones. It may be that there is such a relation to be drawn: parchment is still being made today in numerous locales and at various scales, from the bookmaking workshops of sub-Saharan Africa to the Pergamena tannery in Montgomery, New York, which manufactures fine quality parchments for book artists and furniture makers. I have made parchment myself, from curing hide to pumiced vellum, in the course of researching and writing this book.

Nor is it accurate to suggest that parchment was simply a byproduct of meat consumption in the premodern diet. This is still a widespread assumption in the field of book history, and it certainly gels with modern common sense and industrial practice (vastly more hides and hoofs are discarded than sold by contemporary slaughterhouses). I will have more to say in later chapters about this aspect of parchment culture. For now I would simply point out that the historical record rarely allows us to determine whether hide and membrane were secondary rather than primary products of animal slaughter, and in any case the very notion of a byproduct is largely foreign to the economies of scarcity that characterized much of the medieval world. If you were to pose the byproduct question to the residents of a remote medieval abbey, my guess would be that the monks might answer in a way that hopelessly complicates the issue. We can survive without meat, which we are forbidden to eat during Lent in any case, and in some instances (and in some religious orders) to consume at all; but we cannot survive without the holy books that transmit the Word or the charters and other membrane records that define and sustain our community. For many subcultures of the premodern world, parchment for writing (whether documents or books) was of much more everyday practical and spiritual importance than flesh for consumption. At the same time, eating and reading were never far apart in medieval communities of the book. St. Augustine had some wicked fun tormenting his dualist opponents for hypocrisy when it came to the fine distinctions they drew between their parchment manuscripts and their vegetarian diets. *Hypocrites, all of you, abstaining from meat while writing on skin!*

As the era's writers themselves often reveal, searching questions of violence and power, innocence and culpability are built into the nature and history of the parchment medium. "Is not this a lamentable thing," Shakespeare's Jack Cade wonders, "that of the skin of an innocent lamb should be made parchment; that parchment, being scribbled o'er, should undo a man?"[30] Tongue in cheek, perhaps, though the disposition of the inscribed skins of myriad creatures could often be regarded as a matter of life or death. The practice of *genizah* among Jewish communities demanded the ritual disposal of a range of documents, both holy and unholy, both parchment and (more commonly) paper: "sacred trash," as one study of the great Cairo Geniza describes these repositories.[31] The written object remains alive in some sense by virtue of the words surviving on its vibrant surface and consubstantial with its processed materiality.

My own approach to such complexities has been guided in part by the ethical environment of the parchment epoch itself: the forms of self-justification and modes of moral thought in the medieval world that sought to enlist and justify the slaughtered, flayed, and written animal as integral to the transmission of culture. Such premodern ethical reflections on the subject of parchment are important to take seriously not only for their inherent interest but for the challenges they pose to some long-standing assumptions about the era's indifference to the animality of its written medium—for example, the assertion by one of the world's leading scholars of the medieval book that, when it came to parchment, "most medieval scribes and readers of manuscripts neither knew nor cared what the animal had been when alive."[32] Most medieval gentile scribes and readers, perhaps. But this blanket pronouncement would shock readers and copyists of the Torah and the Talmud over the centuries, as well as the many Jewish *sofrim* or scribes who cared passionately about the derivation of the medium that helped define their religious and professional lives. If many premodern readers and writers show indifference to the creaturely aspects of their written culture, many others enlist these same aspects into often elaborate arguments and justifications for the taking of animal life as indispensable to the preservation of human tradition.

Figure 1.3. Oracle bone of tortoise plastron from the Shang Dynasty. China, ca. 1300–1050 BCE. British Library Or. 76941595 (Couling-Chalfant collection).

→ ←

One of the searching questions we can ask about any civilization, past or present, concerns its self-reflections on the medium through which it represents its greatest aspirations and preserves the preponderance of its thought. If, as Marshall McLuhan once put it in a dictum (now something of a cliché) that helped found the field of media studies, "the medium is the message," what is the message of parchment?[33] Part of this message can be found in those many moments of recognition, contemplation, and even compassion that acknowledge the individual creatures taken for the making of written culture: an ancient legend that extols the ram who gave its hide in lieu of Isaac's skin, so that the holy book might survive; a great Old English riddle that speaks, if only for a few lines, in the voice of the animal killed and rendered for the page; the story of an Irish saint and his treasured cow. Other messages can be found in the visual register of the membrane folio, which puts the dead animal in plain view on leaf after leaf in sometimes self-conscious and often moving ways.

The preponderance of membrane in Euro-Mediterranean book history opens important sightlines into the role of animal parts in other written cultures. The earliest forms of writing to survive from China are inscriptions carved on prepared ox scapulae and tortoise plastra from the Shang dynasty (ca. 1600–1046 BCE). These so-called oracle bones represent a practice that must have involved extensive husbandry and butchering and persisted until the Zhou dynasty at least five centuries before the Common Era (see fig. 1.3).[34] Indigenous book cultures of the Americas also made frequent use of mammal hide both before and after the contact period, with membrane artifacts featuring prominently among the tens of thousands of native codices burned by the Spanish conquerors. Thus a seventeenth-century account speaks of "27 rolls of hieroglyphics and signs on deer skin" as among the objects torched by Franciscan friars attempting to purify the religious life of the indigenous laity.[35] Certain other world cultures, such as Hinduism and Buddhism, have traditionally eschewed the written animal for well-developed moral and theological reasons. Belary Shamanna Kesavan, called the father of Indian bibliography, once wrote that Indians of the premodern world "would have viewed with horror both the slaughtering of young animals for their skin (cf. parchment), and the writing of sacred texts on such material."[36] The animal archive studied here is a largely Abrahamic inheritance, a habit of interspecies inscription elaborated in poetry and chronicle, an artisanal craft practiced among Islamic, Jewish, and Christian textual communities, and a cultural disposition justified across a range of theological positions over many centuries.

Like any part of the historical record, then, the parchment record challenges us to reflect on the cultural biases and assumptions we bring to the study of the written past. Yet it also asks us to embrace our own emotional and affective relation to these myriad objects of study, and to find ways of recognizing the occasional bursts of intimacy and empathy with this creaturely medium on the part of both our predecessors and ourselves. The love and gratitude felt by St. Ciarán toward his dun cow and her skin may seem worlds apart from the scientific distance required of the bibliographer or the paleogeneticist. But we might learn from the spirit of their story even while recognizing the historical distance and ethical dispositions that separate us from its actors, human and nonhuman alike.

CHAPTER TWO

>‹ ›‹

HAIR, FLESH, SENSE

St. Ciarán loved his dun cow, though he had to be brought back from the dead to write on her skin. We can only imagine the saint's reaction upon his resurrection: finding the hide of his long-lost cow laid uncannily before him as a writing surface, joined with her again in the act of literary creation on this incarnate totem of her death. What might our Irish saint have been thinking about as he settled down with his parchment and began to write out and thus reinvent the *Táin* on this particular creature's flesh? What sentiments and emotions moved him as his fingertips once again rubbed the skin of his beloved cow?

My own fingers first brushed the surface of a parchment folio in Columbia University's Butler Library, during my initial semester of paleography. I was one of a dozen or so graduate students finishing coursework or drafting dissertation proposals. We all gathered around a long seminar table and gazed, most of us for the first time, at *actual medieval manuscripts.* Though we were there to learn, we shared a mostly silent thrill in the presence of objects invested with all the auratic charge of a Rembrandt self-portrait or a saint's relic.

Then we touched them, the pads of our fingers and thumbs separated by each folio. Our nerves discerned the gossamer thinness of fine vellum, the uneven thicknesses of the rougher parchments. We intuited the difference between the nearly pristine condition of one example and the discolored, much-thumbed aspect of another. Those who work with old books, whether parchment or paper, know such sensations well, though the variability of parchment from book to book and leaf to leaf can be a vivid lesson in the diverse character of a medium. Parchment books and records teach you quickly that a manuscript is a sensual object: each has a certain smell, a certain feel, a certain look and sound, all derived in part from the distinctive origin, treatment, and history of the animal membranes that comprise them, and from the oily human fingers paging through them over the intervening centuries. When we start touching and transcribing and reading from these books for the first time, such realizations are vividly new. These reactions can be as memorable as the thrill experienced by the paleontology student brushing dirt from her first hominid bone.

One of the early reading assignments that semester was the first chapter of Bernhard Bischoff's *Latin Palaeography: Antiquity and the Middle Ages*. In those days Bischoff's was a standard text for introductory courses in medieval manuscript studies. Its opening chapter likely represents the first exposure by thousands of scholars of the last several generations to the nature of the medium that forms their primary objects of study. Section 2 of the chapter "Parchment" begins with a frank description of the craft process:

> Parchment is normally prepared in the following way: the skin of the animal is not tanned but soaked in caustic calcium lye. This loosens the hair and removes the fat. Then the skin is cleaned with a sickle-shaped scraping iron and sometimes soaked a second time. It is then stretched on a frame to dry. Whether the parchment was further treated, and in what way, differed from country to country and from century to century, and seems to have depended mainly on the nature of the raw material (*Ausgangsmaterial*), that is animal species used.[1]

Like many scholarly and pedagogical accounts of parchment making, Bischoff's begins postmortem. The verbs are passive (the skin is soaked, is cleaned, is stretched), the animal skin already conceived as "raw material" from its moment of entry into the manufacturing process. The colon bisecting the first sentence above thus stands in for complex agrarian processes of husbandry, selection, and seasonal butchering that yield the "skin of the animal" before its transformation into parchment can begin. Bischoff might have started a few steps earlier in the process: *Parchment is normally prepared in the following way: an animal is culled from a herd or flock, then killed and flayed. The skin of the animal is not tanned but soaked in caustic calcium lye.* A tendentious point, though worth an affective pause: that each folio we touch and read entailed the death of some individual calf or sheep whose life came to a premature end, at human hands, and whose remains now make up part of the book we touch. Indeed an individual skin makes up not one but two, four, eight, sometimes as many as sixteen or more separate folios depending on how many times each hide was folded and cut in the process of book production. The same beast whose skin gives a book its second folio may reappear as the donor of its seventh, or (in the case of very small books) its first sixteen, helping us recognize the potential extent of an individual animal's bodily contribution to a manuscript.

Now we turn a page. To lift a parchment folio and separate it from its sur-

Figure 2.1.
A hinge in folded parchment allows for repeated opening and bending (here of a seventeenth-century notarial document). Westminster, 1667. Charlottesville, University of Virginia Ms. 9772-a, box 1, folder 51.

rounding volume is to see and hear in another way the creaturely life of the medium. "Through very careful treatment both sides can become equally white," says Bischoff, "but even then they are distinguished by their curvature: the flesh side is convex, while the less stretchable hair-side is concave (!), a fact which can be very helpful in the reconstruction of manuscripts that are preserved only in a very fragmentary state."[2] The exclamation point is Bischoff's, and it speaks to the persistence of the animal body as the texture and contour of the page, as well as the often surprising contortions introduced into membrane by the process of parchment manufacture, by the animal still ghosting the book. It is this same stiff, fibrous quality of parchment that allows the membrane to bend without breaking. This peculiar flexion can create a membrane hinge (see fig. 2.1) that endures for centuries: an essential feature of the nested bifolium and thus the codex, as well as the folded charter.

Perdurance and delicacy. A hardy softness, gossamer and steel.

When scholars first learn about medieval manuscripts, whether through introductory textbooks such as Bischoff's *Latin Palaeography* or in seminars on codicology, bibliography, and book history, we inevitably learn about their derivation from the skins of animals: part of the "carnal dimension of texts."[3] There is no secret about this aspect of premodern literate cultures, plain to our senses in the presence of the era's written objects, this "porous, almost palpable living quality" manifest in the parchment object.[4] Indeed the animality of medieval manuscripts has long helped shape the canons and conventions of bibliographical description, in some cases for centuries. Several of the Old Norse kings' sagas take their names from an eighteenth-century editor's sense of the quality of parchment on which the copies available to him were written: there is the *Morkinskinna* (the book on moldy or rotten skin), the *Fagrskinna* (the book on beautiful skin), and the *Hrokkinskinna* (the book on wrinkled skin), all now standard monikers in the study of Icelandic literature.[5] "Well, what is Insular vellum, Insular membrane?" the great paleographer Julian Brown asked a half century ago. "It has a kind of rough, suede-like finish. You can generally see the mark of the scraper on both hair and flesh side; and the hair-side and the flesh-side are very alike in surface as well as colour. When it is badly made, it can be transparent, greasy, stiff, too thick."[6] The codicologist as restaurant reviewer, commenting on the relative greasiness and thickness of a folio as if it were a tenderloin. Yet the same attunement holds true on some level for all who work on parchment books and documents. We see the skins there on the table, opened to our view. We touch them, smell them, listen to the whisper of turning pages, transcribe and read from them, even as we move beyond and beneath such surface impressions to experience them as the material phenomena that they are and as the affective subjects that we are.

A phenomenology of parchment: a rigorous openness to that earthy blend of stimulation, doubt, and intuition arising the moment we touch a membrane page; a set of experiences in which we bracket, even for a moment, the store of literary, historical, and bibliographical knowledge that recognizes the objects before us as familiar books or documents rather than peculiar assemblages of animal remains; a mode of consciousness that integrates a spatial and temporal awareness of parchment-qua-animal-skin into our embodied encounters with these objects without reducing such encounters to an amalgam of sense-data or surface impression; and an intuitive, even empathetic awakening to our intersubjective intimacy with the myriad creatures whose flesh constitutes that which we claim as our archive. Thus Catherine Brown calls for an "empathetic codicology": a "feeling-into" the study of the manuscript codex as a thing of hand and flesh that fully implicates our affective selves into the processes of reading and reception; Jennifer Borland writes of "the consuming role of touch" in the experiencing of medieval manuscripts; and Sarah Kay proposes a "speculative phenomenology" of the parchment book "as an extension of the reader's own skin."[7] For modern readers of medieval manuscripts, the animal is a tangible and visible part of the reading process, always at the edges of our awareness, whether as the fuzzy folio that slips along our thumbpad or as the unrepaired flaw in the membrane allowing a glimpse of the next page.[8]

Such sensual reactions can delight and disgust. Open up some medieval codices and you will be greeted by a miasma of odor, the stink of slaughter and animal rot that has lingered there for centuries. And yet even the most seasoned of manuscript scholars can tend to shy away from exploring the olfactory dimensions of the medium. "I have no vocabulary to define this," Christopher de Hamel writes upon opening the Codex Amiatinus, "but there is a curious warm leathery smell to English parchment, unlike the sharper, cooler scent of Italian skins."[9]

Perhaps we need to recover some of our childish delight and repulsion, even our naivete in the face of these creaturely phenomena. This reaction, certainly, is the pose taken by the so-called Anonymous of Bern, a writer of the second half of the eleventh century who left behind a fragmentary treatise on the craft of manuscript illumination. The portion of the treatise that survives speaks in animated and loving detail about the tempering of color: *De Clarea* or "About Glair," a binding medium for pigments made of egg whites either beaten or pressed. A committed artisan, the writer is fiercely devoted to the craft, casting aspersions on the "many workers shirking perfection in their profession" by taking shortcuts, contaminating the whites with the dirt and grease of their fingers, paying insufficient attention to the particulars of their practice.

At one point in the treatise, the Anonymous pauses to apologize for his scrupulous and perhaps puerile insistence on detail. Here, a topos of childish triviality yields to an expertly geographical parsing of beasts and their varying skins:

> I may reasonably be critized for taking time, that is in writing, for such childish and trivial matters [*puerilia seu inutilia*]; but God Almighty can convert these things to good fruits. He is my witness that it is not for vanity, but rather as a friendly response to the requirements of many people, that I write this work, which I now desire to carry out, with God's aid, for the purposes of instructing others.
>
> Not every parchment will take a single tempering of color or glair, for this reason, that there are several sorts of parchment, namely, calf, sheep, goat [*vitulinum, ovinum, caprinum*]. But when sheep or calf parchment is uniform in color, that is, all white, and smooth and handsome [*planum et pulchrum*], like that of Flanders and Normandy, for instance, the tempering described above is suitable . . . But when the parchment is rough, and mottled, and thin, and very ugly, and uneven in color, gray and black and white, like the sheep parchment of Burgundy [*pargamenum* {sic} . . .

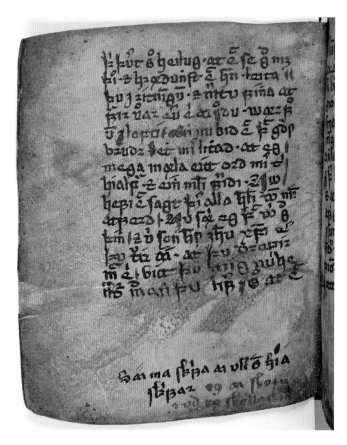

Figure 2.2.
Scribes complaining about parchment quality in the lower margin of the *Margrétar saga*. Iceland, ca. 1500. Reykjavik, The Árni Magnússon Institute for Icelandic Studies, Ms. AM 433a 12mo, fol. 25v.

ovinum de Burgundia], which is very seldom found well painted by anyone, you conduct the tempering of the glair as follows.[10]

A bit of regional snobbery, perhaps, though also a discriminating sense of species difference and quality control in the continental parchment trade. The Anonymous takes some alliterative pleasure in counterposing the "smooth and handsome" (*planum et pulchrum*) Flemish and Norman parchments against their "rough, and mottled, and thin, and very ugly" counterparts. *Hispidum, et maculatum, et macrum, et turpissumum*: joying here in the descriptors piled onto the poor Burgundian sheepskins that rarely lend themselves to art.[11]

Premodern readers wrote and read with varying degrees of attunement to the sight, feel, and smell of the animal parts before them. Despite the era's wide-ranging theological investments in the medium, in practice they must often have regarded it as inconsistent at best, even an incidental annoyance, particularly in those periods and locales in which the fine vellums associated with later, more urban centers of book production were unavailable. In an Icelandic manuscript of the *Margrétar saga*, the main scribe comments despairingly on the poor quality of the sheepy parchment on which he must scratch: "He might as well write on wool [who] writes here." A later scribe responds, "and on skate-skin and fox-hide."[12] The book in question is rough to the touch, its drape poor, its folios blackened and almost cardboard-like in their consistency (see fig. 2.2). It is not difficult even centuries on to comprehend the scribes' acerbic reactions to the resistant quality of the writing surface. In such phenomenal reactions to parchment we perceive the power of the empirical, the observed thingness of the book-as-animal-object, even as beyond and beneath it move those intuitive capacities of touch and recognition that render the parchment folio into an agent of transcendence: a rough-and-ready specimen of rendered animal skin yet also a transhistorical medium of cultural transmission, preservation, and survival. To take a medieval manuscript *zu den Sachen selbst*, as the thing that it is, entails an orientation toward embodied contact with that bookish object before us that awakens our intuition (these "childish and trivial matters," in the words of the Anonymous of Bern) to the shared animality that parchment has always kept before our eyes and beneath our fingertips.

The classroom can be a natural staging ground for an affective openness to the animality of the archive. When I bring students into our Special Collections library, the derivation and the incarnate sensuality of parchment tend to provoke more comment than anything else. The creaturely medium is one of the aspects of medieval manuscripts that our students can find most fascinating, alluring, and also a bit eerie, like a visit to the catacombs or the Capuchin Crypt in Rome.

In recent years I've purposefully lingered over this most basic element of medieval writing, asking my students to think for a while about the fact that these books are made mostly of animal parts.

That's the hair side. Can you feel the fuzz?

Omigod.

Ew!

I ask them what it's like, to touch the skin making up each unique page, to realize the words they see are written on animal flesh. The responses vary widely.

It's weird.

Kind of gross.

Doesn't seem like a big deal.

A student leaves the room with a hand over the mouth.

One comment in particular crops up again and again: But there are so *many* of them!

To which another student sensibly responds by pointing out the obvious: Well, I mean, half of us are wearing leather shoes.

They look down at their shoes, back at the leaves and manuscripts, caught in that strange space between the marvel and the meh of the medium.

Early in Dante's *Paradiso*, the pilgrim gazes upward, at Beatrice's direction, and asks her to explain to him the origin and nature of moon spots. Beatrice in turn asks the pilgrim to relate his own explanation: "Now tell me: what are the dark marks on this planet's body that there below, on earth, have made men tell the tale of Cain?"[13] The "tale of Cain" refers to the folk belief that Cain, as a punishment for the murder of Abel, was exiled by God to the moon, where he was forced to carry a bundle of thorns for all eternity, visible to humans on earth as the *segni bui* or "dark spots" on the moon's surface.[14] In responding to his guide's query, the pilgrim repeats the explanation that Dante had earlier offered in the *Convivio*: that the relative density of matter at different points explains the varying amounts of light refracted through the moon.

Beatrice responds with a series of anti-determinist objections, including the following tercets against the theory of varying density:

> Ancor, se raro fosse di quel bruno
> Cagion che tu dimandi, o d'oltre in parte
> Fore di sua matera sì digiuno
>   Esto pianeto, o, sì come comparte
> Lo grasso e 'l magro un corpo, così questo
> Nel suo volume cangerebbe carte.
> (PAR. 11.73–78)

> And more, were rarity the cause of the
> dim spots you question, then in part this planet
> would lack matter through and through,

or else as, in a body, lean and fat
can alternate, so would this planet
alternate the pages in its volume.

Ernst Robert Curtius, in a classic reading of this passage, interprets Beatrice's simile in the second tercet as follows: "as fat and lean alternate in an animal body, or the
pages of a book with one another."[15] The passage turns to craftsmanship even at the
heights of sublimity, and here the vehicles are, at first glance, mundane. While she
rejects material causation as an explanation for moon spots, Beatrice draws an analogy with the messy materiality of a slaughtered animal. If the moon were of varying
thicknesses, it would either be a void in places ("lack matter through and through"),
an impossibility; or, just as implausibly, it would, like the carcass of a beast that is
lean in some places and fat in others, alternate between thin and thick or light and
dark in the quality and thickness of its pages.

The moon would be, that is, like parchment, its varying qualities the mark of
its material inconsistency. Beatrice has turned from Cain's "dark spots"—from the
stigmatized sign of the fallen human—to the rendered flesh of the animal. Particularly alluring in this sedimented metaphor is the displacement of one creaturely vehicle by another, *corpo* by *carte*. In *un corpo*, the carcass of an animal, fat and lean
are marbled together, creating flesh of differing thicknesses and consistencies; in the
carte, the parchment sheet, the distinctions between hair and flesh as well as the vagaries of the parchment-making process determine the relative feel, hue, and thickness of the page. Beatrice, though, cannot countenance either of the analogies she
invokes. Neither marbled meat nor scraped hide, neither body nor page, *corpo* nor
carte, the spotted moon is instead a manifestation of God's powers, its spots expli-
cable not as concrete manifestations of the pilgrim's vulgar materialism but as signs
of the ineffable yet fully rational diffusion of divine omnipotence throughout the
universe.

As Beatrice's thoughtful if discarded analogy hints, however, the moon *looks*
or *feels* like the slightly marbled surface of blank parchment, with patches of dark
and light across its face—patches perhaps created by the uneven movements of the
lunellum, the half-moon knife used to remove flesh from soaked animal hide during
parchment manufacture; or from the goatskins common in Italian bookmaking of
this period, mottled in ways that can indeed resemble the craters of the moon. The
canticle heightens these effects of materialist exposition by immersing the subjects
within the medium that Beatrice invokes. Throughout this exchange, the pilgrim
and Beatrice stand within some mysterious space in the sphere of the moon, which
receives the travelers like a water drop receives the sunlight, allowing their bodies to

occupy the same physical place as its corporeal substance in a way the pilgrim cannot fathom.

Later in the *Paradiso*, parchment appears in an equally immersive milieu, this time as part of an analogy explaining the effects of the Holy Spirit upon the believer. The pilgrim here encounters St. Peter, who asks him, "What is the origin of the dear gem that comes to you, the gem on which all virtues are founded?" Dante, reaching for a metaphor, finds his answer in an image of rainwater flowing over the incarnate pages of the Old and New Testaments:

> E io: "La larga ploia
> de lo Spirito Santo, ch'è diffusa
> in su le vecchie e 'n su le nuove cuoia,
>
>> è silogismo che la m'ha conchiusa
> acutamente sì, che 'nverso d'ella
> ogne dimostrazion mi pare ottusa."

> And I: "The plenteous rain
> of the Holy Spirit which is poured
> over the old and over the new parchments
>
>> is a syllogism that has proved it to me
> so acutely that, in comparison with this,
> every demonstration seems obtuse to me."
> (*PAR.* XXIV.91–96)

Note the poet's literalism in the midst of a dense allegory. The rain of the Holy Spirit suffuses not simply the pages, but precisely the *skins* of scripture: *vecchie e . . . nuove cuoia. Cuoia*, or treated skins, is the plural of *cuoio*, a term often referring to leather. The *silogismo* embeds a spiritual reversal of a mundane and ubiquitous threat for any medieval bibliophile: what would normally be water damage to a membrane codex becomes here a process of typological unification through the touch of the Holy Spirit that emphasizes the physical parchment Book as a thing of the material world.[16] The image of the neglected but redemptive page had appeared just two cantos earlier, during the pilgrim's encounter with St. Benedict, who laments the abandonment of his monastic Rule by the neglectful as a physical assault on the pages that transmit it: "e la regola mia / Rimasa è giù per danno delle carte" ("and my rule lies now neglected, a waste of the page") (*Par.* XXII.74–75). Fat and lean, hair and flesh, moon and page, skin and scripture: a beautifully intuitive reach for a phenomenology of parchment, that medium of earthy animality and spiritual transcendence that continually challenges the poet to push against the limits of metaphor and mere thought.

Few meditations on parchment's sensual materiality approach the sublimity of Dante's—and few can rival the visceral disgust apparent in an earlier and jazzily detailed account of the medium's shortcomings. Abū 'Uthmān 'Amr ibn Baḥr al-Jāḥiẓ was a theologian, traveler, and jack-of-all-trades who died in Basra in the late 860s. Al-Jāḥiẓ was also a prolific bibliophile (indeed a "bibliomaniac," as one scholar has recently called him), and he lived during just the years in which parchment was giving way to paper as the preferred writing surface in the Islamic world.[17]

Al-Jāḥiẓ, it seems, was an eager adopter. Most of his writings survive in paper manuscripts, several of them in his own hand, though he would almost certainly have relied on parchment at many points in his career—much to his annoyance, evidently, for the work of al-Jāḥiẓ gives us the most extraordinary polemics against parchment to survive from the medieval world. One such rant survives in a long, complaint-ridden letter to a certain Muhammad, whose enmity al-Jāḥiẓ has incurred over certain obscure financial disputes. The letter covers a wide range of topics, from the politics of taxation to the immorality of gossip to the nature of male friendship, at one point coming around to the relative virtues of Chinese and Khurasani paper over parchment. Though the letter rings of tongue-in-cheek hyperbole, Al-Jāḥiẓ's assessment of parchment as a medium of writing and textual transmission leaves little room for doubt about his low regard for what had been a predominant medium in early Arabic-speaking lands since well before the coming of Islam. As he writes, "What is it to you if all my books are of Chinese paper or of Khurasani sheets? Tell me why you extol writing on skins [al-naskh 'alā al-julūd] and urge me to use parchment [al-adam] when you know that skins [al-julūd] are thick in bulk and heavy in weight?"[18]

The sense of bibliographic geography here is quite specific: the paper medium he touts derives from Khurasan, "the factory of Islamic culture," as a recent history of paper describes it, and carries in its fibers all the prestige of its origin.[19] His friend's parchments, on the other hand, exhibit all the wretchedness of their beastly derivation:

> If water touches them, they are spoiled. If it is a humid day, they go limp. That they make their master hate a downpour and their owners dislike rain is sufficient warning for people to avoid them. You know that the copyist at those times does not write

a line or cut a single skin. When dry, they do not return to their shape but rather are much shrivelled and marred by contraction. They have a more fetid odor, are more expensive and more subject to counterfeiting . . . They are aged to remove their odor and to clear away the hair. They have more knots and bulges, more troughs and dips. They turn yellow faster. Writing on them is more commonly worn away quickly. If a scholar wishes to carry a sufficient quantity of them on a journey, a camel's load would not be enough.[20]

Even in condemning the membrane book, al-Jāḥiẓ is alive to its familiar phenomenality: the thickness and weight of skins, the shape and shrivel of membrane sheets, the fetid smell even of the finished product, the knots, bulges, and dips marring its surface. Al-Jāḥiẓ speaks from experience here, experience grounded in intimate and years-long contact with the parchment books that would have made up a good portion of the writings he read, consulted, and carried with him over the course of his long career and travels.

The stinking, messy beastliness of the stuff! Only when al-Jāḥiẓ mimics the voice of the letter's addressee do the virtues of parchment manuscripts come in for some mention: "they hold up better under scratching out and correction, last better through successive borrowing and handling. They have a value even when discarded. Their palimpsests [li-ṭirsihā] are recovered and when restored can be substituted for new ones."[21] These virtues, though, cannot convince the writer that parchment is a suitable substitute for the paper he adores. The phenomenal yields to the practical as al-Jāḥiẓ dismisses the membrane medium as an assault on written culture as well as on the human senses. For a lover of Khurasani sheets and Chinese paper, parchment will always carry with it the weight and stink of slaughter, the palpable signs of its origin in the animal bodies flayed and rendered for the making of books. The nature of this violent process of animal translation, from pen and pasture to pen and page, is the subject of the next chapter.

CHAPTER THREE

➤ ✦

GRISTLE, STINK, SKIN

If we added or omitted anything, either wittingly or not, forgive and bless us for ever and ever. Amen. And bless the makers of parchment [*sarāhta berānnā*], because they labored much.

—GE'EZ COLOPHON, FROM THE PISTOLA OCTOTEUCH (ETHIOPIA, 15TH C.)

A stack of hides, cut and flayed from the carcasses of a dozen deer, slumps on the concrete floor of the Pergamena tannery in Montgomery, New York. The hides have been delivered by local hunters, who sometimes charge five dollars apiece, though often they are dropped off for free, particularly during hunting season. Coated in salt, the hides will cure on the floor for several weeks before the makers deem them ready for processing. Along with hundreds of cow, calf, goat, lamb, and other skins curing elsewhere in the warehouse, the deer hides create a smell unique to these institutions of creaturely processing: partly the stench of butchered flesh (a certain amount of which still clings to the hides), partly the salty perfume of rotting skin.

"The Divine Presence is found on the western side" of any given town, Talmud Bava Batra warns, "and therefore it is inappropriate to set up a tannery there with its foul odors."[1] That distinctive aroma, the smell of animal parts in large numbers, is one of the first sensations that reaches the visitor to a tannery, whether in a converted warehouse in small-town New York or in a market square in North Africa. The same smell permeates the renowned tannery in Fes, Morocco, which occupies a large space in the middle of the city's great medina. In Fes the tradition of skinwork goes back over a thousand years, with parchment making once a thriving subset of the industry. Here young men and boys by the dozen stomp hides into the treatment bins, baste their legs and saturate their lungs in the noxious chemicals used to dye the leather in myriad hues, from the sunniest yellows to the inkiest blacks.

Just a few crowded blocks from the tannery sits the site of al-Qarawiyyin, founded in 859 CE and often identified as the world's oldest university. Before the wide-scale transition to paper in much of the Islamic world, parchment was made in great quantities here for the teachers and students of al-Qarawiyyin, who copied scriptural texts and commentaries for the purposes of instruction and prayer.[2]

Pergamena has its own impressive legacy. The Meyer family has been making leather goods since the Reformation, and Pergamena is only the latest incarnation of the family business. Jesse Meyer is one of a number of contemporary artisans who have devoted significant portions of their lives to the art, craft, and industry of parchment making. Meyer is a sculptor by training and inclination, and his earlier interests tended toward textured and cruder materials: brick, terra-cotta, unfinished metal, distressed woods. Once he started working in the family business, surrounded by animal hides every day at the tannery, he started experimenting with skin as a sculptural medium. Only after receiving his degree and continuing to experiment with parchment did he begin interacting with scholars in library conservation and medieval studies with an academic interest in his practice, as well as craftspeople working in the historical book arts. Their engagement and feedback encouraged him to refine his craft through a long process of trial and error that has established him as among the most respected parchment makers in the world.[3]

One of the services Meyer and Pergamena provide is a series of two-day workshops on the hands-on practice of parchment manufacture. With one or two workshops a year during the last fifteen years, Meyer has trained hundreds of interested parties in the fine points of parchmentery, and thousands of others have handled his products and assayed his craft at conferences and traveling workshops. The sessions at Pergamena allow participants to bring their own hides if they so desire, though the tannery will usually provide each of those enrolled with a single skin to see through the process from start to finish. After the heads, tails, and other parts are removed, the cured hides are heaved into a rotating drum and drenched with a mixture of water, sodium sulfide, and, later, lime. This chemical bath slowly burns and sloughs the hair from the skin.

When removed from the brine the hides feel like raw squid and look something like a wet shirt. After more processing outside the drums (hand-scraping, several runs through a defleshing machine, maybe some bleaching), the hides are stretched on frames to dry in preparation for finishing work, traditionally done with a *lunellum* and then a pumice stone—though Meyer favors a belt sander for some of these final steps. As I discovered in Pergamena's parchment loft, there's a strange thrill to the act of taking a loud power tool to a width of skin, removing flecks of dried gristle from a stretched animal membrane. If you pause to flick your fingernail against the taut surface the membrane will sound something like a tympani drum, a percussion instrument often covered with parchment provided by contemporary makers.[4]

Pergamena is a for-profit corporation, and while the market for its parchments began with book conservators, artists, binders, printers, and calligraphers, its customer base has expanded dramatically in recent years to include manufacturers of furniture, lampshades, and other products far from the book arts—even interior wall surfaces in luxury hotels. It's not unusual these days for the tannery to receive orders for two to three hundred skins at a time, a demand that requires the provision of large quantities of fresh hides on a continual basis. Deerskins come from hunters and hide buyers in the area during hunting season, sheepskins from wool processors, and calf and goat hides from dairy and meat farmers throughout the northeastern United States, speaking to the increasing interest among end users in knowing the origins of the products they purchase. Pergamena plays well to such concerns, emphasizing the locally sourced and the humanely husbanded.

On the other side of the Atlantic is perhaps the world's busiest parchment manufacturer, William Cowley, a business in operation since the 1860s in the market town of Newport Pagnell in Buckinghamshire.[5] What distinguishes Cowley from other contemporary producers is the company's relationship with the government of England, for which it serves as the exclusive provider of parchment—and in quite large quantities. Until 2017 it was a matter of law in the United Kingdom that public Acts of Parliament had to be be produced and maintained on parchment rather than on paper, deposited in duplicate in two separate repositories—the House of Lords Public Record Office, which holds the acts going back to 1497, and the Public Record Office at Kew. (This requirement has been debated occasionally yet fiercely in Parliament, most recently in 2017; see chap. 15 below.) Like Pergamena, Cowley emphasizes what it calls the "ethical sourcing of raw materials" used for its parchment and vellum, stressing its environmentally friendly manufacturing processes and its reliance on byproducts rather than slaughter. "No animals are bred to make parchment," the company's publicity materials proclaim. "The cattle, goat and sheep skins used for parchment are all obtained from farms where livestock has been reared for wool, milk or meat."[6] Despite the larger scale of its parchment business, Cowley has practiced the same hands-on techniques throughout its existence. Watch a master maker at work long enough and you will appreciate the demanding physicality of the craft (see fig. 3.1 and fig. 3.2). The scraping of parchment is a balletic play of hand, knife, skin, and frame, as the maker bends and twists to address the tautened hide with the adequate pressure and from the correct angle. A foot might be lifted onto the edge of the frame for greater leverage; the spine must be bent, sometimes twisted to accommodate the subtle glide of the blade. There is an enchanting so-

Figure 3.1. Paul Wright, general manager at William Cowley in Newport Pagnall, works on tightly stretched calf skins, scraping off unwanted layers to create vellum.

nority to the process as well that cannot be replicated in image or print. The resonance of the stretched skin creates a gorgeous ringing tone as the blade strikes and scrapes, as flesh peels from flesh and the membrane imperceptibly thins.

One aspect of the craft that emerges quickly in discussions with individual artisans concerns the many differences among the types of hides rendered for parchment and vellum. Makers appreciate that particular species and breeds can produce wildly distinctive qualities and grades of membrane sheet (contemporary sheep breeds, for example, tend to be greasy and a bit of a mess). Meyer has made parchment from the hides of ostrich and bear, some of it dyed in exotic colors and showing veins. Zeger Hendrik de Groot, a parchment maker based in Rotterdam, has rendered the skin of eels and frogs for his artisanal books.

A parchment artisan who has long brought his craft talents to bear directly on the study of medieval manuscript culture is Jiří Vnouček, a maker and scholar based in Copenhagen and York with a remarkably intimate visual and tactile knowledge of skins. A true parchment whisperer, Vnouček can discern the species and often the relative age and size of individual mammals scattered across multiple folios and gatherings in single manuscripts. Striation and follicle patterns, production flaws and natural imperfections, the positioning of flanks, shoulders, and tails, the plays of light and shadow created by the impressions of hip bones or the pressure of protruding joints: these are Vnouček's warp and woof, the creaturely traces that make up the membrane books and documents he variously interprets, repairs, and makes, and he has long been attuned to what he calls "the life of the beast from whose skin the parchment was made."[7]

Alongside the work of individual makers such as Meyer, Groot, and Vnouček,

Figure 3.2. Parchment making at William Cowley, ca. 1924.

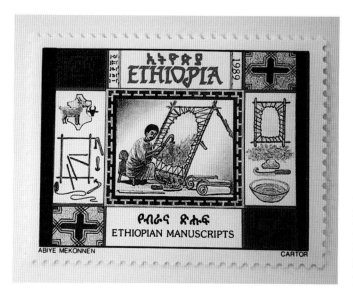

Figure 3.3.
A parchment maker, goat, skins, and equipment, from the Ethiopian Manuscripts postage stamp series. Designed by Abiye Mekonnen, issued June 16, 1989. Printed by Cartor Security Printing S.A., L'Aigle and Paris.

parchment is also made today in certain religious communities with living craft practices that go back a thousand years and more. The Ethiopian Christian Orthodox Church promotes parchment making and traditional book arts as an integral part of its evangelical mission, a practice that extends back through the Aksumite period of Late Antiquity through the present—in the words of Denis Nosnitsin, "the organic and conservative continuation of [an] ancient tradition."[8] Churches across Ethiopia house tens of thousands of membrane codices, stored in often precarious conditions yet dating from as early as the twelfth century.[9] Parchment makers serve these churches through the provision of skins to replenish the supply of manuscripts intended for the purposes of liturgy and private prayer.[10] A typical Ethiopian parchment maker might slaughter several dozen goats a year, flay the animals himself, and spend days rendering parchment under the eye of villagers while instructing young parishioners in the techniques of the craft.[11] The nation's tradition of membrane bookmaking was even commemorated on a series of postage stamps in 1989 (see fig. 3.3). One particularly vivid stamp, a work of art in its own right, displays the instruments and techniques of parchment craft while celebrating its animal derivation. In the central panel, a maker scrapes an unfinished hide, shown complete and smooth in the right panel. To the left we see the creaturely donor: a goat, still alive, standing alert before the rendered skin the animal will soon become.

A counterpart to these sub-Saharan micro-cultures is the thriving parchment industry serving Jewish faith communities around the globe. If a synagogue in Europe or the United States or Japan desires a new Torah scroll, the parchment will likely come from one of a number of specialty shops in Israel that provide kosher parchment expressly for this purpose, with each sheet selected individually by the *sofer* or scribe commissioned to write the scroll. The Tamid synagogue in Manhattan recently commissioned a new Torah from Julie Seltzer, a scribe based in Israel and New York.[12] In order to procure the prescribed number of parchments for the scroll (sixty-two separate sheets, each rendered from a single hide), Seltzer visited an ultra-Orthodox shop in Jerusalem known as Klaf Bak (fig. 3.4). Israeli parchment makers such as Klaf Bak contract with slaughterhouses in Argentina and the United States, purchasing the skins of fetal animals by the hundreds for the soft and supple parchments their hides can render. (It's an open secret in the global meat industry that approximately 5 percent of female cows and sheep killed in industrial slaughterhouses arrive pregnant.)

Shoshana Gugenheim, an artist and scribe based in Portland, Oregon, seeks alternatives to the industrial-scale rendering and sourcing of parchment. Gugenheim was one of the first women in the modern world to train and be commissioned as a *soferet*, a Torah scribe. Along with Linda Motzkin, a rabbi and *soferet* in upstate

Figure 3.4. A stack of uterine calf vellum at Klaf Bak, a parchment maker in Tel Aviv.

New York who renders her own parchment from hunter-supplied deerskins, Gugenheim has sought to bring awareness in Jewish communities of the book to the vital connection between the lives of the animals and the sacred writing done on their skins. Motzkin soaks her treated deerskins in a stream running through her backyard before removing them and stretching them in the sun, a small-scale process that provokes appreciation for the individual creatures whose hides she renders.[13] Gugenheim partners with ritual slaughterers [schochetim] to source skin from free-range and yard-raised animals. As she asks, "How does the Jewish community reconcile . . . the inhumane treatment of animals upon whose backs we are literally writing and the sacred texts inscribed on these very skins?"[14] The movement toward ethically sourced parchment emphasizes the local origins of skins as a mode of remediation against industrialization as well as a means of spiritual connection to the parchment craft as it was practiced in centuries and millennia past.

Today's parchment makers, then, form part of thriving local and global networks dedicated to maintaining a craft that was central to the transmission and preservation of written culture for a good portion of the Common Era. Their knowledge is indispensable to a robust understanding of the medium in its past and present incarnations, forming lines of continuity between ancient and modern textual cultures.

Yet craft can be a difficult aspect of tradition to assess with the seriousness it deserves. "Any craft develops an orthopraxis," Mary Carruthers writes, "a craft 'knowledge' which is learned, and indeed can only be learned, by the painstaking practical imitation and complete familiarization of exemplary masters' techniques and experiences. Most of this knowledge cannot even be set down in words; it must be learned by practicing, over and over again."[15] The histories of such familiarizations—repetition, painstaking hands-on experience, trial and failure—remain difficult to recover and thus largely unrecorded, even as we sense them in the surviving objects of their artisanal labor.[16] No surprise that our traditions of academic criticism have tended to relegate craft to the status of an after-effect or secondary evidence: a study of made things left behind rather than the day-to-day handiwork and in-the-moment frustrations endured by practitioners. Lisa Cooper, citing Hugh of St. Victor, points to this transhistorical interplay between labor and artifact: "Though medieval artificers are no longer directly available to our admiring gaze, we certainly have continued to this day to 'look with wonder' at the mundane and magnificent products of their skill—the many books and buildings, paintings and sculptures, and articles of furniture, clothing and jewelry still extant today."[17]

Yet craft's somewhat antiquarian tinge has led to its persistent imaginative role in the history of labor and the organization of work as a quaint formation largely left behind; as Terry Smith puts it, in certain ways "modernity defined itself, centrally, against craft":

> Craft became the primary instance of the not-modern, the anachronistic. The over-whelming success of mass production/consumption modernity in the early and mid-twentieth century left craft as the obvious signifier of modernity's opposite: tradi-tion. All the basic elements of craft—learning through apprenticeship, accumulated knowledges of past practice, individual conception, ingenious adaptation, adjust-ments between utility and decoration, fashioning by hand, tooling skills, close com-munities of taste—were displaced from the centres of our working, public, domestic, and private lives.[18]

One of Smith's points here concerns periodization: in the modern world, as indus-trial mass production avowedly displaced the traditional work of handicraft, craft in turn came to embody the premodern remainder, the residual afterlife of individ-ual artisanship. In this sense, craft is to be distinguished from mere competency: "Competency implies little of the virtuosity, guile and rhetoric of craftsmanship. Competency is more protocolic, denoting a kind of technical criterion of success."[19] Craftsmanship, on the other hand, must be adapted to circumstance, customized to the occasion: craft entails a level of improvisation that lends itself to various ap-plications and interpretations over time. The long history of parchment making is just such an improvisational practice: adaptable, learned yet learnable, full of sur-prises along the way.

The modern craft of parchment making is thus both indispensable and inevita-bly limited as a lens on parchment manufacture in the Middle Ages. Indispensable because a contemporary maker will possess a unique and hands-on perspective on certain techniques (of stretching, of drying, of scraping) unavailable through even the most scrupulous study of a medieval codex or legal document; limited because the medieval craft of *parchmenterie* remains an elusive art. Many of its idiosyncratic techniques have been largely forgotten, recoverable only partially, and only through years of persistent labor or moments of serendipitous discovery. Indeed, as Ronald Reed contended some fifty years ago, in most respects medieval parchment makers exceeded their modern counterparts in technical know-how and specialized crafts-manship.[20] The contemporary makers I know would readily agree. They stand on the shoulders of medieval giants, peering in awe at the prayerbooks and Pentateuchs written on tissue-thin vellum, the impossible handiwork of forebears who labored in anonymity and over dozens of generations to craft and scrape the stuff of written culture.

The recipes and instructions for the making of parchment that survive from the premodern world, while relatively few in number, are quite diverse in the sensibilities they bring to bear on the enterprise they describe.[21] Paleographers and historians of the book have often characterized these instructions as detailed and pragmatic. As modern-day makers who have tried them will be the first to say, however, such instructions can be surprisingly unhelpful when it comes to the specific hands-on elements of the craft.[22] While they might prescribe a bath of water and lime for the flayed hides, for instance, they rarely specify even approximate proportions of each, and provide little detailed information about the proper techniques for stretching, scraping, and finishing the rendered skins; what detail they do convey will often be incomprehensible to modern scholars and makers.[23] Anyone following these formulas will face a long process of trial and error, reverse engineering, and experimental archaeology before reliably producing usable samples, let alone the thinnest parchments held up as the ideal outcome of medieval artisanship. Like any craft, that is, parchment making generally required a lengthy apprenticeship for its practitioners. Most of the scattered recipes and directions found in medieval sources should be regarded less as specialized instructions than as schematic formulas, their aim more to describe than to teach the craft.

This makes them no less relevant as testaments to the assumptions and cultural sensibilities with which the lineaments and hands-on technicalities of this craft work are described. Even the earliest examples contain enough technical information to give a good sense of certain elements of the practice and often loving attunement to detail, as in a recipe or set of guidelines in Coptic compiled in a papyrus codex of the sixth or seventh century. The surviving portion touches mainly on the finishing of the skins, which the anonymous artisan sees in terms of their texture, contour, and tactile quality: "Then you shall wipe it and write on it . . . When you see that it is shriveled you shall polish it and write on it . . . If it be one that is all in wrinkles . . . If it be one that has a corroded skin [*ouamshaar*], you shall scrape it well with the hard pumice and write on it with a fine reed . . . If it be one that is sticky you shall pumice it with the soft sort and shall not wipe it at all."[24] The term translated here as "corroded skin," *ouamshaar*, is a Coptic compound formed from *ouam-* (a verbal adjective meaning "eater," from the verb *ouōm*, "to eat"); and *shaar*, "skin." A "skin-eater," then, is the organic agent responsible for corroding the surface of the membrane. Though written down on papyrus, the fragmentary treatise addresses its careful scrutiny to the already widespread medium of skin.

Another early set of guidelines occurs in a Latin miscellany containing a num-

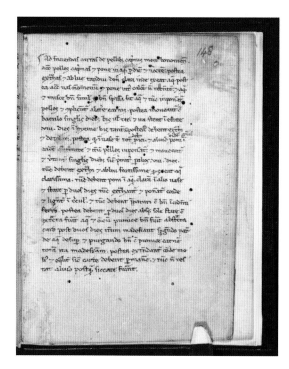

Figure 3.5. *Ad faciendas cartas de pellibus caprinis* (How to render folios from goatskin), from a miscellany of technical, alchemical, and medical texts. Germany, second half of the twelfth century. London, British Library Ms. Harley 3915, fol. 148r.

ber of practical treatises, recipes, and formulas for various artisanal usages. *Ad faciendas cartas de pellibus caprinis*, written on one side of a folio in a twelfth-century German manuscript (fig. 3.5), provides a rough schematic guide to the processes of soaking, liming, dehairing, and scraping necessary to the making of the commodity:

> To make parchment from the skins of goats [*cartas de pellibus caprinis*], as is done in Bologna, take goat skins, and place them in water for a day and a night, then take them out and wash them until the water has cleared. Then take a new vessel, and put in it aged lime and water, and mix them thoroughly so the water is thickened. Now the skins should be placed within, folded on the flesh side. Then stir this with a rod two or three times a day. And let the tub sit thus for eight days, in winter for twice as many. After this the hides must be taken out and dehaired.[25]

The writer prescribes additional days of soaking and rinsing; then "the skins must be taken out and suspended by cords and placed in a circular frame; and then they must be prepared with a keenly sharpened knife [*cum bene incidenti ferre*]." The last phrase is indicative of the vagueness of most such instructions: any old keenly sharpened knife will do, it seems. But the formula has nothing to say about the most demanding and precarious part of the process: the actual technique for scraping the hide to remove the remaining flesh. The recipe concludes with similarly vague instructions for pumicing the surface and tightening the frame cords to give the parchment its permanent form.

Other recipes for making parchment are more stylized, sacrificing technical specificity for literary license or artful paradox. One example comes to us in the form of a Latin poem from the thirteenth century. The author, the Zurich rector Conrad of Mure, composed the stylized recipe for his *De naturis animalium* (ca. 1270), a metrical compendium of practical knowledge, wisdom, and folklore concerning animals.

ON SKIN, HOW A PAGE IS MADE FROM IT
> The skin of a calf is flayed and deposited in water.
> Lime is added, to gnaw away everything rough,
> To clean it well, and to remove the hairs.
> A circular frame is fashioned, on which the hide is stretched.
> It is placed in the sun, so that moisture may be driven out.
> Now comes a sharp knife; it rips out flesh and hairs;
> It renders the skin fine and pleasing.[26]

The subsequent lines go on to detail the preparation of the scraped and dried calfskin [*pellis vituli*] with pumice, chalk, and rulings. The poem describes the parchment-making process in technically vague terms, though what comes across is the figurative brutality of the operation. The knife "rips out" hair and extraneous flesh from its surface, the skin is drowned in acid then stretched on a frame, and even lime is an aggressive agent that exiles moisture through the acidic action of the *calx* upon the flesh. The poem closes with a moralizing couplet that plays on the commonplace medieval association of flesh and page: "Skin from flesh, flesh from skin removed: You, too, must withdraw your carnal lust from the flesh" [*Pellis de carne, de pelle caro removetur: / Tu de carne tua carnea vota trahe*].

Formulas for the making and treatment of parchment often give practical tips for the removal of grease or stains, with the use of powdered quicklime, wood ash, or animal bones; and the effacing or erasure of writing, for which one Italian text of the fifteenth century prescribes orange juice. A set of fifteenth-century guidelines in Middle English provides instructions on how to "done awey what is wreten in Velyn or Parchement withowte any Pomyce"—that is, how to erase words from vellum and parchment without the use of a pumice stone, a common tool for finishing parchment sheets: "Take the juice of rew and of nettle, in March, April, or May, and mix it with cheese, the milk of a cow or of a sheep, add dry lime, mix them well together, and make a loaf, and dry it in the sun, and make powder out of it."[27] The powder must then be cast on the letters once they are moistened with saliva or water; after that, a quick scratch with the fingernail is all that is required to "done awey the lettres." "This medicine," the writer avows, "when made with the cheese or milk of a cow, is good for vellum, and [with the cheese or milk] of a sheep, good for parchment": implying (quite charmingly) that the species derivation of the cheese or milk will determine the effectiveness of the erasure.

Early visual depictions of parchment making are few, though they provide a rich counterpoint to the descriptions of the process in written sources.[28] A well-known image of the craft appears in an initial from the Hamburg Bible, a magnificent three-volume pandect produced for Catherine of Hamburg in 1255 (see fig. 3.6).[29] In this sequence of the pandect, the program of decorated initials follows the process of book making, from the craft of parchment making through the art of illumination. At the opening of the Book of Daniel, in the historiated D in the incipit of Jerome's prologue [*Danielem prophetam*], a parchment maker plies his wares, holding a rolled bundle of membrane sheets beneath his right arm while displaying a sample for his prospective client. The miniature has often been reproduced in modern scholarship on the subject—though without regard for its own surrounding codicological context, which lends an imaginative depth to the image (fig. 3.7). At the feet of the two figures, an unfinished skin stretches across a wooden frame, bound by dark chords attached to pegs along the sides. The illuminator has left two shaded tongues on the white surface of the unfinished parchment, suggesting hair or gristle still to be scraped from its surface with the *lunellum* that rests against the bottom of the frame. The text rulings, still plainly visible between prickings on the left and right margins, link the ruled Latin in the text box with the two pieces of parchment open to the viewer's eye. The folio as a whole features two stitched repairs, pied striations from the finishing blade, and clear curvatures in the skin at the base, marking its derivation from the edge of a membrane—and resonating subtly with the appearance of the unfinished parchment sheet framed in the initial.

A series of images similarly associating finished manuscript page with parchment craft begins a twelfth-century collection of various works of St. Ambrose, a figure often associated iconographically with the practice of writing (see fig. 3.8). Here, ten roundels depict various aspects of the life of texts and books: the tonsured

Figure 3.6. A parchmenter, interrupted in mid-scrape, sells finished product. From the Hamburg Bible, Germany, middle of the thirteenth century. Copenhagen, Royal Library Ms. G.K.S. 4.2, fol. 183r (detail).

Figure 3.7. The initial in figure 3.6 appears on a folio featuring several notable flaws and original repairs to the membrane.

Figure 3.8.
Book-making
roundels from the
Bamberger Schrei-
berbild (Bamberg
scriptorium scene),
in a manuscript of
Ambrose, *Opera
varia*, from Bamberg,
Kloster Michelsberg,
middle of the twelfth
century. Bamberg,
Staatsbibliothek Ms.
Msc. Patr. 5, fol. IV.

Figure 3.9. Parchment-making roundel
from the Bamberger Schreiberbild (detail of
fig. 3.8).

subjects write, read, teach, sharpen a quill, rule a page, write in a wax tablet, tool a binding. The third roundel on the left register (detail, fig. 3.9) features a maker of parchment, his miniature *lunellum* scraping a skin (not much larger than his head) stretched in a frame. The outline drawing of the distended parchment leaves the hide's surface unshaded, unlike the brownish-red tint given to the wax in the roundel just above. Jonathan Alexander suggests that the illustrations on the page represent "the self-sufficiency principle within a Benedictine community, since all the stages of book production from preparing the parchment to binding the completed book are being performed by the monks themselves."[30] The membrane of the manuscript's folio is the same parchment being worked by the craftsman, an appropriately bookish overlay of illustrated medium and visual message.

In these and other medieval images of the craft, the depiction of parchment making remains closely tied to the sacred purpose of the surrounding text. The work of the maker is often at the service of *lectio divina*, the practice of contemplative reading that ideally governs the process of book making. This emphasis on parchment craft as devotional work gives way in certain later representations to a heightened realism and a stronger sense of proportion, emphasizing the full-body labor entailed in the production process. Consider a depiction of *der Permennter*, made from a copper engraving by Jost Amman for *Das Ständebuch*, produced in Nuremberg in 1568. The *Ständebuch* or Book of Trades was a popular compendium of verse and image depicting 113 representatives of various modes of employment at their work, beginning with the pope and descending all the way to the street cleaner. Amman places his *Permennter* in an outdoor setting with a soaking bucket at his feet, leaning over the stretched membrane with two additional framed parchments behind him (see fig. 3.10). The verse on the page, composed by Hans Sachs, presents the craft in four couplets that capture the rhythm of the process in its creaturely detail:

> I buy the skin of sheep, cow, and goat
> I put the hides in the tub,
> After that I rinse them clean
> Stretch out each skin in a frame
> Scrape it next, make parchment [*Permennt*] therefrom
> With great labor in my house.
> From ear and hoof I make glue,
> And sell it all from home.[31]

Amman's engraving of the parchment maker also appears in a contemporaneous trade book, Hartmann Schopper's *Panoplia omnium illiberalium mechanicarum aut*

Der Permennter.

Ich kauff Schaffell/Böck/vñ die Geiß/
Die Fell leg ich denn in die beyß/
Darnach firm ich sie sauber rein/
Spann auff die Ram jeds Fell allein/
Schabs darnach/mach Permennt darauß/
Mit grosser arbeit in mein Hauß/
Auß ohrn vnd klauwen seud ich Leim/
Das alles verkauff ich daheim.

Figure 3.10. A parchment maker from *Das Ständebuch* (Book of Trades). Woodcuts by Jost Amman, text by Hans Sachs (Frankfurt am Main, 1576), p. 93.

sedentariarum artium (1568), this time accompanied by Latin verses recounting the legend of Pergamon and the invention and uses of parchment.[32] In roughly the same genre is the *Hausbuch der Mendelschen Zwölfbrüderstiftung zu Nürnberg*, or House-book of the Mendel Foundation of Twelve Brothers in Nuremberg, a paper manuscript produced over a number of centuries that illustrates a range of crafts practiced by members of the Mendel Foundation.[33] Following the book's conventions, the parchment maker here is given a fitting moniker: Fritz Pyrmenter, his surname reflecting the practice of his craft (see fig. 3.11). The robed Fritz stands before the frame with the *lunellum* held in both hands, scraping a large rendered hide pinned

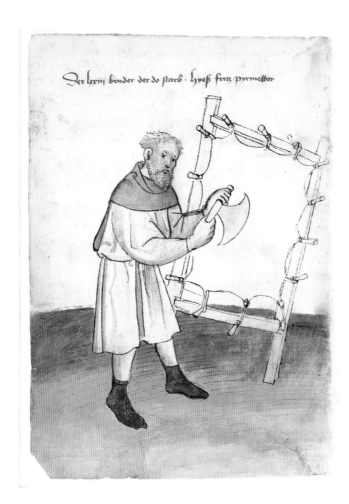

Der ħrɲij bruder der do ſtarb · hieß fritz pyrmeñter

Figure 3.11.
Fritz Pyrmenter
(Fritz the Parchment
Maker), from the
Mendel Housebook.
Nuremberg, ca. 1425.
Stadtbibliothek
Nürnberg Ms. Amb.
317.2°, fol. 34v.

tightly to the frame. And in an eighteenth-century etching by the great Augus-
burg engraver Martin Engelbrecht (fig. 3.12), a female parchment maker [*Eine Pergamenterin*] stands proudly displaying and playing her membrane wares: a fan, parchments in their frames, a drum, and other products of her craft.

    All of these early depictions of the parchment-making process shy away from
the subject of animal slaughter, favoring the milky-smooth surfaces of the medium
in its final stages of processing over the bloody mess of killing and flaying. The same
cannot be said of one of the more remarkable representations of parchment making
to survive from the medieval world. The image appears in a luxurious and richly illustrated fourteenth-century copy of the *Roman d'Alexandre*, a massive adventure-
romance-cum-biography of Alexander the Great composed and compiled over the

Figure 3.12. *Parchementiere.*
Eine Pergamenterin. A female
parchment maker surrounded
by parchment fans and frames
with stretched skins, striking
a large parchment-covered
drum. Hand-colored
etching and engraving from a
series by Martin Engelbrecht.
Augsburg, 1730–50. British
Museum no. 1996, 1103.85.

course of the twelfth and thirteenth centuries. The membrane is itself testament to
the investment and industry embodied by the book, of fine quality with few flaws
and repairs, clearly well selected by the book's makers.[34] At one point in the legend, Alexander's forces engage in a battle against the Duke of Palatine, who has ab-
ducted the wife of Candeolus, son of Alexander's rival and lover Queen Candace.
The battle scene (fig. 3.13) features the forces of the duke arrayed against Alexander's
men: swords drip with blood, helmets appear cleft on both sides, lozenge-shaped
head and leg wounds gaping as black gashes from the page, outlined in blood.

While this spectacle of martial carnage occupies the folio's featured image, the
bas-de-page comments bookishly on the violent waste of flesh above. On the left, one
monkey uses a pumice stone over a piece of stretched parchment in a frame, per-

Figure 3.13.
Folio with battle scene from *Roman d'Alexandre*. Tournai, completed 1344. Oxford, Bodleian Library Ms. Bodley 264, fol. 84r.

forming the final step in the parchment-making process (detail, fig. 3.14). The monkey on the right holds a hammer while fashioning a piece of plate armor, or perhaps a crown (though the image also suggests a *lunellum* to remove bloodied gristle and fat from a piece of animal hide, even as the hint of a face peers out from beneath the monkey's labor). The juxtaposition of the two images—bloodied humans in battle spearing and slaying their fellow human animals, grinning monkeys scraping and rubbing the hides of fellow creatures—at first glance seems to equate the violent carnage of war with the grisly process of parchment manufacture.

Yet there is also an ecological theme here in the juxtaposition of human warfare and primate craftsmanship. Unlike war, which entails the extravagant expenditure of flesh and blood of horse and human alike, parchment making is founded on an

economy of efficiency, in which the hide is made useful through the rendering process rather than left as carrion on the battlefield or decomposing in the grave. All of
this takes place on a parchment page, on animal skin we can plainly discern through
and as the carefully scraped hide stretched on the frame before us. The manuscript's
adjacent pages situate parchment and the slaughter it necessitates within the many
material economies elaborated in the illustrations: a team of smiths beating iron
and gold with the agency of hammer, fire, and air; a peasant bearing grain to a wind-
mill; a tired cook boiling the carcasses of slaughtered animals; a shepherd's feeding
of a sheepdog (some of his charges cousins, perhaps, to the lambs making up the vol-

Figure 3.14. In the *bas-de-page* a monkey makes parchment, while another fashions a
crown or plate (detail of fig. 3.13).

ume before us). All these scenes form part of a larger pastoral ecology that lends an uncanny realism to the spectacle of monkeys making parchment.

The surviving recipes for parchment making in writings from the Christian tradition tend to steer clear of intra-craft controversy. There is little or no disagreement in these formulas about the proper way of going about the business of rendering acceptable sheets from slaughtered beasts, and they rarely acknowledge the existence of earlier discussions of the subject. The same cannot be said for the numerous early treatments of parchment making in the Jewish tradition, which provide a sharp contrast to the often vague and morally neutral discussions of the process in gentile sources. Rabbinic authorities are often quite frank about regional and sectarian biases that differentiate one custom of parchment craft from another, even to the extent of investigating the accuracy of each other's claims.

A fascinating example of such controversy occurs in medieval and early modern discussions of so-called split parchment. The twelfth-century philosopher and theologian Moses Maimonides has this to say on the matter of parchment made from hides that have been split:

> If, after removing the hair, the hide had been split through its thickness into two layers . . . so as to make of it two skins, one thin, namely, that which had been next to the hair; the other thick, namely, that which had been next to the flesh . . . the layer which had been next to the hair is called *klaf*, and the one which had been next to the flesh is called *dukhsustos*.[35]

Maimonides takes it for granted that artisans regularly split hides in two, creating discrete membranes of distinct thicknesses, textures, and qualities, all of which impact their suitability for one kind of writing or another. Certain Talmudic discussions of split skins similarly assume technological know-how among parchment makers sufficient to divide animal hides by hand and render the separate layers of *klaf* and *dukhsustos*.

Such evident confidence in the theological literature, though, was very much misplaced. We get a much more skeptical note on the feasibility of splitting parchment in the writings of Benjamin Mussafia (1606-1675), a Kabbalist, philologist, and court physician to the Danish king Christian IV during the 1640s. Mussafia was also an encyclopedist, producing a compendium of Talmudic knowledge, the *Musaf he-'Aruk*, published in 1655 following his move to Amsterdam (and never translated).

Mussafia's long entry on parchment in the *Aruk* ranges over a number of technical and cultural aspects of the medium, including the matter of splitting skins, on which he actually consults with local parchment makers in his adopted city. Here he is commenting on the technical meaning of the term *dukhsustos*:

> The word in Greek means an animal skin which has been prepared on both sides. The understanding the legal authorities have of this word is especially difficult for me. Firstly, we don't find that animal skin is actually split into two parts. Indeed, I asked numerous skinworkers about this, but to them I seemed to be joking. They told me that if they had the ability to do such a thing, they would double or quadruple their profits by making two skins out of one, or two thin skins out of one thick one. Secondly, the matter is so difficult that, given that it is preferable to write a *mezuzah* on *dukhsustos*, none of the rabbis make pains to have *dukhsustos* available to them! Far be it from me to dispute the words of the legal authorities—I am only trying to practice my [academic] skill . . . Whoever told Rabbenu Tam that *dukhsustos* means flesh in Greek lied to him.[36]

The passage hints at the often unspoken tension between learned theological authority and hands-on craft experience. Rather than settling for the received wisdom of the commentary tradition or even relying on his own theological expertise, Mussafia turns to local makers (most of them probably gentiles) with an everyday knowledge of the parchment craft. As these artisans disdainfully inform him, the dividing of skins in the way implied by the Talmud is a practical impossibility, despite intriguing evidence of the practice in earlier rabbinic sources (see chap. 11 below). As in Mussafia's day, the subject of split skins remains a matter of some controversy among scholars and makers alike (see the discussion of uterine vellum in chap. 5 below).

A similar reverence for craft knowledge informs the wide-ranging entry on *parchemin* included in the *Encyclopédie, ou Dictionnaire raisonné des sciences, des arts et des métiers, par une Société de Gens de lettres*, the great compendium of Enlightenment knowledge published between 1751 and 1772 and overseen by Diderot and d'Alembert—though the through-reader of the *Encyclopédie* will encounter the parchment entry several volumes and years after encountering the long entry on the Qur'ān (*"Alcoran ou al-Coran"*). Here the encyclopedists tell an origin story for Islam's holy book that resonates strangely with the tale of St. Ciarán and his cow:

> But the Muslims believed, as an article of faith, that their Prophet, who they say was a simple and unlettered man, put nothing of his own into this book, that he received

it from God through the ministering of the Angel Gabriel, written on a parchment made of the skin of the ram [*sur un parchemin fait de la peau du belier*] that Abraham sacrificed in place of his son Isaac, and that it was communicated to him only gradually, verse by verse in different times and in different places, over the course of twenty-three years. Thanks to these interruptions they claim to justify the confusion that reigns throughout the work, a confusion that it is impossible to clarify, that their most able Doctors have worked vainly upon, for Mohammed, or if you prefer, his copyist, had gathered pell-mell all these supposed revelations, and so it was no longer possible to find in what order they had been sent from Heaven.[37]

The medium of the Qur'ān, in this account, is the skin of the sacrificed ram, the animal that Abraham found entangled in the bush and slaughtered in place of his son. The ram's parchment carries the faulty and confused text of the work, supposedly bungled by years of delay and interruption in its transmission. The peculiar legend was repeated in numerous encyclopedias and handbooks of practical knowledge throughout the eighteenth and nineteenth centuries and on both sides of the Atlantic.[38] Though its specific source is unknown, the legend bears a close resemblance to a medieval Jewish legend about the origin of the *Zohar* (see below, chap. 11) and may have resulted from a confusion in the early modern period between the two Abrahamic texts and traditions.

The author of the *parchemin* entry in the *Encyclopédie* can be identified as Joseph Jérôme Le Français de Lalande, who in 1762 released his own *Art de faire le parchemin*.[39] This exhaustive study of the craft was published as one of a series of books from the royal Académie des sciences on various technical trades (Lalande also authored the volume on the art and history of paper making).[40] Lalande's redaction in the *Encyclopédie* begins with a skeptical account of the long history of the medium since the ancient world.[41] The technology of parchment was only perfected in the modern era, or so Lalande claims: the entry describes a thriving contemporary international trade in parchment between England, the Low Countries, Spain, and Portugal, making little mention of the medieval history of the medium. The entry includes a detail-oriented description of the parchment-making process, evoking the sight of skins soaking in a river and describing the process of stretching the wet hides on a frame before their drying and scraping, then their bundling for sale and delivery in packets of thirty-six skins [*bottes de parchemin*]. The entry emphasizes the brute force required to scrape skins into the correct thinness, though also the delicacy and lack of damage to the surface at the hands of a skilled maker. Once the parchments have been prepared, the entry goes on, they must be cut into the correct sizes for their designated uses: as quittances or receipts, patents, parliamen-

Figure 3.15. Robert Bénard, "Parchemi-nier," from *Parchemin* entry in Diderot, *Encyclopédie, ou Dictionnaire raisonné des sciences, des arts et des métiers par une Société de Gens de Lettres*, Plate I (Paris, 1768).

tary and legal records, marriage licenses, chancery documents, and so on, with the size of each specified. The entry concludes on a skeptical note concerning the putative origin of one particular variety of vellum ("so called because it is made from the skin of a dead calf," the author notes): "There is also parchment made from the skin of a stillborn lamb, but it is extremely thin and only used for delicate work, such as in the making of fans; it is called virgin parchment; some believe that this kind of parchment is made from the membrane that covers the heads of some newborns; but this is an error engendered by superstition."[42]

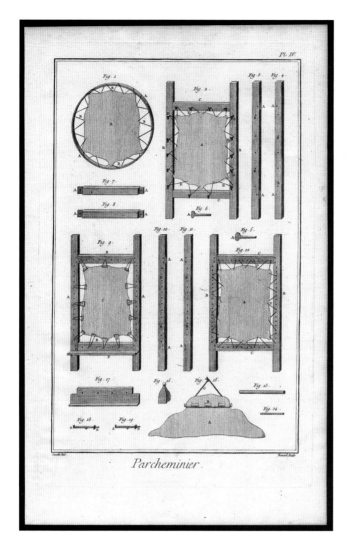

Figure 3.16. Robert Bénard, "Parcheminier," Plate IV.

Lalande's entry on parchment is accompanied by seven engravings, created by Robert Bénard, showing the craft and tools of the *parcheminier*. Along with the other engravings commissioned for the *Encyclopédie*, this sequence was published in a subsequent volume and appears to represent an expansion of the three included in Lalande's *Art de faire le parchemin*. In a well-ordered workshop occupying the top panel of Plate I (fig. 3.15), six men labor through various stages of the craft: soaking, stretching, scraping, finishing, and so on. The lower register shows their instruments of finishing: pumice stones, sandpaper, benches for the seated work illustrated in the upper panel. Plate IV (fig. 3.16) displays skins stretched on wooden frames of various sizes, depicted with their components both separated and conjoined.

The *Encyclopédie*'s illustrations of parchment manufacture present the craft as a thriving and ordered industry, with neat arrays of tools and equipment, no sign of besmeared laborers or flayed carcasses, a workshop neat as a pin. In true eighteenth-century fashion, Lalande's entry on *parchemin* exhibits all the Enlightenment confidence about an endlessly complicated and refined practice, here stripped of its animality and its mess, the gristle and stink that suffused the parchment industry of the premodern world. Printed on paper and intended for mass consumption, the entry and its plates present the craft in terms of its transparency: clean lines, a clear process, a known history of utility from the beginnings of human civilization to modernity's nascent industrial present. The parchment, in this worldview, is flawless.

⇥ ⇤

CHAPTER FOUR

THE FLAYED FOLIO

Those were the days of ups and downs,
Of bloody fingers and cloven crowns.
Never a thought had they of law,
Of a title's strength or a parchment's flaw.
—GEORGE HENRY BOKER, "THE FIDDLER"

Killing, butchering, bleeding, flaying, soaking, stretching, scraping, drying, pumicing, sanding: to make parchment, then as now, requires an aggressive, even combative approach to the organic matter destined to receive ruling, word, and image. Medieval and early modern artisans possessed widely varying levels of competence and care as they addressed the stretched hides before them. Modern parchment makers, too, working with splitting machines and industrial-sized soaking vats, contend with the limits of their own craftsmanship while processing hides into usable sheets of parchment: the slip of a hunter's knife, a belt sander held at too sharp an angle in the workshop.

The membrane record bears innumerable artifacts of these human inflictions on the hides of rendered creatures, alongside myriad traces of animal life and death inhabiting their inscribed or illuminated remains.[1] These flaws and sutures, curves and cockles, veins and bites, hairs and holes populating the folios of codices, scrolls, and records are persistent reminders of the medium's irreducible animality, prompting readers past and present to imagine the nonhuman creatures on and from which they wrote and read. The art of description, Mark Doty writes, is an art of distinction: an attunement to "those braiding elements of the *sensorium*—that continuous, complex response to things perpetually delivered by the senses, the encompassing sphere that is such a large part of our subjectivity."[2] To observe and linger over the animality of a written object is to inhabit the sensorium of reading and seeing in new and often unfamiliar ways, as an enlivening dimension of textual experience.

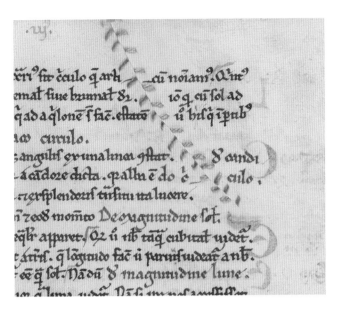

Figure 4.1. A sutured repair in a manuscript of Isidore of Seville, *Etymologies*. Italy, late twelfth/early thirteenth century. New York, Columbia University Libraries Ms. Plimpton 125, fol. 29r (detail).

Of course, the sciences of codicology and collections care have hardly neglected or obscured these zoological elements of membrane writings. As we have already seen, the creaturely substance of written artifacts has sparked its own unofficial idiom of bibliographical description. Conservationists, too, work regularly with animal products—hide powder, gelatin sizing, goldbeater's skin (aka bovine intestinal lining), fish skin bladder, sturgeon glue, sausage casing—in the repair of membrane and other artifacts.[3] Such observations only reinforce the extent to which every vellum folio, every parchment charter is simultaneously a unique and tangible record of faunal life and death, decomposition and dismemberment. Yet each one is also a product of craftwork, a unique hand-made artifact that survives as a testament to human ingenuity in the historical rendering of fellow creatures for the recording and preservation of culture.

This entanglement of animal death and human artisanship plays out on and within the written record, lending each parchment object its own thickness and grain, textures and contours, its own tangible proof of bygone life. A suture's width forces scribal skips across nine lines of Latin (fig. 4.1). A gaping hole swerves an otherwise vertical column of Irish words (fig. 4.2); another nudges the notated chants in a Ge'ez antiphonary to the side (fig. 4.3). Over a long tear at the base of a page, a silken string gathers seven small holes into a floral pattern along a ladder of stitches (fig. 4.4). Scribes faced with gaps in the parchment surface will often stray from the rulings on the page to arc or dip sentences around a hole in the

Figure 4.2.
Parchment hole in
Leabhar Ua Maine,
an Irish miscellany.
Connacht, late four-
teenth century. Dub-
lin, Royal Irish Acad-
emy Ms. D II 1,
fol. 20v (detail).

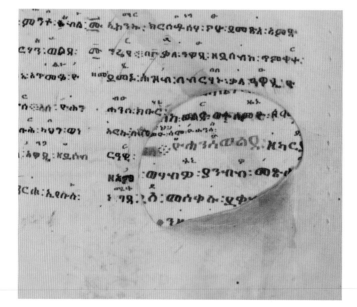

Figure 4.3.
Parchment hole in a
Ge'ez Antiphonary
for the Year. Ethio-
pia, nineteenth cen-
tury. Princeton,
Princeton University
Library Ethiopic Ms.
No. 26, fol. 6r.

Figure 4.4. A petaled parchment repair in the *bas-de-page* of a manuscript of Ovid's *Metamorphoses*. Italy, thirteenth century. Palo Alto, Stanford University Library CODEX M0414 CB, fol. 35v (detail).

skin; a hole's contours might shape the beginning or ending of one or more lines of text or dilate within an entire text block (fig. 4.5).[4] Others will simply leap the pen over them, continuing a word on the far side, as in a twelfth-century Bavarian compilation of geometrical texts; here, a large lozenge-shaped hole bisects the Latin word *longitudine* between the third and fourth syllables (fig. 4.6). Elsewhere in the same book, two lines of Latin text are cut short to compensate for a tear-shaped gap (fig. 4.7), while an awkward indentation compensates for another (fig. 4.8).

The creaturely aspect of the membrane manuscript can often determine the shape of a finished page or charter. The flayed hide of an animal is hardly a perfect rectangle, as we have seen in depictions of stretched skins during the production process. Membranes often betray the original curves of the haunches, necks, and shoulders of the donor animals, whether the wavy curves at the base of a folio (fig. 4.9) or scooped cutaways along bottom edges (fig. 4.10). Figure 4.11 and figure 4.12 suggest how an eighth-century charter from St. Gallen might have been cut from a piece of sheep parchment along with other sheets for documents of various sizes and shapes.[5]

Figure 4.5.
A parchment
hole in an Arabic
martyrology. Egypt,
tenth century. Mount
Sinai, Saint Cather-
ine's Monastery Ms.
Sinai Arabic 461,
fol. 31v.

The contours of a flayed hide could thus often result in a quite misshapen folio, the skin's curvature arcing through a substantial portion of the page to determine the contours of a marginal gloss (fig. 4.13). Sometimes such cutaways and edge
pieces will afford a glimpse of layered skins of varying hues and thicknesses making
up the subsequent pages (fig. 4.14). An extreme example appears in a Merovingian
florilegium in which the words of a dictum attributed to St. Ambrose hunch within
a heavily striated triangle created by the meandering edge of a drastic cutaway
(fig. 4.15).[6]

A twelfth-century Middle English work, the *Ormulum* (so named for its monastic author and compiler, Orm), survives in a single autograph manuscript made
mostly from edge pieces—leading generations of scholars to deride it as a grotesque
mockery of proper codex form (fig. 4.16). As J. A. W. Bennett once described the *Ormulum*, "only about one fifth survives and that in the ugliest of manuscripts."[7] And
yet there is a sober beauty to this book, its membranes folded along their full length,

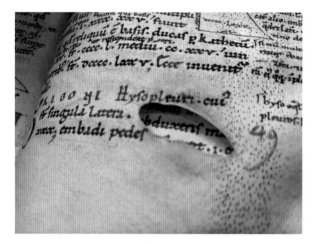

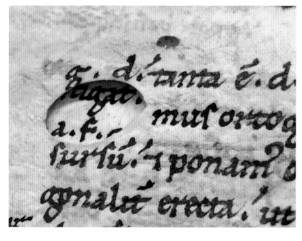

Figures 4.6, 4.7, and 4.8.
Scattered membrane flaws
in a copy of the *Geometria*
of Pope Sylvester II
(ca. 945–1003). Austria (?),
1125–1175. Details from
Philadelphia, University of
Pennsylvania Ms. LJS 194,
fols. 40r, 37r, and 30v.

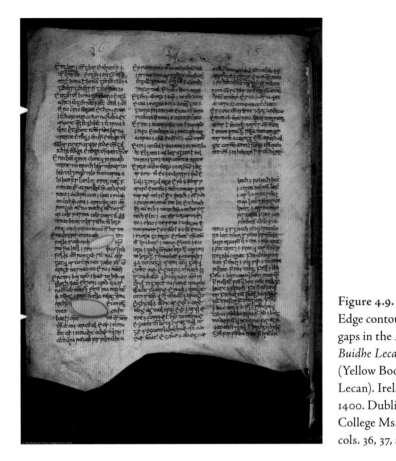

Figure 4.9.
Edge contours and gaps in the *Leabhar Buidhe Lecain* (Yellow Book of Lecan). Ireland, ca. 1400. Dublin, Trinity College Ms. 1318, cols. 36, 37, and 38.

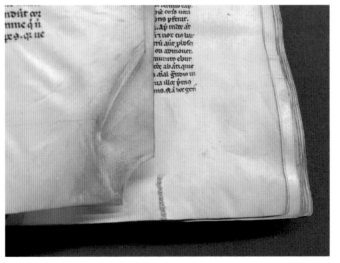

Figure 4.10.
Overlapping membrane edges and repairs in a copy of Isidore of Seville's *Etymologies*. Catalonia, last third of the thirteenth century. Philadelphia, University of Pennsylvania Ms. LJS 184, fols. 103r, 104r, and 105r.

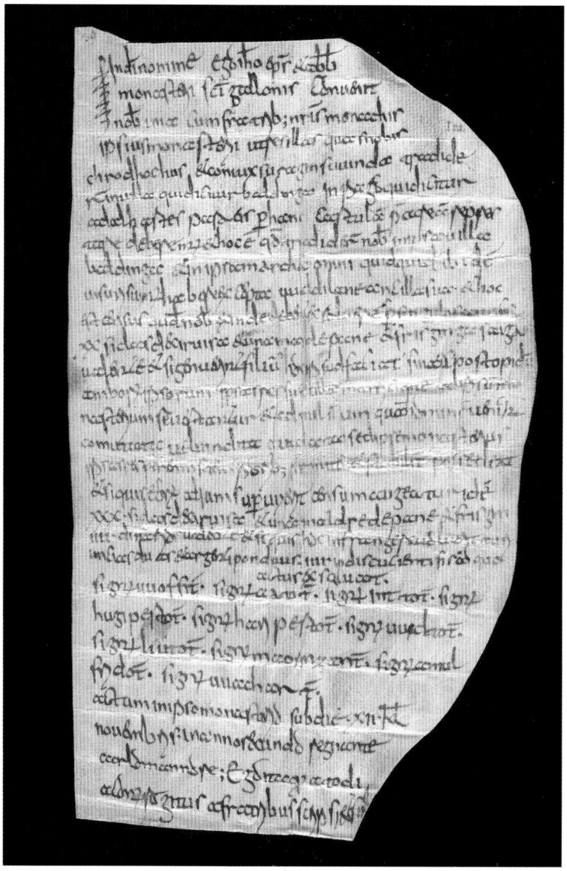

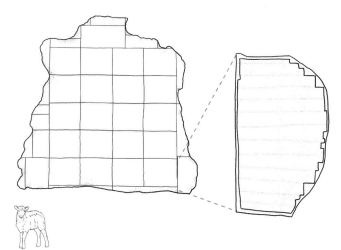

Figure 4.11. An eighth-century charter from the monastery of St. Gallen in Switzerland, rendered from a contoured offcut. St. Gallen, Stiftsarchiv Cod. cart. I 39 (October 21, 769).

Figure 4.12.
A rendering of a sheepskin, showing possible offcuts for documents such as the charter in figure 4.11.

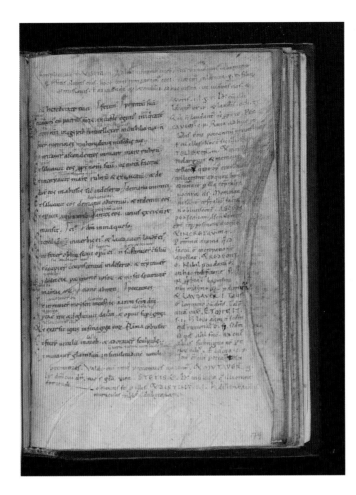

Figure 4.13.
A thickly contoured membrane at the edge of a glossed psalter page. France, ca. 1100. Philadelphia, University of Pennsylvania Ms. Codex 1058, fol. 74r.

lending a striking oblong shape to the whole; nor is there any evidence to suggest that Orm himself regarded his membranes as waste product or castaways.[8]

As in the case of the *Ormulum*, the workaday density of any given manuscript's animality may govern not only mise-en-page but the reader's tactile or haptic experience of all or part of a book. Harley 3698 transmits the text of *Practica dicta Lilium medicine* (*Practical Sayings: The Lily of Medicine*), a summa of medical knowledge written by Bernardus de Gordonia, who taught on the medical faculty at the University of Montpelier in the early decades of the fourteenth century. The manuscript is characterized throughout by numerous holes and flaws in the skin, some of them repaired, some not; and by an irregular pattern of page preparation that

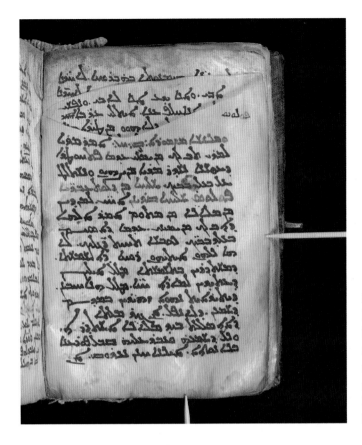

Figure 4.14.
Layered offcuts in a Syriac lectionary. Sinai, Egypt, eleventh century. Mount Sinai, Saint Catherine's Monastery Ms. Sinai Syriac 13, fol. 22v.

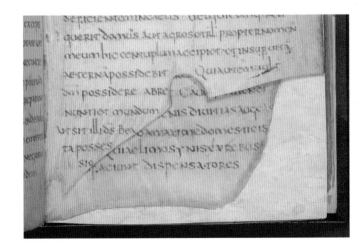

Figure 4.15.
Curvature in two folio edges of a patristic florilegium. France, second quarter of the eighth century. British Library Ms. Harley 5041, fol. 13r (detail).

Figure 4.16. A shapely opening in Orm's *Ormulum*. Lincolnshire, ca. 1180. Oxford, Bodleian Library Ms. Junius 1, fols. 9v–10r.

has left a consistent record of animal palpability within and among the folios. The book's 105 folios divide into twelve quires or gatherings (the smaller membrane booklets which, when bound together, make up a larger codex). The second quire (see fig. 4.17 and fig. 4.18) consists of six folios (fols. 9–14), each of which represents half a bifolium—that is, a single membrane making up two folios that may or may not be adjacent. Thus one bifolium or folded parchment sheet gives us folios 9 and 14, another 10 and 13, and, in the middle of the gathering, a third bifolium yields folios 11 and 12. Within the space of the single gathering, then, the reader encounters the hides of what were most likely three distinct beasts, each with its own characteristic textures, shades, shapes, and contours left by the processes of rendering, flaying, and making. These include stitched repairs snaking across several inches in the margin and base of the page (fig. 4.19), prominent holes (fig. 4.20), and, in the case of the innermost bifolium, a stark vestige of the skinner's marks in the cut of a thick and darkly contoured shoulder or haunch (fig. 4.21). The most efficient way to flip to the verso here is to finger these stiff, cardboard-like arcs marking the curved edge of a flayed skin and turn the page.

Though artisans may have done their best to rid their skins of any remaining hairs in the finishing process, examples abound of flaws, holes, and gaps to which hair and wool still cling to the edges. In an eleventh-century copy of Gregory the Great's *Moralia in Iob* now at the Beinecke Library (fig. 4.22), a hole in the skin divides two phrases of Gregory's Latin (*et in / igne ostenditur* on the first line, *quia quicunque illo / pleni sunt* on the second). A thousand years on, the circumference still bristles with tufts of calf hair left behind, exposed to our eyes, resilient to our touch—as in a Hebrew grammatical miscellany from fourteenth-century Italy, where a hole, gristle-rimmed, bristles with stiff hairs (fig. 4.23).

Parchment veining is another prominent sign of animal derivation, the result of incomplete or insufficient bleeding of a butchered animal before flaying. "Veined parchment may make an interesting bookbinding today," says Leila Avrin, "but in the Middle Ages it never would have been acceptable for a text page."[9] A strong claim, belied by at least a dozen blackly veined folios in a luxurious presentation manuscript of works by Christine de Pizan and others (fig. 4.24); in the Codex Aureus, an eighth-century insular Gospel book in which spidery veins on multiple folios add to the vividly marbled aspect of the membrane (fig. 4.25); and in a tenth-century copy of John the Deacon's *Life of St. Gregory the Great* (fig. 4.26) whose creamy parchment exhibits stark veining that spiders well into the text block.[10] On multiple folios of these books, networks of veins and capillaries run alongside and within the written text, leaving the vascular system of the rendered beast often as legible as the words on its skin.

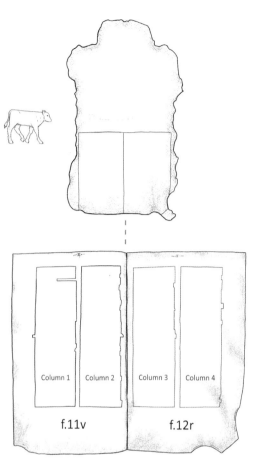

Column 1 Column 2 Column 3 Column 4

f.11v f.12r

Figure 4.17. Diagram showing how a sheet of parchment (such as the irregular bifolium pictured in fig. 4.21) might be cut from the middle and edges of a hide.

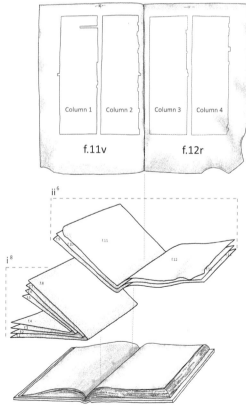

Figure 4.18. Rendering of the first two quires of British Library Ms. Harley 3698. The same irregular sheet shown above becomes part of a quire in a manuscript, in this case the middle two folios of the second quire (ii), which contains six folios in all (indicated by the superscript 6).

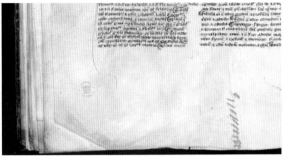

Figure 4.19. Signs of parchment production and repair in the second quire of the *Practica dicta Lilium medicina* of Bernardus de Gordonio. France, first quarter of the fourteenth century. London, British Library Ms. Harley 3698, fol. 9v (detail).

Figure 4.20. A parchment hole in the same quire, fol. 10r (detail).

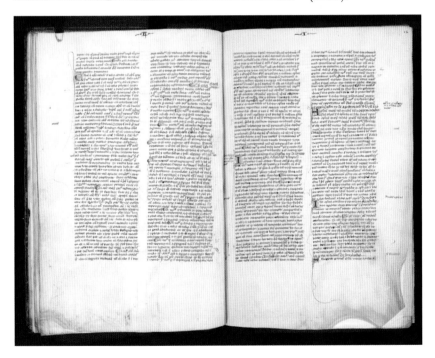

Figure 4.21. The middle bifolium of the quire, showing the thick edges of the membrane (fols. 11v–12r).

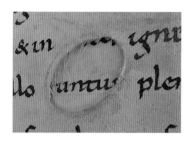

Figure 4.22. A hair-lined gap in the parchment in Gregory the Great, *Moralia in Iob*. Merseburg, Germany, ca. 1000. New Haven, Yale University Beinecke Ms. 1107, fol. 15r (detail).

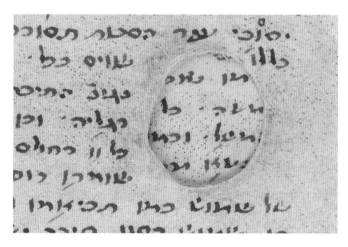

Figure 4.23. The cartilaginous circumference of a parchment hole in a Hebrew grammatical miscellany. Italy, fourteenth century. London, British Library Ms. Or 14058, fol. 64r (detail).

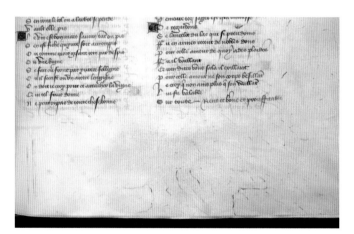

Figure 4.24. Trace veining in *The Book of the Queen*. France, ca. 1410–1414. London, British Library Ms. Harley 4431, fol. 67r (detail).

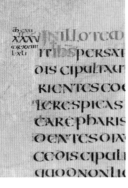

Figure 4.25. Marginal and interlinear veining in Codex Aureus, a Gospel book of the eighth century. Canterbury, ca. 750. Stockholm, National Library of Sweden Ms. A. 135, fol. 27v (detail).

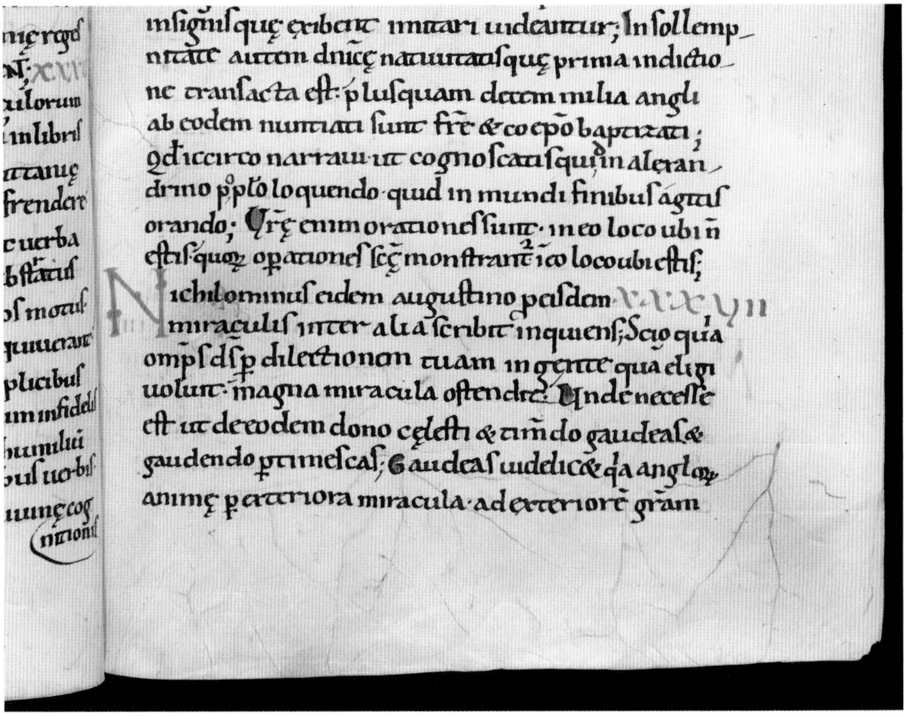

Figure 4.26. Prominent veining in a manuscript of John the Deacon's *Life of St. Gregory the Great*. England, late eleventh century. Oxford, Jesus College Ms. 37, fol. 35r.

Figure 4.27. Follicles in the margin of the Old English translation of Orosius, *Historia adversus paganos*. Winchester, late ninth or early tenth century. London, British Library Ms. Additional 47967, fol. 62v (detail).

Figure 4.28. Molding on the edge of an Esther scroll in Sefardi square script. Sixteenth century (n.p.). London, British Library Ms. Additional 11833, first membrane.

Membrane manuscripts thus bear numerous marks of the myriad beasts constituting their pages: hair follicles, the cockling and bulging and molding of the skin, ghostly impressions of epidermal and hair pigmentation signatures in calves and goats (see figs. 4.27, 4.28, 4.29, and 4.30). The contours of the animal body and the preparation of the membrane also determine the malleability and bendability of the finished page. Some call this dimension of membrane the drape, the compara-

Figure 4.29.
Extreme parchment
cockling and bulging
in a Privy Seal book
awaiting preserva-
tion. Westminster,
1665-1659. Kew,
National Archives E
403/2570. © Crown
copyright (2017).
Licensed under the
Open Government
License v3.0.

tive "softness and flexibility" of a given folio or document.[11] Much like a carpet or a bolt of cloth, some parchment will have good drape, while some (such as the medical manuscript described above) will have poor drape resulting from the stiffness of the membrane—though drape can also change over time depending on frequency of use and nature of storage. Certain larger medieval choir books from the later Middle Ages were assembled not just with quires or booklets but sometimes with singletons, one trimmed hide per folio, leaving dark traces of animal spines running up pages that feature graphic juxtapositions of luxury and utility (fig. 4.31). Against the beauty of the illuminated initial and the expense of the gold leaf, the imprint of spine follicles evokes the corporeality of such massive books. At each turn of the page, the drape may betray a skeletal axis by flopping over at the spine of the rendered beast.

Other sorts of parchment records display their faunal origins in more forthright ways, their zoomorphic shapes retained in whole or in part during the crafting process to become integral to their appearance and even function. Diplomatic

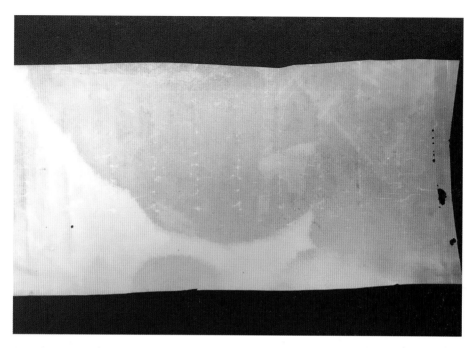

Figure 4.30. Epidermal pigmentation on the dorse of a notarial scroll. Padua, 1555. University of Virginia Albert and Shirley Small Special Collections Library, Ms. 9772-a No. 70.

Figure 4.31. Epidermal pigmentation and the ghost of a spine in a large choir book. Italy, early sixteenth century. University of Virginia Albert and Shirley Small Special Collections Library Accession #229, fol. 14r.

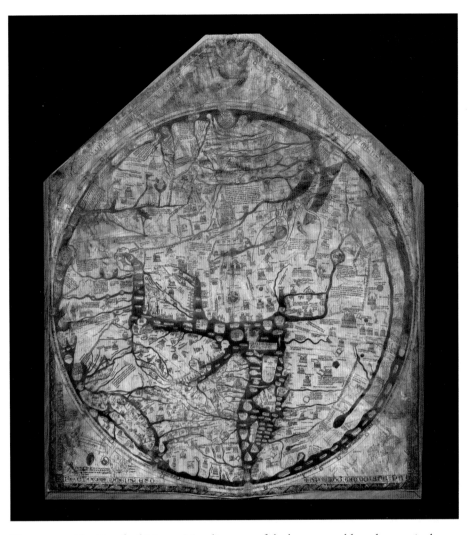

Figure 4.32. The Hereford Mappa Mundi, a map of the known world made on a single membrane. Lincolnshire, ca. 1300.

records from numerous eras and regions survive on whole-hide membranes, such as a pair of Greek charters of the late eighteenth century, their necks repurposed to hold pendant seals.[12] More well known is the Hereford Mappa Mundi, a thirteenth-century *carta* or map of the world written and illustrated on the flesh side of a single membrane, heavily cockled with age and moisture and with the animal's vascular system visible in several places (fig. 4.32). The figure of Christ enthroned sits

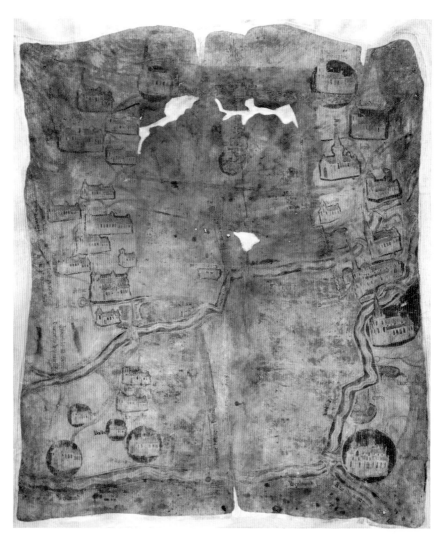

Figure 4.33. The Pinchbeck Fen Map, displaying settlements, churches, and granges on a single skin. Lincolnshire, middle of the fifteenth century. Kew, National Archives PRO MPCC 7 (recto).

at the top of the map, displaying the wounds on the skin of his open palms as his eyes gaze out from the neck of the calf whose flayed hide encompasses both his body and the known world.[13] The map includes a high degree of documentary self-consciousness, displaying a parchment charter complete with seal in the lower left margin.[14] A lesser-known example, more moderate in its cartographic aspirations, is the Pinchbeck Fen Map, a vividly painted chart of the Lincolnshire fenland dating from the fifteenth century (fig. 4.33). Drawn and painted on a whole sheet of parchment, the map is oriented with the spine running the vertical axis and dividing the green-hued fen, the animal's contours providing the natural boundaries of the cartographic range.[15] Another more mundane example is the map of Sherwood Forest long held at Belvoir Castle in Leicestershire (fig. 4.34). The map details the lodges, deer parks, chapels, and other structures dotting the environs of the forest. The top of the skin has been cut into an ogee-like curvature that culminates in the sharp point at the neck.

Mapmakers of the premodern era worked regularly with such zoomorphic parchment sheets, often leaving their shoulder, neck, and haunch portions intact and even incorporating them into the design of their charts. The most arresting ex-

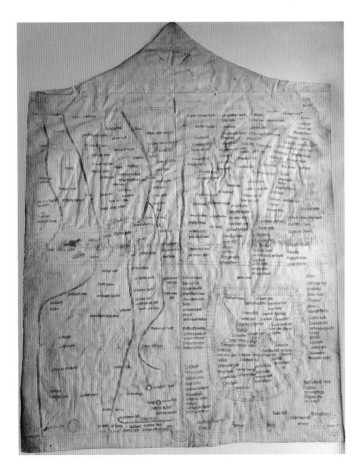

Figure 4.34. Map of Sherwood Forest, drawn on a single piece of sheepskin parchment. Leicestershire, late fourteenth century. Belvoir Castle archives, Map 125.

amples of this cartographic practice are the so-called portolan charts, maps of the Mediterranean Sea and, later, the Atlantic coast of Africa produced from the middle of the fourteenth century through the end of the sixteenth. Nearly two hundred of these charts (so called after the Italian *portolano*, a gathering of sailing charts) survive. Once called the "first true maps," they have been described as "one of the most important turning points in the whole history of cartography," indeed as "a living record of Mediterranean self-knowledge."[16] An apt description for a form of *carta* that nearly always presents its cartographic knowledge on the visibly apparent hide of an animal, and very often integrates the contours of the creature's hide into the chart's decoration, embellishment, and usage (see fig. 4.35).

This is particularly true of the neck, which could serve as a medium for presenting a family's coat of arms, a portrait of Madonna and Child, the signature of the artist or cartographer, or calendrical notations. A fifteenth-century medical doctor, Ibrāhīm Al Mursī, produced his chart in 1461 on a single piece of gazelle skin and filled the animal's neck with a drawing of the Islamic calendar.[17] The neck also served cartographic purposes: as the Atlantic Ocean and the western span of the Mediterranean took on increasing importance for trade into the early modern period, the orientation of the neck shifted in some cases from east to west, with a westward rotation allowing for more detailed renderings of newly mapped territories. In some cases the space of the neck allowed mapmakers to capture both real and imagined islands and archipelagoes in the Atlantic.

Mateus Prunes (1532–1594), scion of a family of Majorcan mapmakers, produced a spiritedly detailed portolan chart in 1559, now held by the Library of Congress. The Prunes chart (fig. 4.36) embraces portions of the Black Sea and the Red Sea as well as the entirety of the Mediterranean, along with the northernmost portion of the Atlantic coast of Africa as far south as Senegal and the coast of continental Europe up to Norway. Like any number of portolan charts, the Prunes map enlists the contours of the hide to embrace various features of the map and its apparatus. Winds are embodied as puff-cheeked cherubs (one of them in the neck) blowing across the sea from every direction, numerous creatures (both mythical and not) frolic on several continents, while parchment scrolls are unwound to show the unpainted membrane beneath (detail, fig. 4.37).

Why would so many makers of the portolan charts have left these vellum or parchment sheets intact? How is it that a revolution in cartography could be tied so intimately to the unvarnished animality of the medium that supported it? It's simple enough to cut parchment sheets into rectangles and sew or glue them together to create larger charts; given the central importance of scrolls to legal procedure and record-keeping, such a documentary practice must have occurred to navigators.

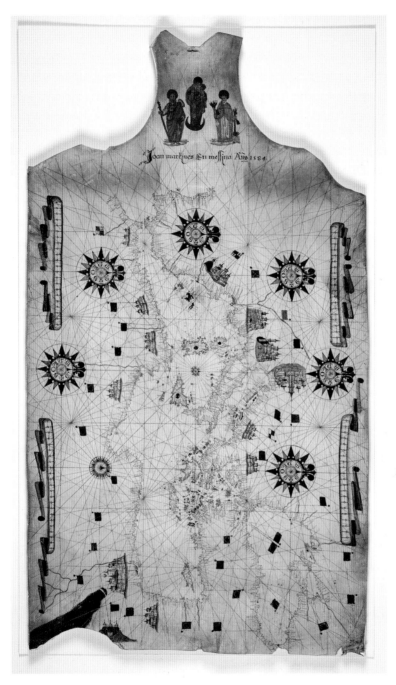

Figure 4.35. Joan Martines, portolan chart on vellum. Messina, 1584. Cambridge, Trinity College Ms. R.4.50 (recto).

Figure 4.36.
Mateus Prunes, chart
of the Mediterranean
Sea, Black Sea, and
the coasts of western
Europe and north-
west Africa. Majorca,
1559. Washington,
D.C., Library of
Congress Geography
and Map Reading
Room G5672.M4P5
1559 .P7 (recto).

Figure 4.37.
Scrolls and unicorn
in the Prunes chart
(detail of fig. 4.36).

Perhaps many of these cartographers were simply following convention, preserving the zoomorphic character of the charts so they would be recognized as part of an established and authoritative cartographic genre. The preservation of the neck had a practical logic as well: a hole pricked in the neck for a cord or thong allowed for easier binding when the map was rolled up.[18] Whatever motivated these generations of cartographers to retain the zoomorphic features in their charts, though, the maps themselves remained visibly and texturally vestiges of skin. Though it has been said that the portolan chart "seems to have emerged full-blown from the seas it describes," the genre's predominant medium derived from hoofed quadrupeds grazing on the same lands that first nourished its human makers.[19]

A more eccentric crafter of membrane *cartae* was the polymath Opicinus de Canistris (ca. 1296–1353), a priest, cartographer, and visionary who spent the latter portion of his career at the papal curia in Avignon. Opicinus was clearly indebted to the early portolan tradition, incorporating its conventions and schemata into the design of much of his idiosyncratic production.[20] In addition to writing treatises defending the papacy against its enemies and opponents, Opicinus was the creator of two major compilations, Vat. lat. 6435, a paper codex of 87 heavily illustrated folios consisting in large part of allegorized maps of the Mediterranean world; and Vat. Pal. lat. 1993, among the most inventive and astonishing bibliographic artifacts of the premodern world.[21] The extraordinary manuscript compilation consists of a series of single pages each derived from a whole sheet of parchment still exhibiting its cutaways for limbs, haunches, and neck (see fig. 4.38 and fig. 4.39). Opicinus likely purchased his membranes in whole uncut form from a parchmenter and decided against trimming the processed hides himself before beginning his magnum opus; rather, he left the membranes in their original flayed shape, and exploited their zoomorphic forms to create a series of illustrations full of bodily reference and doubles entendres that make the compilation a fascinatingly self-reflexive evocation of parchment as medium and message.

Here there is space to glimpse at just one of Opicinus's "body-worlds," as Karl Whittington has helpfully characterized them: "visions of continents and oceans transformed into human figures."[22] Such figures are multiply visible on Folio 10 (fig. 4.40), a membrane dominated by the large image at its center (either God the Father or the Church), whose body contains and organizes the others: the four evangelists on the sides, top, and bottom whose wings help shape the surrounding lozenge; as well as the Crucifixion depicted within and below the central medallion, with the Virgin Mary and St. John the Evangelist standing at either side. Whittington has pointed to the figure's indebtedness to the Zodiac Man, a tradition of illustration that associates human body parts with particular astrological signs, one of

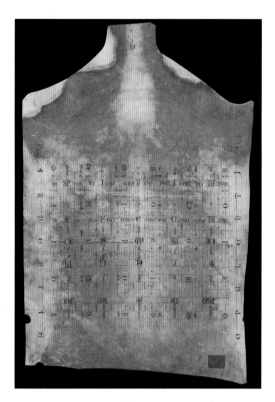 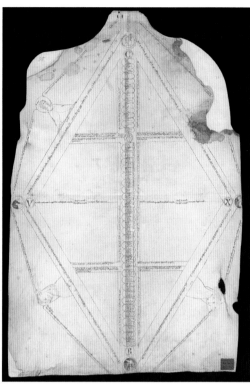

Figures 4.38 and 4.39. Opicinus de Canistris, membranes from the Palatinus manuscript with spine pigmentation and edge cuts. Avignon, second quarter of the fourteenth century. Vatican City, Biblioteca Apostolica Vaticana Ms. Pal. lat. 1993, fols. 8r and 26r.

many cartographic, exegetical, and other sources Opicinus enlisted to create the folio in all its embodied complexity.

The human is not the only mode of embodiment explored on this skin, however. Opicinus also exploits the palpable materiality of his medium to draw the reader's attention to an array of creaturely significations, all part of the often dizzying theological vision of its maker. Most obvious is the alignment of the spinal impression of the rendered animal (perhaps a calf or goat) with the spine of the crucified Christ. The darker impressions at the head and base of the folio suggest more care taken with the cleaner, somewhat lighter membrane above and below the lozenge, a distinction that has allowed the spine's shadow to linger and darken over the centuries. The verso depicts the names of Old Testament prophets as well as medieval theologians as so many vertebrae along the segmented spine of another

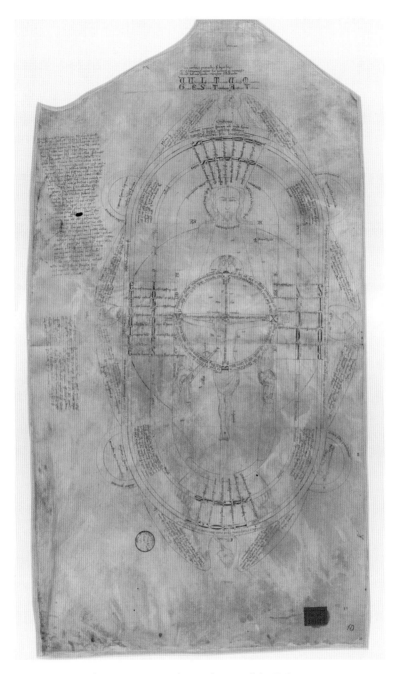

Figure 4.40. Opicinus de Canistris, tenth membrane of the Palatinus manuscript. Avignon, second quarter of the fourteenth century. Vatican City, Biblioteca Apostolica Vaticana Ms. Pal. lat. 1993, fol. 10r.

crucified Christ, this one inverted. An inscription near the top of the recto figure, *Christi membra mortalia*, points up the "mortal members of Christ" depicted below, but also the *membra* from which (according to a common medieval etymology) is derived the *membrana*, the very parchment of the folio. The body parts of Christ are also the parts of the animal from which the skin has been flayed, as detailed in the flowing red-letter list that streams down a band in the center left side of the main lozenge, including *caput* (head), *humerus* (shoulder), *pectus* (chest), and *stomachus* (stomach), all the way down to *genua* (knees) and *pedes* (feet). And the irregular ovoid shape dominating the page evokes a flayed hide stretched on a parchmenter's frame, complete with cut-outs for neck, limbs, haunches, and tail formed by the curved shapes of the four evangelists. The entire drawing seems executed so as to suggest the shape of a rendered hide, embedding the figure of the human-divine body of Christ within the animal medium on which it is drawn.

A calmer mode of animal visibility in the membrane archive inspires the so-called swan rolls. One method that manors and greater households employed to signal their holdings of bevies of swans involved the distinctive marking of the birds' bills. These marks were recorded in turn on narrow rolls of parchment, which would then become a verifiable legal record of avian property. The surviving swan rolls contain dozens and in several cases hundreds of bill designs corresponding to the proprietary markings on the animals themselves (see fig. 4.41). To examine one of these rolls is to encounter a layered record of human-animal relations in both form and content, the outward signs of possession marking the birds' bodies reinscribed on the narrow rolled skins of other beasts. The marks were also compiled in books: an exceptionally fine pair on vellum is at Yale, in the Lewis Walpole Library, the birds' beaks rendered in a vivid red that brings out the hundreds of diverse geometrical marks of ownership (fig. 4.42).

Such collocations suggest a play of dominion and intimacy also evident in the decoration and repair of production flaws and other gaps in membrane. Scholars will often describe such production flaws as "wounds in the parchment,"[23] and indeed such decorative techniques can seem to suggest a subtle association of parchment holes with the bleeding injuries of a slaughtered animal rather than simply the result of poor butchery or hasty craftwork postmortem. Parchment holes in codices are frequently found outlined in red, a common technique across centuries and regions, most likely to alert readers to hiccups in the text (see figs. 4.43, 4.44, 4.45, and 4.46). Yet there can be an uncanny sense of reparation in such gestures, as in the use of embroidery to highlight the vulnerability of the flesh. In a manuscript of the Rusticanus de Sanctis, a cycle of sermons on the Virgin Mary and other holy women by the Franciscan preacher Berthold of Regensburg, embroidered repairs

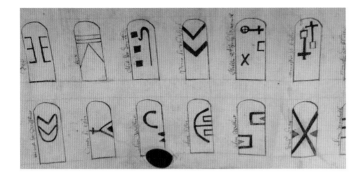

Figure 4.41. Twelve of the several hundred swan marks from the environs of Redgrave Hall, Suffolk. British Library Ms. Additional 40072, recto of third membrane.

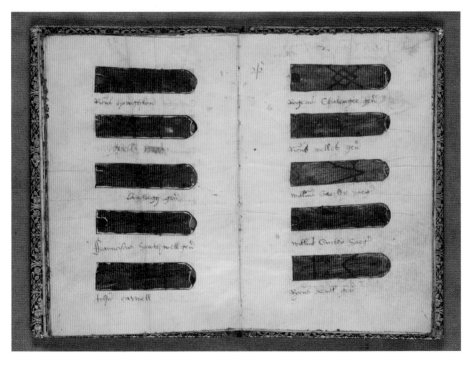

Figure 4.42. Swan marks drawn on vellum, from a two-volume set owned by Horace Walpole. Norfolk, sixteenth century. New Haven, Lewis Walpole Library Ms. LWL 49 2601, vol. 1.

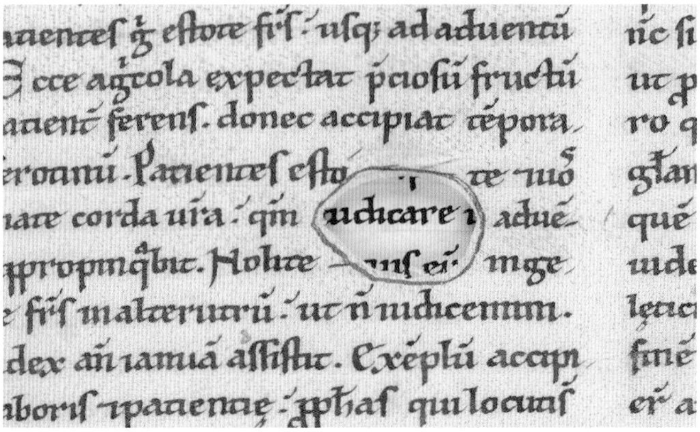

Figure 4.43.
Parchment hole outlined in red, from a vellum Bible. France, twelfth century. New Haven, Yale University Beinecke Ms. 414, fol. 183r (detail).

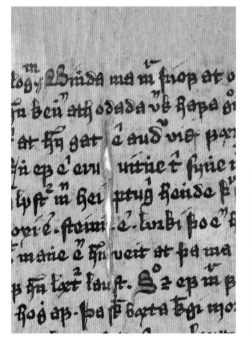

Figure 4.44.
A gap in the parchment traced in red, from *Jónsbók*, Iceland, ca. 1500. Copenhagen, University of Copenhagen Arnamagnæn Collection Ms. Rask 72 a, fol. 11r (detail).

include several crimson discs cross-hatched in bruise-like purple, perhaps as a spur to contemplation (see fig. 4.47 and fig. 4.48).[24] As Nancy Vine Durling has argued, "scribes were closely attuned to the possibility for play presented by parchment imperfections," an attunement to mise-en-page that comes out in myriad ways—for example in a series of Passion meditations in Harley 2253 that seem to incorporate parchment holes as anthropomorphic wounds in the body of Christ.[25] Sarah Kay has suggested that "tears and stitching" in medieval bestiaries "reinforce readers' awareness that human sexual and sensory orifices are just like those of the animals depicted" on their pages.[26]

More subtle adjacencies of human and animal abound in the membrane record, as in an eye-catching pair of drawings in a book of Latin devotional works by St. Bernard of Clairvaux. Here, in the midst of Bernard's treatise *De diligendo Dei* (*On Loving God*), three proximate holes in the membrane inspire a two-part invention (fig. 4.49 and fig. 4.50). On a folio containing twenty-two lines of text, five of them break to frame the face of a man, the second *i* of *diligendi* extending into

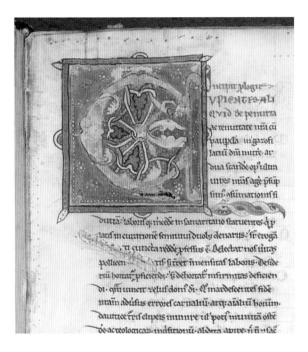

Figure 4.45. A jagged repair in the membrane limned in red ink, from a copy of Peter Lombard's *Sentences*. France, third quarter of the twelfth century. London, British Library Yates Thompson Ms. 17, fol. 2r.

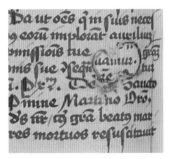

Figure 4.46. An irregular parchment hole traced in red, from a Latin prayerbook. Switzerland, first quarter of the sixteenth century. New York, Columbia University Western Ms. 037, fol. 120v (detail).

Figures 4.47 and 4.48. Embroidered parchment repairs from Bertholdus Ratisbonensis, *Rusticanus de Sanctis*. Germany, ca. 1300. Uppsala, University Library Ms. C 371, fols. 108v (detail) and 162r (detail).

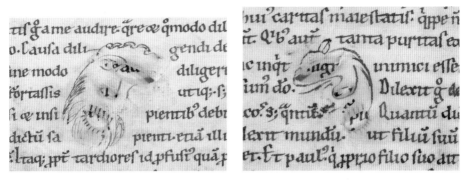

Figures 4.49 and 4.50. Decorated parchment holes from a manuscript of Bernard of Clairvaux's devotional works. Bamberg, Kloster Michelsberg, middle of the twelfth century. Bamberg, Staatsbibliothek Ms. Msc. Patr. 41, fol. 69r (detail) and fol. 69v (detail).

a continuity dash that then traces the figure's curly hair, merging script and body in the space of a pen flourish. The skin of the beast is also the skin of a bearded man, his head and facial features so many traces on the animal ground. On the verso, the same holes trace the contours of a rabbit or squirrel, its bushy tail positioned beneath a corrected abbreviation mark. The relay of these figures from recto to verso conjoins human and animal in a play of difference and commonality rung on crafted skin.

Zoomorphic designs are differently at work in the Old English Orosius, a tenth-century codex containing an insular translation of the *Historia adversus paganos* of the early Christian writer Orosius (ca. 375–420). This lightly decorated manuscript exhibits numerous production flaws, gaps, sutures, corners of pages cut from tails, shoulders, haunches. More than these common codicological features, however, this book displays a degree of self-consciousness about the derivation of its medium. In several places throughout the manuscript (see fig. 4.51 and fig. 4.52), small holes in the parchment blossom into tiny heads of sheep protruding from fluffs of wool drawn around the gaps. A reader who peers through one of these cloud-like tufts will see the next folio lying there beneath the (empty) disc of wool, as if the drawn sheep were flayed and rendered into parchment before our eyes. Such winking scribal gestures are legible both as bursts of creaturely empathy and as subtle nods to the raw utility of animals in the service of written culture.

Just as often, though, membrane repairs will be managed with the workaday practicality of the busy maker impatient with such precious niceties. A jagged scar divides a passage of Arabic at a diagonal, repaired with twine-like thread (fig. 4.53). The repair was likely done prior to inscription, as the scribe has carefully avoided

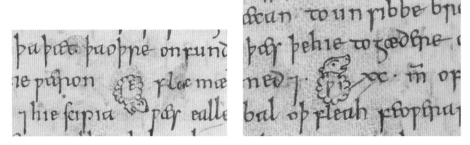

Figures 4.51 and 4.52. Ovine drawings around a single parchment hole in the Old English Orosius. Winchester (?), early tenth century. London, British Library Additional Ms. 47967, fols. 62r (detail) and 62v (detail).

Figure 4.53. A stark and rough repair to a folio from a compilation of martyrdom accounts. Egypt, tenth century. Mount Sinai, Saint Catherine's Monastery Ms. Sinai Arabic 461, fol. 31v.

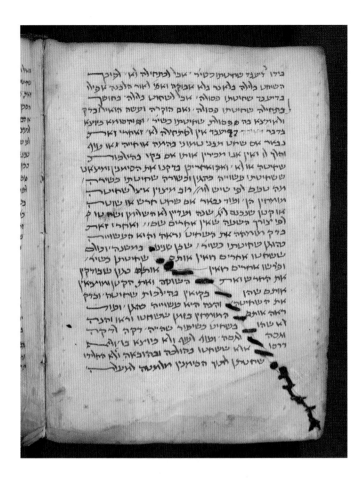

Figure 4.54.
A vividly stitched repair in an Ashkenaz miscellany. Late thirteenth or early fourteenth century. Oxford, Bodleian Library Ms. Huntington 404, fol. 21v.

the Frankenstein-like bisection of the page, leaving two distinct trapezoidal text blocks on the folio. A gap descending through eleven lines of Hebrew is sewn up with a length of red silken cord that remains a vivid element of the page (fig. 4.54).

No account of the creaturely dimensions of the written record would be complete without some consideration of bookbindings, which lie outside the scope of this study though obviously play an important role in defining the animal archive. The skins of pigs, deer, horses, seals, and many other animals were regularly exploited as cover material for codices, whether tanned, tawed, or limed to produce thicker sheets suitable for the purpose, and with widely varying degrees and qualities of fin-

Figure 4.55.
Sealskin wrapper
on Old Icelandic
Homily Book.
Iceland, ca. 1200.
Stockholm, National
Library of Sweden
Ms. Perg. 4to no. 15.

ish. A collection of charters from St. Paul's was long known by its moniker *Liber A sive pilosus*: "Book A, or, the hairy book," though its original hirsute binding has been lost.[27] One such cover that does survive houses the so-called Old Icelandic Homily Book (fig. 4.55), a collection of sixty-odd treatises, prayers, sermons, and liturgical and miscellaneous devotional materials written in the closing years of the twelfth century. The parchment codex was wrapped in a cover of seal hide, a single skin with much of its hair intact that folds over the front, rendering a cover with rounded corners and a curved flap. A combination of runes and script have been traced into the leather in places and also cut out of the seal's hair, which remains a tactile part of the reading experience.[28] A similar example is a glossed Book of Genesis produced at the Abbey of Rievaulx (Yorkshire) in the later twelfth century, and bound in what may be sealskin, with patches of fur still visible (and strokable) on the front and back covers as well as the spine (fig. 4.56 and fig. 4.57).

One of the world's most hirsute early books is the *Ruige Blauwe Register*, or

"Rugged Blue Register," as the volume has come to be known. This manuscript served as a commissions register for the Court of Holland in the early decades of the sixteenth century, documenting the names and positions of royal and civic officials. The pages themselves are a mix of parchment and paper, not an uncommon codicological feature for this period. What is quite unusual is the register's binding (fig. 4.58), fashioned of a limp sheepskin that retains a full head of whitish-grey

Figures 4.56 and 4.57. Sealskin binding of a glossed Book of Genesis. Rievaulx, England, second half of the twelfth century (binding before 1600). London, British Library Additional Ms. 63077, front cover and spine.

wool (hence the Dutch *ruig,* or rough: that is, rough to the touch). The only wool-free patch on the cover is a small rectangular label scraped into the front of the register containing inscriptions about the original contents and subsequent additions. While we know nothing about the bookmaker's eccentric choice of a wooly sheepskin, a later volume, now at the Folger Shakespeare Library in Washington, D.C., was bound deliberately in thickly haired deerskin as a bibliographical nod to the book's content (fig. 4.59). The volume is a copy of George Gascoigne's *The noble art*

Figure 4.58. The woolly cover of the *Ruige Blauwe Register* (Rugged Blue Register). Holland, sixteenth century. The Hague, Nationaal Archief Grafelijkheidsrekenkamer Registers 3.01.27.01, inv. 493 (front).

Figure 4.59. George Gascoigne, *The noble art of venerie or hunting* (London, 1611), in deerskin. Washington, D.C., Folger Shakespeare Library, STC 24328.

of venerie or hunting (London, 1611), a popular compilation of practical wisdom guiding its readers in fifteen types of chases, as well as "how to hunte and kill euery one" of the creatures so pursued. The volume was rebound by Robert Lunow, a German artisanal bookbinder employed at the Folger for a number of years in the first half of the twentieth century.

Parchment books and documents teem with their own rendered animality, the vestiges of faunal life and death, alongside the marks of the butchers, skinners, and makers who transformed countless living beasts into readable commodities. These and innumerable other examples of animal visibility in the written record reinforce the nature of the membrane book as a stack of animal remains never entirely forgotten. For producers and consumers of membrane documents and codices, this creaturely mise-en-page forms part of the lived experience of the written text. Wounds, scars, and gaps, whether pre- or post-mortem, whether repaired or left gaping, were not simply endured as flaws in the writing surface but sensed as irruptions at the scene of writing, as forced alterations in the movement of the eye, the finger, the *yad*, the quill. The flayed page: an integral and often unavoidable part of the *Rezeptionsästhetik* of the parchment inheritance in all its creaturely diversity.

✧ ✧

CHAPTER FIVE

UTERINE VELLUM
AND THE PAGE UNBORN

The texts are heavy to hold in the arms, and awkward as if they breathed;
their pages are made of slunk vellum from stillborn calves, reveined by the
illuminator in tints of lapis and leaf-green.

—HILARY MANTEL, *WOLF HALL*

On the ninth day of their self-imposed exile from the plague-ridden city,
the company of Florentines depicted in Giovanni Boccaccio's *Decameron*
listen to a story of lust, adultery, and a magic parchment scroll. The narrator is Fiammetta, and her story begins when four men, among them Bruno, Buf-
falmaco, and Calandrino, receive a commission from a wealthy man to paint fres-
coes in his house in Camerata. The rich man's son frequently brings prostitutes
home with him. One of them, Niccolosa, who happens to be visiting for an as-
signation during the commission, encounters Calandrino by the household well.
Stricken with love for the woman, who teases him mercilessly, Calandrino seeks
solace from his friend Bruno, who contrives a fake spell to make the prostitute
fall in love with Calandrino. The seduction requires a number of special objects to
effect:

> "Then," said Bruno, "go and fetch me a little piece of parchment from a stillborn an-
> imal [*carta non nata*], a live bat, three grains of incense, and a candle that's been
> blessed. You can leave the rest to me." Calandrino spent the whole of that evening
> trying to catch a bat my means of various contrivances. Finally, he managed to snag
> one and brought it to Bruno along with the other things. Withdrawing into another
> room, Bruno wrote some nonsense in made-up characters on the parchment and took
> it back to Calandrino. "Now be aware, Calandrino," he said, "if you touch her with
> this scroll, she'll come with you immediately and do whatever you want."[1]

Bruno here writes the nonsensical spell on a piece of membrane allegedly taken from the skin of a premature, aborted, or stillborn animal (whether lamb, calf, or goat is unspecified in the text). *Carta non nata*: a more literal translation of this peculiar phrase would be "unborn page" or "not born sheet." The mysterious powers of this freshly incarnate writing surface must be harnessed for the scroll to work its magic: only the touch of unblemished animal skin to flesh will ensure the effectiveness of the incantatory love words Bruno has written on its surface. The story concludes when Calandrino's wife, ushered in to witness her husband's adulterous union with Niccolosa, falls upon him, tears up his face, and torments him once the couple returns to Florence.

Bruno's trick evokes a range of similar spells found in medieval manuals of ritual magic that prescribe the use of "virgin parchment" or similar material for various rituals of sexual conquest—many of them, such as the version in Boccaccio, without the consent of the enchanted. Among the most remarkable of these is the *Clavicula Salamonis*, a pseudepigraphal grimoire (or book of magic) attributed by legend to King Solomon and dating from the fourteenth or fifteenth century.[2] The *Clavicula Salamonis* devotes an entire chapter to the preparation of "virgin parchment":

> Virgin parchment is necessary in many magical operations, and should be properly prepared and consecrated. There are two kinds, one called virgin, the other unborn. Virgin parchment is that which is taken from an animal which hath not attained the age of generation, whether it be ram, or kid, or other animal. Unborn parchment is taken from an animal which hath been taken before its time from the uterus of its mother.[3]

The chapter goes on to describe the ritual slaughter of the uterine beast and then the process of skinning—"thou shalt commence with this Knife to flay the Animal, whether it be Virgin or Unborn"—and closes with an intricate set of instructions on how to inscribe the "unborn parchment" with magical numbers, words, and symbols. The writer takes care to emphasize again (and in highly gendered terms) the unsullied nature of the medium: "No woman . . . should be permitted to see this parchment; otherwise it will lose its virtue. He who maketh it should be pure, clean, and prepared."[4]

The modern term for the type of membrane writing material invoked in these and many other works is *uterine vellum*, a phrase accompanied by a long history of controversy, squeamishness, and scholarly discomfort—and inspiring more than a few flourishes of literary imagination. Both a magical ground for otherworldly incantations and a preferred medium for certain types of book, uterine vellum plays

Figure 5.1. Measurements of membrane thickness from a thirteenth-century French Bible and a sixteenth-century Italian choirbook, taken with a digital micrometer.

diverse imaginative and practical roles in the parchment cultures of the premodern world. Before turning to its modern literary reinventions, it may be worth lingering along this peculiar byway of the bookish imagination. For it is here, in the sober idiom of bibliographical objectivity, that uterine vellum casts its most alluring and repulsing spells.

A first touch of uterine vellum makes it easy to understand why. The stuff is just remarkable: tissue thin with lovely drape, pliant but oddly tough to the pull, and usually without any visible marks of its animal derivation. No surprise that the medium became so explosively popular from the twelfth into the thirteenth century, with the concordant miniaturization and portability of books that such fine material allowed. Chiara Ruzzier has suggested that the thirteenth century alone saw the production of some twenty thousand portable Bibles on uterine vellum, from France, England, Italy, and Spain alike.[5] Flipping through one of these so-called Paris Bibles is an exercise in transhistorical awe, as these books represent the apogee of the parchment craft: no modern maker has been able to replicate with any regularity or precision the techniques that rendered the fine membranes making up these thousands of surviving medieval books. As one craftsman, Rabbi Benjamin Vorst, put it some years ago, "such vellums are forgotten."[6] The folios of one portable medieval Bible at my own institution measure around .07 millimeters in thickness—about a seventh the thickness of those in a large sixteenth-century choirbook whose leaves I measured for the sake of comparison (see fig. 5.1).

So what exactly is uterine vellum, this "unborn parchment"? "A vellum made from the very thin skins of still-born or unborn calves," the book designer William Dana Orcutt's *The Author's Desk Book* defined it a century ago.[7] From the early nineteenth century and well into the twentieth, the question of the origin of uterine vellum remained relatively uncontroversial. Thus John Lumsden Propert's *A History of Miniature Art* (1887): "The finest vellum of all, which goes by the name uterine vellum, or, in the quaint language of the 17th century, 'the skin of abortives,' was obtained from the skin of calves prematurely born, and on this delicate material some of the best of the early miniature portraits were limned."[8] John William Bradley's *Illuminated Manuscripts* (1905), in a discussion of calfskin vellum, specifies "that of the stillborn calf . . . called 'uterine vellum,' and considered the finest and thinnest"; while Sir Edward Maunde Thompson's *Introduction to Greek and Latin Palaeography* (1912) identifies "uterine vellum, taken from the unborn young, or the skins of newborn animals" for its "special purposes" in the book trade.[9] Compilers of nineteenth-century auction lists and library catalogues show no hesitation in designating manuscripts in this manner as a matter of course. An 1898 auction catalogue of the manuscripts and early printed books of the recently deceased William Morris lists six codices on uterine membrane: "MANUSCRIPT ON UTERINE VELLUM *by a Norman French scribe, written in minute clear* gothic letter, *in double columns of 46 lines*."[10] Over the first era of descriptive bibliography, the derivation of uterine vellum remained an uncontested part of the history and technology of the book.

Only in the middle decades of the twentieth century did scholars begin to question the crafting of this material from the flayed bodies of unborn, stillborn, or abortive animals, even as other specialists continued to work with the existing definition. In 1979, Bernhard Bischoff could still define uterine parchment as a medium "prepared from the skin of unborn lambs."[11] Yet an extended note of skepticism had already come from Daniel Varney Thompson, a Harvard art historian and author of an influential 1933 book on the materials and techniques of medieval painting. Thompson, in speculating on the diverse animal origins of the material, eschewed the magical thinking (as he saw it) found in the work of his fellow scholars of the book arts:

> The Latin word *abortivum* occasionally applied to fine parchment in the Middle Ages (though rarely) has given rise to another form of superstition which has become widespread, namely, that the finest medieval parchment, and particularly the very thin, flexible, opaque, small, thirteenth-century French Bible vellum was made from the skins of still-borne calves. There is as nearly as possible no evidence for this belief. It may be true. I have no figures on infant mortality among livestock in the Middle Ages; but I should be inclined to think that animal husbandry must have been in a very precarious condition if enough calves were stillborn in the thirteenth century to provide all the pages which pass for "uterine vellum." It is quite possible that the skins

of deer and other game that people ate were made into parchment, too; and it would not be altogether surprising if it turned out, as a result of experiments now in progress, that some of what now masquerades as "uterine vellum" was actually rabbit or squirrel parchment.[12]

For Thompson, the existence of uterine vellum is nothing less than a "superstition," a misguided belief with no medieval evidence to support it. The medium becomes little more than a "masquerade," unsupported by hard evidence from the records of animal husbandry. Similarly, while Albert Delorez, in *The Palaeography of Gothic Manuscript Books*, allows that this "extremely thin and white parchment . . . is often called uterine vellum (*carta abortive, virginea*)" by medieval writers, he regards it as "doubtful whether this writing-material, apart from a few exceptions, was really made from the skin of unborn calves or lambs."[13] Christopher de Hamel voices an even sterner note of skepticism, objecting to the continuing usage of uterine vellum as a catch-all phrase for the material on the grounds of distaste and common sense:

> It is with reluctance that one mentions, albeit briefly, the vexed and unresolved question of uterine vellum. Old-fashioned books about medieval manuscripts assert that the finest medieval parchment was made from the skin of aborted calves . . . There is some medieval evidence that aborted skin was valuable and desirable, and it is true that parchment made from this rather unappealing material or from the skins of very new-born animals does indeed look and feel like that which antiquarians call uterine vellum . . . But it is very difficult to believe that thousands of cows miscarried for generations, or were deprived of their foetuses in such numbers to supply the booktrade economically . . . If the term uterine parchment must be used at all, it should perhaps refer to a quality of skin and not to its origin.[14]

As Janetta Benton quips, echoing de Hamel, "So very many manuscripts are claimed to be on uterine vellum as to suggest an unfortunate, and unlikely, situation for medieval cows!"[15]

An attempt to drive a final nail in the coffin comes from Ralph Hanna III, who is convinced that premodern references to uterine membrane have nothing to do with the age or state of the rendered animal, but refer exclusively to a craft process involving the splitting of animal skins into thinner layers suitable for rendering into the familiar tissue-like sheets: "In actual fact, as several commentators have surmised, book-producers were not waiting around for extensive supplies of aborted calves. Rather, they wrote the books on skins that had been split."[16] This is common sense, Hanna suggests, supported by the putative ubiquity of the technique among artisanal bookmakers of the Middle Ages: "Such parchment-production will have [been] a well-known procedure across thirteenth-century western Europe, although not perhaps originally among Christian parchmenters. But it was (and remains) a normal procedure among a widely dispersed European minority community, Jewish bookmen."[17] Hanna finds evidence for this claim in rabbinical theology, particularly the writings of Moses Maimonides, which echo other medieval treatises in distinguishing between various types of skin for Torah scrolls and other written objects. As I have already suggested in chapter 3, however, many of these specifications are repetitions of ritual convention rather than descriptions of craft.[18] Nevertheless, Hanna proposes the phrase "split vellum" as the more accurate description for ultrafine membrane than its uterine counterpart.

Such deductions are questionable on a number of levels, and go against considerable historical and contemporary evidence to the contrary (and indeed against several of the very sources and authorities Hanna cites). The splitting of hides by hand, while occasionally practiced with the pelts of certain animals (mostly sheep, whose skin naturally divides into two layers), is a difficult and inordinately time-consuming task; while some premodern artisans may have perfected the technique, and some contemporary artisans have shown its feasibility, others mocked the very notion that animal skin could be divided in such a way, even laughing at academics inquiring as to its feasibility.[19] Cowskin and goatskin are largely homogeneous, making their splitting by hand quite difficult; yet as recent research has shown, uterine vellum was rendered historically from the skins of cow, goat, or sheep depending on overall regional preferences. While there is convincing evidence that the technique of splitting skins was known among early Jewish communities of the Eastern Mediterranean, "rabbinic authorities in western Europe betray no real acquaintance with such a practice," as Menahem Haran puts it quite definitively: "This skill was not passed on to Europe and in the course of time seems to have been forgotten (until the splitting of hides was reinvented, with greater refinement, in the modern period)."[20] Nor should such intercultural exchanges between Jewish and gentile scribes and bookmakers be romanticized: in thirteenth-century Germany, Colette Sirat writes, "It was evidently so difficult for Hebrew scribes to obtain parchment that ordinary books are made up of irregular folios, the parchment is grey and thick, and there are many holes."[21]

As for "Jewish bookmen" past and present, here, too, Hanna's claims about the derivation of uterine membrane do not square with the customs of any practicing Jewish artisans of my acquaintance, nor with the historical testimony of actual Jewish intellectuals and craftsmen. The Catalan rabbi Menahem Hameiri (ca. 1250–1315), in his *Kiryat Sefer*, was crystal clear on the subject: "In our times, the craftsmen

Figure 5.2.
A display of "Unborn Calf Skins: B Grade, Medium," available from Chichester, Inc., in Niagara Falls, New York.

aren't expert or even familiar with the process of splitting the skin into two, such that one could be called *qelaf* and the other *dukhsustos*. They only know how to produce *gevil*, which is made with gall-nuts, and the only part that can be written on is the hair-side, as the ancients did."[22] As for the parchment used by today's scribes for Torah scrolls and tefillin, while rendered in Israel, it is practically all sourced from slaughterhouses in the United States, New Zealand, and especially South America—and nearly 100 percent of this commodity derives from fetal calf skin, a by-product of industrial beef production (see fig. 5.2 for a commercially available sample of "unborn calf skin" from Argentina).[23] Halved membranes today are split with industrial splitting machines, of the sort employed in tanneries such as Pergamena and William Cowley. In Jewish communities, the trade in parchment has long relied fundamentally on the consistent availability of uterine skins. As the author of the *Keset ha-Sofer* (a primer for scribes) memorably put it in 1835, "The skin of an embryo is considered to be a skin and a sefer torah, tefillin and mezuzah may be written on it. It is the best."[24]

I belabor these points simply to temper the overconfidence that can seep into such discussions, guided as they so often are by modern versions of common sense.

For those unacquainted with the modern livestock industry, the proportion of in utero deaths and stillbirths can sound quite shocking. The Canadian National Dairy Study of 2015 estimated that 7 to 10 percent of calves in both small-scale and industrial farms are either born dead or die within the first twenty-four hours, with some herds approaching a 20 percent stillbirth rate.[25] A study conducted at the Spooner Agricultural Research Station in the 1990s found that "a total of 5,425 lambs were born (alive or dead) during the last 9 years (1989 through 1997). Five hundred-thirty-six lambs (9.9%) were born dead or died before weaning."[26] A surprisingly high percentage, though it obtains more or less consistently across five breeds and cross-breeds of sheep, and on large and small ranches alike. As for animals spontaneously miscarried before term, modern studies suggest that a rate of 5 to 7 percent can be normal in a given herd or flock, while so-called abortion storms can produce a much higher percentage in certain seasons or years. A longitudinal study of perinatal mortality among lambs in Norway showed an increase in stillbirths from 3.3 percent in 2000 to 4.7 percent in 2010.[27]

Modern data should be used with extreme caution when approaching historical practices of animal husbandry, of course. As Mark Page points out, the accurate reporting of quadruped death rates on medieval estates and holdings "depended to some extent on the honesty of the reeves and the vigilance of the auditors who examined their accounts."[28] Yet the scattered figures on reproductive mortality rates for medieval livestock suggest corresponding percentages of uterine deaths and stillbirths. A pipe roll from the bishopric of Winchester (1208–09) records only "750 lambs born from sheep this year because 20 were sterile, and 30 aborted"—a uterine yield of 4 percent.[29] A fourteenth-century survey of Crawley Manor suggests that out of 385 bearing ewes, as many as thirty may have miscarried, nearly 10 percent of the annual yield; of the lambs who survived birth, fully forty-one died before they were weaned—a total yield of 71 uterine or newborn skins.[30]

Agrarian historians have shown that livestock mortality rates at all ages improved throughout the Middle Ages, yet even in the fifteenth century numerous surviving accounts point to what would have been great quantities of uterine skin if rendered. Thus in 1435 at Colingbourne "the lambs of 240 ewes were stillborn and are called slynkettes"—a word that yielded "slunk" as a term of art for uterine vellum.[31] Even if the stillbirth rate of sheep, cows, and goats remained at 4 or 5 percent from the twelfth century through the fifteenth, such a figure would easily have accommodated the need for sufficient uterine hides for that small portion of the trade that relied on such skins. No one would have had to "wait around" for cows to miscarry, nor would "thousands of cows [have] miscarried for generations" to furnish the needs of the artisanal book trade for the finest specimens. It's important to bear in mind that a substantial majority of membrane manuscripts produced during this era were documents, not codices, and, further, that the proportion of codices written on ultrafine vellum was quite small, despite the impressive size and quantity of pocket Bibles and similar books on this type of membrane. There is simply no difficulty in reckoning a sufficient proportion of uterine parchment to render the quantity of books surviving on the medium.

Such gleanings from the history of pastoral husbandry make it easier to understand why myriad literary and historical sources from the Middle Ages through the eighteenth century take the facticity of the uterine medium for granted, indeed as a commonplace of the preindustrial book trade. An inventory recorded in 1382 by William Wyntershulle of St. Albans describes "books in various volumes and languages . . . with clasps, boards and tissue for their making" stored in the almonry. The entry then speaks of "parchment, vellum, abortive membrane [*motlyn abortif*] with horse-skins, horns and doe-skins . . . and calf-skins to cover [their boards] and bind them, with paper for [covering and binding] them."[32] Notable in this entry is that *motlyn abortif* is differentiated from both parchment [*pergamenum*] and vellum [*velym*] as a distinctive form of membrane suitable for writing. Here is none of the modern bibliographer's squeamishness or bemusement about the origins of the medium, nor any suggestion that the word *abortif* is being used figuratively rather than literally.

The same holds true for writings in the magical tradition of Boccaccio's story in the *Decameron*. Thus in Charles Sorel's *The Extravagant Shepherd* (1654), a burlesque antipastoral novel, a recipe for a spell recounts an injunction given to neighboring shepherds regarding the skins of their newborn animals:

> The Stars were now ready to fall on the other Hemisphere, and Night by little and little drew her curtains wherewith she had hidden the face of heaven, when it came into my mind that there liv'd neer this place a *Magician* of whom *I* might hope some assistance, if it were possible *I* could receive any. All the Shepherds in our quarters or neer us, were charg'd to look to their sheep when they should cast their lambs, for to fley them and bring their skins to him to make *virgin-parchment*. The Midwives also were in like manner very careful to preserve those thin Cawls wherewith there are some children born. The Falconers, who made in other Countries all Birds their

game, durst meddle with nothing but Dormice and some other unlucky birds; and all this for to provide materials for the enchantments of *Zenocritus*, that was the name of this Magician.[33]

Here the object of acquisition is "virgin-parchment" rather than strictly uterine vellum, though the passage foregrounds the watchfulness of the shepherds, eager to snatch up and flay the newborn lambs sacrificed to make virgin parchment for the conniving of a magician. Newborn babies are not themselves sacrificed, though their "cawls," or amniotic sacs, are given over to the incantatory cause.

A more technical example comes from a work in the tradition of learned magic, Robert Turner's translation of the so-called *Fourth book of occult philosophy* (1665), spuriously attributed to the sixteenth-century German lawyer and polymath Heinrich Cornelius Agrippa von Nettesheim, and printed at the Lamb at the east end of St. Paul. At one point in the treatise, the anonymous author is instructing readers in the crafting of a book of incantations: "Now this book is to be made of most pure and clean paper that hath never been used before; which many do call *Virgin-Paper." The asterisk indicates a marginal note (see fig. 5.3) to a local supplier: "Which *Virgin-paper* is to be had at Mr. *Rooks* shop at the holy lamb at the East-end of St. *Pauls* Church: and likewise the *Virgin-Parchment*, and the best abortives."[34] This frank marginal annotation, likely from a London printer intimately familiar with the accoutrements of the book trade, clearly distinguishes between "Virgin-Parchment" and "abortives" as different qualities of fine membrane available at the shop of a certain Rooks.

We get many such plainspoken accounts of uterine membrane's availability from early modern figures similarly connected to the book industry, whether as printers, artists, or illuminators. Alexander Browne's *Ars Pictoria* (1669), a practical manual on the crafts of drawing, etching, painting, and limning, recommends the medium for the painting of miniature cards. After polishing a card with the tooth of a dog until the surface is smooth and free of blemish, Browne instructs, "Choose of the best abortive *parchment*, a *Piece* proportionable to your *Card*, which piece with *fine* and *clean starch paste* fast on the *card*."[35] In a discussion of "drawing and limning" included in *The Gentlemans Exercise* (1661), Henry Peacham instructs readers to take "the fine skin of an abortive, which you may buy in Paternoster Row, and other places (it being the finest parchment that is), and with starch thin laid on, and the skin well stretched and smooth-pressed within some book or the like, prepare your ground or tablet."[36] As in the marginal note described above, the wording is quite particular: "the fine skin of an abortive"—a construction that identifies the medium in question not by the quality of the skin but by the prenatal death of the beast.

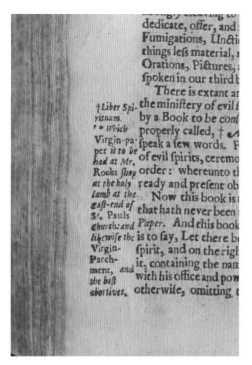

Figure 5.3. Marginal note on the availability of "*Virgin-Parchment*, and the best abortives" at a shop near St. Paul's churchyard. From Agrippa von Nettesheim, *Henry cornelius agrippa his fourth book of occult philosophy* (London, 1665), p. 54. Wing A786. From an amalgamated copy at the Beinecke Rare Book and Manuscript Library, Yale University.

One of the most explicit and detailed descriptions of the medium and its derivation we owe to Nicholas Hilliard, a goldsmith and artist widely famed for producing some of the most important miniature portraits of English royals and aristocrats. Asked by a friend for a guidebook to his artistic practice, Hilliard wrote a brief treatise that was roughly copied and, in the eighteenth century, given a title, *The Art of Limning*, though as far as we know, the work circulated only in manuscript until the early twentieth century. Hilliard insists that the only suitable material for the fine art of limning is "virgine Parchment," though not just any kind:

> Knowe also that *Parchment* is the only good and best thinge to limme one, but it
> must be virgine Parchment, such as neuer bore haire, but younge things found in the
> dames bellye. Some calle it *Vellym*, some *Abertive* derived from the word *Abhortive*,
> for vntimely birthe. It must be most finly drest, as smothe as any sattine, and pasted
> with starch well strained one pastbourd well burnished, that it maye be pure without
> speckes or staynes, very smoothe and white.[37]

Hilliard is closely attuned to the lexicon of the skin trade. Some call the finest membrane vellum, some *abhertive*, some virgin parchment. But the terminological ambiguity is trivial here. What matters is the biological origin of the medium itself, its rendering from the hairless bodies of "younge things found in the dames bellye." The exacting rhetoric suggests Hilliard's close familiarity with the wares of his suppliers: their texture and fineness, their manner of origin, the specific stage of life and death at which they surrendered their skins.

This is a crucial point, for Turner, Browne, Peacham, and Hilliard were not addressing a general public in their commentaries on the most suitable writing material. Rather, their manuals are all directed toward a specialized audience of active artisans like themselves. All four would have had regular interactions with the dealers from whom they commissioned and bought their variegated stocks of membrane. They were clearly picky about the fineness of their medium, and it is hard to imagine them not inquiring after the sourcing of the skins that represented their stock in trade, and describing it accordingly. The extent to which the uterine origin of the medium was taken for granted in this period can be discerned in an *Alphabetical Dictionary of English Words* published in London in 1668. The entry for "Virgin-parchment" specifies that the material is "made of the skin of an abortive."[38]

When it comes to the question of uterine vellum, then, it seems that an abundance of caution has led to the anthropomorphizing of medieval animals and the romanticization of medieval animal husbandry, casting belief in the historical verity of the medium as something of an embarrassment. Yet discomfort, disbelief, and disdain are inadequate substitutes for evidence, and there is good reason to be suspicious of all the scholarly tut-tutting and outright condescension that have greeted the question of uterine vellum over the decades. Again, this is not to say that all of what we call uterine vellum derived from abortive animals. Its production likely resulted from the regular usage of uterine or newborn skins *and* from a craft process that worked equally well regardless of species—surely sometimes a combination of both. Yet well into the modern period, the arts of the book have clearly entailed the widespread usage of uterine beasts.

We get an on-the-ground glimpse of the medium's continuity in Norman Salsitz's autobiographical account of growing up in Kolbuszowa, Poland, before World War II. At the center of the town's Jewish community was an admired *sofer* named Fischel Saltz, who produced tefillin, mezuzahs, and Torah scrolls with scrupulous attention to the sourcing of his raw materials:

> To produce a completed Torah, for example, might take a year, probably two. In part this was because every element he prepared himself, including the parchment from the skin of an unborn calf, thread from its veins, and the ink and the quills with which he produced the letters, then the words. That a scribe should be worthy to

write the holy words was an obligation he assumed with awesome seriousness. Such purity, such exceptional holiness![39]

Before each inscription of God's name onto the scroll, Saltz would walk to the *mikvah* for a purifying bath, believing that "the name of God should not be inscribed by a man not altogether cleansed, not entirely pure." The skins of unborn calves formed a ritual part of his sacred craft, coming to the *sofer* with a cyclical regularity that helped shape the textual labor of his creation.

Uterine vellum has long had the capacity to inspire both credulity and skepticism, to enchant and repulse. No surprise that modern novelists and poets enlist the medium's imaginative charge to limn this strange curiosity of book history onto the margins of their own writings: an exoticizing detail as suited to the period descriptions of historical fiction as to the lush meditations of contemporary lyric. In Blake Morrison's historical novel, *The Justification of Johann Gutenberg* (2000), the eponymous printer must search out sufficient skins of good quality to produce one of the early print runs of his Bible. During a visit to a parchmenter's workshop, he catches an unsettling glimpse of a finer commodity on offer:

> We made our way past brindled cow-hides drying hairside-out on wooden beams. Holding a knife shaped like a newly risen moon, the brother was paring hairs from a pelt held drum-tight in a wooden frame. The pelt was so small and pristine-white I could scarcely credit it.
> "Uterine," he said, catching me looking. "The dearest of all vellum."
> "You abort the calves?"
> "It is not official practice. But if a cow, for some reason, should miscarry and its calf be stillborn . . ."
> I stroked the pelt's soft silk, then turned to the two brothers. Mean-faced and hatchet-eyed, they looked no more fond of each other than of me—the Cain and Abel of the meat trade.
> "I have in mind an order for five thousand skins," I said.
> "Of uterine vellum? Impossible."
> "Not uterine. It is a larger beast I have in mind."[40]

Stretched on a frame, "small and pristine-white," the pelt inspires wonder, even disbelief, until that beguiling word, "Uterine," springs from the lips of the parchmenter. When Gutenberg inquires as to the material's sourcing, he is told that purposeful abortion "is not official practice"—though who knows? Hard to miss the suggestive ellipsis after "stillborn," as if to imply some dark intent toward the calves shared by the two brothers, figured as "Cain and Abel": one a worthy biblical sacrificer of beasts, the other a murderer in the making.

Other writers enlist uterine vellum less for its sensationalism than for the cold sobriety of historical reappraisal. Hilary Mantel, in the opening of Part II of *Wolf Hall*, sets a vivid scene at York Place. The year is 1528, and the house of Cardinal Wolsey is being ransacked by the dukes of Norfolk and Sussex in preparation for its occupation by Lady Anne, "who needs a London house of her own":

> They are overturning chests and tipping out their contents. They scatter across the floor, letters from Popes, letters from the scholars of Europe: from Utrecht, from Paris, from San Diego de Compostela; from Erfurt, from Strassburg, from Rome. They are packing his gospels and taking them for the king's libraries. The texts are heavy to hold in the arms, and awkward as if they breathed; their pages are made of slunk vellum from stillborn calves, reveined by the illuminator in tints of lapis and leaf-green.[41]

The scene of relentless pillage plays up the distinctive medievalism of the biblical manuscripts, heavy and breathing with an archaic Catholic past. The passage takes it for granted that the vellum is in fact "slunk" rendered from calves dead at birth, the veins still latent in the uterine folios relined by the illuminators. The pulpy grotesquery of the membrane here evokes the nasty Catholicism of Mantel's Thomas More: "You rise before dawn," Cromwell sneers at him, "shuffle to your familiar cell and flog yourself, call for your bread and water, and by eight o'clock back in your hair shirt, and over it your old woolen gown, that blood-colored one with the rent in it."[42] More's hair shirt and blood-colored old gown are of a piece with the "reveined" uterine vellum, their sacred purpose a thing of an already archaic past embodied in the ghoulish nature of their production. If Mantel's readers pause over this freakish historical detail ("slunk vellum from stillborn calves"?!), the dukes' goons go about their destructive work with no regard for the bookish value of what they destroy.

Today's poets, too, will often enlist the ghostly mystique of uterine vellum in a medievalist mode that animates the incarnate textual culture shared by fellow writers past. Chelsea Woodard's 2014 collection, *Vellum*, includes an eight-line elision-heavy lyric, "Uterine Vellum," that begins by returning its subject to the womb:

Never exposed to cold or light, to wind.
Not to be licked or scraped with a rough
laboring tongue or herding barb, the skin
weathers scudding instead, the deft prick of the quill tip.

Suckled by neither air nor mother, on its back
this calf carries the gestations of strangers:
unburdenings inked into words, to tattoos
read by fingertip, born flesh.[43]

The subject here is the skin itself, free from a mother's care and human husbandry. The process of parchment manufacture is a "scudding" over a membrane sea before the gentle assault of the pen and the "gestations of strangers," the febrile imaginings of writers. The poem's play with temporality thinks the calf alive again to carry the "tattoos" of human culture—themselves, like the skin, "born flesh."

The title of Catherine Byron's absorbing collection *The Getting of Vellum* (1999) reflects the Irish poet's creative process, which involved an extended collaboration with the visual artist and calligrapher Denis Brown as well as her own immersion in the business of slaughter and flaying for one of her earlier collections, *The Fat-Hen Field Hospital*.[44] The poems in *The Getting of Vellum* meditate in various ways on the rendition of writing from flesh, always with an attention to the animal lives that make this transition possible. The title piece is a long meditation on the rendering process:

Who would have thought it needed
a winch and a steel hawser
to slowly, steadily, undress a calf?
Sure I can skin a rabbit
with my bare hands,
take its soft vest of fur
up and over its head—
rather too like
undressing a baby.
But skinning a calf,
a three days dead calf,
is another thing altogether.
It's like watching a birth,

not a flaying,
seeing the calf being born
a second time,
this headfirst slow entrance
from its skin
as if from the birth canal.
So dainty and delicate
in its glassy, gleaming pinks
and whites, its untried
muscles and tendons,
its organs—lungs, gut, heart—
never used ex utero.
Uterine vellum. Slunk.[45]

The opening lines immediately locate the flaying process in a modern, industrial context, where winch and hawser help "undress" the corpse of a new calf in a process that resembles a second birth rather than the entailment of a death. The "gleaming pinks and whites" already promise the illumination such a sheet, once processed, will ultimately receive.

Another lyric in the collection, "Renderers," Byron sets in the "Vale of the River Tas, South Norfolks." Part 1, "From calf to vellum," distantly recalls the great Bible riddle from the Exeter Book (see chap. 9). The poem begins with a stillbirth and explores the tangled agencies of animal parts and those who render and use them:

The milch cow slipped her calf
a slink, stillborn.
It gave her the slip
and sank through a fault in the earth—
a swallow-hole to Hades.

The knacker picked it up:
a casualty calf.
He winched off its skin
and laid the hide flat in hide-salt.
Its flesh boiled up for dogs.

The vellum-maker slipped the skin
into his vat.

He turned the paddles
and agitated the cream of slake lime.
The hairs let slip their roots.

And now the nib of the letterer
bites the nap.
Scoured skin drinks ink
as if it were paper. Is inscribed
where once veins ran.[46]

Slipped, slink, stillborn, the winch pulling hide from flesh. The process of making uterine vellum ranges across the successive grammatical subjects of the stanzas and lines: the milch cow, the knacker, the vellum-maker, a pen's nib, written skin. The poem embraces the unsullied membrane medium while lingering on the bruter facts of death and flaying, the twinned acts of agitation and inscription that together form the manuscript rendered from the uterine skin of the unborn. Now, as in *Bring Up the Bodies*, lines of ink appear "where once veins ran." *Carta non nata*: in Byron's poems, Boccaccio's unborn sheets awaken to drink an ink that gives them a new if diminished kind of life.

CHAPTER SIX

QUESTIONS OF QUANTITY
Membrane and Archival Scale

Mr. Snagsby is behind his counter in his grey coat and sleeves, inspecting an Indenture of several skins which has just come in from the engrosser's; an immense desert of law-hand and parchment, with here and there a resting-place of a few large letters, to break the awful monotony, and save the traveller from despair.

—CHARLES DICKENS, *BLEAK HOUSE*

How large is the parchment inheritance, and in what sense does its size matter? In the prologue I suggested that the surviving membrane record may consist of some one to three billion discrete pieces of animal skin: a loose and statistically untested figure that will strike many specialists in the history of the book as a gross exaggeration. While this numerical range was derived through a process of information gathering, extrapolation, and informal consultation with archivists and fellow scholars, it goes without saying that any attempt to quantify the extant membrane record of the premodern world with any precision will be largely quixotic. If a single nineteenth-century indenture "of several skins" can be imagined, in Dickens's jaundiced estimation, as "an immense desert of law-hand and parchment," the parchment record as a whole is a universe of written skin.[1] In any archive, Juan Ilerbaig writes, "what surrounds the text is virtually infinite," and questions of why, whether, and how many particular archival objects are treasured and saved at the expense of others have long informed the theory and practice of conservation.[2] Parchment epitomizes the "tough materiality" of the archival assemblage, in Aleida Assmann's felicitous phrase: its perdurance in quantity and variety as those membranes that have survived the gnawing teeth of time.[3] Scale is a simultaneously empirical and emotional attribute of the animal archive, resistant to our calculations, subject to our wonder and awe.

A famous manuscript helps illustrate the provocation such questions of quan-

Figure 6.1. Codex Amiatinus, on display at the British Museum. Florence, Biblioteca Medicea Laurenziana, Ms. Amiatino 1.

tity and scale represent for the history, theology, and science of parchment more broadly. Codex Amiatinus is a Latin Bible produced at the behest of the English monk Ceolfrith in the early eighth century (see fig. 6.1). Ceolfrith served as abbot of the Benedictine monastery of Jarrow, which he founded and led until his death in 716. In the year 692, Ceolfrith commissioned three pandects (or complete Bibles), one of them intended as a gift to the pope in Rome; only scattered leaves of the other two volumes survive, and Amiatinus now represents the earliest extant more or less complete text of Jerome's Vulgate Bible.[4] Codex Amiatinus and its companion volumes eventually made the journey to Rome, though the volumes took so long to produce that Ceolfrith did not live to complete the voyage himself—and not simply for the amount of scribal labor they required, which was considerable. Amiatinus has always been celebrated for its size, and for the scale of its endeavor: an "immense manuscript codex," George Forrest Browne described it in 1903, "so large that two men carry it on a stretcher when it is brought out for the study of some highly privileged person."[5] The manuscript features early on in Bernhard Bischoff's *Latin Palaeography*, where it inspires a famously quantitative passage in his chapter on parchment: "The acquisition of parchment must be viewed also as an economic problem. For the production of the Codex Amiatinus alone—and it had two sister manuscripts—over 500 sheepskins were required at Wearmouth or Jarrow."[6] That phrase "over 500 sheepskins" is still cited or paraphrased frequently in the literature, though the figure may represent merely a third of the hides required for the three pandects. As Richard Gameson puts it in a study of the cost of Amiatinus and its sister books, "The slaughter of the 1,545 calves [sic] whose hides became the parchment of the three Bibles was not a single act of preparation: on the contrary it represents the accumulation of an uncertain but undoubtedly considerable number of years."[7] Such expropriations of skins over years and decades would have been commonplace for prestigious scriptoria commissioned with the making of luxury books at large scale. For chanceries producing written legal and administrative instruments, the needs were more frequent and day to day. M. T. Clanchy estimates that the provision of parchments to the king's justices for a county eyre during the thirteenth century would have required approximately a village's annual yield of sheepskins—not a vast amount for an entire county, though enough to suggest the beginnings of a "new industry in writing materials" that included a sharp increase in the manufacture of parchment.[8]

What comes across in such calculations is the magnitude of animal consumption that allowed for the transmission and preservation of writing on membrane: the seeming reduction of entire flocks and herds, whole pastures and multiple generations of animals, into a single book, library, plea roll, or monastic cartulary. The evidence for such reductions lies everywhere in the written culture of the premodern world, every psalter the remains of twenty-odd sheep, every thick cartulary the hides of a village's annual yield of cattle. As Marcel Thomas and others have cautioned, scholars have tended to overestimate the number of hides required for typical codices, and flock sizes could vary widely within and between regions.[9] In 1283, for example, the Blackbourne Hundred maintained a flock of 17,127 sheep; by contrast, the flocks owned by the Cistercians of Valmagne, an abbey in south-central France, were capped at a thousand.[10] Yet questions of quantity consistently inform our reception and comprehension of monumental books such as Codex Amiatinus or, for other reasons, Codex Gigas. This, perhaps the largest surviving codex from the medieval world (see fig. 6.2), has long inspired marvel both for its size and its alleged creaturely composition. Codex Gigas is "just under a metre tall, half a metre wide, and twenty centimeters thick," writes Mark Forsyth. "It weighs slightly more than I do, and its parchment reputedly contains the skins of 160 donkeys."[11] A book the weight of a grown man! One manuscript, 160 donkeys!

The great mass and myriad forms of the membrane record are discernible in the eccentric and wildly inconsistent zoological idiom informing the modern era's bib-

Figure 6.2. A postcard from 1929 showing the size of the Codex Gigas, printed by the National Library of Sweden, Stockholm.

liographical practices, as attested by the words of scholars and cataloguers past and present. Of a medieval Torah scroll: "The Pentateuch in *Hebrew*, written on a roll of basil goat-skins, 156 feet in length, and 22 inches wide."[12] Of some tenth-century fragments of the Qur'ān: "Ten sheets of gazelle parchment, precise date unknown."[13] Of a Premonstratensian mortuary roll: "Attached to the head is a . . . limp sheepskin wrapper, backed with linen and inscribed in ink with the word 'Wynevale'."[14] Of a fifteenth-century edition of Thomas Aquinas's commentary on the Epistles of St. Paul: "An incunable in its contemporary binding of blind-stamped pigskin."[15] Of a fourteenth-century copy of the *Speculum humanae salvationis*: "Manuscript on Vellum . . . original oak boards, deerskin (a portion of the deerskin cover torn off)."[16] Of a series of early modern bindings: "Dark calf binding . . . White deerskin binding . . . Pale calf binding . . . Brown calf binding."[17] Of a twelfth-century Qur'ān: "written on fish skin parchment and decorated with droplets of gold."[18] Of an undated Hebrew Esther scroll: "Written on goat skins, on a roll fourteen feet eight inches long by 10½ inches wide."[19] Of a royal memorandum book: "There are eighteen leaves, four of which are of ass's skin" (a likely reference to paper or parchment treated to allow erasure).[20] Of a twelfth-century copy of Ovid's *Tristia*: "written on pigskin with a characteristically rounded script."[21]

And the lists go on, and on, and on, in all their randomness and speculation and faunal immensity, the parchment and vellum missals, the charters, scrolls, and mezuzot, the Torahs and Bibles and Qur'āns, the psalters and Gratians and Chaucers. The collective catalogue of the parchment epoch is a grand creaturely litany of sorts, though of undifferentiated animals rather than their human counterparts named in liturgy and private prayer.

The survival rates of premodern books and records vary so widely that any quantitative extrapolation of the shape of medieval holdings from the scale of modern collections (or vice versa) will be an exercise in approximation. As a result, there have been few attempts at enumerating the extant medieval manuscripts from around the Western world. One exception is Eltjo Buringh's *Medieval Manuscript Production in the Latin West: Explorations with a Global Database* (2011), which seeks to construct a statistically rigorous survey of all manuscript books to survive from Western Europe between about 500 and 1500 CE, and to quantify this surviving manuscript record accordingly. Buringh argues against simple arithmetical enumeration and in favor of more sophisticated statistical methods: "We should stop counting, start sampling and let chance and large numbers help us in our endeavour."[22] His first task was to assemble a "general random library collection" consisting of some 2100 modern printed books and journal articles referring in some way to manuscripts: library catalogues, auction lists, essays on medieval book lists, and so on. The books in this library (assembled over a period of twenty-five years) were "put together haphazardly," and thus became a reliably random "repository of the available worldwide literature on manuscripts."[23] A database was then extracted from "a sample of manuscripts described in the books from the library"; from this "fuzzy set" of extant codices, Buringh designed a complex statistical model that includes book production and loss rates as well as separate variables for spatial calibration, scaling, reciprocal survival, selection biases, and a number of other technical factors that allowed him to work outward from the extensive database compiled from his library. Using his statistical model, Buringh arrives at a figure of 2.9 million as the total number of Western manuscript books surviving in the world's collections.[24] Of these, he suggests, the portion of books extant from the millennium between 500 and 1500 BCE is somewhere in the neighborhood of 1.2 million. Accounting for the rough proportion of medieval books on paper (and assuming even a very low average of ten to twenty hides per codex), Buring's figure equates to roughly ten to twenty million distinct specimens of animal membrane.

Yet this is hardly the whole story. Despite its exhaustiveness (and this is a crucial point), Buringh's database includes only those manuscripts surviving in codex form: "We limited ourselves to manuscript books," he notes, excluding "texts that are single sheet manuscripts (as deeds or charters) . . . We did not consider single sheet writs or charters to be manuscripts."[25] An understandable choice, though in sheer quantitative terms, codices represent a minute subcategory of the written record produced on membrane during the medieval and early modern periods. (As Andrew Prescott notes, "By comparison with administrative archives, the manuscript collections containing the literary texts of the Middle Ages are very small.")[26] Animal skin also makes up a substantial proportion of surviving legal and administrative records: charters, pleas, memorandum rolls, property deeds, rents, quitclaims, and so on. In many parts of Western Europe, until about the fifteenth century and in some localities well into the eighteenth, parchment remained the preferred medium for writing down and preserving many such records, due in part to tradition, in part to the proven durability of the material. Nor were parchment codices and membrane records part of separate written cultures; one of Thomas Hoccleve's jobs at the Privy Seal, for example, was to purchase parchment for the office, sheets of which appear in his autograph manuscripts.[27]

The Norfolk Record Office in Norwich, England is an archive of county history that holds local records dating back to the eleventh century. To walk among the archive's shelves is to begin comprehending the scale of the parchment record in its voluminous wealth. By the estimates of the curators and conservators at the Norfolk Record Office, there are currently ten to twelve million discrete parchment items in their collections: everything from rents inscribed on pieces of skin no larger than a small index card to charters taking up a single hide to court and manor rolls on numerous parchments sewn together by the dozens and hundreds (see figs. 6.3, 6.4, 6.5, and 6.6). The vast majority of these parchment records have never been individually described or even examined in the modern era; most remain folded, covered, bound and assembled much as they have been since the later Middle Ages, stored in the thousands upon thousands of boxes lining many miles of shelves, with dozens or hundreds of parchment records per box.

Though the Norfolk Record Office is one of the larger county holdings in England, such a remarkable figure reflects the animal membranes held in a single record office from just one of England's many counties. The Archives of Kent County boast of fourteen kilometers of collection, of which nearly half consist of parchment. The five miles of shelving at the North Yorkshire County Record Office likewise preserve something on the order of ten million discrete parchment records, translating to many more membrane specimens. An archivist at the Shropshire County Record Office estimates the holdings at "about 835 cubic metres of archives," and could give me no rough estimate for the quantity of parchment except "millions of items."[28] The Essex Record Office touts its eight miles of shelves with approximately half of its holdings consisting of parchment. Four miles of parchment: a car traveling an average speed on a highway would take four minutes to drive past all that animal skin.

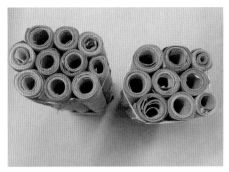

Figures 6.3, 6.4, 6.5, and 6.6. A variety of the many millions of bundled parchment records at the Norfolk Record Office, Norwich.

A parchment repository no less impressive than the county archives is the Parliamentary Archives in Victoria Tower at the Palace of Westminster. The institution's Act Room holds one of two membrane copies of the Public Acts of Parliament, mandated by statute to be inscribed on vellum and stored in duplicate in separate locations. The Act Room resembles nothing so much as a great carpet emporium, with rolls upon rolls of sheepskin stored in shelves that reach from floor to ceiling (see fig. 6.7). The longest act, the Land Tax Act of 1821, is written on 757 skins and records the names of 65,000 tax commissioners; when unfurled the act would equal the length of the palace itself, over a quarter mile (fig. 6.8).

The Public Record Office (now part of the National Archives at Kew) represents a parchment repository of considerably greater vastness than all of these. In a 1903 report to the Prime Minister of Australia on the subject of European Archives, barrister F. M. Bladen remarked on the "enormous accumulations" of archival materials in the record office, as well as the "forty miles of shelving, closely packed" he found there: "The close rolls of the Court of Chancery comprise considerably over 19,000 rolls; whilst the Coram Rege and De Banco rolls, which are also numbered by thousands, contain, in some cases, as many as 500 or 1,000 skins of parchment each."[29] Bladen is likely citing here from a roughly contemporaneous reference work, Samuel Scargill-Bird's *Guide to the Principal Classes of Documents Preserved in the Public Record Office* (1896), which, in a footnote in the introduction, evokes the "enormous bulk" of the PRO's parchment holdings.[30] Anyone who has worked with the written law of medieval and early modern England will be familiar with both the individual bulk and collective vastness of these rolls and record books. Figure 6.9 shows a collection of Court of Chancery orders and decrees from

Figure 6.7.
The Act Room,
Parliamentary
Archives, Victoria
Tower, Westminster.

Figure 6.8.
Land Tax Act of
1821 on parchment
roll, Westminster,
Parliamentary
Archives 1/B/7/3,
Victoria Tower,
Westminster.

the year 1610 (7 James I). This stack of parchments, 1134 folios long and over a foot thick, represents just one type of Chancery record produced in the course of only half a year; the surrounding decades yield many thousands of membrane volumes of similar or greater magnitude and weight.[31] Figure 6.10 pictures one of thousands of surviving plea rolls (in this case from King's Bench), parchments most often bound together by legal term (yielding four per year) such that they resemble a flip book the size of a husky child. In figure 6.11, Mabel H. Mills, who worked for a time with the University of Chicago's Chaucer Research Project, is depicted examining a massive roll in the Round Room at the National Archives, hung on a large viewing rack (or "horse") capable of bearing the weight and bulk of the record.[32]

The rolls, memorandum books, and other records of the Common Law courts

Figure 6.9.
Court of Chancery
Orders and Decrees,
7 James I (1601), PRO
C 33 B 1610.

Figure 6.10. Court of King's Bench Plea Roll, PRO KB 27/1/1364/1.

Figure 6.11.
Mabel H. Mills,
a member of the
British research team
hired by University
of Chicago Chaucer
Research Project,
examining a large
roll at the National
Archives, ca. 1930.

and the Court of Exchequer demanded an immense provision of skins on an almost daily basis.[33] "A roll of parchment is sixty skins," notes an 1858 catalogue of the "collection of animal parts belonging to her majesty's commissioners" for an exhibit at the South Kensington Museum: "The government offices in London alone use upwards of 80 rolls a-week, while fully 400 rolls of parchment per week must be made in other parts of the United Kingdom."[34] Three thousand skins a week, then, and only for one subset of government business.

The profound dependence of English law on the animal medium shapes its own institutional memory as well as its historiographical afterlife. In his list of the named offices within the Court of Exchequer, Scargill-Bird includes the "Clerk of the Pells, so called from his parchment rolls or 'Peles Receptorum'." [35] The *clericus pelle*, "clerk of the skins," a seventeenth-century overview of the Exchequer terms the office.[36] The clerk was housed in the eponymous Pell Office, a department founded in the fifteenth century and abolished only in 1834. Closer to our own time, the great legal historian J. H. Baker, asking why the historical study of English law has not neared completion, adduces the staggering extent of the written record as the primary obstacle: the "enormous bulk" of these "mountains of parchment," these "thousands of miles of abbreviated Latin."[37] In fact, Baker's Dickensian assessment is a masterpiece of zoological understatement: "Over a million sheep, during six centuries, gave their skins to make the 'record'—the continuous parchment memorial of the proceedings and judgments in the king's court. Indeed the common law owes a large debt to sheep-farming." [38] The true debt is far greater than even Baker imagined, by a factor of ten or more. Colleagues I have consulted at the National Archives speak of entire categories of writs, returns, and bundles in the tens of millions, unquantified and uncatalogued, yet archived for an intended eternity.[39]

Tens of thousands of codices in national, university, and local libraries; five, ten, twenty million parchments housed in individual county records depositories; a mountain of membranes in the Public Record Office: as even this superficial overview suggests, it would be folly to suggest anything approaching an exact count of total parchment specimens currently extant in England from before 1800. A conservative estimate would easily exceed one hundred million; a figure of five hundred million or even one billion is not out of the question.

A step across the channel to France perhaps doubles this figure. Though the various traditions of written law on the Continent do not display the same organization and continuity as the English common law system, the quantity of parchment preserved in national and local records offices, ecclesiastical archives, and numerous other holdings rivals its insular counterpart—this despite the creation of monastic cartularies beginning around the turn of the first millennium, which often entailed the neglect and loss of early charters and a "carelessness with original documents."[40] Daniel Lord Smail, speaking only of the surviving notarial records from late medieval France, describes "notarial casebooks and parchments piled up in great drifts in the medieval archives of regions, cities, and small towns all over the southern lands and, by the fifteenth century, in the north, as well."[41] David Nicholas speaks of the "massive written records" generated by European cities from Sicily to Scandinavia, entailing what Daniel Waley terms a "spectacular consumption" of parchment, paper, and other writing materials.[42] Something of the scale of this consumption can still be measured in the current parchment holdings of many hundreds of archives of nations, cities, and localities across Europe and into the Near East. The National Archives of Bavaria estimates its holdings at "half a million parchment documents," including many membrane rolls made up of multiple skins.[43] Local records depositories in eastern Europe and Russia may house up to one hundred million parchment records from before 1800 (the state archives of the Polish city and province of Wrozlaw lists "1,117,154 archival units including parchment documents"),[44] with additional tens of millions accumulated in the various state and local archives across the Scandinavian lands and down into Germany and the Low Countries. Despite the early turn to paper among Islamic and other communities of medieval Spain, there are massive stores of parchment records in the archives of Catalonia and other regions and municipalities, with dependable estimates in the tens of millions (one scholar speaks of the "daunting superabundance of archival records" as a factor discouraging the study of east Pyrenean societies).[45] The legendary vastness of the archives at the Vatican Library has not been exaggerated. Paul Maria Baumgarten, writing of the Vatican's great parchment folio Registers alone, notes their "colossal size," while avowing that "it is quite impossible to form even an approximate idea of the number of documents contained in these volumes. Any attempt at an estimate might be millions wide of the mark."[46]

Numerous sources give us glimpses well into the modern period of the number of skins still being employed for the routine business of courts and other administrative cultures requiring the creaturely medium in dependable quantity and bulk. Charles Vernon, an officer of the Dublin Stamp Office, was questioned in 1823 over the provision of stationers' supplies the previous summer. Vernon, as warehousekeeper of unstamped goods, was responsible for the receipt, storage, and inventory of blank paper and parchment received by the office and stored before official use. His office was also required to record the quantities of goods received from suppliers, one of which was a parchment distributor in Dublin. During his testimony, Vernon consults his record of receipts in response to a question from his examiner regarding the quantity of parchment received from the Dublin supplier over three months; the quantity included "250 skins of parchment," "205 half skins," and "15,030 eighths" (probate documents), "15,030 sixteenths" (for use as "small writs for the courts"). On a later date, "10,000 eights" are identified as probates and 2100 as latitats (a form of small writ).[47] These figures, again, represent the quantity of parchment supplied by just one distributor in a single city over three months. That such an eye-popping amount of parchment was still being supplied as late as the second decade of the nineteenth century points to the continuing vitality of the medium as a written record well into the industrial age.

So, how much is out there, and why should we care? The rough figures posited above suggest that well over one billion distinct parchment specimens may be extant from the era before 1800, and perhaps as many as two or even three billion, housed in the world's archives and libraries. A billion discrete pieces of parchment does not equate to the hides of a billion discrete organisms, of course: Depending on the size of a codex, two, four, eight, or sixteen folios might be rendered from the same hide, while in the case of legal documents such as small charters, deeds, or rents, one hide could furnish several dozen blank slips for scribal use; conversely, though, dozens or even hundreds of skins may make up a large roll, represented by a single entry in a catalogue. In zooarchaeological terminology, the parchment record contains many more distinguishable *specimens* (discrete animal parts) than discrete contributing *elements* (individual mammals).[48] The low billions, then: a very conservative estimate would be five hundred million parchment specimens, a liberal estimate three billion, with highly variable modes of access and degrees of interest in their contents. And there they sit, an immense faunal record consubstantial with the cultural and institutional memories of a human civilization.

Literary scholars these days tend to regard large-scale quantitative questions as the purview of the Digital Humanities, particularly the computational approaches (such as text mining and topic modeling) that guide scholars working with large data sets. As Johanna Drucker has aptly objected, "quantity is an effect of cultural conditions, not a self-evident fact."[49] It may be that the analog humanities have ceded questions of quantity somewhat too readily to the more digital and computational quarters of our disciplines in recent years, notwithstanding the fact that the ongoing digitization of the parchment record is proving by far the most effective means of making its scale visible in new and palpable ways (see the Epilogue below). Yet "scale is a fearsome thing," as Claire Vaye Watkins's narrator puts it in *Gold Fame Citrus*: "Scale is analogy," too, and thus able to capture in unique ways the archival imagination of written cultures.[50] In the case of parchment, the sheer quantity of the stuff that survives in the world's archives presents dimensions of scale and magnitude ungraspable by algorithms; archival scale is a problem less of computation than of imagination, as much a moral or theological conundrum as a machine-searchable set of data.

The scale of the membrane record is a matter not only of quantity and scope but also of temporality, and its study demands methods and approaches that, like parchment itself, transcend and defeat human time-frames. As Jo Guldi and David

Armitage put it, "The return of the *longue durée*" to humanistic study "is intimately connected to changing questions of scale": questions which, in the case of the written record, speak to the tendency of membrane documents and books to survive over vast periods of time.[51] This is an aspect of the medium that registers in different ways depending on the particular discipline or discourse that studies or imagines it: in the contemporary palaeogeneticist's recovery of strands of DNA and collagen from the surface of a seventeenth-century charter, in the theologian's vision of the "skin of the skies" stretched eternally across the heavens.

It is in this sense that the scale of the parchment record foregrounds the biopolitical burden of this animal archive, the moral weight embodied in the countless specimens of mammal hide making up a significant portion of the Western world's written inheritance. The masses of premodern animal skin surviving in our archives bespeak not only the mundane regularity of animal slaughter, that is, but also the immense human industry invested in the rendering and utilization of these untold millions of animal bodies for the specific purpose of documenting, transmitting, and preserving human culture—even as these same bodies served other, more ephemeral purposes down the same centuries, as food, clothing, shelter, tack, and so on. The use of parchment in such quantity over many centuries represents a deeply engrained technological disposition and cultural habit which, if rarely questioned on ethical grounds, nevertheless shaped the cultures and civilization of the Common Era in fundamental ways, and will help shape its future in eras to come.

Is there another great artifact surviving from the premodern world that puts before our eyes similar scales of dominion over the creaturely world? We might think of the pyramids of Egypt, built by human workers (perhaps enslaved, perhaps not) eating four thousand pounds of meat per day as butchers filled waste pits with the bones of the cattle, sheep, and goats they consumed to sustain their labor.[52] Unlike such monuments to expenditure, though, the parchment record consists of the actual flesh of those countless creatures whose bodies were given over to the instrumental demands of written culture. And unlike such massive stone monuments to human folly and accomplishment, the vastness and ubiquity of the animal archive remain largely invisible, dispersed as myriad rendered remains in most major and numerous local libraries, institutional archives, and private collections across Europe, North Africa, the Middle East, and North America.

The wonder such quantitative imaginings inspire among moderns will occasionally come through even in the most sober historical accounts. Here is Diarmaid MacCulloch, in his magisterial *Christianity: The First Three Thousand Years*, on the Emperor Constantine's lavish expenditures on outward signs of his new faith:

"Among his many other donations were fifty monumental copies of the Bible commissioned from Bishop Eusebius's specialist scriptorium in Caesaria: an extraordinary expenditure on creating de luxe written texts, for which the parchment alone would have required the death of around five thousand cows (so much for Christian disapproval of animal sacrifice)."[53] Irony aside, MacCullouch's parenthetical speaks to the vexed but most often implicit relation between sacrifice and consumption in early economies of parchment. The source he cites for this figure is one of the "Letters on Christian Topics" transcribed by Eusebius in the fourth book of his *Life of Constantine*. In the letter, Emperor Constantine demands the provision of materials needed for the dozens of copies of the Bible he has commissioned:

> [A] great mass of people has attached itself to the most holy Church, so that with everything there enjoying great growth it is particularly fitting that more churches should be established. Be ready therefore to act urgently on the decision we have reached. It appeared proper to indicate to your Intelligence that you should order fifty volumes on prepared skins [διφθέραις], easily legible and convenient for portable use, to be copied by skilled calligraphists well trained in the art, copies that is of the Divine Scriptures, the provision and use of which you well know to be necessary for reading in church. Written instructions have been sent by our Clemency to the man who is in charge of the diocese that he see to the supply of all the materials needed to produce them. The preparation of the written volumes with utmost speed shall be the task of your Diligence.[54]

Constantine specifies here that the copies of the Scriptures are to be written on *diphtherai* or skins, leaving it to Eusebius to gather "all the materials," and thus command the provision of thousands of parchments from the surrounding regions at the emperor's orders. A swiftly growing church requires ever more Bibles, and more Bibles require more parchment, and more parchment requires more creatures for their rendering: all in all a "massive blood sacrifice," Anthony Grafton and Megan Williams call it, at the service of an ambitious and expanding church.[55]

Whether sacrificial or practical, such demands for extensive slaughter and rendering make parchment quantity palpable as a front-end process, a vast entailment of book cultures dependent on animal flesh for their everyday medium. The scale of parchment is equally visible in retrospect, through sobering accounts of archival destruction and loss. In the *Philobiblon* (ca. 1340), Richard of Bury, bishop of Durham, dedicates one chapter to the "Complaint of Books against Wars"—for war, he avows, "is above all plagues injurious to books." At one point the treatise turns to the history of libraries destroyed in war, particularly the great ancient library of Alexandria. Like most medieval writers, Richard assumes the works stored in the library were preserved on parchment rather than papyrus. The chapter casts the destruction of the great repository as a mass slaughter of innocent membranes:

> In sooth we cannot mourn with the grief that they deserve all the various books that have perished by the fate of war in various parts of the world. Yet we must tearfully recount the dreadful ruin which was caused in Egypt by the auxiliaries in the Alexandrian war, when 700,000 volumes were consumed by fire . . . Who would not shudder at such a hapless holocaust [*infaustum holocaustum*], where ink is offered up instead of blood, where the glowing ashes of crackling parchment were crimsoned with blood [*ubi prunae candentes pergameni crepitantis sanguine vernabantur*], where the devouring flames consumed so many thousands of innocents in whose mouth was no guile, where the unsparing fire turned into stinking ashes so many shrines of eternal truth! A lesser crime than this is the sacrifice of Jephthah or Agamemnon, where a pious daughter is slain by a father's sword.[56]

This catastrophic image of a bleeding, burning library of skin captures the mass destruction of hundreds of thousands of books, reenacting the myriad originary sacrifices necessary to the invention of cultural tradition. The destruction of the library is imagined through a metonymy of bibliographical catastrophe in which the "innocents" are at once sheets of rendered parchment, innocent volumes, shrines of learning, and victims of human sacrifice: an anthropomorphizing allegory that makes of the perishing library and its books an inferno of humanity.[57]

Yet the passage also evokes the animality of these membrane victims through the author's dense web of allusions to his Latin sources. The first is Richard's invocation of the famously scriptive account of the Lamb of Mt. Syon (Revelation 14:1–5), standing on the mount, "and with him an hundred forty-four thousand, having his name, and the name of his Father, written on their foreheads" [*scriptum in frontibus suis*]. These many thousands were "purchased from the earth," and "in their mouth there was found no lie": "et in ore eorum non est inventum mendacium," the precise phrase Richard of Bury enlists in the passage above to describe the "thousands of innocents" in whose "mouth was no guile." These myriad exemplars of lambish purity, their earthborn flesh inscribed with the names of animal and god, become in the *Philobiblon* the seven hundred thousand volumes burned by the martial auxiliaries in a "holocaust" of membrane.

The pathos of the scene is sharpened by Richard of Bury's liturgical source for this passage (previously unidentified): a hymn to St. Vincent Martyr sung at lauds on Vincent's feast day. The hymn's first two stanzas depict Vincent of Saragossa's gruesome martyrdom as a spectacle of torn and bloodied flesh, his body suffering even its smallest wounds to be rubbed with salt:

Glorious was the Christian warrior
Deacon Vincent, as with tread
Firm and free, the pile ascending
To that fiery doom he sped;
Where the salt shower fiercely crackling
O'er his tortured flesh was spread;

While the furnace flamed around him,
Crimsoned with his gushing blood;
Yet he still endured intrepid
Faithful ever to his Lord;
And with eyes to Heaven uplifted
Christ upon His Throne adored.[58]

In reworking Vincent's martyrdom as a spectacle of bibliographic destruction, Richard enlists the gruesome particulars of the hymnist's Latin—the crackling flesh [*crepitantis*], glowing coals splashed and reddened with blood [*prunae vernabantur sanguine*]—into a tableau that brings the hundreds of thousands of innocent, lamblike parchments back to life only to make them bleed and burn and die anew, the lone sound from their innocent mouths the noise of their own crackling demise. The passage closes by evoking the story of Jephthah, one of the most notorious incidents of biblical child sacrifice, alongside the abortive pagan sacrifice of Iphigenia—whose death was forestalled by the miraculous substitution of a deer in her place. These countless parchment "innocents" are thus also double victims, the animals whose hides, in the bishop's understanding, perish anew in this immense holocaust of written tradition.

An equally vivid legend of mass membrane destruction in the ancient world derives from a series of accounts surrounding the inscription and fate of the *Avesta*, the great sacred text of Zoroastrianism first promulgated centuries before the Achaemenid era. The *Avesta* was all but lost by the time of the early Roman Empire. The text as it survives today consists of a series of fragments cobbled together during the reign of the Sasanian kings of Iran from the third to the seventh century. A number of Middle Persian sources extant from this era describe a certain tradition that grew up around the writing and safekeeping of the *Avesta*, which, according to legend, required the slaughter of thousands of oxen or water buffalo for its inscription and preservation. Sitting before the king, Zoroaster, according to an epistle by the tenth-century polymath Ibn al-Nadīm, composed the holy book "on twelve thousand water buffalo skins inscribed with gold, in which all the sciences are found."[59] The scriptures, preserved on the beasts' skins, were thereafter hidden in a cave at Persepolis, guarded by holy designates as an eternal record of the faith, until their destruction by Alexander the Great—reviled as "Alexander the Destroyer."

The most influential account of the *Avesta*'s decimation occurs in the so-called *Letter of Tansar*, described by Mary Boyce as "a fugitive piece of Middle Persian literature" and purporting to be an epistle by a missionary serving under Ardashir I (r. 180–242 CE), founder of the Sasanian Empire.[60] The letter frames its account of scriptural destruction within a wider lament bemoaning the loss of Zoroastrian tradition—histories, genealogies, and memory:

> If your concern is for religious matters, and you deny that any justification is found in religion, know that Alexander burnt the book of our religion—twelve thousand skins—at Istaxr. One third of it was known by heart and survived, but even that was all legends and traditions, and men knew not the laws and ordinances; until, through the corruption of the people of the day and the decay of royal power and the craving for what was new and counterfeit and the desire for vainglory, even those legends and traditions dropped out of common recollection, so that not an iota of the truth of that book remained. Therefore the faith must needs be restored by a man of true and upright judgment. Yet have you heard tell of, or seen, any monarch save the King of kings, who has taken this task upon him? With the vanishing of religion you have lost also the knowledge of genealogies and histories and lives of great men, which you have let pass from memory. Some of it you have recorded in books, some upon stones and walls, until none of you remembers what happened in the days of his father.[61]

Particularly striking in the Tansar account is the distinction drawn between animal hide—the "twelve thousand skins" preserving the original sacred text—and other mediums enlisted by the faithful in the age following the destruction of the original *Avesta*: stones, walls, books of unspecified composition, and, worst of all, human memory, an unreliable method of preservation at best. These inferior modes of record-keeping cannot rival the power of myriad hides hidden and guarded in an archival fortress. In a similar account in the *Ardā Wirāz Nāmag*, a Sasanian visionary text dating from Late Antiquity, the bookish ravages of Alexander force a Babel-like catastrophe among the Zoroastrian faithful: "And this religious tradition [*dēn*], the entire Avesta and Zand as it was written on adorned ox-hides [*gāw pōstīhā*] in golden ink, had been placed in Pābak's Istaxr in the Fortress of Archives [*diž ī nipišt*]. That ill-omened adversary, the wicked, evil-doing heretic Alexander the Roman, who lived in Egypt, carried them off and burnt them." Because the Iranians "had no rulers, chiefs, leaders, or judges who knew the religion," the destruction of the massive written tradition represented by the Avestan membranes introduced "many types of sects, beliefs, heresy, doubt, and disagreement" into the world.[62] The term translated here as the "Fortress of Archives," *diž ī nipišt*, evokes a wide range of bookish associations: a "castle of inscriptions," a chamber of written things emptied and desecrated by Alexander during his ravages in Iran.[63]

Both accounts emphasize the physical magnitude of the written record as inherent to its content, as well as the powerful claim animal membrane has on the preservation of tradition against threats of its decimation. The twelve thousand hides inscribed by Zoroaster are a record of seeming permanence destroyed en masse under the devilish ruler of a foreign power. The seven hundred thousand membrane volumes mourned in the *Philobiblon* are innocent victims of war. In either case, the scale of an animal archive renders its destruction all the more unimaginable.

How to account for that shiver of horror produced in medieval chroniclers and modern scholars when evoking these numbers—"700,000 volumes," "12,000 hides," "the death of around five thousand cows," "a massive blood sacrifice"? There is something of the sublime in such awed imaginings, caught as they are between totality and infinity, mired in the frightful magnitude of bibliographic estimation. In the *Critique of Judgment*, Kant introduces the attribute of quantity to the philosophical consideration of the sublime: "in view of the formlessness which may belong to what we call sublime," we must "begin with quantity, as the first moment of the aesthetical judgment as to the sublime" (CJ §24).[64] By quantity Kant means both number and our own collective investment in the natural world beyond us. Indeed, "our power of estimating the magnitude of things in the world of sense is inadequate" to the scale of totality, which forces us to comprehend them instead from an undifferentiating distance. "Yet this inadequacy itself is the arousal in us of the feeling that we have within us a supersensible power" (CJ §25). With respect to objects outside of ourselves, the sublime is a double-edged sword, giving us a sense of dominion over the nonhuman world while attuning us to what Emily Brady calls "the nature we are able to resist within us, that is, nature's determination of us through sensibility."[65] Even as the thunderstorm or the landslide terrifies us, we remain both its subjects and its potential collective victims. As Sarah Novacich reminds us, for medieval theology "Noah the ark-maker" is also "Noah the archivist," maker and preserver of a unique record of a bygone world.[66] At least for certain writers, the archive, like nature for Kant, "excites the Idea of the sublime in its chaos or in its wildest and most irregular disorder and desolation," its "size and might" (CJ §23).

Parchment quantity is thus a subject as fit for the novelist and poet as for the historian. Donna Woolfolk Cross's *Pope Joan* (1996) sets the life of the legendary female pope in the ninth century. The fifth chapter begins with a scene of writing, as Aesculapius, the Greek pedagogue, allows Joan's brother to practice his letters on parchment rather than his customary wax tablet.

> "No, no, no." Aesculapius's voice was edged with impatience. "You must make your letters much smaller. See how your sister pens her lesson? . . . You must learn a greater respect for your parchment, my boy—there's a whole sheep gone to make just one folio. If the monks of Andernach sprawled their words across the page in that manner, the herds of Austrasia would be wiped out in a month!"[67]

Aesculapius's ecological vision, however tongue in cheek, casts the parchment medium as a dilemma of number: the "whole sheep" rendered into a single folio, the specter of half a kingdom's herds decimated for the sake of its books.

A far less sentimental perspective on parchment and scale inspires "Flock," a poem by Billy Collins, former poet laureate of the United States. The provocation for "Flock" appears to have been an unidentified "article on printing" that Collins excerpts as the poem's epigraph and that introduces his unknowing readers to a somewhat obscure fact of book history: that Johannes Gutenberg printed some two dozen copies of his Bible on vellum, procured from parchment makers in Mainz. (As Bruce Metzger estimates, "Since one calfskin provided only two good sheets of [appropriate] size, almost 6,000 calves were needed to supply enough vellum for the 35 parchment copies of this Bible."[68]) The epigraph operates on the same emotional register as the passage from Bischoff on Codex Amiatinus, or Richard of Bury's account of the Alexandrian library. With this bibliographical backdrop established (another "veritable blood sacrifice," one scholar has called it[69]), the poem adduces a vision of Gutenberg's printing press as a house of bookish horrors:

It has been calculated that each copy of the Gutenberg Bible . . .
required the skins of 300 sheep.
—from an article on printing

I can see them squeezed into the holding pen
behind the stone building
where the printing press is housed,

all of them squirming around
to find a little room
and looking so much alike

it would be nearly impossible
to count them,
and there is no telling

which one will carry the news
that the Lord is a shepherd,
one of the few things they already know. [70]

The first five lines create a sobering image of Gutenberg and his crew shoving sheep into the printing press like tree limbs into a wood chipper, churning out sheets of parchment that are then fed into the maw of the bookmaking machine. One of the poem's other deliberate absurdities is the notion that the sheep rendered for Gutenberg's parchment were penned just outside the printing house, this coldly nondescript "stone building" sheltering the press. The grim turn at line 9 brings together the categories of theology and slaughter, as the poem moves toward closure with an omniscient image of dominion alongside a glimmer of nonhuman awareness: the shepherd who confines the flock and sends its numberless members to the press is also lord and master, one of the "few things" the otherwise ignorant beasts know full well. It is left to the knowing reader to complete the death sentence of biblical pastoralism from Psalm 23: "The Lord is my shepherd"—and for parchment, at least, the Word of God shall not want. What the poem emphasizes above all, though, is quantity: the "300 sheep" required for each copy, the individual animals both indistinguishable from one another and "impossible to count." Whether three hundred sheep in a pen or twelve million parchments in a county records office, such impossibilities are entailments, not adjuncts, of the parchment inheritance.

In the preface to *A Sand County Almanac* (1949), his classic work of ecological reflection, Aldo Leopold wrote of the "Abrahamic concept of land," the unending cycle of expropriation and commodification that stymies conservation in the service of human dominion over the great community of flora and fauna that surrounds and embraces human collectivities.[71] The writing practices of the Abrahamic traditions have in turn entailed an immense provision and expenditure of animal membrane for the transmission and survival of written culture: a scale of consumption of which writers of the premodern world are well aware, and take largely for granted.

It is true that the great cultural inheritance embodied by the parchment record is more than a story of continuing and unthinking utility. Alongside the logics of human dominion over animals, these traditions also developed alternative ways of imagining human-animal relations in terms of mutuality, communion, benevolence, and so on, and a range of scholarly works have shown us the wide array of compassionate and even empathetic postures taken by premodern writers with respect to the creaturely world. The numbers, rough and raw, tell a different but equally important story, one latent in the shared biohistory of human beings and the animals whose remains formed a good portion of their archives. As poets, theologians, and encyclopedists recounted sentimental tales of talking hounds and companion horses, they recorded and preserved them, in great part, on the skins of a billion beasts. These great legions of parchment-rendered animals will be a subtext of all that follows, as indeed they served as the incarnate texts of the parchment epoch from its scattered beginnings in the great empires of the ancient Mediterranean world.

PART II

The Medium and Its Messages

➜ ❮

CHAPTER SEVEN

PARCHMENT INVENTIONS

And then (the person) named Pikara,
at the kāšaru, brought those sheep.
Copied on one skin.
—PERSEPOLIS FORTIFICATION ARCHIVE,
TABLET 2178-101 (CA. 500 BCE)

The official story of parchment begins with library envy and a trade war over writing supplies. Pliny the Elder (23–79 CE), the Roman naturalist and philosopher, transmits the most complete version of this famous account, which he attributes to an earlier historian whose version has been lost. According to Pliny, a rivalry had sprung up between Ptolemy, the king of Alexandria in Egypt, and Eumenes, king of Pergamon in Asia Minor, cities that boasted the two greatest libraries of the ancient world. Apparently stoked by envy, King Ptolemy "suppressed the export of papyrus" from Northern Africa; as a direct result, Pliny avows, "the use of parchment [*membranas*] was discovered at Pergamum; and afterwards the employment of the material on which the immortality of human beings depends spread indiscriminately."[1] Pliny carefully distinguishes here between *chartas*, for papyrus sheets, and *membranas*, the treated hides of animals, suggesting that the city's written culture turned entirely to the flesh-based medium once deprived of its traditional plant-based counterpart. The city of Pergamon gave its name to the newly discovered medium, which will ever after be known as *pergamena*, or parchment.

Pliny's intriguing story attributes parchment's long-term success not to the lack of papyrus but to the inherent qualities of the membrane medium. The story registers the exceptionalism of parchment and the peculiar circumstances of its rise, and like many such legends of origin, it imputes the invention of a certain technology to a particular moment, in this case a political crisis pitting two kings and two cultures against one another across the great sea. Already in the first century, a Roman intellectual touts the superiority of animal skin as a vehicle of written culture. The story of parchment's origin becomes in turn a paean to its perdurance, the immortality it promises to the achievements of humanity as their primary medium of transmission and preservation.

Medieval writers, in adapting Pliny's account, found in his legend a locus for robust reflection on the nature of the era's favored medium.[2] An extended elaboration of parchment's origin story occurs in Isidore of Seville's *Etymologiae*, an influential compendium of lexical and etymological knowledge written in the first third of the seventh century. Isidore's work in general is full of false etymologies, many of which have delighted later scholars for the peculiar juxtapositions and puns they create between like and unlike things. The two word origins proposed in Isidore's version of the parchment legend speak to the provenance and creaturely derivation of the medium:

> Parchment [*De pergamenis*]. Because the kings of Pergamum lacked papyrus sheets, they first had the idea of using skins. From these the name "parchment" [*pergamena*], passed on by their descendants, has been preserved up to now. These are also called skins [*membrana*] because they are stripped from the members [*membris*] of livestock. They were made at first of a muddy color, that is, yellowish, but afterwards white parchment was invented at Rome. This appeared to be unsuitable, because it soils easily and harms the readers' eyesights—as the more experienced of architects would not think of putting gilt ceiling panels in libraries, or any paving stones other than of Carystean marble, because the glitter of gold wearies the eyes, and the green of the Carystean marble refreshes them. Likewise those who are learning money-changing put dark green cloths under the forms of the coins, and carvers of gems look repeatedly at the backs of scarab beetles, than which nothing is greener, and painters do the same, in order that they may refresh the labor of their sight with the greenness of these scarabs. Parchment comes in white or yellowish or purple. The white exists naturally. Yellowish parchment is of two colors, because one side of it is dyed, that is yellowed, by the manufacturer. With regard to this, Persius:
>
> *Now the book and the two-colored parchment with its hair scraped smooth.*
>
> But purple parchment is stained with purple dye; on it melted gold and silver on the letters stands out.[3]

This version of the story is stripped of its martial resonance; instead Isidore focuses on the creaturely qualities of the medium, marking the etymological and material connection between membrane and members, between the written skin and the animal bodies from which it is flayed. Parchment, stripped from the *membra* of creatures, will always bear the animality of its derivation. The entry notes the stark visuality of white parchment (the "natural" kind, Isidore avows), with its propensity to afflict the vision of a reader just as a gilt ceiling would harm the eyes of scribes, coins the eyes of money-changers, and gems the eyes of jewel-cutters, who must take frequent breaks to stare at the backs of dark green beetles to relieve their vision.

Likewise with parchment: overly bright parchment will degrade the eyes, he claims, while overly yellowed membrane will appear muddy. The correct manufacturing process will create parchment both naturally white on one side and artificially dulled on the other, the implication of the illustrative citation that breaks up Isidore's account. The passage comes from the *Satires* of Persius (34–62 CE), an Etruscan poet of the Silver Age and a shrewd observer of Roman decadence and social mores. The speaker in *Satire* 3, waking up with a bad hangover and his bile swelling up, experiences the membrane book as a bother, the physical accoutrements of writing as so many obstacles to clear thought, akin to the gunk in his throat and the pounding in his head. He reaches for "a book and the two-tone parchment with its hair removed," along with sheets of papyrus and a pen. He corrupts his thick ink with water, and complains when it goes runny as he writes.[4] The *liber* here, unusually, is made up of both papyrus and pied parchment "with its hair removed" [*bicolor positis membrana capillis*]: a combination that adds to the confusion of the waking speaker, who wants only to write without impediment, though ends up foiled by his medium.[5]

This concern with the coarse animality of parchment continues into the next section of the *Etymologiae*, "De libris conficiendis" ("On bookmaking"), which begins with an overview of the diverse bookish curiosities of the known world. As Isidore observes of pagan books, "They were made not only on papyrus sheets or on parchment, but on the intestinal membranes of elephants or on the interwoven leaves of mallows or palms." Whether as the elephant intestines of North Africa or the bleached parchments of imperial Rome, for Isidore written culture consists in things of the natural world modulated by the genius of human craft.

Though parchment would come into widespread usage in the Mediterranean basin only gradually over the first centuries of the Common Era, the written animal already had a deep and diverse history in the ancient Mediterranean world, one that long predates the full-scale emergence of the membrane codex in Late Antiquity and the parchment cultures of the early Middle Ages. The legend of Pergamon and the invention of parchment emerged during centuries in which papyrus, of course, remained dominant. Yet as recent archaeological excavations and reinterpretations have begun to suggest, membrane played a much more central role in the era's cultures of writing than most histories of text technologies have allowed. Though the evidence is fragmentary and in some cases anecdotal, it reveals a diverse enlistment of the animal as medium in the long material history of writing, from the leather rolls of Early Dynastic Egypt to the scribal practices of the Achaemenid Empire to the written culture of Rome in the time of Jesus Christ.

The oldest extant fragments of inscribed animal membrane date from the late Bronze Age, discovered at a number of archaeological sites around the Mediterranean basin during the early decades of the twentieth century. Camel skin from the second millennium has been found in the Hebron Valley, while preserved sheepskin likely used for some form of inscription has been identified at sites from Kerma in northern Sudan dating from as early as the sixth millennium.[6] A considerable trove of parchments comes from a site at Dura-Europos, an ancient border city on the Euphrates in present-day Syria, a find that includes membranes inscribed with Hebrew liturgical prayers, among other texts.[7] There have also been several intriguing finds from the New Kingdom of Egypt (1550–1069 BCE), an era in which leather was apparently regarded as a more prestigious commodity than other, more common writing materials, such as papyrus or pottery shards. The so-called Egyptian Mathematical Leather Roll (fig. 7.1), discovered at Thebes in the nineteenth century among an assemblage of papyri in the ruins of the Rameseum, consists of a table giving the sums of mathematical fractions, likely the work of a junior official at court.[8] Tissue thin and only slightly yellowed, the membrane is remarkably well preserved after these thousands of years, the script still dark and readily discernible on the webbed and mottled surface.

Another fragment of Egyptian membrane writing is the so-called Berlin Leather Roll, a portion of a scroll created during the reign of Amenophis II during the decades before 1401 BCE (P. Berlin 3029). The document (a palimpsest) is a compilation of texts relating to various aspects of royal administration and bureaucracy.[9] One portion of the roll concerns the construction of the temple of Atun at Heliopolis by the Twelfth Dynasty pharaoh, Sesostris I. The inscription was likely first made on a stela, a monumental stone obelisk in a public area, then preserved by a scribe working from memory some years later.[10] Inscribed on the scroll's verso in hieroglyphic fragments, the temple decree seems to speak in the persona of the membrane scroll itself while taking the voice of a "herdsman" who oversees the land governed by the document's authority:

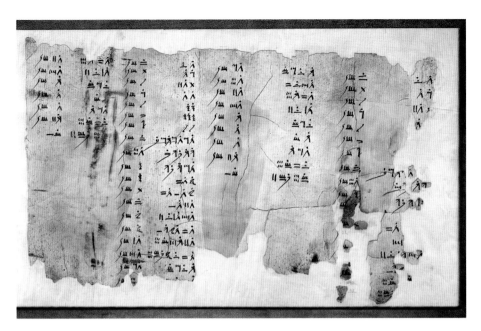

Figure 7.1. Fragment from an Egyptian mathematical roll on membrane. Middle Kingdom Egypt, ca. 1600 BCE. British Museum no. EA10250, 1.

For the future will I make a monument,
I will settle firm decrees for Harakhty
He begat me to do what should be done for him,
To accomplish what he commands to do.
He appointed me shepherd of this land,
Knowing him who would herd it for him.
He gave to me what he protects,
What the eye in him illuminates.[11]

The temple decree concludes with the appearance of the king with diadem and two feathers: "the chief lector-priest and scribe of the divine books stretched the cord. The rope was released, laid in the ground, made to be his temple."[12] The scribe as fashioner of the membrane book constructs the house marked in turn by the stela, completing a creative circuit of stone-to-skin/skin-to-stone transmission of monumentalizing text.

This ancient material should not all necessarily be classified as parchment, as some of it appears to have been tanned rather than limed, though in most cases of membrane records from this epoch the processes of manufacture have yet to be determined.[13] Yet recent discoveries by Laurel Phillipson suggest that the modern Ethiopian process of parchment making may be part of a more or less continuous tradition going back twenty centuries or more.[14] Along with surviving written artifacts are extant several visual depictions from the New Kingdom of figures engaged in what looks almost certainly like parchment craft.[15] The clearest of these representations appears on a tomb relief from Saqqara dating from the late Eighteenth- or early Nineteenth-Dynastic period (fig. 7.2 and fig. 7.3). Here, two figures, one seated and one standing, work over animal skin stretched on a wooden frame and attached at a number of points along the circumference. The standing figure holds the frame upright, while the seated figure scrapes at the surface of the hide with a curved blade. Aside from the subjects' clothing, this realistic depiction of the process could easily derive from sixteenth-century Europe, suggesting a deep-seated continuity in a craft tradition across the Mediterranean world for some three thousand years.

Among the largest assemblages of membrane records extant from before the Common Era are the Arshama letters, a trove of administrative documents dating from the middle years of the Achaemenid Empire (550–330 BCE) and now held at the Bodleian Libraries in Oxford.[16] The eponymous Arshama was a fifth-century *satrap* or prince serving under the Achaemenid emperors Darius II and Artaxerxes II. The membrane letters are all addressed to a steward named Nakhthor, overseer of Arshama's estates in Elephantine, a settlement along the Upper Nile, and concern a wide variety of affairs of concern to Arshama and the running of his properties, from the distribution of food rations among his slaves to the terms of sale of properties to the authorization of travel for his underlings.[17] The letters from Arshama to his steward "would have been spoken in Persian, written down in Aramaic, read by an Egyptian and finally annotated in Egyptian," a history of transmission and translation testifying to the multilingual character of the empire as a whole.[18] Originally the letters would have been folded accordion-style, bound with string and a lump of clay and marked with Arshama's seal.

Today the surviving documents consist of hundreds of fragments of skin, variously identified as leather and parchment by modern scholars, though the precise technique of their original production cannot be determined (see figs. 7.4, 7.5, and 7.6). Some are quite impressive in size, several as large as a medieval quarto bifolium. The original letters seem to have been cut from larger skins in neat rectangles of varying dimensions, with only occasional signs of haunch or shoulder curves at the edges and varying degrees of thickness, though it is impossible to know whether such variations result from original production or the long process of aging. Many of

Figure 7.2. Fragment of a tomb relief on limestone with scene of parchment making, from the necropolis of Saqqara. Late Eighteenth or Early Nineteenth Dynasty, ca. 1300 BCE. Berlin, Ägyptisches Museum und Papyrussamlung, Staatliche Museen, Berlin, Germany. Inv. ÄM 19782/2.

Figure 7.3. A modern rendering of the relief in figure 7.2.

the membranes are lined with what look almost like tree rings, scored and cracked where they were folded; some are mottled and faded with age; still others are quite light in appearance, their follicle marks remarkably preserved. Others survive as fragments the size of fingernail clippings, and give the appearance of a random scatter of dirt in the glass frames that house them. Along with the letters themselves, the Bodleian preserves fragments of the two leather sacks in which they were found. The sacks have the look and feel of old shoes, the larger of them (fig. 7.7) the size of

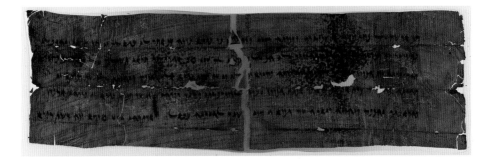

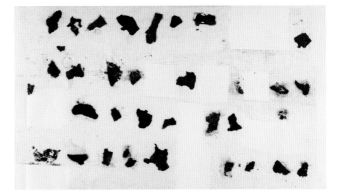

Figures 7.4, 7.5, and 7.6. Membrane letters and fragments from Arshama, the Persian prince of Egypt, to Nakhthor, his steward. Egypt, 500–400 BCE. Oxford, Bodleian Library Ms. Pell. Aram. IX (interior view), XV (interior view), and F1/F2 (fragments).

my hand and the color of an unwashed potato skin, the other in three fragments and much darker in appearance.

These Achaemenid letters represent perhaps the largest trove of membrane documents from the ancient world, and thus provide a unique material perspective on the prehistory of parchment in the centuries before the Common Era—though the scribes who produced them took their creaturely nature largely for granted, at least as far as the texts themselves indicate. Other written records from the Achaemenid era display a surprising degree of self-awareness about animal skin as a medium of administrative writing and record-keeping. This preoccupation comes out with particular clarity in a large set of inscriptions found in the Persepolis Fortification Archive, an array of thousands of clay tablets and fragments speaking to the inner workings and cultural life of the empire. Only in the last several years have certain of these records yielded information about the era's written culture and its dependence on membrane.[19] Though surviving on clay, any number of these tablets refer to their own inscriptions as having been *n'siḥ 'l mšk*: an Aramaic phrase that translates as "copied (literally 'removed') onto a membrane document." Many others (nearly one hundred) enlist the Aramaic epigraph *n'siḥ* to refer to the process of inscribing certain accounts on skin, signaling a widespread understanding of leather or parchment as indispensable to the exercise of administrative authority during the Middle Achaemenid era.

Figure 7.7. Leather letter sack from Elephantine. 500-400 BCE. Oxford, Bodleian Library Sacc. Pell. Aram. Olim cont., pars A, recto.

The Persepolis inscriptions reveal that for a significant period in the imperial capital, Achaemenid administrative culture required a creaturely counterpart to the clay-and-stone archive whose fragments make up the Fortification record itself. Indeed the specific association of writing with animal skin could even define the professional personae of the scribes employing it. Certain Elamite inscriptions from Persepolis refer to the office of "scribes on skin" [tippip kušMEŠ-ukku], distinguishing them quite carefully from "a scribe on clay" [tipira halat-ukku]. Thus one tablet refers to "Itibena? and his 1 companion, a total of 2 in all, scribes [writing] on skin, accountants, sent from Bakabana (at) Babylon to Ziššawiš at Persepolis"—marking these "skin scribes" as a separate class of imperial clerks.[20] As a professional moniker, "leather scribe" or "scribe on skin" implies that the official identities of these copyists derived from the animal membrane on which they wrote. The archive of the animal, mutatis mutandis, is an archive of human labor, though in this case defined and circumscribed by the animal medium governing its transmission from skin to clay and back again.

The Arshama letters and Persepolis inscriptions are compelling windows onto the prehistory of parchment culture, revealing a scattered but strong tradition of membrane as medium in the ancient Mediterranean world. In this respect, they provide a fascinating archaeological counterpoint to the first explicit discussions in Indo-European literature of writing on skins, which occur in the *Histories* of Herodotus of Halicarnassus (fifth century BCE), whose work gives us some of the richest perspectives on the culture and habits of ancient Northern Africa and the Eastern Mediterranean. Herodotus would likely not have transcribed his writings on skins but on papyrus [βύβλος/*biblos*], the predominant medium of elite writing in the ancient world derived from a freshwater reed common in the wetlands of Northern Africa and in the Nile Delta. The historian may have transcribed his notes and narratives onto papyrus rolls suitable for travel, after which they were compiled into longer scrolls circulated among the communities of readers who would become his first audience.

The oldest surviving fragments of the *Histories* survive on Roman-era papyri transcribed centuries after the author's death, while the earliest complete texts are contained in a number of medieval codices from the tenth to the fourteenth centuries.[21] All of these later manuscripts likely derive from one or two exemplars copied from scrolls to parchment codices in the early Middle Ages. This translation of medium at a certain point in the text's transmission history seems oddly suitable, for we owe to the *Histories*, and perhaps to the ubiquity of papyrus in Herodotus's day, the earliest historical account of the practice of writing on animal skin, a habit that the historian notes in part due to its exceptionalism. Herodotus links this creaturely mode of inscription to the very invention of alphabetic writing, siting its emergence within a series of cross-cultural encounters of languages, scripts, and mediums that suggest once again the defining role of parchment at the origins of written tradition and cultural identity.

The fifth book of the *Histories* comprises a linked series of accounts of political and military conflicts stretching over the first decades of the fifth century: the invasion and conquest of Thrace by Persia, the Ionian Revolt, and conflicts between Athens and its various enemies, among others. Interspersed among these accounts come a number of observations on the technological advances and cultural idiosyncrasies characterizing the societies whose history Herodotus reconstructs. Such stories reflect a broader preoccupation throughout Book 5 with the materiality of the written word, tied closely to Herodotus's understanding of the potential of skin as a medium of signification. Near the middle of Book 5, for example, we encounter the story of Sisamnes, a royal judge who had once allowed himself to be bribed into handing down an unjust sentence. The punishment inflicted in turn on Sisamnes by Cambyses, a king, involved the postmortem removal of his skin and its subsequent deployment as a kind of moral mnemonic for Sisamnes's son: "Therefore Cambyses slew and flayed Sisamnes, and cutting his skin into strips, stretched them across the seat of the throne whereon he had been wont to sit when he heard causes. Having so done Cambyses appointed the son of Sisamnes to be judge in his father's room, and bade him never forget in what way his seat was cushioned."[22] The gruesome scene recapitulates a more graphic account of flaying in Book 4 that depicts the Scythians' practice of flaying their conquered enemies and using their skins as personal garments or coverings for their horses. The account in Book 5, by contrast, enlists the preservation of Sisamnes's skin into an ostentatious display of royal power. Taking on his father's juridical role, the son of Sisamnes must perform his own authority while seated on his father's rendered lap, a tangible and infantilizing reminder of the paternal body he has violently displaced.

If the spectacle of dermal furniture speaks to Herodotus's "horrified fascination" with the act of flaying, as Leslie Kurke has argued, the fate of Sisamnes anticipates an equally provocative episode later in Book 5 that literalizes the utility of human skin specifically as a written surface.[23] Soon after the story of Sisamnes comes the account of "the man with the marked head": a slave serving in the household of Histaeus, the tyrant of Miletus and one of the instigators of the great Ionian Revolt against Darius I. While in Susa with Darius (who, according to Herodotus, suspects nothing), Histaeus comes up with an ingenious means of conveying secret military orders to Aristagoras, his subordinate back in Miletus:

> For Histiaeus, when he was anxious to give Aristagoras orders to revolt, could find but one safe way, as the roads were guarded, of making his wishes known; which was by taking the trustiest of his slaves, shaving all the hair from off his head, and then pricking letters upon the skin, and waiting till the hair grew again. Thus accordingly he did; and as soon as ever the hair was grown, he despatched the man to Miletus, giving him no other message than this: "When thou art come to Miletus, bid Aristagoras shave thy head, and look thereon." Now the marks on the head, as I have already mentioned, were a command to revolt. All this Histiaeus did because it irked him greatly to be kept at Susa, and because he had strong hopes that, if troubles broke out, he would be sent down to the coast to quell them, whereas, if Miletus made no movement, he did not see a chance of his ever again returning thither. (5.35)

Herodotus does not tell us whether the slave was aware of what was pricked upon his skin, nor whether the practice was repeated for subsequent military correspondence. Indeed one of the points of the story is to emphasize the pure utility of the slave's skin, a surface of obscuring hair and written flesh. Unlike parchment, dehaired before its inscription to leave a cleared width for words, the skin rather than the words of the slave serve as a provocation to revolt—and the slave must remain alive and speak for the trick to work.

This secretive inscription on the slave's head points to the broader concern throughout Book 5 with the utility of skin as an object of power and dominion—and not exclusively human. These accounts of signifying skin led a rich afterlife, retold in various forms from the Roman Empire through the early modern period. The story of Histaeus and the written slave reappears in the *Attic Nights* of Aulus Gellius, a Roman writer of the Silver Age who includes it as one of several illustrations of "secret writing from times past." Gellius repeats the account largely as he found it in Herodotus, though with one important difference. Histaeus, according to Aulus Gellius, "shaved all the hair from the head of a slave of his who had long suffered from weak eyes, as if for the purpose of treating them. Then he tattooed the forms of the letters on his smooth head" [*caputque eius leve in litterarum formas conpungit*].[24] Here the ignorance of the slave is assumed, entailing an act of deception on the part of the master, and unlike Herodotus's *Histories*, the account says nothing about the slave's trustworthiness.[25]

The final account of written skin recorded in Book 5 occurs as part of the well-known legend of the invention of the written alphabet by Cadmus, the mythical Phoenician king and founder of Thebes who, by Herodotus's rough dating, lived at the turn of the second millennium. In the *Histories* the alphabet legend begins as a story of migration and cultural transmission:

> The Phoenicians who came to Greece with Cadmus, among whom were the Gephyraei, ended up living in this land and introducing the Greeks to a number of accomplishments, most notably the alphabet, which, as far as I can tell, the Greeks did not have before then. At first the letters they used were the same as those of all Phoenicians everywhere, but as time went by, along with the sound, they changed the way they wrote the letters as well. At this time most of their Greek neighbors were Ionians. So it was the Ionians who learnt the alphabet from the Phoenicians; they changed the shapes of a few of the letters, but they still called the alphabet they used the Phoenician alphabet, which was only right, since it was the Phoenicians who had introduced it into Greece. (5.58)

Subsequent retellings of the story usually end there, with this epochal account of the introduction of a written alphabet by the Phoenicians to the Greeks through the Ionians. Cadmus and the Phoenicians are credited with introducing the technology that would eventually be adapted into Herodotus's own Greek alphabet. Without King Cadmus and the Phoenicians, the legend implies, the Greeks would never have discovered how to write, and the Western tradition could not have begun. As Ralph Waldo Emerson would extol in his essay "Civilization," "there is a Cadmus, a Pytheas, a Manco Capac at the beginning of each improvement, some superior foreigner importing new and wonderful arts, and teaching them."[26] Marshall McLuhan is more cynical, imputing the legend's importance to its functionalism: "When the alphabet was a revolutionary novelty, the Cadmus myth was formulated to explain the social operations of the alphabet."[27]

Yet there is a further dimension to the founding story of Cadmus and the written culture of the Greeks. Immediately following the account of the alphabet and its introduction, Herodotus pauses to reflect on the Ioanian written medium and its origins:

> The Ionian term for papyrus rolls—namely 'skins' [διφθέρας]—also goes back a long way, to when they used both goatskins and sheepskins [διφθέρῃσι αἰγέῃσί τε καὶ οἰέῃσι] to write on, because they did not have any papyrus. In fact even today many barbarians still write on such skins [διφθέρας].
> (5.58)

The observation on the Ionian medium suggests in a different way the deep and lasting continuity of membrane usage for cultural transmission in the ancient world. The legendary Cadmus lived some sixteen centuries before Herodotus, who emphasizes the past and present of the written animal even while voicing some ambivalence regarding its enduring affiliation with the "non-Greeks" (or barbarians) who continue to adopt it. In this sense, and despite the dominance of papyrus, the *diphtherai* employed for writing by the ancient Ionians are of a piece with the wider deployment of skin as a signifying medium involved in a long cycle of retribution, slavery, and dominion. Even papyrus volumes—*diphtherai*—have their origin in the animal skins—*diphtherai*—that give them their name. A prominent judge executed and flayed for his disobedience, a slave inscribed with a message of rebellion, generations of beasts rendered into text: by the logic of the historian's account, membrane, living and dead, human and not, serves as a potent bearer of culture, both an instrument of transmission and a written medium of subjugation.

Like their Hellenistic and earlier predecessors, most writers of the Roman epoch preferred papyrus as their primary medium of written transmission, presentation, and preservation, and there is little doubt that the reed-based commodity was manufactured and employed in much greater quantities than its animal-derived counterpart. Yet for several centuries before the wide-scale adoption of parchment in early Christian book culture, the membrane medium was regularly employed throughout the Roman world, both in the capital itself and in imperial outposts, as a rough-and-ready, durable material suitable for traveling notebooks, rough copies of poems, account keeping, and so on. Parchment makes a brief appearance in the Gospels, in the Second Epistle to Timothy (2 Tim. 4:13), where Paul requests that Timothy bring along his books, especially his membranes, when he comes to join him: "When you come, bring the cloak that I left with Carpus at Troas," Paul enjoins his correspondent, "and my scrolls, especially the parchments" (μεμβράνας in the Greek, *membranas* in the Latin Vulgate).[28]

Even as they accorded parchment a workaday status as a durable medium for the transmission and transportation of writings, though, Greek and Latin writers of the era will often register the many ways the animal medium bedazzled its beholders and users, often greeting it with curiosity, delight, and a degree of awed respect. The mystical power of parchment forms the basis of a legend related by Titus Flavius Josephus, the Romano-Jewish scholar and general of the first century CE and author of the *Antiquitates Judaicae* (*Antiquities of the Jews*). Looking back on the ancient Jews and the time of Moses, Josephus describes a ritual for testing the faith of a wife suspected of adultery that involves the inscription and subsequent distillation of parchment into a magical elixir that a suspected wife must drink to demonstrate her marital faithfulness.[29] The chronicler Suetonius records that Emperor Augustus "made a will a year and four months before his death . . . consisting of two skins of parchment, written partly in his own hand."[30] And in the fourteenth book of Martial's *Epigrams*, the writer celebrates a selection of the many volumes he owns on membrane as part of a catalogue of material belongings and amicable gifts:

> VII. Tablets of parchment [*pugillares membranei*]
> Although these tablets are called parchment [*membrana*], imagine them of wax; you will be able to erase and replace the writing at pleasure.

> CLXXXIV. A parchment copy of Homer [*Homerus in pugillaribus membraneis*]
> The Iliad, and the story of Ulysses, hostile to the kingdom of Priam, lie deposited in these many folds of skin [*multiplici pariter condita pelle latent*].

> CLXXXVI. Virgil on parchment [*in membranis*].
> How small a quantity of parchment holds the great Maro. His portrait ornaments the first page.

> CLXXXVIII. Cicero on parchment [*in membranis*].
> If this parchment be your companion on a long journey, you may imagine that you are travelling with Cicero.

> CXC. Livy in a single volume
> The voluminous Livy, of whom my bookcase would once scarcely have contained the whole, is now comprised in this paltry set of skins [*pellibus exiguis*].

> CXCII. Ovid's *Metamophoses* on parchment [*in membranis*]
> This mass, which, as you see, consists of a great number of leaves, contains fifteen books of the verses of Naso.[31]

Martial's parataxis of books emphasizes the skins and membranes that serve as the material medium of his treasured writings, implying a close attunement to the bookish technologies of codex and scroll as well as the practice of scribal miniaturization.[32] The list includes one of the first explicit metonymic conjunctions between written skin and individual subject: "If that parchment [*ista . . . membrana*] is to be

Figure 7.8. A portion of the Temple Scroll (11Q19, cols. 46–48), found in Qumran Cave 11. Late first century BCE–early first century CE.

your traveling companion, imagine that you're taking Cicero himself with you to share your long journeys."[33]

Such a concatenation of written flesh and human person will be a frequent topos in the succeeding centuries, as writers enlist the medium as part of often elaborate allegories to figure the inscribed bodies of the prophets, the saints, and Jesus Christ even while recognizing parchment's mundane materiality. As the next chapter will argue, it was such a doubled conception of parchment that inspired St. Augustine of Hippo in the waning years of the Roman Empire to limn a profound and detailed theology of parchment, embracing scripture, the body of Christ, and the sacrificial skins of both beasts and saints into a single vision of human-divine relation. No wonder that Pliny the Elder evokes parchment in a list of the wonders of human accomplishment, lauding its apparent capacity for a drastic miniaturization of writing: "Cicero states that a copy of Homer's *Iliad*, written on parchment [*in membrana scriptum*], was kept in a nutshell. He also mentions a man who could see a distance of 135 miles" (7.85). We have already seen the same Pliny's homage to parchment as "the material on which the immortality of human beings depends," speaking to a widely shared understanding in the ancient and medieval worlds alike of the ability of membrane to outlive the human creatures and cultures that produce it.

A proof of this comprehension of parchment's unique perdurance can be found among the Dead Sea Scrolls, the famous collection of ancient Jewish texts found in the Qumran Caves in the West Bank in the middle of the twentieth century. Most of the scrolls survive on parchment, with papyrus and (in one case) hammered copper representing only a combined 10 percent or so of the total assemblage. The largest of the membrane writings, the Temple Scroll (see fig. 7.8), consists of sixteen separate membranes rendered extraordinarily thin (less than 0.1 mm.).[34] The scroll, devoted in large part to divine instructions on the construction and operation of the Temple, contains an elaborate set of rules for the maintenance of bodily purity through sexual practices, diet, and the treatment of waste and organic materials, including the treatment and disposition of animal skins:

> Nor are you to consecrate a skin from another city for use in My city; for the skins are only as pure as the flesh from which they come. If you have sacrificed the animal in My temple, the skin is pure for use in My temple; but if you have slaughtered the animal in another city, it is pure only for use in other cities.[35]

Once flayed from animals, skins retain the moral and religious purity or stigma of their creaturely origins. Sacrifice demands locality: the skin of a beast sacrificed in a foreign city will not be suitable for use in the city of God. Though written down centuries before the medieval rabbinical period, the regulations in the Temple Scroll anticipate the more detailed and exacting rules that would govern the treatment of skins as expounded in later Jewish sources, particularly the Talmud.

Even the greatest archives are vulnerable to catastrophe—flood and fire, worms and war, erasure and deletion—and the rates of survival of medieval manuscripts (let alone their ancient predecessors) are often vanishingly small. Yet within these deep histories of archival loss, there are also many stories of fortuitous survival, often against long odds: the *Beowulf* manuscript, rescued from a library fire in 1731; the Cairo Genizah, hundreds of thousands of parchment and paper fragments discovered in a synagogue storeroom in the late nineteenth century. One small but resonant story of survival has as its durable protagonist the *Histories* of Herodotus. His great work of research, Herodotus avows in the prologue, will be "put down here so that human accomplishments will not be blotted out with the passing of time, nor great and marvelous achievements—some displayed by Greeks, some by foreigners—lack renown." One of his primary concerns, shared by innumerable writers over the ages, is the physical survival of his own work, and here Herodotus has both humans and beasts to thank for its endurance. After the Father of History first wrote down or dictated his twinned accounts of Cadmus and the coming of the alphabet, of the Ionians and their long-standing preference for animal skin, they were preserved on papyrus—yet not a single papyrus scrap of the *Histories* is extant from Herodotus's own day. The oldest copies of the complete *Histories* survive, rather, in a handful of codices produced by Greek-speaking monks writing on animal skins between the ninth and twelfth centuries.[36] In one of the great silent ironies of the parchment inheritance, we owe the endurance of the *Histories* (as so much else) to a creaturely medium Herodotus himself regarded as little more than a provincial curiosity.

CHAPTER EIGHT

ST. AUGUSTINE'S (A)THEOLOGY
OF PARCHMENT

The ark of the Old Testament was a cleaner covering for the tables of
stone than the goatskin of their manuscripts.

—AUGUSTINE, *CONTRA FAUSTUM MANICHÆUM*

From the Old Kingdom of Egypt to the height of the Roman Republic, then,
and even as papyrus remained the dominant medium of written transmission, the cultures of the ancient world employed the skins of beasts in myriad forms to record their thoughts, document their transactions, preserve their traditions, and communicate to far-flung corners of empires, even while beginning to
understand the medium's special properties in this epoch of papyrus and clay. Over
the first three centuries of the Common Era, animal begins to challenge plant as
the favored written medium in the Mediterranean basin, due in part to what historians agree was a preference among certain early Christian communities for the codex over the roll. Though papyrus codices survive, by the second century the membrane codex was emerging as an increasingly popular form of book, rising gradually
in prevalence until the middle of the fourth century, when, as Harry Gamble puts
it, the parchment codex "finally came into its own."[1]

Christian writings of the patristic period, Latin and Greek alike, abound in references to parchment, which will often be specified and named by the Fathers of the
Church in their discussions of the Mediterranean book trade and its many byways.
Thus in *De viris illustribus*, written in the early 390s, St. Jerome records an account
of the attempted preservation of the great library of Caesarea (Antioch) by Euzoius,
one of the successors of Origen and Pamphilus, former bishops of the city. Euzoius,
Jerome reports, loved the works of his masters so deeply that he "attempted with
great pain to preserve on skin [*in membranis instaurare*] the ruined library of Origen
and Pamphilus," creating many hundreds of parchment volumes by his own hand
and through instruction to others.[2] Several generations earlier, as we saw in a previ-

ous chapter, Constantine the Great had ordered the copying of fifty completed Bibles "to be written on prepared parchment in a legible manner, and in a commodious and portable form, by transcribers thoroughly practiced in their art."[3]

It would be only a matter of time before the use of animal membrane as the primary medium of Christian writing would receive theological justification, as an incarnational religion centered around the humanation of its deity begins to reckon with the book as a thing of beastly flesh, a humble concatenation of animal skins nevertheless entrusted with the Word of God. As in so many dimensions of early Christian thought, it was the North African bishop Augustine of Hippo who formulated the richest and most provocative theological reflections on the implications and significance of parchment as the incarnate medium of Scripture. The *Confessions*, his great spiritual autobiography, imagines the heavens as a great membrane book, a *firmamentum* cloaked by the same *pelles* (skins) that clothe men after the Fall. Parchment assumes a very different guise in Augustine's *Contra Faustum Manichaeum*, written in reply to a polemic against the Hebrew Bible by Faustus the Manichee, in whose ambit Augustine moved before his turn away from the sect's radical dualism. In *Contra Faustum* we find what I am tempted to call an *atheology* of parchment: a stingingly ironic and wonderfully matter-of-fact rebuke of a school of thought unwilling to think critically about the fine line separating books from meat, codex from carcass. The theological implications of parchment as flesh and parchment as scripture receive their most elaborate treatment in the *Enarrationes in psalmos*, an exegetical work written at the height of Augustine's theological powers. In these and other works we can discern one of the great intellects of the premodern Mediterranean world puzzling over a creaturely medium—its potential and its paradoxes—that would serve the written culture of Christianity for the next thousand years.

The thirteenth and final book of the *Confessions* casts a wide net, touching on the role of the Trinity in the creation, the spiritual meaning of Genesis, and the promise of eternal rest. In the fifteenth chapter, following an intensely personal meditation on the nature of God's omniscient sight and his division of light from darkness, Augustine offers a bookish meditation on the *firmamentum* created in Genesis 1:

> Or who but Thou, our God, made for us that firmament of authority over us in Your divine scripture? As it is said, 'For heaven shall be folded up like a scroll; and now it is extended over us like a skin.' For Your divine Scripture is of more sublime author-

ity, since those mortals through whom You dispensed it unto us underwent mortality. And You know, O Lord, You know, how You with skins clothed men when by sin they became mortal. Whence as a skin have You stretched out the firmament of Your Book [*sicut pellem extendisti firmamentum libri tui*]; that is to say, Your harmonious words, which by the ministry of mortals You have spread over us. For by their very death is that solid firmament of authority in Your discourses set forth by them more sublimely extended above all things that are under it, which, while they were living here, was not so eminently extended. You had not as yet spread abroad the heaven like a skin [*nondum sicut pellem caelum extenderas*]; You had not as yet spread everywhere the report of their deaths.[4]

This much-studied passage imagines the *firmamentum auctoritatis* as *scriptura*, and vice versa: the firmament spread over the earth is the book, while Scripture itself is coterminous with the heavens above. The celestial firmament covers humanity "like a skin" [*sicut pellem*], signifying the flesh of the "mortal men" or evangelist-martyrs whose death would spread its message throughout the postlapsarian world.

Though most immediately inspired by the account of creation in Genesis 1, this sequence develops out of Augustine's interpretation of several later verses from the Hebrew Bible and the New Testament that were commonly read in the early Christian era as references to membrane books. The first occurs in Isaiah 34, in the midst of an apocalyptic prophecy of vengeance to be delivered upon the nations of the earth:

> For the indignation of the Lord is upon all nations, and his fury upon all their armies; he hath killed them, and delivered them to slaughter. Their slain shall be cast forth, and out of their carcasses shall rise a stink: the mountains shall be melted with their blood. And all the host of the heavens shall pine away, and the heavens shall be folded together as a scroll [*et conplicabuntur sicut liber caeli*]: and all their host shall fall down as the leaf falleth from the vine, and from the fig tree.
>
> (ISAIAH 34:2–4)

The biblical chapter includes the promise of slaughter to be visited on domestic animals: "The sword of the Lord is filled with blood, it is made thick with the blood of lambs and buck goats, with the blood of rams full of marrow" (32:6). Despite the chapter's creaturely preoccupation, the *liber* invoked in the simile here is almost certainly meant to refer to a papyrus scroll, as in a New Testament echo of this verse in Revelation 6:14: "The sky disappeared like a scroll rolling up [*sicut liber involutus*], and all the mountains and islands moved from their place." There are also a number of verses in the book of Psalms that cast God's heavenly construction in similar terms: "Bless the Lord, O my soul: O Lord my God, thou art exceedingly great. Thou hast put on praise and beauty: And art clothed with light as with a garment. Who stretchest out the heaven like a skin [*extendens caelos ut pellem*]" (Psalm 104:1–2).

None of these verses on the celestial *liber* and the heavenly *pelles* can be taken as referring to a parchment codex, and it is doubtful that the original term translated in the Latin Bible as "ut pellem"—*like a skin*, translating a Hebrew word for curtain or tent—had anything to do with written media in its original Psalmic context. For early Christian commentators, however, the treatment of these particular verses shows us, in Ernst Robert Curtius's words, "how the book-metaphors of the Bible develop and multiply" as the epoch of parchment begins in earnest among the reading communities of Late Antiquity.[5] Indeed the subsequent discussion in the *Confessions* only muddies the waters, juxtaposing *codex* and *liber* in its account of celestial reading:

> Other waters there be above this firmament, I believe immortal, and separated from earthly corruption. Let them praise Thy Name, let them praise Thee, the supercelestial people, Thine angels, who have no need to gaze up at this firmament, or by reading to know of Thy Word. For they always behold Thy face, and there read without any syllables in time, what willeth Thy eternal will; they read, they choose, they love. They are ever reading; and that never passes away which they read; for by choosing, and by loving, they read the very unchangeableness of Thy counsel. Their book is never closed, nor their scroll folded up [*non clauditur codex eorum nec plicatur liber eorum*].
> (13.15.18)

Angelic reading and human reading are both practices that seek the face of God in the expanse of Scripture. For humans, though, even during the reading process this face will be obscured by both the physical medium and the occluded message. The fallen, human act of reading a physical book (and deciphering these "syllables in time") by necessity obscures the sight of God with mere signs. The angels, by contrast, are "ever reading" a text that "never passes away." The passage invokes the book as simultaneously *codex* and *liber*, capturing both the constant unfolding of the celestial scroll and the binary open-or-shut action of the codex; the competing text technologies evoke the eternal openness of the angelic book in what Brian Stock argues is one of the first recognitions of parchment and pen as "media."[6] As Gillian Clark puts it of Augustine's densely metaphorical rendering, "Skin can be made into parchment: is heaven a parchment scroll to be rolled up, or a parchment codex to be closed? Either way it is skin that makes a text."[7]

Despite the insistent attention in the *Confessions* to the physical matter of the book (as skin, as scroll, as codex), the animal remains largely invisible here. Augustine seems uninterested in the creaturely source of these *pelles* that cover the sky, and only the specifically human "mortals" are imagined as clothed with skin at the creation—presumably their own, though the sequence makes no distinction between skin-as-organ and skin-as-clothing. Of course, the theological tradition of the heavenly book can often entail the enlistment of human skin for its more earthly incarnations: the wounded skin of Christ on the cross, the flayed skin of the martyr. As the passages above suggest, however, in the *Confessions* this skin emerges only from a more sublime encounter with the "skin of the skies," the celestial book removed from the roiled world of material things below—though it was from this world that the faithful rendered the messy membranes constituting their books.

One of the formative moral and spiritual dilemmas in St. Augustine's life was his difficult encounter with the dualist theology of the Manichaeans, a struggle he recounts in the *Confessions* as a deeply personal process of reckoning with the origin and place of sin within his soul. Peter Brown, Augustine's great biographer, points out that Manichaeism had been Augustine's primary source of faith as a young man, and "provided him with an extreme and distinctive mould for his feelings."[8] In his earlier years Augustine had himself been under the sway of the charismatic Mani, founder of a sect of radical dualists whose influence would be felt across the Mediterranean and into the Near and Far East. The allure of dualism was far reaching—geographically, intellectually, and morally—as it provided an idiom of escape and release from the corrupted things of this world. For the Manichees, the radical evil of our half-darkened existence is embodied in the fleshly and material things of the earth and the depravity to which they lead: sexual sins such as adultery and fornication, the eating of animal flesh, even the killing of plants. Indeed the Christian dualism of Late Antiquity furnishes one of the early chapters in the history of vegetarianism, and there are contemporary schools of deep ecology that have found inspiration in the era's anticarnivorous writings.[9]

In the late 390s, Augustine began writing back against the now despised doctrine that had shaped his early years. One of his most compelling responses to the dualist cosmology of the Manichees appears in the form of a sparky, quite vitriolic letter addressed to Faustus of Mileve, a bishop and leader of an influential sect of

Manichaeans based in the northern African city of Carthage. *Contra Faustum Manichaeum*, written right at the turn of the century, consists in part of a vigorous defense of the allegorical reading of the Old Testament against its literalist rejection by the Manichaeans, who found much to condemn in, say, the scandalous behavior of figures such as Abraham, Solomon, and others. Augustine concedes the moral failings of the patriarchs while recuperating their spiritual role as types of Christ, a gesture typical of the period's effort to reconcile the two biblical testaments.[10]

Yet Augustine's intellectual assault on Faustus relies on a relentlessly literalist pursuit of the Manichee's theological purism. The greatest weakness of Faustus's position, he says, lies in its dualist insistence on the imprisonment or confinement of God in the material things of the world—a state of vulnerability embodied in the figure of Jesus, "who, suspended from every tree, is the life and salvation of human beings."[11] Nothing we can see, touch, taste, or smell is free of the taint of the diabolical darkness that subsumes the earthly realm after the division of evil from good, and God is trapped in the worldly objects around us. "For they say that flesh is unclean," Augustine writes of the Manichaeans, "and it follows that God, in the part which is detained by the flesh, is made unclean."[12] Nor is flesh alone vulnerable: even plants and vegetables bear the stain of primal evil, leading to a condition in which the Manichaean Elect cannot be bothered to harvest food for themselves for fear of contact with God's "members in fruits and vegetables," which are nevertheless "purified by your mastication and digestion": "you, in your rest, wait till one of your followers takes his knife or hook into the garden, to get food for you by murdering the vegetables, and brings back, strange to say, living corpses" (6.3). "One of your silly notions," he writes later in the same chapter, "is that the tree weeps when the fruit is pulled."

These are not mischaracterizations of his opponent's positions. The Cologne Mani Codex, a miniature parchment book from the late fourth or early fifth century, transmits a treatise on Manichaean theology (titled "Concerning the Origin of His Body") that corresponds in remarkable detail to Augustine's summations regarding dualism and the natural world. At one point in the fragmentary text a date-palm tree speaks its pain: "If you keep the pain away from us trees, you will not perish with the murderer." The human interlocutors recount the "agony of the date-palm tree," while vegetables taken from the garden inspire laments from their butchers: "Alas! Alas! The blood was streaming down from the place cut by the pruning hook . . . they were crying out in a human voice on account of their blows."[13]

The Manichaeans are particularly vulnerable, Augustine recognizes, in regard to their books—both the doctrine and tradition they convey as well as the material medium of their transmission. In the Cologne Mani Codex, it is papyrus that

Figure 8.1. An opening from the Cologne Mani Codex, University of Cologne, Codex Manichaicus Coloniensis. Egypt, fifth century. P. Köln inv. 4780, seite 57 (64).

serves as the imagined writing support of Mani's revelation: "Wherefore take and write these things which I reveal to you on most pure papyrus, incorruptible and insusceptible to worms"—though the miniature codex itself is written on a fine and creamy parchment (see fig. 8.1).[14] Augustine addresses the materiality of Manichaean textual culture in book 13, perhaps the most blistering portion of *Contra Faustum*, where Augustine is at his most contemptuous. Book 13 as a whole is devoted to the Manichaean rejection of the Hebrew prophets of the Old Testament, whom Faustus holds up as the equivalents of mere pagan prophets such as the Sibyl, Hermes, or Orpheus. Augustine replies with a detailed defense of the value and utility of prophecy, coming around near the end of the book to the broader implications of the Manichaean rejection. If Faustus dispenses with the Old Testament as well as the divinity of the incarnate Christ, why not also the Gospels—or even the books of the sect's founder himself?

> If believers are to throw away all the books which have led them to believe, I see no reason why they should continue reading the Gospel itself. The Gospel, too, must be worthless to this inquirer, who, according to Faustus' pitiful supposition, rejects with ridicule the authority of Christ . . . By this principle, you should throw away the books of Mani, on the authority of which you already believe that light—that is, God—fought with darkness, and that, in order to bind darkness, the light was first swallowed up and bound, and polluted and mangled by darkness, to be restored, and liberated, and purified, and healed by your eating, for which you are rewarded by not being condemned to the mass of darkness for ever, along with that part of the light which cannot be extricated.
>
> (C. FAUSTUM 13.18)

By the logic of the Manichaeans, a book, no matter how sacred in its doctrinal or spiritual content, is inevitably and inherently tainted—"polluted and mangled by darkness," in Augustine's words—by its earthly incarnation, even if this comes in the form of the Gospels or indeed the books of Mani himself. Augustine's response is to argue for the fully reciprocal values of the New and Old Testaments: "And if the Gospel should be read by the believer, that he may not forget what he has believed, so should the prophets, that he may not forget why he believed. For if he forgets this his faith cannot be firm." Both laws have a particular spiritual function in the soul of the believer, and neither should be discarded on a dualist whim.

Augustine does not stop here, intent as he is on pursuing the Manichaean logic of the book to its most extreme ends. What follows at the end of book 13 is one of the most forthright statements in early Christian writings regarding the animality of the parchment book, though it appears in the guise of a savage dig at the sect's hypocrisy. As Augustine knew well, the Manichaeans invested a great deal of wealth and prestige in the manufacture and decoration of their books, an observation supported by modern study of the many surviving fragments of codices and scrolls produced as the order spread east along the Silk Road from the ninth to eleventh centuries, many of them from Toyok and the Turfan Oasis. The Manichaeans employed "the finest calligraphy with a copious use of paint and gold leaf," commissioning rich programmes of illustration and polychrome embellishment of the parchment, leather, silk, and paper on which they inscribed and preserved their writings.[15]

This bookish luxury was an aspect of the sect's written culture clearly vulnerable to theological critique. For Augustine, the Manichaean rejection of the words of the Old Testament should properly entail a rejection of the creaturely medium of its transmission:

> Why do you seek for the testimony of books, and add to the embarrassment of your God by the consumption of strength in the needless task of writing manuscripts? Burn all your parchments [*membranas*], with their finely-ornamented leather binding [*decoris pellibus*]; so you will be rid of a useless burden, and your God who suffers confinement in the volume [*codice*] will be set free. What a mercy it would be to the members of your God, if you could boil your books and eat them! There might be a difficulty, however, given the prohibition of flesh [*carnis*]. Then the writing must share in the impurity of the sheepskin [*quae corio inhaesit agnino*].
> (C. FAUSTUM 13.18)

In this delicious take-down, Augustine quite logically equates the production, ownership, and use of membrane books with the practice of eating animal flesh. Particularly striking here is his appositive diction: that is, the array of word choices used to connote Manichaean books. The passage delights in the sheer number of fleshly terms thrown at Faustus to signal the sect's reliance for the transmission of its sacred texts on the same animal flesh it spurns as the embodiment of evil. Books are *membranas* (membranes), *pellibus* (skins), *carnis* (flesh), and *corio agnino* (sheepskin). For any self-respecting Manichee, the codex is a house of beastly horrors. And yet the sect refuses to acknowledge its bookish hypocrisy:

> Indeed, you are to blame for this, for, like what you say was done in the first war between light and darkness, you brought what was clean in the pen in contact with the foulness of the parchment [*immunditiae membranarum*]. Or perhaps, for the sake of the colors, we may put it the other way; and so the darkness would be yours, in the ink which you brought against the light of the white pages [*ad lucem candidarum paginarum*]. If these remarks irritate you, you should rather be angry with yourselves for believing doctrines of which these are the necessary consequences.
> (C. FAUSTUM 13.18)

Membranarum, paginarum; skin, book: for Augustine, animal flesh is animal flesh, and the Manichaeans have no good reason to reject meat while embracing parchment. Even in its sarcasm, the argument exposes the self-evident absurdity of the Manichaean position as Augustine presents it, an absurdity highlighted yet again in book 15, when the treatise comes around to Faustus's utter rejection of the Old Testament in favor of the New. Here the issue involves Faustus's failure to understand the allegorical relationship between two passages of Scripture, both cited by Augustine in the course of his argument: "And I will give them one heart, and will put a new spirit in their bowels: and I will take away the stony heart out of their flesh, and will give them a heart of flesh" (Ezekiel 11:19); and "You are our epistle, written in our hearts, which is known and read by all men: Being manifested, that you are the epistle of Christ, ministered by us, and written not with ink, but with the Spirit of the living God; not in tables of stone, but in the fleshly tables of the heart" (2 Corinthians 3:2–3). These passages together render an allegorical understanding of the heart, flesh, and law that the Manichees are too blinded by their dualism to discern:

> For by the heart of flesh and the fleshy tables is not meant a carnal understanding: but as flesh feels, whereas a stone cannot, the insensibility of stone signifies an unintelligent heart, and the sensibility of flesh signifies an intelligent heart. Instead, then, of scoffing at thee, they deserve to be ridiculed who say that earth, and wood, and stones have sense, and that their life is more intelligent than animal life. So, not to

speak of the truth, even their own fiction obliges them to confess that the law written on tables of stone was purer than their dead parchments [*pellibus morticinis*]. Or perhaps they prefer sheepskin to stone, because their legends make stones the bones of princes. In any case, the ark of the Old Testament was a cleaner covering for the tables of stone than the goatskin of their manuscripts [*caprina pellis codicem istorum*]. (C. FAUSTUM 15.4)

What is common to all of these passages against dualist rejections of various kinds is Augustine's steadfast devotion to the vital status of "animal life," as he calls it, whether sheep or goat: that organic continuum that links books to beasts to humans and ultimately to God. Even while holding up the animal materiality of the membrane codex as the hallmark and touchstone of the movement's hypocrisy, the bishop grounds his righteous vision in the very "goatskin of their manuscripts."

In *Contra Faustum*, then, books are beasts, and parchment is as much a product of the butchered animal as is the meat spurned by the Manichaean Elect. This is an element of Mediterranean book culture that Augustine had studiously avoided in the *Confessions*, which, as we have seen, imagines the heavens-as-*pelles* in purely symbolic terms while holding up the material book as an earthly obstacle to be overcome. Together the two works confront us with the simultaneously spiritual and fleshly character of the membrane book. When Augustine returned some years later to the provocative notion of a stretched skin covering the sky, he would do so with a more particularized attention to the animality of the book—a sensibility perhaps instilled by his indelicate assertion of the commonality of books and meat in *Contra Faustum*.

The *Enarrationes in psalmos*, written over the first ten years of the fifth century, consists of a long series of sermons preached on specific occasions before their compilation into a multi-volume set of exegetical reflections on each of the Psalms. The sermon on Psalm 93, a meditation on divine justice, takes up the question of God's tolerance for evildoers, and his seeming indifference to human affairs. How are the just to tolerate the deplorable actions of the unjust, particularly when the latter are rewarded with worldly fame, riches, and seemingly boundless fortune, often at the expense of the righteous? Augustine enjoins his auditors to put aside such transitory concerns, and to recognize that they represent a mere temporal scratch on the smooth surface of eternity. When pressed with such doubts, we should emulate the "luminaries," whose "citizenship is in heaven," by keeping our own eyes and souls fixed on the firmament, "the unrolled book of the sky":

> The sky, or more properly the firmament, is to be understood figuratively as the book of the law. Somewhere it is said, *He stretched out the sky like a skin [sicut pellem].* It is stretched out as a book is unrolled [*tamquam liber est extentus*], so that it can be read. But when the proper time has passed, it is read no longer. The law is read now because we have not yet reached that Wisdom who fills the hearts and minds of those who contemplate her; when we come into that presence there will be no need for anything to be read to us. What is read to us now consists of syllables that become audible and then die away, but the light of truth does not fade . . . Reading is necessary at present, as long as we *know only in part, and utter partial prophecies,* as the apostle says, *but when perfection comes, what is partial will be superseded.* [In that city, Jerusalem, no book will be necessary, nor shall we read,] where the angels live, the city from which we are absent like travelers abroad, groaning in our exile.[16]

The passage exemplifies the Christian platonism informing all of Augustine's mature works of theology, drawing a mystical relationship between the celestial book, that figurative scroll that God stretches across the sky, and the physical books of our earth-bound existence, the material scrolls and codices from which we read "syllables that become audible and then die away"—including, of course, the book from which we are reading Augustine's sermon on Psalm 93. In an intriguing expansion on this notion (contained in a variant in the manuscript tradition, bracketed in the passage above), the sermon explains the implications of the bookish transformation to come. In the heavenly Jerusalem, "no book will be necessary, nor shall we read": that is, the incarnate books that have guided our spiritual lives on earth will disappear, obviated and obliterated by the eternal light of truth, in which there will be "no need for anything to be read to us."

If Psalm 93 focuses the auditor's attention on the "skin of the sky" as a practice of tolerance and patience in the face of worldly adversity, Augustine takes Psalm 103 as an occasion to marvel at God's practical craftsmanship in assembling this firmament as an ornate covering for the earth: "We behold a vast fabric consisting of sky and earth and all things within them, and from the greatness and beauty of all that is crafted we have some inkling of the greatness and beauty of the craftsman [*fabricatoris*] himself" (103.1.1). This attention to the *craft* of creation, the skilled work of an artisan or *fabricator*, allows for a more deliberate interpretive pace, as Augustine takes delight in unpacking first the literal sense of the psalm verse *He stretched out the sky like a skin*: "The comparison, *like a skin*, is added to illustrate the ease with which it was done, if you take it at face value. You have looked at this vast construction, and you reflect on how hard it is for a human being to put up even a small vault or arch, how much effort and trouble he has to put in, and how long the job takes" (103.1.7). Initially the emphasis is on the original sense of the phrase "like a skin," which in the Hebrew, again, referred to a tent or pavilion rather than a membrane scroll. But we should not imagine that it took the same effort for God to stretch out the sky as it takes for us to erect a vault or arch as a ceiling; indeed, "to rule out such a misunderstanding the psalmist used a symbol of effortless operation which you can grasp." The verse, Augustine insists, should on one level be read in a comparative sense: God stretched out the sky like we stretch out a skin: "With the help of this comparison you may begin to believe that God works with ease, and not suppose that he stretched out the sky in the way that you put a roof on your house. It was as easy for him to spread out this vast sky as it is for you to spread out a hide [*unam pellem*]."

The sermon turns almost teasing in tone, as Augustine proposes an experiment in magical thinking, with a crafted animal hide conjured as the object of a fruitless mental exercise: "Imagine that a hide [*pellis*] is laid down in front of you, crinkled or folded [*vel rugosa, vel plicata*]. Order it to stretch out flat. Stretch it out simply by your command. 'I can't,' you say. Even in your action of spreading out a skin [*extendenda pelle*] you are a long way from God's easy act, then, for *he spoke and all things were made* (Ps 148:5)" (103.1.7). The distance between this failure of the human mind to stretch out a mere hide and the instantaneous ease of God's creation of the universe is immeasurable, of course; yet it illustrates more than our abject separation from divinity while trapped in our fallen condition. It also hints strongly at the process of parchment manufacture, which demands the stretching or *extensio* of an animal hide as part of the physical process of book making—though for Augustine these books are embodied in the mortal skins of God's preachers, as well as the "skin tunics" of Adam and Eve after their expulsion from Paradise.

Just as Augustine oscillates between the literal and figurative senses of Scripture, the absent animal is slaughtered, skinned, and rendered, written, read, and worn, all for the purposes of a salvation promised in the words inscribed on "this skin of the divine scriptures." I quote this culminating passage at length for the range of experiences and meanings it invests in the sacrificial life of skin and the bookish results of its rendering:

[T]he psalm speaks of God stretching out the sky like a skin because it means us to understand this as a reference to holy scripture. God established the authority of scripture in his Church first of all, and from it other things flowed, as also he established the sky, stretching it out like a skin. Now this comparison, *like a skin*, was not chosen without good reason. The first thing God did in his Church was to spread the name and fame of his preachers, a fame that was like a skin because skin symbolizes mortality [*pellis mortalitatem significat*]. The symbolism is unmistakable, because after our first parents, Adam and Eve, the progenitors of the human race, had spurned God's command in paradise, and at the serpent's persuasion and proposal had transgressed the law God had given them, they became mortal and were driven out of paradise. As a sign of their mortality they put on skin tunics [*tunicis pelliceis*], for they had been provided by God with tunics made out of animal hides; and hides are not usually taken from animals until after they are dead. Thus in our psalm skin symbolizes mortality. What are we to understand, then, when the psalm speaks of God making the sky out of skin, and spreading it out like a skin, if divine scripture is represented by this comparison? It means that those who promulgated the scriptures to us were mortal men.

Those who believed were to be saved through the foolishness of preaching, and so God chose mortal creatures, human beings subject to death and destined to die. He employed a mortal tongue and uttered mortal sounds, he employed the ministry of mortal men and made use of mortal instruments, and by this means a sky was made for you, so that in this mortal artifact you might come to know the immortal Word, and by participating in this Word you too might become immortal. Moses lived and died, for God ordered him, *Go up onto the mountain, and die* (Dt 32:49). Jeremiah died, and all the multitude of prophets died, but the oracles of these dead men remain for their posterity, even for us, because those words, spoken through them, were truly the words of him who *stretched out the sky like a skin*. Think about it: the apostle who declared that to die and to be with Christ would be far the best for him has been released from this life and now lives with Christ, just as all the prophets are living with Christ now; but what did God use to make available to us these scriptures that we read? He used what was destined to die, their mouths, tongues, teeth and hands. The apostle produced what we read through the instrumentality of these bodily organs; but his soul commanded them, and God was commanding his soul. Thus was the sky spread out like a skin [*sicut pelles*]. We read now under this sky, under this skin of the divine scriptures [*sub pelle divinarum Scripturarum legimus*] spread out for us.

(*EN. IN PS.* 103.1.8)

This long passage crystallizes a sacrificial theology of parchment in the Christian tradition, one that will find its way into myriad reflections on the role and meaning of animal skin in later medieval accounts of the membrane book. In this vision, the book is a concatenation of word and flesh: a convergence of nonhuman membrane and human skin, of the rendered animal making up the hide or the book and the bodily parts of the prophets instrumentalized to produce "what we read"—the Scriptures.

Yet what grounds the passage is Augustine's wonderful sense of skincraft: the tunics made out of animal hide, flayed from the carcasses of beasts after they have died; the stretched skin of the sky that becomes a "mortal artifact" in order to teach us the immortality of the Word; the "mouths, tongues, teeth, and hands" of the prophets crafted by God into human instruments spreading the Word; and the apostle who "crafted what we read"—the physical books of the Bible written on similarly rendered skin—through the instrumentality of these same physical parts. The result is a circuit of creaturely and celestial reading in which membrane books open under the same sublime sky—"this skin of the divine scriptures spread out"—that covers the animals and humans given to their making.

For St. Augustine, then, parchment serves a variety of theological and polemical ends. A scroll that covers the sky with the divine Word. A material thing of earth every bit as chewable as a piece of meat. The skins of the prophets and the preachers as well as the holy teachings they embody with their bookish evangelizing. Augustine's writings help us discern the medium's simultaneous utility, mystery, and sanctity: the enabling paradoxes of parchment culture that later writers will puzzle in new and enigmatic ways.

→ ←

CHAPTER NINE

RIDDLED FLESH

What's slender, smooth and fine,
and speaks with power while dumb,
in utter silence kills,
and spews the blood of lambs?
—JUDAH HALEVI (HEBREW RIDDLE, 12TH C.)

My enemy, a fiendish man, ripped me from my life. Once I was dead he threw me in a tub of water. Then he took me out, stretched me in the sun, and left me there. I lost all my hair as his knife cut into me and thereby scraped me clean of my filth and infirmity. Then his fingers folded me up, and with a bird's feather he spread the dark of tree dye across my barren field. He dressed me then with boards, and wrapped me in the skin of another, and decked me out in gold and in the finery of smiths. Now, in my blushing glory and through luxurious trappings, I proclaim the glory of God, and thus only fools would complain about the use of me by men. By putting me to use they shall be made sound and victorious and wise, bold of heart and joyful of mind. They will gather through my use more and truer friends who will shower them with glory, favors, and love. Who am I, useful to men? My name is renowned, holy and good.

A baggy rendition, though I hope it captures some of the uncanny qualities of the medieval poem it paraphrases. The work in question is one of the gems of the insular literary tradition: a twenty-seven line poem written in the idiom of an *ænigmatum* or riddle, and preserved in the Exeter Book, a manuscript compiled in the tenth century and containing some of the most significant works of Old English poetry and prose.[1] Among the vernacular writings preserved in the Exeter Book is a series of ninety-odd riddles on a variety of subjects, from everyday household items such as keys and plows to weapons of war and bagpipes. The riddles present a subject or tableau, often in the language of paradox (and occasional bawdiness), while asking the reader to provide the solution.[2] (Those unfamiliar with the medieval riddling tradition might recall the exchange between Bilbo and Golum in *The Hobbit*; in a chapter titled "Riddles in the Dark," the two characters engage in a game of riddles deriving from Tolkien's own work on Old English literature as a scholar of medieval culture.[3])

The poem paraphrased above is one of several in the anthology that take up the subject of textual culture and bookmaking, exploring elements of the craft through the lens of the natural and often the animal world: a feather quill and three fingers journeying across the sky; a reed-pen that moves from the water's edge to the mead hall to speak a cryptic tongue; a moth or bookworm that eats words and swallows men's speech.[4] Riddle 24 imagines the making and sharing of a holy text, the Bible, from the singular moment of animal slaughter to the common eternity of human salvation. The poet limns each step in the process as a distinctive part of a wondrous metamorphosis that transforms beast into book. Here is the riddle in full, accompanied by Craig Williamson's vivid translation:

Mec feonda sum feore besnyþede,
woruldstrenga binom, wætte siþþan,
dyfde on wætre, dyde eft þonan,
sette on sunnan, þær ic swiþe beleas
herum þam þe ic hæfde. Heard mec siþþan
snað seaxses **ecg**, sindrum begrunden;
fingras feoldan, ond mec fugles wyn
geond speddropum spyrede geneahhe,
ofer brunne brerd, beamtelge swealg,
streames dæle, stop eft on mec,
siþade sweartlast. Mec siþþan wrah
hæleð hleobordum, hyde beþenede,
gierede mec mid golde; forþon me gliwedon
wrætlic weorc smiþa, wire bifongen.
Nu þa gereno ond se reada telg
ond þa wuldorgesteald wide mære
dryhtfolca helm, nales dol wite.
Gif min bearn wera brucan willað,
hy beoð þy gesundran ond þy sigefæstran,
heortum þy hwætran ond þy hygebliþran,
ferþe þy frodran, habbaþ freonda þy ma,
swæsra ond gesibbra, soþra ond godra,

A life-thief stole my world-strength,
Ripped off flesh and left me skin,
Dipped me in water and drew me out,
Stretched me bare in the tight sun;
The hard blade, clean steel, cut,
Scraped—fingers folded, shaped me.
Not the bird's once wind-stiff joy
Darts often to the horn's dark rim,
Sucks wood-stain, steps back again—
With a quick scratch of power, tracks
Black on my body, points trails.
Shield-boards clothe me and stretched hide,
A skin laced with gold. The bright song
Of smiths glistens on me in filigree tones.
Now decorative gold and crimson dye,
Cloisoned jewels and a coat of glory
Proclaim the world's protector far and wide—
Let no fool fault these treasured claims.
If the children of men make use of me,
They will be safer and surer of heaven,
Bolder in heart, more blessed in mind,
Wiser in soul: they will find friends,

tilra ond getreowra, þa hyra tyr ond ead	*Companions and kinsmen, more loyal and true,*
estum ycað ond hy arstafum	*Nobler and better, brought to new faith—*
lissum bilecgað ond hi lufan fæþmum	*So men shall know grace, honor, glory,*
fæste clyppað. Frige hwæt ic hatte,	*Fortune, and the kind clasp of friends.*
niþum to nytte. Nama min is mære,	*Say who I am—glorious, useful to men,*
hæleþum gifre ond halig sylf.	*Holy and helpful from beginning to end.*[5]

The riddle begins in the voice of an animal of indeterminate kind, perhaps a calf, perhaps a lamb or kid, recounting its own physical death at the hands of a fiendish enemy. This death takes place through the theft of the beast's *woruldstrenga*: a compound word (or kenning) rich with complexity. The *woruldstrenga* here may refer simply to the beast's life, but it may also imply the part of the animal that faces the *woruld*: perhaps the skin, though Williamson translates the term to connote a general attribute of strength in the world. Almost immediately, though, indeed by the end of the second line, the skin itself begins speaking, and this flayed hide remains the first-person subject for the next several lines as it endures the process of parchment making: the speaking skin is dipped in water, taken out and placed in the sun, scraped with a knife, rid of its impurities, folded by human fingers. Soon the writing itself begins, and while the riddle is still speaking at this point in the persona of the parchment folio, the process of transformation continues as the swift drops of ink trace patterns across the surface before the whole is enclosed by shield-boards, which in turn are covered by another *hyde* to complete the binding. It is only here, as the gatherings are brought together under one protective covering, that the riddle begins to speak as the whole book, the codex that promises safety, strength, and happiness to those who use and enjoy it.

This sequential voicing of the book's components is one of the more striking aspects of the riddle. Corinne Dale finds in this self-conscious bookishness "an echo of the colophon tradition," the common practice of accounting for a manuscript's origin in the labor of the scribe.[6] Most of the vernacular *ænigmata* in the collection tend to move from beginning to end in the voice of the singular object of speculation, speaking as one thing, however elusive or ambiguous. Here, however, the poet creates a layered assemblage of speakers each of whom riddles from and as a distinct component of the membrane book. *Frige hwæt ic hatte* ("Ask what I am called"), the riddler implores the reader in the antepenultimate line. This injunction to identify the riddle's solution is common across the Exeter corpus, and a staple of the medieval genre. Yet the answer here is an impossible one—or at least a multiply ambivalent and collective one. Am *ic* the beast robbed of my *woruldstrenga* in the opening line? Or am *ic* the finished parchment after I have been dipped, scraped, and dried?

Or am *ic* the gilded book itself, bound with a stretched and tooled *hyde* and promising joy and salvation to those who take me up? What is *nama min* (my name), and what shall I properly be called?

There can be no single solution to this riddle.[7] The animal whose life was taken for parchment is not identical with the flayed hide, which in turn is not identical with the finished piece of parchment, which in turn is not identical with the multiple membrane sheets folded into the many pages of a book, which in turn are not identical with *the* Book, which in turn cannot be identical with the singular animal speaking in a postmortem first person in the opening lines. The poem's breathless refusal of singularity keeps our focus on the process of transformation itself, the paired logics of sacrifice and rendition that create a Bible out of mere flesh. Yet the stark evocation of death and deprivation in the opening lines continually pulls us back to the imagined scene of animal slaughter that commences the making of the book. Through the grammatical and descriptive multiplicity of its subject, the riddle slides us along an uncanny continuum from beast to book and back again, putting the animal in view both before and after its slaughter by holding up the raw materiality of skin against the enobling sentiments of Scripture. The poem thus asks us to see our own human community of reading, if only for the moment of this riddle, from the creaturely outside.

While Riddle 26 presents a dynamic image of the whole book and the process that brings it into being, another poem in the Exeter collection may refer more specifically (if more allusively) to the craft of parchment making itself. Riddle 28 begins in a *dæl*, a field or portion of cultivated earth planted with the hardest and sharpest of humanity's possessions. What these keen things might be remains unsaid, as does the specific reason they are cut, cleaned, bleached, and taken away into human culture through our doors. Once they arrive, however, adorned and arranged, they give us joy while they linger for a very long time, speaking and perhaps boasting to us:

> Part of the earth grows lovely and grim
> With the hardest and fiercest of bitter-sharp
> Treasures—felled, cut, carved,
> Bleached, scrubbed, softened, shaped,
> Twisted, rubbed, dried, adorned,
> Bound, and borne off to the doorways of men—
> This creature brings in hall-joy, sweet
> Music clings to its curves, live song
> Lingers in a body where before bloom-wood

Said nothing. After death it sings
A clarion joy. Wise listeners
Will know what this creature is called.[8]

The more obvious solution to the riddle is ale or beer, the products of cultivation and processing that come from the field and enter doors, loosen tongues, lengthen mirth. Other proposed solutions include metal weapons (a knife or sword) and musical instruments. Yet the final line beguiles us with the folly of easy answers. What other product is taken from the earth, cut and cleaned, turned, dried, bleached, bound, then adorned and beautifully arrayed before entering the spaces of human culture? What other commodity rendered from the field sings and talks—but only after death? If parchment is one of the riddle's potential solutions (as Waltraud Ziegler first suggested), certain elements of the poem come into focus as the grinding work of the grisly craft, realized in the trochaic pulsations of the fourth and fifth lines—"*corfen sworfen cyrred þyrred / bunden wunden blæced wæced*"—that evoke the repetitive actions upon animal bodies the rendering process entails.[9] For "living creatures" these speaking membranes give joy; the creatures rendered for their sake talk big only "*æfter deaþe.*"

The ingenious parchment paradoxes that inspire these insular vernacular poems have close analogues in the Anglo-Latin tradition of literary riddling, practiced widely among educated clerics in Britain prior to the tenth century. Like the Exeter riddles, the Latin *ænigmata* on the theme of animal skin and writing exploit the sophistication of parchment as an extended conceit, though with a more economical balance of themes and somewhat less florid figurations.[10] One of the earliest of these parchment riddles comes from Tatwine (d. 734), a Benedictine monk and Archbishop of Canterbury in the early eighth century. Tatwine was the author of an influential book of grammar modeled in part on the work of Priscian, whose love for philosophical obscurities and grammatical intricacies also inspired his collection of forty riddles written as Latin verses on a variety of themes. The fifth riddle in Tatwine's collection, "De membrano," opens with a violent attack on the speaking subject:

Efferus exuuiis populator me spoliauit,
vitalis pariter flatus spiramina dempsit;
in planum me iterum campum sed verterat auctor.
    Frugiferos cultor sulcos mox irrigat undis;
omnigenam nardi messem mea prata rependunt,
qua sanis victum et lesis prestabo medelam.[11]

(A savage thief robbed me of my raiment,
stripped my pores of their life's breath.
but then an author transformed me again, into a level field.
A farmer soon waters the fruitful furrows in waves;
my meadows furnish a harvest of nard, of every variety,
whereby I shall give sustenance to the healthy and cure to the ill.)

This riddle, at least in its opening lines, is perhaps the closest analogue to Exeter 24, beginning with the action of the "savage thief" ("Efferus . . . populator") who despoiled the speaker—in this case of his raiment or *exuuiis*: a word that can mean covering, clothing, or surface, and here connotes the skin. Unlike the Old English version, this Latin riddle begins, then, with an explicit reference to the act of flaying, the excruciating removal of the beast's hide. The human actors are also the grammatical subjects of the riddle's first three sentences: *populator, auctor, cultor*: thief, writer, farmer, the agents of the parchment-making process and the act of writing. The next grammatical subject, "my meadows" [*mea prata*], evokes the rich medieval metaphorics of writing as a form of cultivation (the "vineyard of the text," in Ivan Ilich's phrase), the fragrant harvest of words and inspiration that make of the writing surface a site of teeming fertility, and also cultivation: it is the auctor who returns the flayed animal to the *planum . . . campum*, the smooth field or smoothed surface of the parchment.[12] The switch to a first-person verb in the final line (*prestabo*, "I shall give/grant") allows the *membranus* to speak to the reader in a tone of futurity brought out all the more by the changing verb tenses (from past to present to future) that have preceded it. Tatwine's careful grammatical modulations throughout the short riddle create an implied argument about its subject: parchment is the flesh-and breath-deprived animal that continually lives on as writing and thereby promises endless sustenance and continuing nourishment to its consumers.

One of the ubiquitous themes in the history of parchment is its ability to triumph somehow over death, whether by preserving the culture of its human makers or coming to animal life again, as in the story of St. Ciarán and his cow. This topos informs the parchment riddle found in the *Ænigmata Bernensia*, or Berne Riddles, a collection originating in Italy and likely known to Aldhelm, the most influential of the insular riddlers. The riddle shows no hesitation about openly displaying the butchery entailed in the rendering of the medium it describes:

Lucrum viva manens toto nam confero mundo
et defuncta mirum praesto de corpore quaestum.

Vestibus exuta multoque vinculo tensa,
gladio sic mihi desecta viscera pendent.
Manibus me postquam reges et visu mirantur,
miliaque porto nullo sub pondere multa.[13]

(While life remains I spread riches over all the world,
and once dead bestow wondrous profit from my body.
Stripped of my raiment and stretched hard by many cords,
my ripped flesh hangs, rendered thus by a blade.
Kings, bearing me in their hands, then gaze at me, marveling:
I hold many thousands of weightless things.)

Here the distinction between living animal and dead parchment seems at once more tenuous: the first-person verbs in the opening two lines, *confero* and *praesto*, both convey a sense of bestowal or conferral. The beast's body spreads its wealth over the world (in the form of milk, or perhaps manure) while the animal is alive; the same body bestows great profit (written words) once the animal is defunct. As in the Exeter riddle, though, the speaker is not singular. Neither solely *membranum* nor solely *animalium*, the first-person voice here must be both at once, separated self-consciously from both the living animal and the ripped, objectified flesh stretched and cleaned on the frame. The emphasis here on the viscera pushes subtly against the frequent denigration of parchment as the lowly stuff of flesh, made truly valuable only through translation into human use for largely sacred purposes.

A third Latin analogue comes from the *Enigmata* attributed to the pseudonymous Eusebius, likely identifiable as Hwætberht, abbot of Wearmouth from 716–45. The riddle (headed "De membrano" in the collection) contrasts the before and after of parchment while touting the mystery of its present-day incarnation:

Antea per nos resonabat vox verba nequaquam;
distincta sine nunc voce edere verba solemus.
Candida sed cum arva lustramur milibus atris,
viva nihil loquimur, responsum mortua famur.[14]

(Once a voice resounded in us with no words,
now, without voice, we produce distinct words.
White fields, yet we glisten with a thousand points of black;
alive we say nothing, when dead we give answer.)

The brief riddle abounds in Latin terms—*resonabat, voce, verba responsum*—reflecting a liturgical culture invested in the resonance of words, voices, and responses from the pages of membrane books. The voice of parchment here is the voice of animals making wordless cries in life as well as books forming silent words in death. Despite their voices, the animals "say nothing" when alive: mute servants to the human culture of the book.

The Old English book riddles and their Latin analogues unfold in an incarnate idiom of familiarity and enigma, in which poets discover potent words and resonant juxtapositions that reflect the uncanny double life of the animal medium on which they themselves survive—on which those who wrote them down surely hoped their riddles would survive long after their own deaths. Despite their deliberate artifice, the bookish riddles also represent some of the most direct attempts on the part of medieval writers to give voice to the animals flayed for the sake of the written medium and its human users. The rendered beasts come alive to speak their own paradoxical double natures while giving themselves willingly to the humans who rob them of their lifeblood, deprive them of their skins, manufacture them into books and documents. These human creatures are murderers, they are thieves, they are butchers; but they are also shepherds, they are farmers, they are authors and makers, they are givers of voice and evangelizers of the Word of God.

The *ænigmata* thus present a remarkably frank sense of the ethical entailments of parchment culture, particularly the strong sense of sacrifice inspiring a certain understanding of the medium. You humans kill us, skin us, put our hides through a brutal and alienating craft process that leaves us utterly transformed, both physically and ontologically; we in turn give you the gift of writing, the blessing of the physical book. We, the animals, have to believe the sacrifice is worth it in the end given the many blessed words we know you will inscribe on us, and for the manifold rewards you, our captors and killers, will preserve on and as our flesh. We die for your words, yet even as we die we shall sing for you and for your salvation.

Easy for us to say, of course. The rich medieval vein of creaturely thought that gives us the parchment riddles derives from the same bookish paradox at play in a number of later medieval texts that draw on the ethical register of parchment to explore the boundaries between the human and the nonhuman, the earthly and the divine. Medieval literary animals rarely speak of their own or others' rendering into parchment, though when they do, they often exploit its double nature as a medium of life and death, evoking the shock value of parchment as both a provocation to slaughter and an agent of creaturely transformation.

Such envoicings of membrane can take on a quite violent cast, as in the Latin mock-epic *Ysengrimus*, a mid-twelfth-century fabliau that features an ongoing struggle between Ysengrimus, a doltish and monkish wolf, and Reinardus, a trickster fox who labors constantly to get Ysengrimus into mortal peril. The conflict grows increasingly violent as the story progresses, as the fox puts the wolf through a series of trials and attacks, including a severed tail, a severe beating at the hands of angry sheep, a kick in the head from a deceptive horse, a booby-trapped pile of false relics, and other indignities. Though the poem's violence is often slapstick and cartoonish, it can take on a darker cast, particularly around issues of gender and sexuality. Thus at one point Reinardus invades Ysengrimus's home and rapes his wife after urinating on their children, an incident that reveals the poet's taste for casual brutality and victimization.

The longest sequence in the poem, centered around a conceit to which the writer often returns, concerns the fate of the wolf's skin as it transforms from the animal's hide to written surface—a sequence that Sarah Kay has read for its "identification between skin and the page" and the implications of this identification for the human and nonhuman identities of the reader.[15] *Ysengrimus* might also be understood as an extended anti-allegory of parchment making and repair, as the poem explores the troubling consequences entailed when animals take the craft process into their own hands. The poet takes special delight in an obsessive "working" of the wolf's skin, which is subjected to repeated processes of dehairing, piercing, and pummeling: "Ysengrimus was, in his much-pierced body, a mass of wounds, like someone who was covered with a net gaping with holes. His broken bones were almost coming away from his sinews; not one of his veins remained hidden beneath his skin [*venarum penitus sub cute nulla latet*]."[16] So rent and fouled is Ysengrimus's hide that he seeks new skin from other animals encountered throughout the poem: "The wretch hoped to patch up his gaping slits with your hides [*exuviis vestris*]," a group of cows is told, "and that hope was illusory, for the holes gape bigger and more numerous than before" (2.637–40). By the end of Book 2, Ysengrimus lies half dead and bloodied in a field, his skin bitten, rent, and pierced beyond recognition through the wiles of his intimate enemy, the fox.

Much of the action in Book 3 takes place in the court of a lion king who has fallen ill and seeks a cure from his subjects. After summoning a representative of every animal group, the king is prescribed a remedy requiring "the skin of a wolf who is three and a half years old. Nature has blessed the hide of a wolf of that age with so wonderful a gift of medicinal power that, if you sweat under its covering when you have taken the herbs, sleep will quickly invade and refresh your limbs as of old" (3.447–52). Ysengrimus, justifiably afraid for his hide, puts up a valiant defense (involving the age of his skin and his many grey hairs) even as the other animals gathered at court try to convince the wolf to surrender his body to the king: "Give, Dom Ysengrimus, give your claws in their entirety; give skin and flesh [*corium et carnem*], and don't wish to keep back anything" (3.923–24). The wolf loses the argument and soon hangs before the king, ready for sacrifice to the sovereign lion. His flayer and the first *lector* of his skin will be another of the king's servants, a bear:

> De super ergo ac subtus et hinc atque inde relectum
> > grandaevi iuvenis restrofat ursus ephot;
> unde altum medias discriminate occiput aures,
> > postremas calces mensus adusque metit.
> Horrida non alio falx pervolat impete faenum;
> > non alio candens unguina crassa calibs.
> Anteriora tamen restant suralia nec non
> > aure tenus tegmen frontis ab aure patens,
> porro super nasum caudale ut tortilis ibat
> > nervus ab exortu frontis adusque labrum.
> Unguibus incussis citra nimis, ursus utrimque
> > liquerat haec, nimia mobilitate volans.
> Clamavitque alacer: "Comites, haec lectio lecta est;
> > nunc melius, cui non complacet ista, legat.
> Sed sic Teutonicae membrana est nescia linguae,
> > tamquam Pictavi corpore rapta lupi.
> Carcophas, quid ais? Video regisse venuste?
> > At tu dic, vervex, et caper!" Ambo tacent.
> Reddidit haec asinus: "Peream, nisi legeris apte,
> > hactenus et placide sustinet ille legi.
> Legeris ulterius, iam sentiet; ecce pusillum,
> > quod modo legisti, senserat ipse fere."

(So, having read off the priestly robe of the aged youth up and down and from side to side, the bear sheared it off, taking the measure and slashing from where the middle of his skull separated his tall ears, right down to the heels of his back feet. With just such a swoop does the fierce scythe slice through hay, or glowing-hot steel through thick fat. But there remained behind the socks on his forepaws, and also a covering for his forehead, visible between his ears—or rather a ribbon, like a crooked sinew, ran over his nose from the swelling of his forehead as far as his mouth; the bear had plunged his claws in too much to each side, and had left this behind in the excessive haste of his rush.

He called out cheerfully: "Comrades, this Lesson has been read; now anyone who doesn't like it can read it better. But this parchment is as innocent of the Germanic language as if it were torn from the body of a Poitevin wolf. Carcophas, what do you say? Do I seem to have read pleasantly? You at least, sheep and goat, speak up!" They were both silent, but the ass replied as follows: "Let me die if you didn't read excellently. And so far, he has patiently borne being read. If you read further, he'll soon feel the effects; you see he's hardly felt the little bit you've just read.")
(3.951–72)

In a sequence of graphic and extended violence, the poem transforms the scene of the wolf's flaying into a textual spectacle with parchment at its gruesome heart. Before flaying Ysengrimus, the bear "reads" the wolf's skin from side to side and top to bottom, then proceeds to cut and tear it off his flesh, as a scythe slices through hay or a blade through fat. The bear has flayed the wolf too hastily, we are told, leaving strips of skin behind; nevertheless, once the wolf hangs skinned and bleeding before the crowd, his hide can be read anew, and interpreted accordingly. The precision of the diction here, particularly the string of terms associated with reading and interpretation—*lectio/lecta/legit/linguae/legeris/legisti*—suggests a twisted parable for monastic *lectio divina* or sacred reading: both a hermeneutical satire and a hagiographical parody.[17]

Yet the intensely textual idiom of the flaying episode might also be understood as a send-up of that mode of gentle utilitarianism inspiring the book riddles in their approach to parchment as creaturely sacrifice. If the riddles imagine their membrane-giving animals as useful both before and after their deaths, *Ysengrimus* inverts the process into a scene of gruesome horror. The wolf is less a docile sacrificial lamb here, giving itself willingly and even happily to its human readers, than a terrified and unwilling victim, poised below the knife (claw) and all too aware of the consequences of the rendition he is about to endure. As the bear says of his victim's skin, "this parchment [*membrana*] is as innocent of the Germanic language as if it were torn from the body of a Poitevin wolf." Later, in Book 6, this logic of utter dominion returns as a comment on the various uses of a sheep when sheared, skinned, or dead: "A sheep is better sheared than skinned [*decoriata*], and even when skinned is some good, but is utterly useless when destroyed" (6.325–26).

A more mundane approach to envoicing the skin-giving animal is taken by the late medieval English poet John Lydgate in "The Debate of the Horse, the Goose, and the Sheep" (ca. 1425), one of a number of vernacular debate poems among assemblages of beasts to survive from the later Middle Ages. Here the three animals engage in an extended exchange regarding the virtues of their respective kinds, including the utility of their bodies to humanity. Thus the sheep extols the value of its flesh and wool for a variety of human needs, including the enrichment of owners. "Of sheepe al-so comyth pilet & eke fell" (fur and skins), commodities that may be "Gadrid in thys lond for a gret Marchaundise," and transported "ovir see where men may it sell."[18] These "wolle skynnys," the sheep avows, grant men "gret richesse in many sondry wise": "The sheepe al-so turnyth to gret profite, / To helpe of man berith furris blak & white." The next stanza turns to the products of the hide and guts, beginning with the skin which, once flayed, may be rendered into many other products for the benefit of humans:

> Ther is also made of [the] Sheepis skyn,
> Pilchis & glovis to dryve awey the cold.
> Ther-of also is made good parchemyn,
> To write on bookes in quaeirs many fold.
> The Ram of Colcos bare a flees of gold;
> The flees of Gedeon of deun delectable
> Was of Maria a Figure ful notable.
>
> His fleesh is natural restauracion;
> As summe men seyn aftir gret siknesse,
> Rostid or sodyn holsom is moton:
> Wellid with growel phisiciens expresse,
> Ful nutritiff aftir a gret accesse.
> The sheepe also concludying doutelees
> Of his nature louyth rest & pes.[19]

The two stanzas proclaim the variety of ways we meet our most pressing needs with the bodies of sheep, first the hide, then the flesh: the need for warmth and protection (the hide can be used for gloves and "pilchis," or coats made of skins); the need for restorative food after sickness ("rostid . . . moton" is particularly healthful when stewed or "wellid" in gruel); and the need for "good parchemyn," the rendered hides making up "bookes in quaeirs many fold" ("quaeirs" here refers to quires or fascicles, the folded booklets bound together to make up a codex).[20] Lydgate notes two famous examples of sheepskins, the Golden Fleece of the winged ram of Colchis, as well as Gideon's Fleece, the hide laid down on the threshing floor in the Book of Judges (Judges 6:36–40) that was a common figure for the Virgin Mary's dewed flesh in medieval Christian allegories of incarnation. The concluding couplet hails sheep for their natural love of peace and restfulness—an ironic close to a sequence that imagines repeated violence to flesh that also serves as a form of "natural restauracioun."

I want to conclude this chapter with a rather different sort of riddling "restauracioun" of the animality of parchment, one that pushes back against the inevitability of animal sacrifice for the making of the book, or at least reverses its logic. Andrew Waterhouse was an English poet and environmental activist whose first and only collection, *In*, was awarded the Forward Prize for the year 2000. Waterhouse died shortly afterward while working on a commission to commemorate the Lindisfarne Gospels.[21] As part of his preparation for the commission from the Mid-Northumberland Arts Group, Waterhouse had already been reading in book conservation and history, which led him to confect a passage that serves as an epigraph from an imaginary volume on manuscript restoration by a certain "J. Makepeace": "The vellum pages of old manuscripts will take on the curves of their original shape over time." Take away the translative epigraph and the poem becomes a musing riddle that reverses the acts of slaughter, flaying, and rendering that underlay the parchment *ænigmata* of the Middle Ages:

> After various centuries the Book's pages
> finally bent and realigned, escaped
> their tight gatherings and the library,
> stood upright once more, four legged, wet nosed.
> The covers sat in place on the animal's back,
> like a saddle or stunted wings. Some words
> became clearer: on its tongue *caelorum*,
> along the tale *beau quisant*. Fine initials
> followed the lines of the ribs, in the fur
> grew spirals and knots between the eyes
> a cross flamed. Of all the evangelists,
> poor Mark came off worst, being far too close
> to the arse for comfort. Now, Luke's healing hand
> settles over the calf's heart and it shivers

in the rain, takes a second first breath,
kicks out, begins to gallop across the grass.[22]

This is book restoration in a movingly literal sense: the uncrafting of the membrane codex back into the singular animal composing it, the calf that now takes "a second first breath" before galloping away. The calf retains its covers as well as certain words written on the vellum, initials that limn its ribs, and a cross set between its eyes. The reborn animal is still tattooed or branded, that is, with the words and art that once embellished its bookmade skin, just as the vellum had been marked (as the poem's epigraph has it) with the "curves" of the calf's "original shape." While certain passages in the Gospel of Mark are a bit too close to the calf's ass for comfort, the words of Luke cup the beast's heart, and shepherd the animal back to a second life in the meadow from whence it came.

CHAPTER TEN

THE HUMAN BOOK AND
THE BODY OF CHRIST

To prepare the independence act, we need the skin of a white man for parchment, his skull for a writing-case, his blood for ink, and a bayonet for a pen.
—LOUIS BOISROND-TONNERRE (1804)

At the consummation of created things there will be a resurrection of all people. At that time their manner of life will be represented in their own persons and their bodies will become parchment skins for the books of justice.
—THE TEACHING OF ADDAI (SYRIAC, CA. 400 CE)

Two visions of inscribed human skin, recorded thirteen centuries apart. The first, a proclamation by a Haitian historian and revolutionary, displays all the fervor of a targeted massacre and a human vehicle; the second, an anonymous early Christian meditation on the resurrection of the body, casts the end times as a universal transumption of written skin. Both visions enlist the human hide as a spectacular medium of juridical writing: for an act of national independence, for a record of eternal justice.

The first epigraph derives from an anecdote related by Thomas Madiou, author of *Histoire d'Haïti* (1847), the earliest attempt to write the complete history of the Caribbean nation in its first decades of existence. Madiou is recounting the years around the ratification of the Declaration of Independence in 1804, which represented Haiti's official break from European colonial rule after a revolution that had lasted nearly fourteen years.[1] Composed by Jean-Jacques Dessalines, the formerly enslaved governor-general of the newly independent nation, the Declaration was transcribed by Louis Boisrond-Tonnerre, identified among the signatories as the secretary of the revolutionary army. According to witness accounts of the days leading up to ratification, it was Boisrond-Tonnerre who would sit up all that New Year's night drafting the Declaration and make the ominous if tongue-in-cheek proclamation about the materials required. As he was reported to have quipped to Dessalines at one point, "All that has been done is not in harmony with our current frame of mind; to draw up the declaration of independence, we need the skin of a white man for parchment [*la peau d'un blanc pour parchemin*], his skull for an inkwell, and a sword for a pen!"[2]

Boisrond-Tonnerre's notorious parchment quip would become part of the revolutionary legend of Haiti's founding, the potent symbol of an era of rebellious fervor and widespread anticolonialist violence. Though the Declaration itself was written, printed, and distributed on paper rather than on the pale human medium Boisrond-Tonnerre imagines, the anecdote casts its composition as a brutal reversal of the logic of dominion underlying the long history of parchment, "reduc[ing] the slaveholders to an assemblage of exploitable body parts: bones, blood, skin."[3] Through the scribal agency of Boisrond-Tonnerre, Haiti imaginatively writes itself into constitutional modernity on the written bodies of its colonial oppressors, now the flayed object and animalized medium of its national origin and independence.

Nor was Haiti's the only revolution to be cast as a retribution written on the rendered skin of its antagonists. The secretary's gruesome aside evokes an urban legend that circulated widely regarding the French Constitution of 1793: the story of the so-called Montagnard Constitution, a radical document whose provisions were never officially implemented before its replacement two years later by the official Constitution of 1795. A version of this earlier legend appears in the work of Sydney Owenson (Lady Morgan), author of the wildly popular *The Wild Irish Girl* (1806), an epistolary novel and a founding work of Irish nationalism. Owenson spent a period of months in her later, less political years residing in Paris, publishing the account of her sojourn as *France in 1829–30*. At one point in the memoir (a chapter titled "Private Collections"), Owenson and a companion visit the library of a certain Monsieur de Villenave, "a little Vatican in its way." There they inspect one of the monsieur's bibliographical treasures:

> Among the curious books in his collection was a horrible relic of modern times—a printed copy of the constitution of 1793, bound in human skin. It had been the property of a terrorist, who paid the forfeit of his atrocity on the scaffold. The temperament that could lend itself to such a dereliction of all human feeling must, at all times, form a monstrosity, for which nature is accountable; but its untamed development in the bosom of society, is the consequence of institutions; and the terrorists were the children of the ancient monarchy.[4]

Owenson's horror at the bookish spectacle is tempered by her ambivalent sense of its temporality: the skin-bound constitution is both a "horrible relic," a "monstrosity" derived from an "ancient monarchy," but also a thoroughly modern spectacle, "the consequence of institutions" that have only recently awakened Europe and the world to a post-Enlightenment modernity.

The "skin of a white man" desired as parchment, a nation's constitution bound in the hides of slain reactionaries: these revolutionary anecdotes and their prurient afterlives rely on the shock value of "anthropodermic bibliopegy," a phrase evidently first rendered into English in 1946 by Lawrence Thompson, a librarian at the U.S. Department of Agriculture, to denote the fashioning of books and other written documents from the skin of human beings (more properly "using human skin for book-binding," though Boisrond-Tonnerre's fantasy entails a parchment writing surface rather than a leathern cover).[5] The practice has a long if thin and sensationalized history, consisting of equal parts anecdote, pseudoscientific prurience, bibliographical inquiry, and scientific investigation. The subject has been much written about, most often for the distasteful images and morbid imaginings to which it has given rise.[6] A cottage industry has grown up in recent years around the investigation of books claimed by museums, libraries, and private collections to be written on or bound in human skin. The Anthropodermic Book Project, founded by a team of librarians and scientists (including Megan Rosenbloom, author of a definitive new study of the practice), devotes itself to confirming or debunking claims of anthropodermic bookmaking, combining archival research with biomolecular techniques such as peptide fingerprinting in order to confirm or rebut the allegations around individual volumes.[7] As of July 2021, the Project's rolling census of tested books had identified 50 volumes alleged to be anthropodermic in whole or in part, of which they have tested 31, confirmed 18 as human, and rejected 13 (the current count is available at https://anthropodermicbooks.org).

There is clearly much more to the story of anthropodermic binding and writing than a gruesome byway in modern textual tradition, more than a literalization of Kafka's *Strafkolonie*, with its spectacular machine inscribing punishment on the skin of the condemned. In its material history, anthropodermic bibliopegy is a biological record of human atrocity; in its imaginative spectacularity, an enduring subject of curiosity and disgust. Yet for its most prominent practitioners as well as its chroniclers in memoir, fiction, and descriptive bibliography, anthropodermic bibliopegy entails an unspoken confluence of membrane and modernity, evoking the animality that underlies the long shared histories of human embodiment and the technology of the book. These were congruences that the premodern world thought about in fascinating detail, and even theorized as part of the era's own textual imaginings, as the second epigraph above suggests. If the Enlightenment fashioned the anthropodermic book into an instrumentalizing spectacle of all-too-human cruelty and punishment, medieval parchment cultures embraced the difficult animality that formed the common substrate of the written word. Thinking about these two traditions in tandem will help clarify the stakes of each, and show their distinctiveness as alternative imaginings of the human book.

From the early decades of the nineteenth century, the alleged human binding of the Constitution of 1793 and other revolutionary volumes became a charged topos in the afterlife of the French Revolution. Accounts of anthropodermic media appeared across numerous fields of knowledge and written genres, from history to art history, from memoir to fiction, from philosphy to descriptive bibliography and the history of bookbindings—and the Constitution was not the only piece of revolutionary writing in France so imagined. A review essay by Abraham Hayward, appearing in the *Edinburgh Review* for 1866, includes an account of the "emptying of the tombs" during the Reign of Terror: the patroness of an establishment in Paris, he reports, "stood at the door distributing copies of the Rights of Man, bound in human skin supplied to the binder by the executioner." Hayward swears that "M. Villenave possessed one of these copies": likely the very volume earlier examined by Sydney Owenson.[8]

Many of the legends surrounding the anthropodermic books and pamphlets of the revolutionary era grew up around scattered reports of a tannery in the suburban municipality of Meudon outside Paris. The tannery, according to contemporaneous reports, specialized in the rendering of human skin for all sorts of purposes. Sir Thomas Carlyle, in his epochal study *The French Revolution* (1837), cites the Abbé Montgaillard on the unique horrors of "that Tannery at Meudon; not mentioned among the other miracles of tanning!" as a loaded symbol of revolutionary excess:

> "At Meudon," says Montgaillard with considerable calmness, "there was a Tannery of Human Skins; such of the Guillotined worth flaying: of which perfectly good washleather was made;" for breeches, and other uses. The skin of the men, he remarks, was superior in toughness and quality to shamoy; that of the women was good for almost nothing, being so soft in texture!"[9]

The Abbé's cold description of the gendered qualities of human leather appeals to Carlyle as part of the more general catalogue of horrors afforded by the conflict, much like the lists of "thousands guillotined, fusilladed, noyaded, done to dire death" compiled by the revolutionaries.

Carlyle, with his intimate ties to the European publishing industry, would have been particularly taken with the purported role of the Meudon tannery in the revolutionary publishing industry—or so a fellow writer imagines. The story appears in *Doctor Claudius* (1883) by Francis Marion Crawford, an American novelist and memoirist later renowned for his creative supernaturalism, which here lends itself to Carlyle's ghoulish response to the prattlings of an ignorant man:

> It was at a dinner-party, and Carlyle sat silent, listening to the talk of lesser men, the snow on his hair and the fire in his amber eyes. A young Liberal was talking theory to a beefy old Conservative, who despised youth and reason in an equal degree.
>
> "The British people, sir," said he of the beef, "can afford to laugh at theories."
>
> "Sir," said Carlyle, speaking for the first time during dinner, "the French nobility of a hundred years ago said they could afford to laugh at theories. Then came a man and wrote a book called the *Social Contract*. The man was called Jean-Jacques Rousseau, and his book was a theory, and nothing but a theory. The nobles could laugh at his theory; *but their skins went to bind the second edition of his book*."
>
> Look to your skin, world, lest it be dressed to morocco and cunningly tooled with gold. There is much binding yet to be done.[10]

The emphasis is in Crawford's original, as is this footnote to the anecdote: "There was a tannery of human skins at Meudon during the Revolution."[11] This novelized Carlyle takes the existence of the tannery as fact, part of the same horrific machinery that covers the revolutionary volumes of Rousseau, Payne, the radical constitutions of nations young and old. So provocative was the notion of the anthropodermic revolutionary book that by the last decade of the century, the *Journal de Lois* would include an advertisement touting an original anthropodermic copy of the Constitution and open to public display: "One of our subscribers has forwarded to us, as a worthy memorial of the tyranny of the Decemvirs, a copy of 'The Constitution of 1793,' printed by Causse at Dijon, and bound in human skin resembling tawny calf. We shall be pleased to show it to any who are curious to see it."[12]

The same image gets picked up (and Carlyle quoted verbatim) in "An Original Edition," a neogothic short story published anonymously in *Cornhill Magazine* in 1888, edited by William Makepeace Thackery. The story transforms Carlyle's creepy account of Rousseau and the human tannery into a tale of bibliographic horror that begins when the narrator picks up a copy of *Du Contrat Social* at a secondhand bookstore. The volume, he speculates, "was evidently an original edition, octavo, bound in—what I couldn't exactly say; it wasn't calf, but had rather the appearance of vellum or parchment of some description, as far as I could judge, who was no connoisseur of books or bindings."[13] The bookshop owner engages him in some suggestive banter about the binding, the "most uncommon and costly beyond anything of the sort ever met with"—though the narrator negotiates him down to a mere two shillings. Upon taking the book home, he records his own observations of the binding, "a species of parchment or vellum . . . yellowed and discoloured by time and use" (284–85). Soon the volume takes on a life of its own, "slowly and deliberately opening of its own accord," and always to a particular chapter: "'Du droit de vie et de mort' . . . 'the right of life and death'" (286). Our rattled narrator finally places the odd book under his pillow, only to inspire a horrific dream of a vast charnel-house, filled with "recumbent forms" and hurled skulls, thousands of "brothers and sisters of the guillotine" who approach the "stranger" and are ordered by an unseen leader to "take him; he is yours, serve him as they served you at Meudon!" (288). The narrator casts the book out his window only to have it found and returned by his friend Jack, a "capital French scholar" who takes the book away to investigate its properties and is treated in a similar uncanny way by the volume.

When Jack returns three days later, the narrator confesses all. The friends come up with a scheme to rid themselves at last of the book, only to have it returned to them once again by "a tall dark figure" (obviously Death)—whereupon they finally decide to burn it. An explanation for these bookish horrors finally offers itself only as the two men prepare to throw the volume into the flames, as words written in invisible ink magically appear in the margin, illuminated by the fire:

> 'At Meudon, in 1794, there was a tannery of human skins, where such of the guillotined as were deemed worth the flaying were tanned, and their skins made excellent soft leather for the binding of books and many other purposes, but it is said there is a curse upon all things thus made. This book is bound—' The writing was fading out again as I looked over his shoulder while he read these words.
>
> Snatching the volume from his hand, I turned to the title-page—'Meudon, 1794.' We both saw the inscription and looked at one another in blank horror and amazement. The next moment I had cast the accursed thing upon the blaze. There it curled and writhed like a living thing, until a tongue of flame caught it, and in a few seconds there was nothing left but a handful of white ashes. (292)

The story conjures all the spectacular horrors of the Revolution, crystallized in its gruesome practices of publication: an industrial-sized tannery of human skin, the flayed skins of the victims ("sons and daughters of the guillotine") serving as the

Figure 10.1. Pocket notebook bound in dark tanned skin with silver corners and clasps; appended inscription claims anthropodermic origin. Lieutenant Thomas Laurence, former owner. London, Wellcome Library, ref. L0043480. Photograph courtesy of Wellcome Collection.

bindings of Rousseau's *Social Contract*, a symbolic hallmark of revolutionary modernity with all its attendant atrocities and, here, its postmortem retribution figured as a large-scale practice of anthropodermic bibliopegy.

Such long memories of the tannery at Meudon inform the descriptive language of artisans as well. Here is Émile Gallé, a renowned Art Nouveau designer and glassmaker, recounting his crafting of a cover for a copy of *Salammbô* by Gustave Flaubert, a historical novel set in ancient Carthage, in order to achieve "a harmony with the book, romantic and brutal" to match the wanton and spectacular violence featured in the novel: "my old friend Flaubert's *Salammbô*, for whom I invented a true Carthaginian binding, made of a Japanese brownish leather, which looks like human skin, from tannery Meudon, and the end-papers made from wild silk, representing owls woven in gold on blood-colored background."[14] With the eye of a true connoisseur and practitioner, Gallé summons the anthropodermic specter of Meudon to capture the horrors of his friend's brutal narrative.

A final example of the revolutionary implications of the practice derives from a volume now at the Wellcome Institute for the History of Medicine in London. The unassuming notebook consists of random annotations from a Mr. Thomas Laurence of Borough, London, including an account of election returns in 1786. The volume (see fig. 10.1) is accompanied with a paper tag, affixed by string to the book's clasp, that reads as follows: "The Cover of this book is made of *Tanned Skin* of the Negro whose *Execution* caused the War of *Independence*—." No further information is provided, though the man referenced here is almost certainly the renowned Crispus Attucks, a Boston servant (perhaps enslaved) of mixed African and Wampanoag descent who was reputedly the first victim of the Boston Massacre, and thus the first American resident killed in the Revolutionary War. Testing has shown that the skin covering the Wellcome volume is not human; as Tavia Nyong'o suggests, the book is rather "a fiction of tanned black skin secreted into the archives of the colonial modern," though a compelling enough fiction to summon all the rhetoric of dissent and retribution embodied by a book bound in human skin.[15] At issue here is the role of anthropodermic bibliopegy precisely in the dehumanization of Attucks, whose imagined flaying serves a history of the book as a spectacle of enslavement and dehumanizing utility.

Other cases of anthropodermic bibliopegy (whether verified or alleged) derive from more mundane circumstances, incidents of minor criminality and even scientific voluntarism. Alfred Wallis, in a note on a "Book Bound in Human Skin" published in *Notes & Queries* in 1889, reports on a such a find at the Albert Memorial Library in Exeter. The book is a copy of Thomas Tegg's edition of *The Poetical Works of John Milton* (1852) from the library of Ralph Sanders, Esq., also of Exeter. Wallis found the following inscription on the inside covering:

> This Book is bound with a part of the skin of George Cudmore, who with Sarah Dunn were committed to the Devon County Gaol on the 30th of October, 1829, by Francis Kingdon, Esq., Coroner, for murdering and poisoning Grace Cudmore, his wife, in the Parish of Roborough, on the 14th day of October, 1829.
> Tried at the Lent Assizes, March, 1830.
> George Cudmore was Executed March 25th, 1830.
> Sarah Dunn was Acquitted.
> Judge—Sir John B. Bosenquet
> Sheriff—J.B. Swete, Esq.
> Under-Sheriff—H.M. Ellicombe, Esq.
> County Clerk—H.M. Ford, Esq.[16]

According to Wallis's description of the binding, "the skin is 'dressed' white, and looks something like pigskin in grain and texture." Wallis also reports that the material was furnished to the binder by Cudmore himself, formerly a rat catcher, who insisted that his accomplice witness his execution. Cudmore's sentence included the dissection of his body, after which his hide was reportedly tanned and then repurposed as a new binding by a denizen of the Exeter book trade.[17]

A public dissection was also the fate of John Horwood, executed in 1821 for the murder of Eliza Balsum, whom he had been threatening in the months prior. Following the dissection and accompanying lecture, Horwood's skin was tanned and apparently kept by the surgeon for many years before being used to bind a volume of documents relating to Horwood's case. The book (now in the Bristol Archives) includes transcripts of the trial, a hand-drawn map of the crime scene, and even a bill for the binding process that made the anthropodermic book.[18]

Yet the annals of anthropodermic bibliopegy also evidence a fair amount of voluntarism: cases of the condemned who faced their deaths with enough equanimity to offer their own hides for bibliographic posterity. One such case is that of James Allen, a New England thief whose criminal memoir, *Narrative of the life of James Allen: alias George Walton, alias Jonas Pierce, alias James H. York, alias Burley Grove, the highwayman: being his death-bed confession, to the warden of the Massachusetts State Prison*, was published in Boston by Harrington & Co. in 1837. The memoir itself takes the unremarkable form of a first-person autobiography dictated to an unnamed scribe, and includes a conventional narrative of conversion to Christianity and a deathbed confession. Though the text makes no mention of the disposition of Allen's corpse, it was apparently at his direction that two copies of his *Narrative* were, upon publication, bound in his tanned hide. The front cover of one of these volumes, now at the Athenæum in Boston (fig. 10.2), is affixed with a small plate engraved with the words *HIC WALTONIS CUTE COMPACTUS EST*: "This book is bound in Walton's skin"—human membrane "treated to look like gray deer skin," as the catalogue description has it.[19]

Perhaps the most abjectly horrifying instance of anthropodermic bibliopegy is the case of Mary Lynch, an Irishwoman admitted to the Philadelphia General Hospital in 1868. Presenting with unremitting pain in her limbs, she was diagnosed with phthitis, a tubercular condition that was greatly worsened when family members brought her tainted pork products to supplement her institutional diet. When she died in January 1869, Lynch's body cavity was discovered to be filled with roundworms. The autopsy on Mary's body was performed by John Stockton Hough, who later wrote up and published a report on her likely cause of death and her postmortem condition for the *American Journal of the Medical Sciences*.[20] It was also Hough, a prominent Philadelphia bibliophile, who flayed portions of Lynch's corpse and tanned the skin of her thighs in a chamber pot in a hospital cellar. Hough af-

Figure 10.2. *Narrative of the life of James Allen: alias George Walton, alias Jonas Pierce, alias James H. York, alias Burley Grove, the highwayman: being his death-bed confession, to the warden of the Massachusetts State Prison* (Boston, 1837), with engraved cover plate claiming anthropodermic binding. Boston, The Athenæum.

terward used Lynch's tanned skin to bind three books on female reproduction and anatomy, in each of which he left an inscription attesting to his utilization of her remains.[21] The longest appears in Hough's copy of Robert Couper's eighteenth-century work *Speculations on the Mode and Appearances of Impregnation in the Human Female* (see fig. 10.3). "The leather with which this book is bound was tanned from the skin of the thigh of Mary L_____," Hough writes, "who died of consumption in the Philadelphia Hospital, 1869." Her skin was then tanned by Hough himself, and the books were bound in Trenton, New Jersey, some years later.

The case of Mary Lynch brings to light the hidden circuits of bibliographic obsession, human subjection, and dark skincraft that inhabit the peculiar history of anthropodermic bibliopegy, a practice that has often been cast as a kind of murderous spectacle worthy of a horror film. In *Original Skin*, her memoir-cum-history of

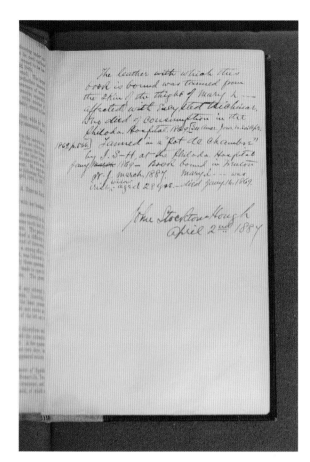

Figure 10.3. Anthropodermic inscription by John Stockton Hough, dated April 2, 1884, in Robert Couper, *Speculations on the Mode and Appearances of Impregnation in the Human Female*, copy owned by the Historical Medical Library of The College of Physicians of Philadelphia.

the human hide, Maryrose Cuskelly likens anthropodermic books to actual killers: "To me, such volumes are the Hannibal Lecters of cultural objects, with the unholy allure of the serial killer swirling around them. There is the whiff of the occult about them, but also of the slaughterhouse."[22] Here the anthropodermic book assumes the agency of a murderer, the anonymizing stench of the slaughterhouse yet clinging to its pages.

Unlike the countless slaughtered nonhuman animals whose skins make up the bindings or pages of parchment books and documents, the human animals whose hides are employed for anthropodermic volumes will nearly always be endowed with names, biographies, and histories.[23] It is unusual, in fact, to see an account of anthropodermic bibliopegy in which a specific book is alleged to be bound in an *unnamed* person's skin (the urban legend of the tannery at Meudon is an exception that helps prove the rule). One of the entailments of the practice is its specification of the individuals whose body parts have been repurposed toward bibliographic ends. Stories of human-bound books achieve much of their allure and fascination through association with a rendered victim's prior life, whether defined by criminality or treason or sickness. This resistance to anonymity is a distinguishing feature of the practice, and may help explain why such a large proportion of anthropodermic books are enlisted to the cause of revolutionary modernity—and why its premodern antecedents have been consigned to near-oblivion in accounts of the practice's history. The modern practice of anthropodermic bibliopegy, in other words, obscures the longer history of imaginative renderings of human skin into books and documents: not simply the binding but the page, the hair and flesh of the parchment folio that both embodies our beastly abjection and, though only for some, promises salvation.

A florid manuscript page, illuminated with peacocks, flowers, pink stems and leaves, all on a ground of rich yellow (fig. 10.4). At the upper center of the folio, John the Baptist, standing beneath an arched window, gestures with his right hand at a book and a beast cradled in his left. Reclining on the book, a lamb gazes back at John's hand, the beast's front hoofs and tail dangling from the cover. The text block (first in red letter) enjoins readers to offer prayers *de sancto Ioanne baptista*, beginning with the antiphon (in black letter): "Among those born of women there arose none greater than John the Baptist who prepared the way of the Lord in the wilderness." John the Baptist performs a bookish husbandry to the lamb, though the scene is hardly pastoral. The Evangelist stands here before a sweeping forest, a river or creek visible over his right shoulder, both background elements meant to represent the wilderness [*heremo*] as the setting of his evangelical mission.

This representation of John the Baptist and the reclining lamb comes from the Spinola Hours, a luxury book illuminated by a Flemish master and his collaborators in the early sixteenth century. *Saint John the Baptist Preaching* holds a special place in the manuscript, for it is the only full-page untexted miniature, painted on one side of a tipped-in folio left blank on the reverse.[24] The image depends on a series of common associations to make both theological and practical sense of its various elements, beginning with John himself, clad in "his garment of camel's hair" (Matthew 3:4), alongside the fluffy lamb seated upon a book. The lamb in the Spinola Hours, of course, is Jesus Christ, prophesied by John in the years before Christ's arrival in Galilee: "Behold the Lamb of God, behold him who taketh away

Figure 10.4. Master of
James IV of Scotland, *John
the Baptist Preaching*, with
lamb perched on book. From
the Spinola Hours. Bruges,
ca. 1510–20. Los Angeles,
J. Paul Getty Museum, Ms.
Ludwig IX 18, fol. 249v.

the sin of the world." The book here is *the* Book, the Word made flesh by the incarnation of God in the person of his Son, and depicted in careful codicological detail. The Baptist's fingertips touch not the wooly lamb but the fore edge of the volume, all but the pinkie finger positioned between the two golden clasps that hold the codex closed. The Baptist's own skin grazes the edges of the pages, the skins of the multiple beasts making up the book: the Word of God literalized as a parchment codex, the Lamb of God suggested as its sacrificial *materia*. As the Middle English "Charter of Heaven" puts it, "the parchment . . . is neither of sheep nor of calf but it is the body and blessed skin of our Lord Jesus lamb."[25]

Numerous medieval representations of the Baptist with the Lamb of God depict the holy creature reclining on a book, associating the lamb's hide and wool with the leathern cover or the membrane folios of a codex. In some images, the lamb's

Figure 10.5. Initial P with St. John the Baptist pointing to the Lamb of God merged with binding, from a fragment of an Augustinian sermon lectionary. Austria, second quarter of the fourteenth century. Philadelphia, Free Library of Philadelphia, Rare Book Department, Ms. Lewis E M 042:14 (detail).

hoofs will touch the book's fore edge, its woolly legs matching the bright sheen of the parchment and contrasting vividly with the darker binding of the volume. In an initial in a fourteenth-century lectionary, the lamb adheres to the book's cover so as to suggest an embossed or stamped binding, raised into a three-dimensional figure within the bounds of the cover (fig. 10.5). In a fifteenth-century book of hours, the codex lies open with the lamb sprawled across the parchment, its body obscuring the script and its wool visually merging with the text block (fig. 10.6). A related iconographical tradition, derived from Revelation 5, envisions a "horned lamb" standing to open a book sealed with seven seals, taking the volume from the hand descending from the heavens (fig. 10.7). The bookish Lamb may be the subject of evangelical reverence, the harbinger of apocalypse, the husbandry of John the Baptist, the pastoral care of Christ, the Word made flesh.

Similar associations of Lamb of God with membrane medium inform the iconography of the Mystic Lamb from Revelation 5:6, the subject of the Ghent Altarpiece as well as a popular theme for prayer books and the decorative arts. In the frontispiece to the Gospels of Saint-Médard de Soissons (fig. 10.8), a set of early Christian prologues to the four evangelists, the Lamb stands guard over a scroll, the rolled-up parchment *carta* resting parallel to his torso in the immediate foreground of his hoofs. Below the lamb the four evangelists appear in the form of their respective iconic beasts, each holding a membrane book, presumably opened to his respective Gospel, and gesturing to the text with the equivalent of a *nota bene* hand (or *nota bene* talon, as the case may be). The Lamb-qua-animal often gives way to a more explicit association of Christ's body with the membrane pages of the Book. Kathryn Rudy has discovered a number of places in which Eucharistic wafer souvenirs or to-

Figure 10.6. John the Baptist Preaching, with white lamb emerging from the parchment, from a French Book of Hours. Lyon, 1484. New York, Morgan Library Ms. M.1162, fol. 172r (detail).

Figure 10.7. Apocalypse, Lamb Opening Book, from French Book of Hours, Use of Rome. Bourges, 1520s. New York, Morgan Library Ms. M.1135, fol. 15r (detail).

kens have been impressed upon, sewn into, or painted into the parchment folios of late medieval devotional manuscripts. Figure 10.9 reproduces an opening from one such book in which the roundel has been affixed to the verso at four points with a needle and thread, facing the crucified body of Christ. As Rudy describes the juxtaposition, "Perhaps the owner likened these four punctures with the needle to the four nails with which Jesus was hung on the cross. Indeed, on the recto side of the folio [not pictured], one can see that the threads have formed a cruciform shape, as if the body of Christ had symbolically been crucified on parchment with silk."[26]

These associations reach an apogee of sorts in twinned depictions of Jesus Christ in the Rohan Hours, a manuscript that combines a book of hours with a moralized Bible presented in a series of French-captioned scenes on each folio alongside the Latin prayers. In a sequence of images from a central portion of the codex, the basket carrying Moses becomes the holy book, the Word of God that bears him and embodies him in the world: "Mary cries because she sees her brother Moses discovered in the water. This signifies that the synagogue cries for Jesus Christ whom she sees is revealed as divine in the world." Mary here is to be understood as Miriam, a common type of the Virgin Mary from the Old Testament. Christ's divinity is an emphatically bookish divinity (fig. 10.10), complete with a black book clasp across

Figure 10.8. Lamb of God over parchment scroll, from the frontispiece to the Monarchian Prologues from the Gospels of Saint-Médard de Soissons. Aachen, first quarter of the ninth century. Paris, Bibliothèque nationale de France, Ms. Lat. 8850, fol. 1v (detail).

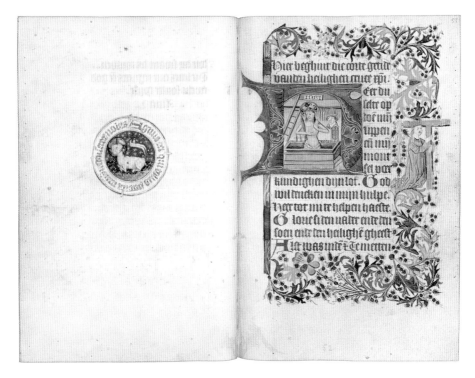

Figure 10.9. Sewn-in Lamb of God medallion in Book of Hours, Haarlem, ca. 1450. Delft, Prinsenhof Ms. PDC 939, fols. 52v–53r.

Figure 10.10. Infant Christ bound to book, from the Rohan Hours. France, 1420–1440. Paris, Bibliothèque nationale de France Ms. Latin 9471, fol. 133r.

his midsection, keeping the manuscript closed while hugging the body of the infant Christ tightly to the fore edge of the membrane manuscript (the diagonal may also be a later defacement intended to obscure the infant Christ's genitals). On the next leaf (fig. 10.11), an adult Christ emerges from the pages of the codex as if from the water, his physical body a continuation of the incarnate folios that rebirth him. The legend: "And the daughter of the pharaoh sees the child in the water and has him pulled out. This signifies that the Holy Church sees Jesus partly revealed to the world. And she orders that he be pulled out and revealed in his divinity." Enclosed in a striking red cover, the book reappears throughout the Rohan Hours as a potent symbol of contemplation, evangelization, and ecclesiastical authority, a reminder of the concrete embodiment of the Lamb of God in the pages of the membrane codex.

Such devotional imaginings of Christ's "blessid skyn" as the parchment of a sacred book are a far cry from modern practices of anthropodermic bookmaking, which have rendered volumes bound in actual human skin that can be observed, touched, and tested. Yet as these many earlier images suggest, the modern phenomenon of anthropodermic bibliopegy can have the effect of obscuring a long tradition of bookish thought that associated human skin intimately with the carnality and materiality of writing in its sacrificial immediacy. This rich allegorical vein has its roots in ancient writing, particularly in certain conventions around images of inscription in the Hebrew Bible and elsewhere, and flourishes during the Christian Middle Ages as part of what Ernst Robert Curtius long ago called the "magnificent . . . religious metaphorics of the book."[27] The Book of Nature, the Book of the Heart, the Charter of Christ: these and other topoi draw on the technology and physicality of parchment to conceive membrane books and documents as a symbol, figure, or totem central to the ritual and theological lives of the human subjects who read, touch, and consume them.[28] As the Word of God, the book of skin embodies the sacrificial dimensions of Christian redemption while inducing others to participate through their own scriptive identifications in a great incarnate narrative.

For some early Christian writers, this long bookish story would culminate in

Figure 10.11. Adult Christ emerging from book, from the Rohan Hours. Paris, Bibliothèque nationale de France Ms. Latin 9471, fol. 134r (detail).

the resurrection of the body. Thus a prophetic vision recorded in *The Teaching of Addai* (ca. 400 CE), a Syriac apocryphal text, casts the myriad bodies of the risen as so many parchment skins inscribed with words of justice:

> For the whole of that for which our Lord came in to the world was that he might teach and show us that at the consummation of created things there will be a resurrection for all people. At that time their manner of life will be represented in their own persons and their bodies will become parchment skins [*mgl'*] for the books of justice. There will be no one there who cannot read, because in that day everyone will read the writings of his own book. He will hold a reckoning of his deeds in the fingers of his hands. Moreover, the unlearned will know the new writing of the new languages. No one will say to his companion: "read this for me," because teaching and instruction will rule over all people.[29]

The passage imagines an embodied autodidacticism of writing, a process in which all those resurrected in the flesh will become membrane sheets bound together, perhaps, in the eternal volumes of justice, while learning to read their own inked-up flesh: the Syriac term used here, *mgl'* (pron. *mgaleh*), can refer to the parchment folio in a codex or a discrete membrane in a scroll.[30] Especially striking in this vision is the hagiographical impulse of universality. Christians "produce upon themselves the life of a saint" in a mode of eschatological inscription in which all will participate.[31]

Such participation could take violent form, as in Prudentius's hymn to St. Eulalia of Barcelona (d. 304 CE), a Christian girl martyred during the persecutions in the reign of Diocletian. The hymnic *vita* is cited by Curtius as exemplary of the era's "life relation" to the incarnate book of Christ. After her gruesome wounding by her tormenters, who "tore into her slim breast . . . cutting to the bone," Eulalia cries out: "Behold, Lord, your name is being written on me. How delightful it is to read these letters, for they mark your victories, O Christ! The purple of the blood itself that is drawn speaks your holy name!"[32] As in *The Teaching of Addai*, the saintly body bears its torments as a parchment page bears confessional words. The exemplary membrane, of course, is the body of Jesus Christ. "Jesus's body, the parchment is," avows a Middle English lyric: "With true love he imprinted our seal that is heritage of our bliss."[33] This commonplace medieval conceit imagines the materiality of the book in avowedly human terms, embracing the animalization of person while obscuring the animality of parchment.

Like its modern counterpart, then, this long anthropodermic tradition of bookish thought in premodern Christianity is, mutatis mutandis, an anthropocentric one. Indeed the enlistment of animal flesh in such allegories only points up the dependence of this analogical convention on a relation of utility and dominion. It asks readers to identify with the written skins of animals even while looking away from the beasts whose death and rendering provide its metaphors. Unlike so many modern accounts of anthropodermic bibliopegy, which greet the spectacle with the assertive distance of cold description, the premodern metaphorics of the incarnate book create an intimacy between living person and membrane page, with much of its moral energy directed at the animalization of humans at the hands of (certain) others.

The notion of anthropodermic *imitatio* appealed to a wide array of medieval writers, perhaps none more so than Henry Suso (ca. 1295–1366), a Dominican visionary and theologian whose asceticism famously entailed intensive acts of inscription on his own skin. In *Das Buch von dem Diener* (*The Book of the Servant*, part of Suso's *Exemplar*), a chapter headed "How he inscribed the beloved name of Jesus on his heart" recounts an episode in which the friar seeks a sign that would demonstrate his love for God, their eternal bond "one that no forgetting could ever erase":

> In this state of fervent earnestness he threw aside his scapular, bared his breast, and took a stylus in hand. Looking at his heart, he said, "God of power, give me today strength and power to carry out my desire, for today you shall be engraved in the ground of my heart." And he began to jab into the flesh above the heart with the stylus in a straight line. He jabbed back and forth, up and down, until he had drawn the name IHS right over his heart. Because of the sharp stabs blood poured profusely from his flesh and ran over his body down his chest. . . . The name IHS remained over his heart, as he had wished. The letters were about as thick as a flattened out blade of grass and as long as a section of the little finger. He carried this name over his heart until his death. And as often as his heart beat, the name moved. At first the letters were quite visible. He bore the name in secret, so that no one ever saw it except for one friend to whom he showed it in divine confidence.[34]

Suso's inscribed body functions in some ways like that of the unnamed slave of Histaeus in Herodotus's *Histories*, his shaved head carrying a secret message only divulged to a trusted ally (see above, chap. 7).

An early manuscript of the *Exemplar* vividly realizes this concatenation of writing, blood, and skin. Early in the book (fig. 10.12), the initials "IHS" appear within the text block, five letters in height and surrounded by a waffle pattern in the same vivid shade as the red-word pointings and the blood spatter in the lower margin.

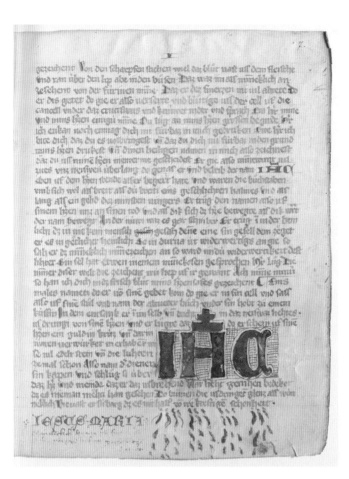

Figure 10.12. Christ initial monogram from Henry Suso's *Exemplar*. Germany, third quarter of the fourteenth century. Strasbourg, Bibliothèque nationale et universitaire, Ms. 2929, fol. 7r.

This "bleeding monogram," as Jeffrey Hamburger terms it, creates of the manuscript's membrane page an incarnate realization of the self-inflicted wound written on Suso's own skin.[35] The scene of reading is spectaculary realized later in the manuscript (fig. 10.13 and detail, fig. 10.14), where Suso bares his chest to reveal the inscription of the holy initals, a hint of blood still pooled in the vee of his garment. On the part of the scribe or artist, to write these letters on the parchment page is to replicate Suso's own ascetic act with pen and ink. The artist has rendered the scene all the more uncanny with subtle visual parallels between *der Diener* and the divine body he imitates. As the seated figure of Suso reaches out to touch Christ's riddled flesh, Suso's own skin breaks out in the same wounds, which spread across his hand and forearm like a rash, or the boils of pestilence.

These imaginative and material manipulations of membrane vis-à-vis the bodies of Christ and Suso himself speak to the array of meanings attached to the parchment medium at various points in Suso's writings. On the one hand, oral devotions in the sacred tongue are vastly superior to those written in the vernacular on dead skins: "Unlike as it is to hear for oneself the melody of sweet strings being played rather than merely to hear someone describe it, just so dissimilar are the words that are received in pure grace and flow out of a responsive heart through a fervent mouth to those same words written on dead parchment [*tote Pergament*], especially in the German tongue."[36] At the same time, Suso clearly treasured parchment as a devotional medium with its own unique properties as material bearer of holy images. He frequently took refuge in private places for contemplation "surrounded by pictures," the *Exemplar* tells us, such as a certain image created for him

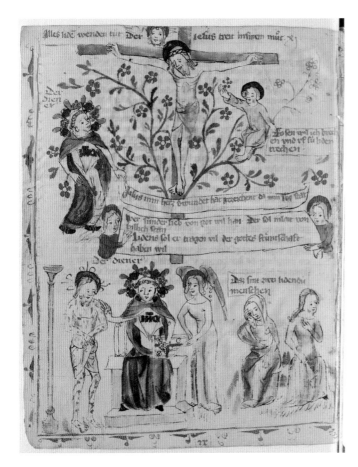

Figure 10.13. Der Diener, with monogram of Christ's name, worshipping the cross and touching Christ's wounded skin. Strasbourg, Bibliothèque nationale et universitaire, Ms. 2929, fol. 109v.

Figure 10.14. Detail of figure 10.13.

years before: "In his youth he had had eternal Wisdom painted on parchment, with heaven and earth in her power, and surpassing in her lovely beauty and pleasing form the beauty of all creatures ... He carried this lovely image around with him in his years of study, putting it in front of him on the windowsill of his cell and gazing at it lovingly with longing in his heart. He brought it back home with him and installed it in the chapel with thoughts of love."[37] This is likely a description of one of the "postcards on parchment" identified by Rudy as a distinctive genre of medieval material text, here put into action as part of the visionary's devotional life.[38] Finally, in a stirring image recalling cosmological reflections on parchment from Late Antiquity, Suso translates the absence of Christ from his presence as a desire to write on limitless membrane the suffering this absence has caused: "Who shall give me the expanse of heaven for my parchment [*das Himmels Breite zum Pergament*] and the depths of the sea for my ink, leaf and grass for my pen, that I might describe to the full the suffering of my heart and the irreparable desolation that this bitter separation from my Beloved has caused me?"[39] Here as elsewhere, parchment erodes the boundaries between death and life, the oral and the written, dessication and eternity.

Other medieval images of anthropodermic inscription turn on the animality of the parchment medium, even enlisting some of the artisanal details of parchment craft to limn their accounts of the Passion, as in the *Fasiculus Morum*, a handbook for Franciscan preachers that imagines Christ stretching his body on the cross "like a parchment-maker is seen exposing parchment to the sun [*sicut pergamenarius ad solem pergamenum explicare videtur*]."[40] Perhaps the most vivid examples occur in a series of Middle English texts collectively known as the Charters of Christ, which combine devotional poetry and prose with the language, formulaic idioms, and in some cases the mise-en-page of documentary writing. In a spectacular illuminated example in figure 10.15, from a Carthusian miscellany of the mid-fifteenth century, the charter text's "physical form becomes as meaningful as its language," in Jessica Brantley's words.[41] The conceit of the Charters holds that Christ grants his human subjects the redemptive promise of his suffering and death through the medium of an incarnate charter, a spectacle figured in textual terms as a violent inscription on his own skin:

> Thyrty wynter and thre þer-to
> Or my dyssese were alle I-doo.
> Parchemyn to fynde wyst I noone
> To make the chartur a-yenst thy foone,
> That wold last withoutyn ende.
> Herkenys nowe to my free wordys hende:
> But as trewer love bad me doo
> Myn owyn skyn to take ther-to.
> And whan I had so I-doo
> Well fewe frendys had I thoo.[42]

The idiom here is almost predatory, as the speaker seeks out a source for the "parchemyn" needed to make a charter. Instead Christ offers his "owyn skyn" in lieu of the animal hide that would otherwise allow him to write. The lines even seem to suggest that Christ flays himself as a sign of his "trewer love," an unthinkable act that leaves him with "few frendys" to witness the sacrifice of his skin.

Notable here and elsewhere in the Charters tradition is the sense of permanence accruing to membrane: the charter "wold last withoutyn ende" due to both the permanence of salvation and the durability of the medium. Yet parchment is also a worldly commodity, an object that Christ seeks but cannot find in the material world around him. Stripped of his cloth and bound to a tree, he stands all night stretched and alone in a parchment-like state:

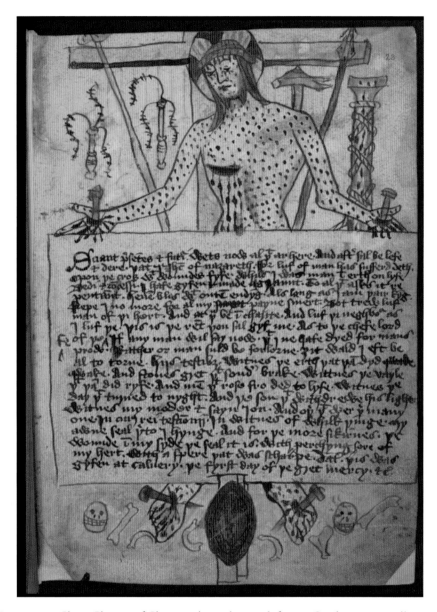

Figure 10.15. Short Charter of Christ with pendant seal, from a Carthusian miscellany. England, second half of the fifteenth century. London, British Library Ms. Additional 37049, fol. 23r.

And so I stood bounde all the nyght
Tyll on the morowe þat it was lyght
Streyned well faste vp-on a tree
As parchemyn owyth for to be
Heryth nowe & 3e shall wetyn
Howe thys chartyr was I-wretyn
Ouer al my face fell the ynke
Thornys in myn hed be-gonne to synke
The pennys þat the letterys wretyn
Were scorges þat I was wytht smetyn...
And redythe vp-on þis parchemyn
Yet ony sorowe be so gret as myn
Stondyth an herkenyth thys chartur rede
Why I am woundid and all for-blede
Siant presentes et feturi[43]

Here Christ is stretched on a tree "As parchemyn owyth for to be"—blank parchment, properly prepared for inscription, which comes in the form of the blood, scourges, and whips that stand in for the ink and pens equipping a scribe. The parchment charter is now consubstantial with the skin of the Savior, marked with wounds that the reader-subject encounters in the same register as the words inscribed on the skin of the page. The poem ends in the formulaic Latin of documentary address, promising knowledge of Christ's death to the present-day and future readers of the charter.

A key couplet in the passage above observes Christ "Streyned well faste vp-on a tree / As parchemyn owyth for to be"—the modal verb *owyth* (ought) making a claim about the parchment-crafting process itself. Other writings similarly exploit the details of parchment craft to bring out certain visual and physiological dimensions of the Passion. A meditation on Christ's wounds once attributed to Richard Rolle imagines how God the Father suffered Christ to be "streyned on the harde cros, moore dispitously & greuously þan euer was schepys skyn streyned on the wal or vp-on þe parchemyn-makeris harowe a3ens þe sonne to drye."[44] The moist sheepskin still drips from a lime bath, stretched (*streyned*) within a "harowe" or frame to dry in the sun before the flesh may be scraped thin. Similarly, in "The Privity of the Passion," an independent vernacularization of one portion of the *Meditationes vitae Christi*, the body of Christ is "sprede o-brode one þe crosse more straite þan any parchemyne-skyne es sprede one þe harowe, so þat mene myghte tel al þe blyssede bones of his body."[45] And in the Digby play of the Burial of Christ, Mary Magdalene remarks on "how many bludy letters beyn writen in þis buke" of Christ's body, so crowded that "Smal margent her is": a codicological detail that brings a keen eye for documentary knowledge to bear on the spectacle of the Crucifixion. Joseph responds, lamenting the piteous sight of "this parchement . . . stritchit owt of syse."[46]

Similar language and imagery can be found well into the early modern period, as in a sermon on Ezekiel and the Passion by John Fisher, Bishop of Rochester, published in London in 1578. The sermon builds an extended visual allegory of Christ on the cross as a book. Just as "a booke hath two boardes," the "two boardes of this booke is the two partes of the crosse"; similarly, "The leaues of this booke be the armes, the handes, legges, and féete, with the other members of his most precious and blessed body." These leaves are formed by the parchment of Christ's flesh:

> Neuer anye Parchement skynne was more strayghtlye stratched by strength vpon
> the tentors then was this blessed body vpon ye crosse. These lorells that crucifyed
> him, drewe by vyolence his moste precious armes, with ropes vnto either braunche of
> the crosse, that the sinowes burst in sonder, and so nayled his handes fast with spy-
> kinge nayles of yron, vnto the crosse. After they stretched his féete lykewyse vnto an
> other hole beneath in the crosse, and there nayled them with the third nayle thorough
> bothe his féete. And so they reared vp this body a loft against the sunne, euen as a
> parchment skinne is sette foorth before the heat of the Sun for to drye. It was set vp a
> loft to the entent that all the worlde might looke vpon this booke.[47]

Though aware of certain elements of parchment craft, however, these later medieval and early modern works tend to avoid mention of its more grisly elements: Christ is not compared to an animal slaughtered for its skin (a notion clearly underlying the earlier medieval book riddles treated in the last chapter), and there is little or no mention of the act of flaying as part of the torture his body must endure.

In fact, one of the more striking aspects of this whole anthropodermic tradition of Passion meditation is its avoidance of animal suffering and death among its catalogue of fleshly torments.[48] In a document among the *Poor Caitiff* tracts that styles itself "a notable chartour of pardoun of oure lorde Ihesu crist," readers are enjoined to be mindful of "þe witte of þis bille: for þe pardoun þerof schal dure wiþouten ende." The pardon includes a long and detailed exposition on the derivation and treatment of its membrane medium:

> þe parchemyn of þis heuenli chartre. is neiþir of scheep ne of calf: but it is þe bodi &
> þe blessid skyn of oure lord ihesu loomb þat neuere was spot|tid wiþ wem of synne | &
> was þere neuere skyn of scheep neiþir of calfe so sore & so hard streined on þe teyn-

ture eiþir harewe of eny parchemyn makere as was þe blessid bodi and skyn of oure
lord ihesu crist. for oure loue streined & drawen vppon þe iebat of þe cros herde neuer
man fro þe biginnyng of þe world til to now. neþir schal hens to domesdai: þat euere
writere wroot vppon schepis skin eiþir on calues wiþ so hard & hidouse pennes. so
bittirli so sore & so depe as writen þe cursid Iewis vppon þe blessid bodi & swete skin
of oure lord ihesu crist. wiþ harde nailes. scharpe spere & sore prickinge þornes in-
stide of here pennes | thei writen so sore & so depe.[49]

The passage is one of the few instances in which writings in this genre pause to remind us explicitly that parchment is animal skin: though imagined here only fleet-
ingly and postmortem, and only to serve the human allegory of the Crucifixion.
Three times the writer emphasizes that the parchment of the charter is "neiþir of
scheep ne of calf," evoking precisely the humanity of Christ in his documentary tor-
ment: the "blessed skyn" of Christ "neuer was spottid" like inferior parchments; no
skin of a sheep or a calf was ever so sorely stretched on a parchment maker's har-
row as the body and skin of Christ; no man has ever written "on schepis skin eiþir
on calues" with such hard and pitiless pens as on the skin of Christ. Yet so unremarkable, so unworthy of comment is the sacrifice of sheep and calf for parchment
that the writer misses the opportunity to identify Christ's own suffering and death
with the slaughtering of the beast. The vehicle of the metaphor is instead the insensate skin stretched on the parchmenter's frame only *after* it has been stripped from
the slain animal: stretching that the beast, being dead, of course cannot feel (unlike
Christ, whose pain is boundless).

Instead the allegory turns on the Jews, reminding us that the charter is part of
a larger "covenaunt" between the Christian God and his faithful subjects. As the
A-text of the Long Charter avows, "þe Iowys fell with gret swynk / Of my blode
þey madyn ynke."[50] In such instances, the writers in this tradition figure the material violence of writing by positioning the Jews as the agents of inscription who carve
with nail, spear, and thorn "instide of here pennes" while making ink of Christ's
blood. The ubiquitous medieval logic of supersession—the displacement of one
"covenaunt" by another, as the Charters have it—undergirds the enduring conceit
of the written body of Christ, which serves as both medium and message of victory
over the "dead letter" of Scripture embodied by the Jews. If, as David Stern puts it,
certain medieval Christian commentators "seized upon the codex's supersession of
the scroll to express Christianity's supersession of Judaism," the processes of parchment making and use gave Christian theology a more intimate but no less comprehensive metaphorical ground for its successionist imaginings.[51] Unlike Christians,
who write on the insensate skins of "scheep" and "calfe," the "cursid Iewis" here write

on the sensing and suffering flesh of the incarnate god-man. These parchment allegories may represent one of Christianity's most avowedly textualist attempts to reclaim the literal sense from the Jews.

The practice of anthropodermic bibliopegy makes clear that the long, strange history of the animal archive inevitably includes our own rendered bodies as potential medium. For the Christian Middle Ages, the written body of Christ, with its parchment skin stretched and wounded like the hide of a flayed beast, served as a potent symbol, openly celebrated as an inscribed charter of salvation. This symbol was also an allegory, endlessly readable, laden with depths of mimetic significance for saints, visionaries, and other holy persons, and a persistent reminder that even the Son of God might be reduced to the status of sheep or calf—worse, to the status of their flayed and stretched skins.

It is tempting to draw clear and fast distinctions between these two modes of writing on and between the hides of our fellow human creatures: the modern practices of anthropodermic bibliopegy proper and the medieval metaphorics of incarnate writing. One is clearly secularizing, punitive, sometimes revolutionary; the other is sacred, sacrificial, redemptive. Anthropodermic bibliopegy relies on the cold distancing logics of medicalization and punishment, the other on the passionate humanization of a deity. Modern imaginings of the anthropodermic book, too, tend toward spectres of mass atrocity, whether in the tannery at Meudon or in the death camps of World War II. During his deposition in the Nuremberg Trials, Franz Ziereis, commandant of the Nazi complex at Mauthausen-Gusen, reported that two of his fellow officers "had human skin specially tanned on which there were tattoos. From this leather they had books bound, and they had lampshades and leather cases made."[52] The horrifying spectacle of such anthropodermic objects summons the raw utility of the nameless butchered over and against the distinctive and individuated medium of salvific skin.

"Our flesh is tender, our hide is mere lambskin," Nietzsche writes in *Thus Spake Zarathustra*—in a fragment on sacrifice and cannibalism, it turns out, where the philosopher considers the perverse allure of ritual life: "We all bleed on secret sacrificial altars," Nietzsche writes, "we all burn and broil in honor of old idols." The collective "we" here elides the selectivity of such sacrifices, and at whose expense they are enacted. "For man is the cruelest animal," pronounces Zarathustra, an utterance fully attuned to the imaginative and material histories of anthropodermic writing in its diverse incarnations.[53]

⇥ ⇤

CHAPTER ELEVEN

TORAH, TALMUD, TEFILLIN

I go and sow flax seeds and twine nets with the flax, and then I hunt deer
and feed their meat to orphans. Next I prepare parchment from their
hides and I write the five books of the Torah on them.

—*TALMUD BAVA METZIA*

An old fairy tale tells the story of Rabbi Loew of Prague, a chemist and magician reputed to have angels and devils at his command. So intimidating
are the rabbi's dark machinations that he is unable to find a servant willing to move into his home to carry out household and workshop tasks—and so he
decides to create his own. The rabbi fashions a mechanical creature, a feminine figure big and strong, though without life. In order to animate it, the rabbi enlists the
tools of his scriptural craft:

> Carefully, in the silence of his mysterious study at midnight, he wrote out the Unpro-
> nounceable Sacred Name of God on a piece of parchment. Then he rolled it up and
> placed it in the mouth of the creature. Immediately it sprang up and began to move
> like a living thing. It rolled its eyes, waved its arms, and nearly walked through the
> window. In alarm, Rabbi Loew snatched the parchment from its mouth and the crea-
> ture fell helpless to the floor.[1]

Parchment animates the automaton, whose ingestion of the skin and the sacred
word vivifies its limbs. Yet the rabbi brings his mechanical creature to life only to
have her perish in a fire she sets accidentally, after a period in his service: "The creature could not be found, and only when the parchment with the Name, which could
not burn, was discovered amid the ashes, was it known that she had been destroyed
in the conflagration." After the fire, town elders summon the rabbi, rebuke him for

attempting to create life, and threaten him with death. Assuring the leaders of his good intentions, Rabbi Loew creates a second automaton, a golem three times the size of his first creation. But this second creature turns out to be quite malicious, eventually attacking the synagogue, intent on destroying the parchment scrolls of the Torah and its people. Frightened for his own life and for the security of his community, the rabbi finally removes the parchment slip from the creature's mouth, whereupon it clatters lifelessly to the ground.

The story of Rabbi Loew and his automata is one of many legends in Jewish tradition featuring the totemic power of parchment as a locus of miracle, magic, and enlightenment. Giving breath and spirit to inanimate creatures, the divine name inscribed on parchment also deprives them of life through its absence, even while remaining alive in its own way as a medium of inscription capable of surviving catastrophe. Once written with the name of God, these magical scraps of animal skin often cannot burn or otherwise be destroyed, and they maintain a peculiar, often confounding status in many such legends as both symbol and embodiment of the tenuous boundary between life and death.[2] In Hebrew manuscripts of the Middle Ages, too, membrane codices, scrolls, and documents are accorded special status as sites of material connection between the animal, the human, and the divine. In the Coburg Pentateuch from late fourteenth-century German, King Solomon sits enthroned with a membrane scroll on either side (fig. 11.1). To the viewer's right, an unfurled scroll looms over his throne, its outer membranes curled and colored to show depth. On the left, a partially unfurled scroll is chained to the neck of a dog, showing Solomon's legendary intimacy with animals. "As [Solomon] ascended the first step" to his throne, *Midrash Esther Rabba* reads, "a lion stretched out an arm to him; at the second an eagle stretched out an arm."[3] The scrolls share their parchment surface with the page, rendering the visual and tactile face of scroll and codex indistinguishable.

The most compelling and detailed perspectives from the premodern world on parchment in its creaturely materiality derive from Judaic tradition, dating back to the centuries before the Common Era. Transmitted in the Babylonian Talmud and its medieval commentaries and extracanonical tractates, in the mystical branches of the Kabbalah, in the *Mishneh Torah* of Moses Maimonides, and in a series of richly suggestive legends and visual conventions accruing around the materiality of the book, the parchment imaginings of premodern Jewish tradition give us a breathtaking inventory of reflection on the animality of written culture—one too often ignored in accounts of parchment's medieval significance based on exclusively gentile sources, and one to which a brief chapter can hardly do justice. The premodern

Figure 11.1. A double scroll motif with micrography in the Coburg Pentateuch. Central Germany, late fourteenth century. British Library Ms. Additional 19776, fol. 54v (detail).

rabbinic literature on the subject of parchment and its meanings is vast, a poetics and practice of animal skin that has been read, commented upon and reinterpreted continuously over many centuries and generations, even during an era when the use of paper for Hebrew manuscripts became increasingly common.[4] Indeed the vastness and continuity of this heritage is part of the point of this chapter, for in their multiplicity and endurance, these myriad reflections on the written animal are unrivaled among world traditions. Together they aspire to capture the totality of the written world, a sentiment expressed in an ancient figure first put into Hebrew by Rabbi Yohanan ben Zakkai, legendary founder of the religious school at Yavneh in the earliest decades of the Common Era: "If all the skies were parchment, and all the oceans ink, and the wood of all the trees were filed down to pens, it would hardly hardly suffice to imprint, not my wisdom, but the wisdom of my teachers."[5] The sentiment, translated into a variety of ancient and medieval contexts, distantly anticipates Henry Suso's aspiration to write on a celestial field of parchment, though predates even Augustine's vision of the heavens as a scroll unfurled. Yet it speaks to the simultaneous intricacy and vastness of membrane imaginings among Jewish intellectuals in the premodern world: a boundless assemblage of "heavenly archives and parchment fragments," in Eva Mroczek's felicitous phrase, that has much to teach other traditions about the history of parchment as well as the animals, both human and non, whose lives this history has touched.[6]

Massekhet Soferim, or *Tractate of the Scribes*, is one of the so-called minor tractates that accreted around the Babylonian Talmud as the text emerged in the early centuries of the Common Era. *Soferim* likely originated in eighth-century Palestine during the Gaonic period (589–1038 CE), and it concerns the rules and regulations governing the scribal work of the learned men engaged in the copying of Torah scrolls, tefillin, and other written texts used for specific ritual and theological purposes.[7] The tractate weds the quotidian with the ritualistic, the practical with the theological, laying out prescriptions on everything from palimpsests and the treatment of spaces between words to the preparation of Esther scrolls and the disposition of textual variants in the Psalms.[8]

The treatise's first nine chapters concern the physical and material aspects of scribal practice: the treatment and preparation of parchment, the making of scrolls, the forms and size of letters and columns, the storage of written objects, and so on. From the opening passage, *Soferim* specifies with frankness and detail the origin and disposition of animal bodies in written culture, and here the processes of consumption and inscription go hand in hand:

> It is not permitted to write the sacred books, *tefillin* and *mezuzot* on skins of ritually unclean cattle or on skins of ritually unclean wild animals. Nor may they be sewn with their sinews, or the parchment rolls of *tefillin* be wound with their hair. It is an oral prescription delivered to Moses at Sinai that all these shall be written on the skins of ritually clean cattle or ritually clean wild animals, be sewn together with their sinews and the *tefillin* rolls wound with their hair. It is also an oral prescription delivered to Moses at Sinai that the parchments shall be ruled with a reed and the writing on the skin be done with ink. This latter requirement has support in Scripture, *And I wrote them with ink in the book*.[9]

Notable in this opening declaration is the claim of originary antiquity. The treatise follows many rabbinic works from this period in grounding its scribal prescriptions in the authority of the Hebrew Bible, with the implication that the Jewish culture of the biblical epoch inscribed and preserved its written culture on skin. Though the earliest surviving Hebrew manuscripts date from perhaps the fourth century BCE, this forthright claim—that for some fourteen centuries before the Common Era Judaism employed animals for sacred and ritual writing—speaks to the power of parchment as a unifying material vehicle of religious transmission in a culture that would long privilege the importance of orality in its intellectual and ritual life.[10] The passage also specifies the kinds of beasts unfit to receive either the words of scripture or the totemic inscriptions on objects such as teffilin and *mezuzot* (small strips of parchment inscribed with Torah verses and employed as ritual objects). Neither the "skins of ritually unclean cattle" nor the pelts of "wild animals" are permitted for writing, nor may the sinews, hairs, and other parts of these particular creatures be used to bind or secure written objects.

Soferim develops this detailed language of zoological prohibition in dialogue with relevant citations from the Hebrew Bible, read in the treatise as regulatory pronouncements specifically on the usage of animals and their hides for written practice.[11] Passages from Deuteronomy, for instance, underlie an internal dialogue with a rabbi over the propriety of using parchment from animals who die in nonritual ways: "R. Joshua the grits-dealer was asked: 'Why is it permitted to write sacred scrolls on the skins of *nevelot* and *terefot*?'" (1.2). The two terms refer to animals' various modes of death; *nevelot* derives from a biblical chapter on pure and impure foods: "But whatsoever is dead of itself [*nevelot*], eat not thereof" (Deuteronomy 14:21). *Terefot* is a broader term for any food not ritually prepared, and can refer more specifically to an animal killed by mishap or accident (for example, roadkill). "'It is stated,' replied R. Joshua"—citing Deuteronomy 14:21—"'You shall not eat any *nevelah*. Scripture has forbidden it, so what can I do for you?' From here it is inferred that it is permitted to write on skins of *nevelah* and on skins of *terefah* and there is no need to consider the possibility of their having been pierced at the animal's heart." The passage evokes a particular sacrificial practice alleged among the "heathen" in which the heart is removed and burned, an act that would render the entire animal, skin and all, unfit for eating or inscribing—though this circumstance does not rule out the procurement of skins from gentile sources: "Skins for the sacred books, *teffilin* and *mezuzot* may be bought anywhere, and one need not consider the possibility that they might be skins which were pierced at the animal's heart" (1.3).

This concern with the modes of animal death is discernible throughout the myriad rabbinic writings on the subject of parchment. *Soferim* lays out as well some of the technological distinctions between various kinds of parchment that will inform (sometimes confuse) subsequent discussions of the subject for centuries to come: "The writing on *qelaf* must be on the side of the flesh, and on *gevil* it must be on the side of the hair, no deviation from this being permitted. It is an oral prescription delivered to Moses at Sinai that if one changed one for the other, the scroll may not be used for the lection in the statutory services" (1.4). Here the ancient authority of Moses is invoked to distinguish between *qelaf*, or parchment derived from the inner layer of skin (with the outer layer peeled or scraped away, derived from *qlf*, "to peel"); and *gevil*, whole-hide parchment containing both layers, with only the hair side suitable for inscription.[12] *Soferim* specifies that the scripture "may not be written on *diftera* or on erased parchment," a clear reference to palimpsests, implying that prior writing on membrane renders it unfit for scriptural use. Other passages in *Soferim* dictate that Torah scrolls "may not be written in gold" (1.9), nor are those written by people of inferior station, gender, ethnicity, loyalty, or age fit for liturgical use: "A scroll of the Torah that was written by a Sadducee, an informer, a proselyte, a slave, a woman, a madman or a minor may not be used for the lection" (1.13). The tractate brings this concern for the proper treatment and disposition of skins to bear on practices of repair and restoration and even the intermixture of species in a single biblical scroll: "A Torah scroll may not consist of half *gevil* and half *qelaf*, but it may consist of half *gevil* and half *qelaf* of deers, although this is not the best procedure" (2.10).

Many of the rabbinic regulations for the treatment of animal skin in written culture derive from *kashrut*, the regime of dietary laws that govern the selection and handling of food, and it is no accident that the close proximity of culinary and scriptural reasoning is always evident in *Soferim* and elsewhere. In several passages on foodstuffs, the treatise draws an analogy between the covering of food and the protection of the Torah scroll against impurities: "R. Simeon b. Gamaliel says: Any foodstuff which has a protection may be used as a covering. One who writes Torah scrolls may not turn over a sheet on its face because this is disrespectful treatment" (3.14); and later: "Foodstuffs may not be eaten with the aid of foodstuffs unless they are consumed simultaneously. If a scroll cannot be covered with a cloth, it may be turned over on its writing" (3.16). Such concerns over the treatment of inscribed skin extend even to the human body as proscribed writing surface: "If a person writes a divine name on his body, he must neither bathe nor anoint himself nor stand in an unclean place. If he must perform an obligatory immersion, he should wind a reed about it, descend and perform an immersion. R. Jose said: He may at all times descend and perform an immersion in the ordinary way provided he does not rub it off" (5.12).[13] A fascinating detail, according the human hide the same status as animal skin when it comes to the inscription of sacred text.

This intimacy between human and animal skin similarly informs the making and wearing of tefillin, leather-boxed parchment scrolls strapped on the arm and head in fulfillment of biblical verses such as Deuteronomy 6:8: "You shall bind them as a sign upon your hand, and they shall be for a reminder between your eyes." One of the other minor Talmudic tractates, *Tefillin*, is devoted exclusively to this ritual practice, detailing, among other subjects, the rabbinic reasoning behind certain biblical prescriptions: "R. Judah says: It is stated *upon thy hand* and it is also stated in the same verse *between thine eyes* the inference being that as *upon thy hand* refers to a place that is susceptible of ritual uncleanness by one symptom of leprosy, so also *between thine eyes* refers to a place that is susceptible of ritual uncleanness by one symptom of leprosy." These concerns extend even to the relative hirsuteness of the body parts conjoined to the leather-boxed membrane scrolls: "It is stated *between thine eyes* and it is also stated, *Nor make any baldness between your eyes*: as baldness occurs where there is hair on the head so you must put the *tefillah* only where there is hair on the hand."[14] The head and the hand, the hairy and the bald, the animal and the human: in these tractates, parchment forms part of a network of scriptural life grounded in the same ancient authority it incarnates in the present. As Talya Fishman puts it, paraphrasing Sefer Hasidim, "Whether the artisan prepares the parchment, pricks the holes used for ruling lines, plumbs the lines, stitches the quires together, or binds the book, his labors build and maintain written vessels of the sacred."[15]

Despite their complexity, the scribal and ritual guidelines set forth in *Massekhet Soferim*, *Sefer Torah*, and *Tefillin* represent practical, workaday counterparts to the elaborate and intricate treatments of parchment found elsewhere in Talmudic writings. These discussions and disputes unfold across the sixty-three major tractates of the Babylonian Talmud, most voluminously in Tractate Shabbat, which is devoted overall to the interpretation of various decrees (both biblical and rabbinical) having to do with proper behavior on the Sabbath: prohibited acts, special regulations regarding worship, the division of work and the household, and so on. Shabbat echoes many of the same proscriptions found in *Soferim* and *Tefillin*, such as the governing Mosaic injunction concerning animal selection for writing material, the modes of animal death allowing or disallowing its use, and the use of other body parts in the sewing and binding of these ritual objects:

> Our Rabbis taught: *Tefillin* can be written upon the skin of domestic animals and upon the skin of wild beasts, and upon the skin of their *nevelot* or *terefoth*, and they are tied round with their hair, and sewn with their tendons. And it is a *halakhah* from Moses at Sinai that *tefillin* are tied round with their hair and sewn with their tendons.

But we may not write them upon the skin of unclean animals or upon the skin of unclean beasts, and the skin of their *nevelot* and *terefot* need not be stated; nor may they be tied round with their hair or sewn with their tendons. (Shab. 108a)

Folios 79a–b are particularly concerned with regulations for the putting away and carrying out of household goods and ritual objects on the Sabbath, many of them measured by the quantity that would fit in the mouths of various animals: "a cow's mouthful of straw, a camel's mouthful of pea-stalks, a lamb's mouthful of ears of corn, a goat's mouthful of herbs," and so on. The Mishnah (the "base text" of the Talmud, redacted around 200 CE) at one point notes the maximum allowable amount of skin and parchment permitted to be carried out: "Skin, for making an amulet; parchment, for writing thereon the shortest passage of the *tefillin*, which is 'Hear O Israel'." This mention of skin and parchment provokes a discussion in the Gemara (the subsequent rabbinic commentary on the Mishnah) of the relative weights, densities, and sizes of animal hide, which can be dressed or undressed depending on its usage. Concerning parchment in particular, the commentary invokes the three canonical varieties supposedly adumbrated in scripture:

Come and hear: It is a *halakhah* of Moses from Sinai that tefillin should be written upon *qelaf*, and a *mezuzah* upon *dukhsustos*; *qelaf* is the skin on the side of the flesh, and *dukhsustos* is that on the side of the hair?—That is for the most preferable observance of the precept. But it was taught: If one does otherwise, it is unfit?—That refers to the *mezuzah*. But it was taught: If one does otherwise, in either it is unfit?—Both refer to *mezuzah*, one meaning that he wrote it on parchment facing the hair [*qelaf*]; the other, on *dukhsustos* facing the flesh. An alternative answer is: The ruling. If one does otherwise in either, it is unfit . . . For the School of Manasseh taught: If one writes it on paper or on a cloth strip, it is unfit; on parchment, gewil, or *dukhsustos*, it is fit. 'If one writes it'—what? Shall we say, a *mezuzah*; can then a *mezuzah* be written upon *qelaf*? Hence *it* surely means tefillin. Yet even on your reasoning, can tefillin be written upon *gevil*? But that was taught of a Torah Scroll.

Shall we say that the following supports him: When tefillin or a Torah Scroll wear out, a *mezuzah* may not be made of them, because we may not debase [anything] from a higher sanctity to a lower sanctity. Thus there is the reason that we may not debase, but if we might debase, we could make [a *mezuzah*]: now, whereon is it written? Surely it means that it is written on *dukhsustos*?—No: It Is written upon parchment [*qelaf*].—But may a *mezuzah* be written upon *qelaf*?—Yes. And it was taught [likewise]: If one writes it on *qelaf*, on paper, or on a cloth strip, it is unfit. R. Simeon b. Eleazar said: R. Meir used to write it upon *qelaf*, because it keeps [better]. Now that you have arrived at this [conclusion], according to Rab too, do not say. *Dukhsustos* is as *qelaf* but say, *qelaf* is as *dukhsustos*: just as a *mezuzah* may be written upon *dukhsustos*, so may it be written upon *qelaf*.

(SHAB. 79B)

The passage displays an intricate concern with the relative purity or impurity of certain animals, as well as the subtle gradations among the variety of skins depending on the way they have been treated post-butchery. Even so, the evident confusion at several points here regarding the distinctions among *kelaf*, *dukhsustos*, and *gevil* is a common thread in rabbinic discussions of parchment, the subject of some dispute at various points in the Talmud and elsewhere.

Shabbat also takes up more originary questions about parchment in relation to biblically prescribed human relations to animals. The portion of the Mishnah in question concerns the many creatures of the land, sea, and sky mentioned in Leviticus 11, a chapter on clean and unclean foods that would become the primal text for the Jewish practice of *kashrut*, foreseen in the opening verses: "The Lord said to Moses and Aaron, Say to the Israelites: 'Of all the animals that live on land, these are the ones you may eat: You may eat any animal that has a divided hoof and that chews the cud'" (Leviticus 11:1–3). Leviticus 11 goes on to name a number of prohibited animals broken down by category: birds, insects, sea creatures, and "swarming things that swarm on the ground," including rats, mice, and many kinds of lizard. It is this last category with which the relevant section of the Mishnah begins:

Regarding the eight ground-crawlers which are mentioned in the Torah, he who catches or wounds them on the Sabbath is culpable; but as for other abominations and creeping things, he who wounds them is exempt; he who catches them, because he needs them, he is liable; if he does not need them, he is exempt; as for a beast or bird in one's private domain, he who catches it is exempt; he who wounds it is culpable.

(SHAB. 107A)

The Gemara on this intensely zoological passage begins with a dispute over whether these reptiles in Leviticus have skin—woundable skin, that is, distinct and separable from their flesh, and thus, by the logic that guides this strain of interpretation, able to heal (the passage also touches on the permanence of animal wounds). The discussion comes around to the topic of bird skins and wings mentioned in the Mishnah (capitalized here):

A BEAST OR A BIRD, etc. R. Huna said: *Tefillin* may be written upon the skin of a clean bird. R. Joseph demurred: What does he inform us? That it has a skin? But we have already learnt it: HE WHO WOUNDS IT IS CULPABLE?—Said Abaye to him, He informs us much. For if we deduced from our Mishnah, I might object. Since it is perforated all over, it may not be thus used; hence he informs us as they say in the West: Any hole over which the ink can pass is not a hole.

R. Zera objected: *And he shall rend it by the wings thereof* [Leviticus 1:17]: this is to teach that the skin is fit. Now if you think that it is a separate skin, how can Scripture include it?—Said Abaye to him. It is indeed a separate skin, but the Divine Law includes it. Others state, R. Zera said: We too learnt thus: 'By the wings thereof': this is to include the skin. Now, if you say that it is a separate skin, it is well: hence verse is required for including it. But if you say that it is not skin, why is a verse required for including it? Say Abaye to him, In truth I may tell you that it is not a separate skin, yet it is necessary. I might argue, Since it is covered with holes, it is repulsive.

(SHAB. 108A)

This complex interpretation of the Mishnah and its lessons for parchment culture extends even to the anatomy of fowl. Is a bird's skin separate from the bird itself, or do birds not possess skin in the same sense that mammals do—thus rendering even "the skin of a clean bird" unfit for writing? And what about the holes left in bird skin once the creature has been flayed? Whether from wounds or feathers, do such holes render the parchment "unsuitable" for the inscription of sacred text?

The Gemara does not stop with bird parchment at this point. Prompted by a question from the son of Ravina (one of the great early Talmudic sages of the fifth century), the text stages a fascinating exchange over the propriety of using fish skin for ritual inscription:

Mar son of Ravina asked R. Nahman b. Isaac: May *tefillin* be written upon the skin of a clean fish? If Elijah will come and declare, he replied. What does 'if Elijah will come and declare' mean? Shall we say, whether it has a separate skin or not—but we see that it has a skin? Moreover we learnt: The bones of a fish and its skin afford protection in the tent wherein is a corpse! Rather he meant: If Elijah comes and tells us whether its foul smell evaporates or not.

Samuel and Karna were sitting by the bank of the Nehar Malka and saw the water rising and becoming discolored. Said Samuel to Karna, A great man is arriving from the West who suffers from stomach trouble, and the water is rising to give him a wlecome. Go and smell his bottle! So he went and met Rav. He asked him, How do we know that *tefillin* may be written only on the skin of a clean animal? Because it is written, *that the Law of the Lord may be in thy mouth* [Exodus 13:9], meaning of that which is permitted in thy mouth, he replied.

(SHAB. 108A)

As in the earlier discussion of avian parchment, one of the points of confusion here concerns the anatomy of fish skin as part of the creature's body. The rabbis seem to be disputing the precise nature of this "separate skin." The bones and skin of a fish may have some kind of power to ward off evil in the presence of a dead body, and should perhaps be regarded as suitably clean material for tefillin. The prohibition against the medium's usage for writing, however, concerns smell: the foul secretions and odors naturally emitted by the skin of a fish (presumably even after it has been rendered into parchment, though the passage is more musing than practical). The speculation on piscine membrane nevertheless prompts the wonderful anecdote that follows, involving a great man's arrival with the rising of a river. "Go and smell his bottle!" Samuel directs Karna, a proverb meant to imply a testing of the learned man's mind. In answering Karna's query, Rav enlists a verse from Exodus to fuse the practices of diet, writing, and ritual into a single decree that puts Tractate Shabbat's parchment questions to rest.

The Babylonian Talmud contains many such deliberations on the nature and meaning of parchment for Jewish ritual life, nearly always conveyed with a sense of speculative openness, and often with a dark humor befitting the subject. In a discussion of the technicalities of biblical writing, a rabbi is asked about the proper size and make-up of scriptural text, and in particular the amount of parchment required to make a Torah scroll. His reply suggests a careful attention to slight gradations in the quality of rendered skins: "With thick parchment, six handbreadths, with thin parchment I do not know. R. Huna wrote seventy scrolls of the Law and hit the exact measurement with only one. R. Aha b. Jacob wrote one on calf's skin, and hit it exactly. The Rabbis looked at him enviously and he died" (Bava Batra 14a). The precise fit of animal hide to biblical scroll serves here as a measure of moral worth, a sensibility reinforced in a dispute found in Tractate Hullin concerning the problem of animal skin naturally riddled with hair follicles. "Surely it is necessary that the writing be perfect, and it is not so?" a commentator inquires. The gloss initially responds in the affirmative: "Since the hair penetrates the hide the parchment made from it must perforce be full of holes, and any writing on it must be interrupted as the pen passes over these holes, and this invalidates the scroll." But, the Gemara counter-objects, "In raising this objection he must have overlooked the statement of the Rabbis in the West, viz., any hole in parchment over which the ink can pass is not considered a hole," an assessment affirmed in the subsequent comment on the passage: "The holes are so minute that the pen passes smoothly over them, even the ink does not collect in these holes"—thus rendering the membrane in question a legitimate surface for inscription (Hullin 119b).

The major and minor tractates of the Talmud, then, offer a wide-ranging yet intimate and often self-contradictory body of commentary on the animality of written culture. At least in spirit, these Talmudic teachings on parchment governed the spirituality and craft of writing in Jewish culture through the early centuries of the Common Era and well into the second millennium, when commentators such as the French rabbi and scholar Rashi (1040–1105 CE) added their own exegetical interventions to these rabbinic guidelines while attempting to clarify the commentary tradition toward various ends. Crucial to this effort was the work of Moses Maimonides, the twelfth-century rabbi-philosopher who would exert a transformative effect on Talmudic interpretation for centuries to come through the *Mishneh Torah*, his great systematization of Talmudic teachings, oral law, and observance that has much to say about the creaturely medium. Writing from Egypt in a moment of profound intellectual change, Maimonides embodied what Colette Sirat has called "a turning point in the history of texts" and their technologies.[16]

Mishneh Torah contains an influential section of *halakhot* or rules titled "Laws of Tefillin, Mezuzah, and Torah Scrolls," aimed at codifying prior teachings on animal membrane into a body of guidelines aimed at *soferim*, rabbis, and others involved in the life of parchment. Maimonides writes extensively about the preparation of skin, expanding on those portions of the Talmud that speak to the relation of animal flesh to the present life of sacred texts. In the process he sharpens several of the Mosaic rules governing the disposition of parchment, beginning with a typology of animal skin:

> 6. There are three types of parchment: *gevil, qelaf,* and *dukhsustos.* What is implied? The hide of a domesticated or wild animal is taken. First, the hair is removed from it. Afterwards, it is salted and then prepared with flour. Then resin and other substances which cause the skin to contract and become harder are applied to it. In this state, it is called *gevil.*

> 7. After the hair is removed, the hide may be taken and divided in half in the manner known to the parchment processors. Thus, there are two pieces of parchment: a thin one, which is on the side where the hair grew, and a thicker one, on the side of the

flesh. After it has been processed using salt, then flour, and then resin and the like, the portion on the side where the hair grew is called *qelaf* and the portion on the side of the flesh is called *dukhsustos*.

8. It is a halakhah transmitted to Moses on Mount Sinai that a Torah scroll should be written on *gevil* on the side on which the hair had grown. When *tefillin* are written on *qelaf*, they should be written on the side of the flesh. When a *mezuzah* is written on *dukhsustos*, it should be written on the side of the hair. Whenever one writes on *qelaf* on the side of the hair or on *gevil* or *dukhsustos* on the side of the flesh, it is unacceptable.[17]

Following the often contradictory guidelines laid down in the Talmud, Maimonides attempts to clarify once and for all the distinctions among the three types of hide (whole, skin side, flesh side) used or prohibited in the making of scrolls, *mezuzahs*, and *teffilin*. What is particularly notable here are the injunctions against writing certain sacred texts or textual instruments on the flesh-facing side of skin. According to Maimonides, a Torah scroll may be written only on the hair side of *gevil*: that is, on the hair side of unsplit, whole-hide parchment. Tefillin, by contrast, should be written on *klaf*: on the layer of prepared skin that has been sundered from the flesh-facing side, distancing the written text as far as possible from the inner flesh of the rendered beast. While *mezuzahs* alone may be written on *dukhsustos*—that is, by Maimonides's definition (contradicting some prior definitions), on that half of split hide that once faced the flesh—they must be written on the hair side of the flesh side.

Here and elsewhere in the *Mishneh Torah*, we can discern a will to instill a particular kind of purity in parchment scripture and ritual instruments. Such regulations are in striking contrast to medieval Christian discourse concerning parchment, which rarely distinguishes between the hair sides and the flesh sides of membrane, and (as far as I am aware) never does so in the intricate legalistic terms guiding the rabbinic dictates found in the Talmud, the *Mishneh Torah*, and elsewhere. For Maimonides, the natural and typological distinctions among mammal, fish, and fowl are less important than the moral writability of their respective flesh, determined in varying degrees by their mode of butchery, the processing of their corpses, and the appearance and feel of their skin once rendered into parchment:

10. [Torah] scrolls, *tefillin*, and *mezuzot* may not be written on hide from a non-kosher animal, fowl, or wild animal. One may write on the hides of [all] kosher animals, wild beasts, and fowl. This applies even when these animals died without being ritually

slaughtered or when they were killed by wild beasts. We may not write on the skin of a kosher fish because of the foul secretions, since the processing of the skin will not cause the foul secretions to cease.

20. The following rules apply to parchment which has holes: One should not write over a hole. If, however, ink passes over the hole without seeping through, the presence of the hole is of no consequence, and one may write upon it. Accordingly, if the skin of a fowl has been processed, it is permissible to write upon it. The following rules apply when a parchment becomes perforated after it has been written on: If the perforation is within the inside of a letter—e.g., in the space inside a *heh*, inside a *mem*, or inside any of the other letters—it is acceptable.[18]

The tenth halakhah repeats the familiar scriptural distinctions among kosher and non-kosher animals, as well as among those who die a "natural" death or are slain by predators, while also returning to the controversy over fish skin as writing surface. In the twentieth Maimonides expounds a kind of avian codicology already familiar from *Soferim* and portions of the Talmud's major tractates. The result is a remarkably frank approach to the haptic aesthetic and the penetrability of the membrane writing surface that accounts closely for the relationship between animal medium and sacred message.

In Kabbalistic mysticism, too, parchment appears as an object of totemic veneration and magical usage, embodied in membrane amulets and captured in descriptions of love spells and charms. The Torah itself was often imagined by its readers and commentators as a "living organism," in the words of the great Kabbalistic scholar Gershom Scholem, "a living fabric" capable of generating leaves, branches, roots, teeming with the flora and fauna of the world.[19] At the same time, the Torah is seen to predate the very existence of the material world, its animal skin medium almost an encumbrance at times—though a necessary and vital one for its perdurance. As *Midrash ʿAseret ha-Dibberot* has it, "On what was the primordial Torah written? On parchment? But the animals had not been created yet, so how could one use their skins for parchment? Maybe on gold or silver? But the metals had not been created, refined, or unearthed! Maybe on wooden tablets? But the trees had not yet been created! So what was it written on? It was written with black fire on white fire and wrapped around the right arm of the Holy One, as it is written: 'On His right arm fiery law' [Deuteronomy 33:2]."[20]

Such passages exemplify the status of parchment as both a totemic object like the mezuzah and a sacrificial garment embodying scripture's metonymic intimacy with human skin, a concatenation that informs numerous early Jewish legends, many of them found in the Babylonian Talmud. One of the Ten Martyrs under Emperor Hadrian, according to a story told in Tractate Avodah Zarah, was Rabbi Hanina, whose death takes place just after the burial of Rabbi Ben Kisma. On their return from the deceased rabbi's burial, the persecuting Romans found Rabbi Hanina reading the Torah while "keeping a scroll of Law in his bosom."

> They took hold of him, wrapped him in the scroll of the Torah, placed bundles of branches round him and set them on fire. They then brought tufts of wool, which they had soaked in water, and placed them over his heart, so that he should not expire quickly. His daughter exclaimed, "Father, that I should see you in this state!" He replied, "If it were I alone being burnt it would have been a thing hard to bear; but now that I am burning together with the Scroll of Torah, He who will have regard for the plight of the Torah will also have regard for my plight." His disciples called out, "Rabbi, what do you see?" He answered them, "The parchments are being burnt but the letters are soaring on high." . . . The Executioner then said to him, "Rabbi, if I raise the flame and take away the tufts of wool from over thy heart, will thou cause me to enter into the life to come?" "Yes," he replied. "Then swear unto me," he said. He swore unto him. He thereupon raised the flame and removed the tufts of wool from over his heart, and his soul departed. The executioner then jumped and threw himself into the fire and burned. And a heavenly voice came out and said: "R. Hanina b. Teradion and the executioner have been invited to the world to come." Rabbi wept and said: "One may acquire eternal life in a single hour, another after many years."
> (AVODAH ZARAH 18A)

The scene of execution involves an intimate and fiery contact between the body of the victim and the membrane scroll, which wraps the rabbi in its scriptural embrace—only to perish along with the rabbi even as the words of the Torah float free, along with the rabbi's soul.[21]

Parchment's uncanny human attachments figure as well in an anonymous theurgic manual from medieval Germany, the "Book of the Putting On and Fashioning of the Mantle of Righteousness" (known as the *Sefer ha-Malbush*, or *Book of the Garment*). At one point the magical text describes a ritual involving a "garment of deerskin parchment inscribed with the magical names of God." An adept dons the parchment garment and performs a series of observations that test his purity (including seven days of a strict vegetarian diet), the performance as a whole enacting the ritual substitution of man for animal.[22] Several early stories feature parchment in scenes of postmortem animation. One such account, preserved in the *Chronicle of Ahimaaz* (Italy, ca. 1050), concerns a cantor who was unable to enunciate the name of God because he was already dead, though his body somehow remained active and functioning. The cantor relates that he had been taken from his mother years before, and a vow had been made that he would be returned to her before he died—but his death would have made such a return impossible, so the name of God was inscribed on a piece of parchment and inserted beneath the skin of his arm. With his last words, the figure of the cantor describes the process and its aftermath:

> "When they saw [my master's] sorrow and mournful tears, they wrote the Holy Name which was written in the Sanctuary, they made an incision in the flesh of my right arm and in the place where they cut the flesh they placed the Name; so I came safely from there, I returned to my home and my mother, and as long as Master Ahima'az lived I fled from isles unto isles. Now I live on ever since those days, if I so desire, forever, for no man can know the place where the Name is, unless I reveal it. But I shall show you and here I am in your hands, do with me as you see fit." Then they brought the shroud, he got up onto it and showed them the place of the incision, the Master made there an incision and extracted from within the Name, and the body was left without soul and the inanimate body fell decayed as if it had been decaying for many years and the flesh returned to dust.[23]

The *Chronicle of Ahimaaz* also tells of a Rabbi Hananeel whose cousin has been turned into a golem, a being dead yet animated by an inscribed parchment inserted beneath his tongue: "To prevent the body from decomposing and becoming putrid, he wrote upon a piece of parchment the Name of God, his master, and placed the parchment under the dead man's tongue." Eager for his cousin to return fully to the dead, the rabbi takes sober measures: "In sadness and anguish R. Hananeel then approached his cousin and said, 'Raise thy mouth, that I may kiss thee.' The body opened his mouth. R. Haneneel, kissing him, put his hand under his tongue, and took therefrom the Name written on the skin. As soon as the Name was taken from him, his body fell back upon the bed. So the body returned to dust and decay, and the soul returned to God who gave it."[24] The story picks up on the same tradition of parchment as an agent of preservation and even resurrection, a not uncommon motif in medieval legends that enlist animal membrane to embody the often tenuous boundary between death and life. The skin of the beast is the mere instrument and medium, a burnable thing that will leave only the words of scripture intact once it perishes; yet this skin also functions as an engine of mysterious life.

What unites these diverse discourses in Jewish tradition about parchment over many centuries—its origin and nature, its preparation, its usage in the inscription of sacred text, its phenomenal dimensions as written medium—is the emphatic persistence of the beast as a vital and fully avowed dimension of the text's enduring existence and role in the world. The Jewish commentary and folk traditions long ago developed and have since sustained over (at least) two millennia a creaturely materialism with respect to written culture, one that shows up in both creative and practical ways across myriad genres and that places unique value on the ritually slaughtered animals whose remains somehow retain the life-giving force of the divine. Jewish divinatory practices, too, relied for centuries on quite precise specifications of the type of animal use for ritual inscription: a name should be written on the skin of a gazelle [*in pergameno algacel*] if on a Saturday; a divination of Solomon should be inscribed "on the skin of a black or white goat" [*in pelle caprioli nigri vel silvestris*], and "the skin should also be hairy and round" [*pillosa et rotunda*].[25]

In the background of many of these sources is that originary substitution of ram for man, a substitution that reveals a fascinating commonality in the Abrahamic religions regarding the very invention of parchment as the privileged medium of divine writing. The primal moment of human-animal displacement occurs in what the Jewish tradition calls the Akedah, the "binding" of Isaac in Genesis 22:

> And Abraham stretched forth his hand, and took the knife to slay his son. And the angel of the Lord called unto him out of heaven, and said: "Abraham, Abraham." And he said: "Here am I." And he said: "Lay not thy hand upon the lad, neither do thou any thing unto him; for now I know that thou art a God-fearing man, seeing thou hast not withheld thy son, thine only son, from Me." And Abraham lifted up his eyes, and looked, and beheld behind him a ram caught in the thicket by his horns. And Abraham went and took the ram, and offered him up for a burnt-offering in the stead of his son.
>
> (GENESIS 22:10–13)

The divinely prescribed substitution of the animal for the human in the Abrahamic tradition leads to that widespread, primal recognition in these sacrificial creeds that the object of offering might have been Isaac—that is, that it might have been us.[26] This originary substitution has given the Hebrew Bible a foundational but contested role in discussions of animal dignity, rights, and compassion over against the

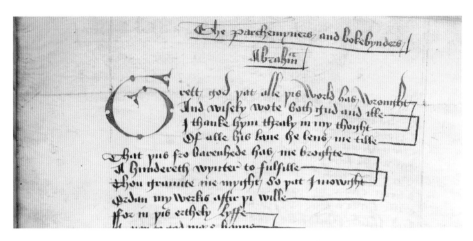

Figure 11.2. Opening lines of the play of Abraham and Isaac from the York Plays, performed by the "Parchemyners and Bokebynders." York, late fifteenth or early sixteenth century. London, British Library Ms. Additional 35290, fol. 32r (detail).

bare fact of animal sacrifice.[27] Rashi avows that after this moment in which God intervened to save his son from sacrifice, Abraham, in every subsequent ritual performance with the ram, prayed to God and said, "May this be acceptable to thee as it had been done on my son . . . as if his blood had been spilled, as if his skin had been torn off, as if he had been burnt and become ashes."[28]

Bookish stories of this sacrificial substitution appear in numerous guises in some of the foundational texts of Judaism, Christianity, and Islam. In the Christian exegetical culture of Late Antiquity, the ram from the Abraham-Isaac story becomes the Word made flesh, as in a letter of St. Ambrose to Justus, bishop of Lyons, written in 381 CE: "Now the ram is the Word, full of tranquillity, moderation, and patience; whereby is shown that Wisdom is a good sacrifice, and that He was well skilled in the mode of meritorious propitiation."[29] There may be a distant echo of the same conflation in late medieval drama. Though none of the six surviving Middle English and Cornish plays representing the story of Abraham and Isaac make any direct mention of parchment, the York play of Abraham and Isaac (see fig. 11.2) was performed by the "Parchemyners and Bokebynders," in one of those crafty homologies for which medieval theater is renowned.[30] During the Enlightenment (perhaps earlier), a popular legend grew around the origin of the Qur'ān, a story in which "God sent the Koran to Mohammed by the angel Gabriel, written on a parchment made of the skin of the ram which Abraham sacrificed instead of his son" (see chap. 3 above).

Perhaps the most direct realization of this translation of ram to book occurs in a Jewish legend appearing in different forms in the Babylonian Talmud, the Midrash, and the Kabbalistic tradition. The story concerns an episode in the life of Shimon bar Yohai, a Mishnaic sage and rabbi active in the last decades of the first century of the Common Era following the destruction of the Temple. A respected teacher and interpreter, Shimon bar Yohai was renowned in later legends as a great Kabbalist, and was even credited (spuriously) with the authorship of the *Zohar* by Moses de León in the thirteenth century. Persecuted and sought by the Romans, the rabbi hides with his son in a cave for fifteen years. In the cave the rabbi and his son study the Torah, plumbing its mysteries as they encounter a number of marvels. One of them concerns the origins of the *Zohar* itself:

> Then a day came when Elijah the Prophet arrived at the cave to study with Rabbi Shimon and his son. Elijah revealed great mysteries that had never been spoken of outside of heaven. And in the days that followed Elijah often returned, and Shimon bar Yohai wrote down those mysteries on parchment that Elijah brought them, which came from the ram that Abraham had sacrificed on Mount Moriah. Now that was an enchanted parchment, for it expanded to receive his words as Shimon bar Yohai wrote. And every letter he inscribed there burned in black fire on white. And the name of the book that he wrote down there, filled with the celestial mysteries, was the *Zohar*.[31]

By the story's compelling logic, the greatest result of Abraham's sacrifice was the invention of a creaturely medium that would make its written preservation possible. The parchment rendered from the ram of the Akedah is the originary writing surface, the membrane that miraculously expands to embrace the entirety of the *Zohar* and sustains Kabbalistic written tradition for perpetuity. The story has much in common with the legend of St. Ciarán and his dun cow, though in this case the rendered animal dies a sacrificial rather than a natural death.

The concatenation of the sacrificial ram and the membrane book receives one of its most intriguing visualizations in an early fourteenth-century Hebrew Bible known as the Duke of Sussex's German Pentateuch.[32] The book contains the text of the Torah accompanied throughout by the Masorrah, an ancient notation system that served as a guide to writing and recitation found in many medieval Hebrew Bibles. On the folio containing most of the Akedah (fig. 11.3), a ram stands at the bottom of the page, its horns caught in a bush, emphasizing that part of the story most concerned with animal-human substitution.[33] More than a mere illustration, though, this ram is part of both the story and its interpretation. For this written

Figure 11.3. Genesis 22:1–9 with masora, decorated with entangled ram from the Akedah in micrography, from the Duke of Sussex's German Pentateuch. Southern Germany, first quarter of the fourteenth century. London, British Library Ms. Additional 15282, fol. 28r.

Figure 11.4. Detail of figure 11.3.

animal is created out of words, written in Hebrew and Aramaic micrography, a common medieval practice of crafting images out of the masoretic and biblical texts (see detail, fig. 11.4). The animal written on parchment acknowledges the divine gift of animal skin that will make up this and indeed every other sacred text in the epoch of parchment. There is no allegory here; instead there is a kind of grateful and graphic acknowledgment of the donor animal for the sacrifice that made possible the words that the beast and its progeny bear on their skin. The written ram here is still living, its life fully available to the viewer even as its death, eyes wide open, creates the sacred membrane page on which this written creature will survive. In its sacrificial immanence, the animal medium is the message of cultural inheritance.

CHAPTER TWELVE

SHAKESPEARE'S PARCHMENTS,
IN LIFE AND DEATH

The law endlessly writes itself on bodies. It engraves itself on parchments
made with the skin of its subjects. It articulates them into a juridical
corpus. It makes them its book.
—MICHEL DE CERTEAU, "TOOLS FOR BODY WRITING"

On March 10, 1613, William Shakespeare went in with three partners on
the purchase of the Blackfriars gatehouse, a residence located above the
gate of the former Dominican priory and near the Puddle Dock wharf,
directly across the Thames from the Globe Theater. To finance the transaction, the
playwright put in £80 of his own funds, which were supplemented by a mortgage of
£60 from the seller, Henry Walker, "citizen and minstrel of London," and guaranteed by the other purchasers acting as trustees.[1] Whether Shakespeare ever lived in
the Blackfriars gatehouse is unknown, as is the exact purpose of the property in relation to his ongoing work with the Blackfriars Theatre located in the same precinct.

The mundane facts of this famous transaction itself, however, are well known,
thanks to the survival of three parchment documents recording the sale: the original indenture, a copy provided to the seller, and the mortgage agreement securing Shakespeare's funding from his partners.[2] The three documents specify, among
other elements of the contract, the purchase price, conveyances, the urban location
of the house and property in relation to local landmarks, mortgage provisions, and
the date of purchase, stated in the indenture's formulaic opening (see fig. 12.1):

This Indenture made the Tenthe day of March, in the yeare of our Lord god according to the Computac[i]on of the Church of England one thowsand six hundred and
twelve, and in the yeares of the reigne of our Sovereigne Lord Iames by the grace of
god king of England, Scotland, ffraunce, and Ireland defender of the faithe &c that
is to saie of England, ffraunce, and Ireland the tenth, and of Scotland the six and for-

Figure 12.1. Henry Walker, Bargain and sale from Henry Walker, citizen and minstrel of London, to William Shakespeare of Stratford-upon-Avon, Gent., and to his trustees, William Johnson, citizen and vintner of London, John Jackson, and John Hemmyng of London, Gentlemen (1612/13 March 10). Washington, D.C., Folger Shakespeare Library Ms. Z.c.22.

tith; Betweene Henry Walker Citizein and Minstrell of London of th'one partie, And William Shakespeare of Stratford vpon Avon in the countie of Warwick gentleman, William Iohnson Citizein and Vintener of London, Iohn Jackson, and Iohn Hem[m]yng of London gentlemen of th'other partie.[3]

The indenture goes on to specify the physical inclusions that came with the gatehouse, among them "that plott of ground on the west side" of the tenement, "lately inclosed wth boord[es] on two sides" and on "the third side inclosed wth an olde bricke wall," the "voyde ground" previously used as a garden, as well as the "soyle" on which the house stood.

The three records of the Blackfriars gatehouse purchase are unremarkable in themselves, the sort of commonplace instruments of legal contract extant in the many millions from the period, though they have come to assume a special place in the modern understanding and appreciation of Shakespeare's life. Two of these re-cords, the original deed of sale and the mortgage indenture, bear Shakespeare's sig-nature, which has otherwise survived in just four instances. Another signature ap-pears among the parchment records of a legal case in 1612, *Bellot v. Mountjoy*, for which Shakespeare signed a deposition of evidence attesting to his role in a fam-ily dispute. There are also three instances of Shakespeare's signature on his original will (made March 25, 1616), which was written on paper before its inscription into a parchment register of wills at the Prerogative Court of Canterbury in London. The only other specimen of Shakespeare's writing known to survive occurs in the man-uscript of *Sir Thomas More*, a collaborative draft (again on paper) of a theater piece that includes a three-page scene likely in his hand.[4]

Though paper was of course the dominant medium of writing and printing in early modern England, parchment continued to play a central role during the period as an official medium of juridical life: a "court of record" was always understood as one whose "acts and judicial proceedings are enrolled in parchment for a perpetual memorial and testimonial."[5] Membrane made up the bulk of legal records of prop-erty ownership and contract, the records and rolls of courts and parliament, and many other written forms governing the relations among persons and institutions. Parchment subtended a large part of written law and on its surface were traced the institutional contours of innumerable official lives. An integral part of the fabric of early modern written culture, then, animal skin forms part of the common ground-work of English legal and documentary culture, as it had since the early Middle Ages, and indeed as it would down into the nineteenth century. As we saw in chap-ter 6, the Public Record Office in London and the numerous county and munici-pal archives are florid with membrane records of transactions both small and grand, some recorded on full, uncut hides straight from the parchmenter's frame, others on snipped-up scraps of animal skin no larger than a Post-it note. And as archivists at these repositories acknowledge, the persistence of early modern parchment in such quantity is due in part to the distinctive quality of membrane as a particularly du-rable medium.

In Shakespeare's case, the parchment record preserves many of the basic facts that scholars have been able to establish about his biography. The first recorded ap-

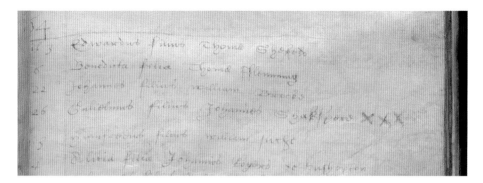

Figure 12.2. William Shakespeare's baptism recorded and highlighted in the parchment parish register of Holy Trinity Church, Stratford-upon-Avon, April 26, 1564. Shakespeare Birthplace Trust, Stratford-upon-Avon, Ms. DR243/1.

pearance of any form of William Shakespeare's name occurs in the parish register of Holy Trinity Church in Stratford-upon-Avon, on the recto of the fifth parchment folio, where his baptism as *Guilielmus filius Johannes Shakspere* (William, son of John Shakespeare) is recorded as occurring on April 26, 1564, scored by a later and perhaps excited reader with three crosses (see fig. 12.2). The register is just one of dozens of membrane records in various forms, sizes, and genres that make up a good portion of the historical evidence attesting to the official lives of Shakespeare and his immediate family. These include pipe rolls, subsidy rolls, account books, cases in the courts of Chancery, King's Bench, and Common Pleas, surveys of manors and boroughs, writs, pleas, records of fines and rents, chamberlains' accounts, precepts and recognizances, writs and feet of fines, and numerous other parchment instruments and records attesting to the various ways that William Shakespeare and his family members moved through the institutions that shaped a good part of their lives.[6] Legal record-keeping, as Kathryn James puts it, "was an important engine of manuscript culture in early modern England, governing every aspect of life," including Shakespeare's.[7] The playwright's own written life, his own biography—from the Greek *bios*, life, and *graphia*, record or account—was one of many that in turn generated and justified the surviving membrane record of the age. An official human life, a life filled with actions and events that both produce and enter the written record, is a life dependent on the lives and bodies of animals for its recording and remembrance.

Take, for example, the registered copy of Shakespeare's will, copied in the Prerogative Court of Canterbury in June 1616 (fig. 12.3). The membrane has been cut from an end piece, as suggested by the slight curve at the lower right of the recto.

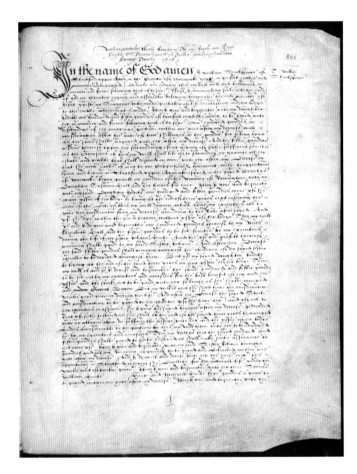

Figure 12.3. Will of William Shakespeare, Gentleman of Stratford-upon-Avon. Prerogative Court of Canterbury, Warwickshire (registered copy), made June 22, 1616. Kew, National Archives, PROB 11/127, fol. 466r.

The verso (fig. 12.4) shows extensive veining in the lower margin, where hair follicles swarm among dusts of finishing chalk on a leathery surface, gouged with old flaws, torn, wrinkled, scratched. The parchment records the desires of the famous testator regarding the disposition of his material life: property, clothing, plate, furniture, and jewels, as well as shillings bequeathed to friends and relations in order to purchase rings. The will embodies the remnants of a man and the remains of an animal, joined together in an instrument that commends Shakespeare's own "bodye" to "the Earthe whereof yt is made."

The professional affiliations of Shakespeare's father would have exposed him daily to the early modern trade in animal skin; as Anston Bosman puts it memorably, "Shakespeare was born into leather."[8] An administrative record from October 10, 1592, names "John Shackspeare, glover" as the subject of a bond; the membrane document bears both his mark and the seal of his ring.[9] Leather gloves and parchment records speak to distinct if complementary sides of the skin trade, the tanner and the parchmenter processing fresh hides in their craft. Like a pair of gloves, the two parts of an indenture of sale (such as the one marking Shakespeare's purchase of the Blackfriars gatehouse) are commodities of skin, each crafted from animal membrane via a specialized artisanal process into a specific form required by their human users. Unlike gloves, however, such documents are not intended to be ephemeral or subject to daily use; they are intended, rather, to survive long after their immediate inscription and authentication, as more or less permanent records of a transaction among and for the subjects creating them. Though they are base things of the body, their transhistorical survival is a testament to both intentional archival preservation and the limits of human memory for which they are saved to compensate.

It is just this super-mundane and quasi-transcendent dimension of parchment that most crucially distinguishes it from other commodities rendered from animal skin in Shakespeare's day: gloves, shoes, saddlery. At the same time, parchment carries a particular juridical and imaginative charge inseparable from its organic derivation from skin and, in certain cases, from its discernible animality. The word *parchment* appears just nine times in the Shakespearean corpus, in eight plays; the word *vellum* appears not at all, despite the growing resonances of the term in early modern England as a distinctive reference to finer sheets supposedly rendered from calfskin. *Paper*, by contrast, appears in over one hundred places, in both the plays and the sonnets, with a looser range of associations than those accruing to its more

Figure 12.4. Detail of Shakespeare's will, fol. 466v.

elusive membrane counterpart.[10] Shakespeare collocates the two terms just once, in a speech by King Edward III in praise of the Countess of Salisbury. After a drum plays offstage, the king declares his infatuation with the wife of his earl:

> What drum is this that thunders forth this march
> To start the tender Cupid in my bosom?
> Poor sheepskin how it brawls with him that beateth it!
> Go, break the thund'ring parchment-bottom out
> And I will teach it to conduct sweet lines
> Unto the bosom of a heavenly nymph;
> For I will use it as my writing paper,
> And so reduce him from a scolding drum,
> To be the herald, and dear counsel-bearer,
> Betwixt a goddess and a mighty king.[11]

The lines play on the variegated meanings accruing to parchment in the Shakespearean corpus: as a "Poor sheepskin" that forms part of a percussion instrument; as a vibrant membrane that "brawls" with the anger of the drum-beater; and as a "writing paper" that will "conduct sweet lines" as a medium of inscription. The metaphor, which wonderfully conflates two mediums, reduces paper to a kind of secondary status: anything can be paper, but only parchment can be parchment, capable of mediating between "a goddess and a mighty king," the divine and the human. Here and elsewhere in the plays, parchment serves as a kind of inflection point, bending the thematic and moral arc of a scene toward searching issues of animality and memory, written law and human subjection: John of Gaunt bemoaning the corrupt state of the realm, Dromio of Ephesus critiquing the brutality of slavery, Hamlet pondering death and remembrance. No two of these parchment figurations are quite alike, yet all share a certain emphasis on the uncanny if often latent potential of membrane as a medium of transition or transformation: from the transitory to the eternal, the human to the animal, the living to the dead.

"Nor brass nor stone nor parchment": *A Winter's Tale*

Leontes, King of Sicily, a jealous man, has convinced himself that his pregnant wife Hermione has taken up with his old chum Polixenes, King of Bohemia. Polixenes has recently extended his visit to the island at Hermione's urging. Though Leontes, too, wants his royal friend to remain in Sicily, the banter between his wife and Polixenes arouses his suspicions—and soon enough his rage. Leontes summons Camillo, a Sicilian nobleman and counselor of admirable moral character, to carry out his vengeance. Acting in his capacity as cupbearer at court, Camillo will poison the visiting king: so orders Leontes, who promises in turn to put his wrath against his wife to rest and "give no blemish to her honor."

Leontes then exits the stage, leaving Camillo alone to contemplate the murderous directive. Torn with indecision, he voices empathy for the queen before raising larger questions about the lessons of precedent on the subject of regicide:

> O miserable lady! But, for me,
> What case stand I in? I must be the poisoner
> Of good Polixenes; and my ground to do't
> Is the obedience to a master, one
> Who in rebellion with himself will have
> All that are his so too. To do this deed,
> Promotion follows. If I could find example
> Of thousands that had struck anointed kings
> And flourish'd after, I'ld not do't; but since
> Nor brass nor stone nor parchment bears not one,
> Let villany itself forswear't. I must
> Forsake the court: to do't, or no, is certain
> To me a break-neck. Happy star, reign now!
> (1.2)

Camillo makes his decision quickly in these enjambment-rich lines. To kill Polixenes means obeying a king who, torn from himself with rage, threatens to create the same condition of inner division in those who follow his lethal commands. Yet it also means some form of "promotion," or royal favor, the coin of the realm for an advising lord such as Camillo. What to do?

Perhaps, Camillo speculates, history will provide a guide, and so in the precise midpoint of the soliloquy his thoughts move to the problem of exemplarity. Even if he could find in history a thousand aspiring regicides who had accomplished their homicidal mission and thrived in the aftermath, he "'ld not do't," presumably constrained by his own personal sense of ethics. Since there are no precedents recorded on brass, stone, or parchment, he will let "villainy itself" warn him away from even contemplating the evil task. Faced with such an easy decision, Camillo vows to leave the court and take his chances in exile.

"Nor brass nor stone nor parchment": parchment as medium, one of three potential bearers of historical precedent. Brass and stone evoke the architectural and plastic modes of exemplarity, in the form of stone sculptures and reliefs, brass effigies, monuments, plaques; parchment represents the bookish and historiographical modes, the written histories of kings and their killers, and also the juridical records of the trials, pleadings, and sentences of their assassins—though few if any who got away with the dastardly deed of regicide. Each of the three mediums implies permanence, activated through distinctive acts of remembrance.

The play's later acts keep these concretizing modes of moral instruction at play, embodied in the various written instruments summoned as the story unfolds. After the departure of Camillo with Polixenes, Hermione gives birth only to see King Leontes order their newborn daughter to be abandoned in the wilderness. Hermione seemingly dies of sorrow, only to return at the end of Act V as a figure frozen in stone who comes to life again after her bereft royal husband recognizes her form—and asks for a rebuke: "Chide me, dear stone, that I may say indeed / Thou art Hermione" (5.3). Meanwhile Shakespeare captures the drama of bookish exemplarity in the idiom of pastoral. Perdita, the abandoned child of Leontes and Hermione, is raised as "a shepherd's daughter" in a rural part of Bohemia among meadows and flocks, though no less susceptible to corruption. "I'll be with you at your sheep-shearing too," vows the pickpocket Autolycus to the character of the Clown, natural son of Hermione's adoptive father. Autolycus vows the Clown will be "flayed alive" even as he prepares to "fleece" the crowd expected for a sheep shearing: "if I make not this cheat bring out another and the shearers prove sheep, let me be unrolled and my name put in the book of virtue!" (4.4). Appropriately, in the brief fourth scene of Act IV, Florizel, Hermione's suitor, praises her transformation at "this your sheep-shearing," anticipating the translation of her person from humble shepherd's daughter to princess.

Sheep, wool, skin, scroll, book: this series of metonymic associations summons the "parchment" from 1.2 on which Camillo searches in vain for homicidal precedent. The medium of notoriety is also a mechanism of a conjured forgetting, as Autolycus imagines himself "unrolled" or scratched out from the membrane lists of worthy thieves: "nor parchment bears not one." Like stories of prosperous regicides, the name of the unsuccessful thief survives in the parchment record only in oblivion.

"If the skin were parchment": *A Comedy of Errors*

Parchment as medium of human exemplarity: in *A Winter's Tale*, a nobleman wrestles with a moral conflict and evokes the animal medium as potential bearer of historical instruction. In *A Comedy of Errors*, parchment evokes instead the political subject of slavery and the human subject of dominion—comically so, though with equally dark implications. The parchment figure in this play arises as part of an extended conceit of bodily inscription and the homologies of skin, serving a story of mistaken identity involving two masters, their matching slaves, and the violence that structures their relationships.

In Act II, the slave Dromio of Ephesus, an identical twin to another slave of the same name, takes Antipholus of Syracuse for *his* twin brother, Antipholus of Ephesus. Antiopholus of Syracuse rebukes then beats his brother's slave for his failure to hand over money he believes to be in the possession of his own Dromio:

> ANTIPHOLUS OF SYRACUSE: In what safe place you have bestow'd my money,
>   Or I shall break that merry sconce of yours
>   That stands on tricks when I am undisposed:
>   Where is the thousand marks thou hadst of me?
> DROMIO OF EPHESUS: I have some marks of yours upon my pate,
>   Some of my mistress' marks upon my shoulders,
>   But not a thousand marks between you both.
>   If I should pay your worship those again,
>   Perchance you will not bear them patiently.
> ANTIPHOLUS OF SYRACUSE: Thy mistress' marks? what mistress, slave, hast
>   thou?
>   (1.2)

If Dromio of Ephesus misrecognizes the identity of his master, both men are familiar with the legibility of master-slave violence, figured here as a series of "marks" on Dromio's skin: the marks of his master on his head, of his mistress on his shoulders. Both lines play on the usage of *marks* as a measure of currency: the marks sought by the master will never equal in value or quantity the marks imprinted on his body.

Antipholus's puzzled question above—his own slave has no mistress, as he has no wife—sows more confusion, as Dromio's attempt to clarify his purpose only further infuriates his master: "What, wilt thou flout me thus unto my face, / Being forbid? There take you that, sir knave." Dromio cowers as he receives the predictable punishment, pleading for leniency: "What mean you, sir? For God's sake, hold your hands! / Nay, and you will not, sir, I'll take my heels" (1.2). Commentaries on the scene often characterize Antipholus's blows as "slaps," though there is no stage direction to mitigate the repeated violence against the slave, who flees the master's wrath rather than stay to endure further "marks" on his already wounded flesh.

The abuse-as-inscription continues after Dromio returns home as ordered. There he awaits the arrival of his master while lamenting to his mistress Adriana (Antiopholus of Ephesus's wife) about her husband's apparent state of mind. Dromio responds to his mistress's imprecations by lamenting his own victimization as a mere thing of skin written with the signs of his subjection:

> DROMIO OF EPHESUS: Quoth my master:
>> 'I know,' quoth he, 'no house, no wife, no mistress.'
>> So that my errand, due unto my tongue,
>> I thank him, I bare home upon my shoulders;
>> For, in conclusion, he did beat me there.
> ADRIANA: Go back again, thou slave, and fetch him home.
> DROMIO OF EPHESUS: Go back again, and be new beaten home?
>> For God's sake, send some other messenger.
> ADRIANA: Back, slave, or I will break thy pate across.
> DROMIO OF EPHESUS: And he will bless that cross with other beating:
>> Between you I shall have a holy head.
> ADRIANA: Hence, prating peasant! fetch thy master home.
> DROMIO OF EPHESUS: Am I so round with you as you with me,
>> That like a football you do spurn me thus?
>> You spurn me hence, and he will spurn me hither:
>> If I last in this service, you must case me in leather.
> (2.1)

In this rough exchange between mistress and servant, Shakespeare works through a dense set of connotations that link Dromio's status as slave to the wounds inflicted on his skin. Adriana will "break" his head "across"; the adverb, misheard by Dromio as "*a* cross," signifies to him a cruciform wound that his master will subsequently "cross with other beating," a line that creates an unsubtle analogy between Dromio's "pate" and the beaten and wounded body of Christ.[12] The correlation is further reinforced by Dromio's double entendre of his "holy head" (sacred and full of holes) marked with the punishments inflicted by mistress and master alike. In its vulnerability the slave's head is "like a football," a leathern plaything subject to masterly abuse that Dromio self-reflexively suggests must be "case[d] . . . in leather," like the bladder inside the same football, for his protection (later, in Act IV, Dromio of Syracuse will invoke "a bass viol in a case of leather").

These marks, holes, breakings, and crosses on the slave's skin all converge at the opening of Act III, when Antipholus of Ephesus returns home and upbraids

Dromio for his apparent confusion: "Thou drunkard, what didst thou mean by this?" Dromio then confronts his master with a documentary metaphor that captures both the physical violence and the juridical force governing the master-slave relation:

> DROMIO OF EPHESUS: Say what you will, sir, but I know what I know:
>   That you beat me at the mart I have your hand to show;
>   If the skin were parchment, and the blows you gave were ink,
>   Your own handwriting would tell you what I think.
> ANTIPHOLUS OF EPHESUS: I think thou art an ass.
> DROMIO OF EPHESUS: Marry, so it doth appear
>   By the wrongs I suffer and the blows I bear.
>   I should kick, being kick'd; and being at that pass,
>   You would keep from my heels, and beware of an ass.
>   (3.1)

The "marks" that Antipholus recalls from the exchange at the market now become the "hand to show" imprinted on Dromio's cheek. The slave figures his own skin as "parchment," the master's violence as "ink," the lingering signs of the assault a mode of "handwriting" readable as the unending story of violent dominion of master over slave.

The scenes recall the series of skin stories in Herodotus, with their clear association of enslavement and the written body, a topos of authoritarian subjection with a continuous history from the ancient world to Kafka. As Michel de Certeau puts it, "The law endlessly writes itself on bodies. It engraves itself on parchments made with the skin of its subjects. It articulates them into a juridical corpus. It makes them its book."[13] De Certeau is writing here about juridical authority vis-à-vis embodiment, "the law's demand to make the human skin one of its surfaces of inscription."[14] This concatenation assumes a familiar guise at the hands of Thomas Nashe, an English dramatist active in the last decade of the sixteenth century. Nashe's comedy *Summer's Last Will and Testament*, first performed in 1592, features Will Summer, a notorious jester in the court of Henry VIII, who invokes a tradition of "hieroglyphical writers," such as the legendary type of scribe "that writes under hair." Nashe's account derives ultimately from Herodotus though with a medicinal twist:

> I have heard of a certain notary Histiaeus, who, following Darius in the Persian wars, and desirous to disclose some secrets of import to his friend Aristagoras, that dwelt afar off, found out this means: he had a servant that had been long sick of a pain in his

eyes whom, under pretence of curing his malady, he shaved from one side of his head to the other, and with a soft pencil wrote upon his scalp (as on parchment) the discourse of his business, the fellow all the while imagining his master had done nothing but noint his head with a feather.[15]

Will's remembered tale recasts the notary's act of espionage by evoking the privileged medium of written law: he writes on the slave's shaved head "as on parchment." The unnamed slave of Histiaeus is beast-like in his blind ignorance of the words inscribed upon his flesh, thinking his master's tattooing a merely curative act.

Unlike the anonymous slave in Nashe and Herodotus, Shakespeare's Dromio is fully aware of the law written upon his flesh, fully capable of interpreting his subjection in the face of his master. Much of the comedy of the exchange derives from the fact that Dromio (for the moment, at least) fingers the wrong scribe. In reading back to Antipholus from the marks on his own skin, though, Dromio claims a kind of practical and resistant literacy built on a metaphor of parchment. The named slave redeploys the written medium of enslavement and thereby exposes the juridical mechanism of its inscription. It is a rare slave, the play implies, who can read back from the parchment that covers and shapes him.

"A parchment with the seal of Caesar": *Julius Caesar*

Act III, and Julius Caesar is dead. At the Forum, before the plebeians, Marc Antony enters with the riddled corpse to deliver, with Brutus's assent, his infamous funeral oration ("I come to bury Caesar, not to praise him"). The speech, though couched in abject obeisance toward Brutus and his henchmen, is intended to start inciting rebellion among the citizenry of Rome. First, however, must come the reading of Caesar's will. As the blade-riddled body of the sovereign lies before the Roman people, Antony recovers himself and evokes the membrane document the sovereign has left behind—"a parchment with the seal of Caesar":

> But yesterday the word of Caesar might
> Have stood against the world; now lies he there.
> And none so poor to do him reverence.
> O masters, if I were disposed to stir
> Your hearts and minds to mutiny and rage,
> I should do Brutus wrong, and Cassius wrong,
> Who, you all know, are honourable men:

I will not do them wrong; I rather choose
To wrong the dead, to wrong myself and you,
Than I will wrong such honourable men.
But here's a parchment with the seal of Caesar;
I found it in his closet, 'tis his will:
Let but the commons hear this testament—
Which, pardon me, I do not mean to read—
And they would go and kiss dead Caesar's wounds
And dip their napkins in his sacred blood,
Yea, beg a hair of him for memory,
And, dying, mention it within their wills,
Bequeathing it as a rich legacy
Unto their issue.
(3.2)

The image of Caesar's parchment will, held up in the theater before the on-stage crowd and the audience, turns the oration from Antony's sardonic put-down of these "honorable men" into a subtle documentary injunction to affiliation and then rebellion. Just as the parchment is inscribed on hair and flesh, so the plebeians, in its presence, may be inspired by Antony to "kiss dead Caesar's wounds," to "beg a hair of him for memory." They in turn will "mention it within their wills," creating a parchment inheritance linking their fortunes forever to the "legacy" of their dead sovereign.

The reading aloud of the parchment will consolidates Antony's counter-plot, goading the plebeians to revolt by encouraging them to "read" for themselves the story of Caesar's heroic life through the material text of his dead body and its clothing. "The will! The testament!" demands the crowd; "the will! Read the will!" enjoins a Second Citizen. Antony seems to comply, first gathering the plebeians around the ruined corpse of Caesar:

You will compel me, then, to read the will?
Then make a ring about the corpse of Caesar,
And let me show you him that made the will.
Shall I descend? and will you give me leave?
(3.2)

But the words that Antony will "read" here are written on Caesar's body itself: in the tears in his clothing, in the wounds and gashes and blood that mar his flesh and thus document his brutal assassination:

If you have tears, prepare to shed them now.
You all do know this mantle: I remember
The first time ever Caesar put it on;
'Twas on a summer's evening, in his tent,
That day he overcame the Nervii:
Look, in this place ran Cassius' dagger through:
See what a rent the envious Casca made:
Through this the well-beloved Brutus stabb'd;
And as he pluck'd his cursed steel away,
Mark how the blood of Caesar follow'd it,
As rushing out of doors, to be resolved
If Brutus so unkindly knock'd, or no;
For Brutus, as you know, was Caesar's angel:
Judge, O you gods, how dearly Caesar loved him!
This was the most unkindest cut of all;
For when the noble Caesar saw him stab,
Ingratitude, more strong than traitors' arms,
Quite vanquish'd him: then burst his mighty heart;
And, in his mantle muffling up his face,
Even at the base of Pompey's statue,
Which all the while ran blood, great Caesar fell.
O, what a fall was there, my countrymen!
Then I, and you, and all of us fell down,
Whilst bloody treason flourish'd over us.
O, now you weep; and, I perceive, you feel
The dint of pity: these are gracious drops.
Kind souls, what, weep you when you but behold
Our Caesar's vesture wounded? Look you here,
Here is himself, marr'd, as you see, with traitors.

(3.2)

The mantle of Caesar and the bloodied flesh of "himself" is the true text of his "will," "marr'd . . . with traitors" and the marks they have left on the sovereign's body. When Antony displays this body to the gathered crowd and relates the story of its ruin, he is translating and interpreting something like an incarnate chronicle, written with his own distant memories of heroic battle, his more immediate recollection of the assassination, and his description of the killing's stains on Rome's built environment (the blood "rushing out of doors" of the Forum) and commemorative art ("the base of Pompey's statue . . . all the while ran blood"). Indeed so moved are the plebeians by Antony's interpretive gloss of Caesar's body that they nearly forget his promise to read them the actual parchment will: as he has to remind them, "You have forgot the will I told you of." The reading of the membrane document is almost an anticlimax in the scene, so primed are the plebeians to revolt against the usurpers.

In the subsequent scene at Antony's house in Rome, Antony discusses with Octavius and Lepidus what to do with the surviving conspirators. Antony reads the names of the condemned from a ghoulish list, its pages "prick'd" to indicate those who are to die:

> ANTONY: These many, then, shall die; their names are prick'd.
> OCTAVIUS: Your brother too must die; consent you, Lepidus?
> LEPIDUS: I do consent—
> OCTAVIUS: Prick him down, Antony.
> LEPIDUS: Upon condition Publius shall not live,
>   Who is your sister's son, Mark Antony.
> ANTONY: He shall not live; look, with a spot I damn him.
>   But, Lepidus, go you to Caesar's house;
>   Fetch the will hither, and we shall determine
>   How to cut off some charge in legacies.
>   (4.1)

Pricking here is both the scoring of a page and the killing of a man: "Prick him down, Antony," Octavius orders, to which Antony responds with a darkly scriptive action on the page: "with a spot I damn him." Only now does Antony order Lepidus to Caesar's house to "fetch the will"—the same parchment document that has served as emblem of his oratory.

"Upon a parchment, and against this fire": *King John*

Another king is dying, poisoned by a monk. Set in the orchard at Swinstead Abbey, the final scene of *King John* finds a group of lords—Prince Henry, Salisbury, and Bigot, soon joined by Pembroke—lamenting their sovereign's perilous mental and physical state ("the end of mortality," in his son's words). Soon the ailing king himself appears, following a stage direction in the First Folio: "*John brought in,*" presumably on a litter or carried in a chair. Once on stage, the king delivers what will be his last words, beginning with a delirious lament on the inner state of his body as it suffers the burning effects of the poison:

> Ay, marry, now my soul hath elbow-room;
> It would not out at windows, nor at doors,
> There is so hot a summer in my bosom,
> That all my bowels crumble up to dust:
> I am a scribbled form drawn with a pen
> Upon a Parchment, and against this fire
> Do I shrink up.
> (5.7)

A remarkable image of physical diminution, likening the decay of an aging body to the burning of a membrane document, though the metaphor is strained. With his body contracting and suffering from the inner heat of illness, his soul now has "elbow-room" within its physical confines. The lines enlist the Platonic notion of body as prison of the soul, which seeks escape from the flesh through the "windows" and "doors" of the body dying around it, now "crumbl[ing] up to dust." The king himself is not the parchment but the form the parchment will destroy as it burns.

The choice of pen on parchment as a figuration of a dying king speaks to the well-known role of documentary culture in shaping the reign and afterlife of King John. One of the features of *King John* that has puzzled generations of critics is the play's seeming failure to engage with the making of Magna Carta, the signature achievement of King John's reign, an achievement regarded even in Elizabethan England as a monumental event in English constitutional history.[16] As Annabel Patterson put it, Shakespeare "notoriously omitted Magna Carta from his play on [John's] reign," and numerous critics over the generations have sought to explain this curious documentary absence.[17] The immediate source for the play, an earlier, anonymous drama called *The Troublesome Reign of King John*, also leaves Magna Carta unrepresented, perhaps as a cautionary gesture in the face of Queen Elizabeth's rising absolutism. Yet the details of the Runnymede negotiations as well as the text of Magna Carta itself are treated at length in Holinshed's *Chronicles*, a source Shakespeare knew intimately and drew on repeatedly for his depiction of King John's reign. Holinshed devotes a large portion of his narrative of this kingship to the details of the negotiations, including long lists of baronial signatories, as well as flourishes of documentary prose that include the incipits to the two charters signed at Runnymede: "when the king measuring his owne strength with the barons, perceiued that he was not able to resist them, he consented to subscribe and seale to such articles concerning the liberties . . . in the two charters Magna Charta, and Charta de Foresta, beginning Iohannes Deigratia, &c." Similarly, at the conclusion of the negotiations, the barons "returned to London with their charter sealed, the date whereof was this: Giuen by our owne hand, in the medow called Kuningsmede or Rimemede, betwixt Stanes and Windsore, the fifteenth of Iune, in the eighteenth yeare of our reigne."[18] The specifically documentary struggle between the barons and the king includes as well "a roll conteyning the auncient liberties, priuiledges, and customes of the realme, signifying that if the [king] would not confirme the same, they would not cease to make him warre, til he shoulde satisfie their requests in that behalfe" (6.186).

Charter, seal, subscription, roll: the density of documentary reference in Holinshed's account of John speaks to the importance of the material text in the historiography of kingship—as in the *Chronicles'* account of the Act of Succession during the reign of Henry VIII, when "euerie lord, knight, and burges, and all other were sworne to the act of succession, and subscribed their hands to a parchment fixed to the same" (6.937). The implied nobility of the membrane medium constrasts vividly with Holinshed's account of parchment remnants found, like old coins and other treasures, among the lost antiquities of the realm, "gotten eyther in the ruines of auncient Cities & Townes decayed, or in inclosed borowes." Thus during the reign of Henry VIII, at an audience with Catherine of Aragon at Peterborough, a ploughman presents the queen with several such finds, including "a few auncient rowles of Parchment written long agone, though so defaced with mouldinesse, and rotten for age, that no man coulde well holde them in hys hand without falling into péeces, much lesse reade them by reason of their blindnesse" (1.92). For Holinshed, parchment is a medium of political cohesion that always risks succumbing to the destructive vagaries of time, and thus historical oblivion.

Holinshed's historiographical presentation of these and other documentary aspects of John's reign may help explain their more figural role in the portrait of kingship presented in Shakespeare's *King John*. Absent the presence of "Magna Charta" in the text or staging of the play, the dying king himself becomes the great charter: a barely living document burning from within, his transcendent written authority shrinking as its material medium curls up in flames around it. This moving image of the parchment king recalls a scene from early in Act II, a moment of similar pathos in which Arthur, King John's nephew and chief rival to the throne, begins to assume his reluctant role as rightful king of England. Here Austria kisses Arthur's youthful cheek in an image that plays on a similar association of royal skin with documentary authority:

> Upon thy cheek lay I this zealous kiss,
> As seal to this indenture of my love,
> That to my home I will no more return,
> Till Angiers and the right thou hast in France,
> Together with that pale, that white-faced shore,
> Whose foot spurns back the ocean's roaring tides
> And coops from other lands her islanders,
> Even till that England, hedged in with the main,
> That water-walled bulwark, still secure
> And confident from foreign purposes,
> Even till that utmost corner of the west
> Salute thee for her king: till then, fair boy,
> Will I not think of home, but follow arms.
> (2.1)

Unlike John's skin, a withering "parchment" in the fire, Arthur's cheek is that of a "fair boy" ("pale," perhaps, like "that white-faced shore" of Dover), and thus suitable to receive the seal of an "indenture," a living membrane that signifies Austria's fealty to the rightful king. The lines that follow the documentary performance cast the realm of England as the political and geographical subject of this indenture, its people "coop[ed]" and "hedged in" with the sea. And like the indenture of sale marking Shakespeare's purchase of the Blackfriars gatehouse, this parchment will be divided in two, figuratively split to signify Austria's own division between his native England and the France he occupies as an exile.

"With inky blots and rotten parchment bonds": *Richard II*

Austria's image of England as a "water-walled bulwark" against foreign invasion evokes the longer and more celebrated "blessed plot" speech of John of Gaunt, the dramatic centerpiece of *Richard II*. The plays were written at roughly the same period in the mid-1390s, when searching debates about Elizabeth's monarchy considerably raised the stakes of dramatizing royalty.[19] At the opening of Act II, Lancaster lies ill at Ely House, waiting for death and the appearance of a king deaf to his "life's counsel," the many attempts the duke has made to dampen Richard's "fierce blaze of riot" that threatens to consume the realm.

A hot-headed king needs a truth-teller, who comes in the form of a powerful but aged duke. After bemoaning the king's increasingly irrational behavior, Gaunt delivers his memorable paean to England and its exceptional geography:

> This royal throne of kings, this scepter'd isle,
> This earth of majesty, this seat of Mars,
> This other Eden, demi-paradise,
> This fortress built by Nature for herself
> Against infection and the hand of war,
> This happy breed of men, this little world,
> This precious stone set in the silver sea,
> Which serves it in the office of a wall,
> Or as a moat defensive to a house,
> Against the envy of less happier lands,
> This blessed plot, this earth, this realm, this England,
> This nurse, this teeming womb of royal kings,
> Fear'd by their breed and famous by their birth,
> Renowned for their deeds as far from home,
> For Christian service and true chivalry,
> As is the sepulchre in stubborn Jewry,
> Of the world's ransom, blessed Mary's Son,
> This land of such dear souls, this dear dear land,
> Dear for her reputation through the world,
> Is now leased out, I die pronouncing it,
> Like to a tenement or pelting farm:
> England, bound in with the triumphant sea
> Whose rocky shore beats back the envious siege
> Of watery Neptune, is now bound in with shame,
> With inky blots and rotten parchment bonds . . .
> (2.1)

The majestic sequence of appositions imagining England as throne, isle, earth, nurse, womb, and so on culminates in the passive verb that serves them all. This England "is now leased out" like a "pelting farm": a phrase evoking the paltry or beggarly state of the rural poor. The word "pelting" as Gaunt enlists it here may be punning as well on the trade in pelts or skins, as in *Lear*: "from low farms / poor pelting villages, sheep cots and mills / enforce their charity" (2.7). The lines paint a grim portrait of rural poverty (human and animal alike) that the "inky blots and rotten parchment bonds" of the realm's weakened administrative apparatus can do nothing to assuage.[20]

The vivid contrast drawn by Gaunt between the transcendent might of England and the base animality of its documentary apparatus thus suggests a corrosion of the juridical force of parchment in governing the realm. Just as kingship has weakened through Richard's corruption and favoritism, so have these membrane embodiments of his authority—writs, indentures, patents, and so on—devolved into meaningless wads of unreadable ink and putrid skin, much like those found parchments "defaced with mouldinesse, and rotten for age" described by Holinshed. The play's image of rotting parchment and blotted ink evokes a venerable habit in English documentary culture of disparaging certain membrane instruments as metonymic of their beastly derivation, as worthless as the animal hides on which they are written. Parchment reduced to its animal materiality: a thing of creature and earth, unequal to the supernatural majesty of a rightful king.

"The skin of an innocent lamb should be made parchment": 2 *Henry VI*

A king, perhaps, such as Henry VI. In 2 *Henry VI*, the power of the parchment instrument is articulated neither by a king nor a duke but by a revolutionary, in a darkly comic assault on royal authority. On Blackheath, during an uprising against the English king, an interlude features two rebels bantering about the promise of revolution. Part of the discussion involves the fate of the spoils: the tanner "shall have the skin of our enemies, to make dog's leather of." Enter Jack Cade, clothier, marked in various ways with his criminal past and his rural affiliations, "burnt i' the hand for stealing of sheep." When I am king, Cade promises, "seven halfpenny loaves" shall be "sold for a penny: the three-hooped pot shall have ten hoops and I will make it felony to drink small beer" (4.2).

Central to Cade's strategy is an all-out assault on documentary culture, the written instruments that force and maintain the bondage of one class by another: even an "anti-writing rebellion," as Roger Chartier has put it in an influential reading of this scene.[21] "I have thought upon it, it shall be so," Cade proclaims. "Away, burn all the records of the realm: my mouth shall be the parliament of England" (4.7). The pronouncement recalls any number of similar acts of destruction aimed at the scribal milieu of administrative culture, many of them remembered in historical accounts from the later Middle Ages on.[22] Throughout the history of dissenting communities in England, the role of documents as means of control and potential agents of rebellion has been a constant theme, suggesting a strong awareness shared by high and low alike of parchment instruments as vital components of juridical authority and control.

These metaphorical and symbolic functions of documentary membrane are clearly part of Cade's purpose in this episode, despite his apparent rhetoric of wholesale destruction. In the following exchange, Cade moves from a promise to obliterate distinctions of aristocratic "livery" to ensure his own lordship to a full-throated condemnation of legal practitioners, including and especially those in the scribal professions:

> CADE: I thank you, good people: there shall be no money; all shall eat and drink on my score; and I will apparel them all in one livery, that they may agree like brothers and worship me their lord.
>
> DICK: The first thing we do, let's kill all the lawyers.
>
> CADE: Nay, that I mean to do. Is not this a lamentable thing, that of the skin of an innocent lamb should be made parchment? that parchment, being scribbled o'er, should undo a man? Some say the bee stings: but I say, 'tis the bee's wax; for I did but seal once to a thing, and I was never mine own man since. How now! who's there?
>
> (4.2)

"Who's there" is a clerk, a poor scrivener of Chatham whom Cade condemns to hang for the simple fault of being able to write his own name: "Away with him! I say: hang him with his pen and ink-horn about his neck" (4.2). Julian Yates reads this passage as a "multispecies impression," a memory that "transfers the pain of the knife that flays the lamb to human skin that is stung by the seal."[23] Documents, we learn, can kill human and animal alike.

Cade's attack on written instruments also draws on his own sophisticated knowledge of documentary jargon, entailments, and mediums, and this sophistication is surely part of the point. As Chartier has suggested, Shakespeare's depiction of Cade's "egalitarian and anti-writing discourse" resonates with a strain of thinking in medieval canon law regarding the comparative authority of the spoken and written word.[24] It also speaks to the venerable distrust of written instruments that was a central component of the long transition "from memory to written record," in M. T. Clanchy's influential phrase—part of which involved a dissenting and often destructive stance toward archives and the notarial apparatus, as a whole and in its parts (seals, parchments, ink, and the like).[25] Cade, a rural rebel allegedly wedded to archaic modes of trust and communication, rebels against the written instruments that embody the bondage of one class by another.

An earlier account that resonates compellingly with this passage occurs in Eadmer's *vita* of St. Anselm, included in his *Historia Novorum in Anglia* (ca. 1123) and adduced by Clanchy to illuminate the ongoing tension between written and spoken authority in the early twelfth century. The story involves a dispute between King Henry I of England and St. Anselm, then archbishop of Canterbury. Each magnate sends emissaries to Rome to receive judgment from Pope Paschal II, who sends them home with official letters on parchment prohibiting the king from certain acts of investiture with respect to ecclesiastical properties. Back in England, a dispute breaks out over the probity of the document versus the remembered words of the bishops, who claim that Paschal had promised them he would go easy on the king, though he wanted to avoid making this promise in writing. Henry, so his episcopal advocates argue, should more readily rely on the word of the bishops than on "the skins of wethers [*vervecum pellibus*] blackened with ink and weighted with a little lump of lead": in other words, the spoken witness of the ecclesiastical hierarchy is more trustworthy than a parchment document in its vulgar animality. The fascinating specificity of Eadmer's language here adds a gendered, even sexualized element to the charge: the word of a bishop should be trusted over words transcribed not on any old sheepskin, but on that of a *vervex*, or a castrated ram. This subtle implication of monkish emasculation only strengthens the monks' defense of the written word:

> ANSELM'S MONKS: But what about the evidence of the letters?
> HENRY'S BISHOPS: As we don't accept the evidence of monks against bishops, why should we accept that of a sheepskin [*ovinæ pellibus*]?
> ANSELM'S MONKS: Shame on you! Are not the Gospels written down on sheepskins?[26]

Another analogy: monks are to bishops as a parchment document is to their sworn words. An ecclesiastical hierarchy figures a hierarchy of medium and communication. In the end, the monks defend the creaturely derivation of the parchment letter by evoking Bibles similarly written on the skins of sheep: the most sacred texts of the scriptural tradition common to bishop and monk alike.

In Eadmer's *Historia* there is no talk of innocence when it comes to the wethers, no idiom of sacrifice. What, then, does the lamb's innocence imply in Shakespeare's play? On one level, Cade is enlisting the animal's lack of legal culpability as a figure for his own: just as an unknowing beast cannot be deemed capable of a crime, so those condemned by the legal system would remain innocent were it not for the juridical apparatus. The lawyers targeted by Cade and his company embody the ruinous designs of documentary culture on the lives and skins of helpless herd animals—a figuration made more powerful by the passage's clear evocation of Jesus Christ, an originary "innocent lamb." Nor is parchment the only animal product implicated in this all-too-human system. It is not the bee that "stings" the innocent man, Cade avows, but the bee's wax: "for I did but seal once to a thing, and I was never mine own man since." When the poor clerk of Chatham enters to face Cade's judgment, it will be no surprise that the condemned scribe will die marked by the instruments of his documentary craft.

"Is not parchment made of sheepskin?": *Hamlet*

Three creatures at a grave. The creatures are human, though what that category might imply at this juncture of the play is an open question.

We are in the fifth act of *Hamlet*. The prince and Horatio stand in a churchyard and watch as a gravedigger blithely tosses up skulls and fragments of bone from the ground. Hamlet's reaction to the spectacle is a mixture of disgust and morbid humor. These skulls could have belonged to anyone, he muses—a singer, a courtier, a politician—yet now they are without tongue and brain, an undifferentiated mass of bones that might as well be objects tossed about in a child's game. On seeing one particular skull, Hamlet speculates that its owner could have been a lawyer; another might have belonged to a buyer of property. In both cases, Hamlet imagines the professional lives of these men in all their messy documentary glory:

> HAMLET: Why may not that be the skull of a lawyer? Where be his quiddities now, his quillities, his cases, his tenures, and his tricks? Why does he suffer this rude knave now to knock him about the sconce with a dirty shovel and will not tell him of his action of battery? Hum! This fellow might be in's time a great buyer of land, with his statutes, his recognizances, his fines, his double vouchers, his recoveries: is this the fine of his fines, and the recovery of his recoveries, to have his fine pate full of fine dirt? will his vouchers vouch him no more of his purchases, and double ones too, than the length and breadth of a pair of indentures? The very conveyances of his lands will hardly lie in this box; and must the inheritor himself have no more, ha?
>
> HORATIO: Not a jot more, my lord.
>
> HAMLET: Is not parchment made of sheepskins?

HORATIO: Ay, my lord, and of calf-skins too.

HAMLET: They are sheep and calves which seek out assurance
in that.

(5.1)

Hamlet, in his disquisition on the skull, could well be describing the Shakespeare life records with which this chapter began: the numerous parchment indentures, feet of fines, conveyances, leases, and other instruments that defined the official life of the Bard and his family—most of whose members would have been well familiar with the prolific membrane apparatus regulating so many of their encounters with legal communities. But where are this man's "quiddities" now, Hamlet asks, the cant and jargon of his profession, and just where are those written instruments that defined his craft? They are, like the putative lawyer himself, gone, and as Hamlet muses, the "very conveyances of his lands will hardly lie in this box." The rotted coffin that now holds his remains, that is to say, is almost too large to hold the imagined stack of deeds to the properties he once owned.

This banter about legal documents provokes Hamlet's haunting query: "Is not parchment made of sheepskins?" The rhetorical question reminds the audience that, despite the dominance of paper by the early seventeenth century, animal membrane remained the preferred medium for legal record-keeping in Shakespeare's England, an aspect of documentary culture also informing Horatio's matter-of-fact response: "Ay, my lord, and of calf-skins too."[27] In a telling riposte, though, Hamlet turns the scene from bookish banter to bleak despondency: "They are sheep and calves which seek out assurance in that." Though animal skin might provide a more durable writing material than papyrus or paper (a fact acknowledged, as we have seen, by ancients and moderns alike), this should provide no comfort to the living, Hamlet avows. Those who would invest any hope in the ability of parchment to effect meaningful survival are dumb beasts themselves, as unknowing as the sheep and cows making up the mute membranes of the legal profession.

Missing records of a successful regicide, violence inked on the body of a slave, and the withered skin of an aging king; the will of a slain emperor, the rotten and unheeded records of a ruined realm, and the skin of an innocent lamb; and finally, in *Hamlet*, the sheepskins and calf-skins on whose survival a common culture long depended. In these membrane imaginings, Shakespeare provides us with a robust if sobering sense of parchment's capacities to shape human memory, relations of power, and forms of dominion. If a parchment document makes up the contested will of Julius Caesar and inspires urban rebellion, the decayed remnants of its modern equivalent are, in Gaunt's words, the "rotting parchment bonds" that signify the shame of a decadent sovereign. If the body of a febrile king can be imagined as "a Parchment" in the midst of "shrink[ing] up" against the fire of death, the body of the enslaved—"if the skin were parchment"—bears the marks of the master and mistress, and "like a football" suffers the violence of a game. Animals, the rendered "sheep and calves" and "innocent lamb" evoked by Hamlet and Jack Cade alike, are the most silent and silenced of all these subjects of human dominion, despite their indispensable role in furnishing the written records of human life.

Life: a fraught and ambivalent word in the long history of parchment. So far this book has left the question of life largely in the margins, though its provocations are everywhere in the parchment inheritance: tactile signs of animal life in hair, flesh, and scar; whispers from once-living animals in riddles and the commentary traditions; the young life of the uterine folio; the gruesome life of the anthropodermic book. The three final chapters usher this study into modernity, in a sense, though as we have already seen, the archive of the animal defeats and surpasses mere chronology, surviving by centuries its human makers just as it survives the creaturely beings who make it up. The "life" of this archive is both fully animal and fully human, in the most literal and the most metaphorical of senses. The merest scrape of parchment teems with biomes past, present, and future—both ours and theirs, intermingled in the glorious chaos of archival life.

PART III

✦✦

The Medium and Modernity

➤ ✦

CHAPTER THIRTEEN

BIOCODICOLOGY

Book History and the Biomolecular Revolution

Before me on the table rests University of Virginia Medieval Manuscript M, a small Latin Bible copied in the thirteenth century (fig. 13.1). Its folios measuring a mere 150x100 millimeters, this portable Bible is one of many thousands of volumes from this era written on the tissue-thin parchment commonly known as uterine vellum. This particular book is a "Paris Bible," a subcategory of biblical manuscript so called for its place of initial production and emergence as well as the standardization of its textual divisions, organization, and elements.[1] I have come to Special Collections today neither to read from this book nor to study its contents, however, but to collect biological samples from several of its membrane folios. In short, I need some skin.

But I won't be using scissors to snip off the tiny corner of a folio, nor a razor blade to slice a sliver from the margin. Instead I will be employing a small white PVC eraser, a fragment cut from a larger polymer eraser to form a cuboid just the right size to be held between two fingertips. With my left hand securing the book firmly in place and my right hand enclosed in a nitrile glove to minimize contamination from my own skin and its microbiome, I gently rub the eraser along a one-inch span in the blank margins of a vellum folio. Anyone who has used an everyday pencil eraser on a piece of notebook paper will know what this process creates: a pile of tiny crumbles where the eraser has rubbed the surface. That rubbery gunk has a (charming) nickname: erdu, for "eraser doo" (see fig. 13.2). With one fingertip, I gently sweep the erdu onto a small piece of folded acid-free paper, then, using the fold as a channel, tap the paper's edge against the side of a 1.5 milliliter microcentrifuge tube until most of the erdu tumbles in. I snap the tube shut, label the lid to identify the manuscript from which its contents have been taken, and set the tube aside.

Despite its unassuming appearance, the eraser gunk I've collected holds a wondrous potency. That small sample of erdu is teeming with proteins and molecules—many millions of them, gathered by the electrostatic charge of the polymer eraser

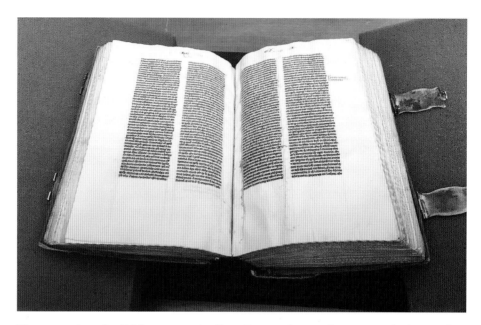

Figure 13.1. A pocket Bible on uterine vellum. France, thirteenth century. Charlottesville, University of Virginia Medieval Ms. N, fols. 124v–125r.

Figure 13.2. A pile of erdu (eraser rubbings) gathered from the surface of a sixteenth-century missal.

against the parchment and abounding with the building blocks of mammalian life: among others, collagen, the triple-helixed amino acid protein that makes up the primary component of connective tissues, skin, and muscle; and DNA, the double-helixed molecule that carries the genetic blueprint of all living organisms. Every specimen of parchment surviving from the premodern world contains these and other microscopic elements, all of them with the potential to yield vital new information about the animal whose rendered skin makes up the folio or document sampled by contemporary investigators, as well as the cellular matter accumulated on the membrane surface over the history of its usage. To take a rubbing of skin from a medieval charter or codex is to collect biomolecular data from a reservoir of boundless variation, one that will inevitably include the remnants of those human users (past and present) sloughed off over the centuries.

The "eraser method" for the biomolecular sampling of parchment was developed by Sarah Fiddyment, formerly a postdoctoral researcher in biochemistry and paleobiology in the Matthew Collins lab in the Department of Bioarchaeology at the University of York. In the summer of 2012, Fiddyment spent several weeks with the conservation staff at the Borthwick Archive, gathering information about the preservation and repair of medieval documents. As she watched the conservators at their work, she noticed that one of the tools used for cleaning parchment books and records was a common PVC eraser. Spying the remnants of this process, she wondered whether the erdu swept from the membrane and discarded willy nilly might contain biomolecular data gleaned from the parchment.

Back in the lab, she subjected the waste samples to a chemical, centrifuging, and heating process that rendered them suitable for analysis in an Ultraflex III MALDI-TOF mass spectrometer, a room-sized machine that the lab uses for ZooMS, short for Zooarchaeology by Mass Spectrometry. This process (pioneered by the Center for Excellence in Mass Spectrometry at York) allows the investigator to read the evolution and durability of the collagen molecule within animal remains as a kind of biomolecular barcode full of information about genus and species as well as material deterioration over time. York's ZooMS method has been applied most often to ancient animal bones as a means of identifying species type in archaeological digs, though it also has present-day applications in controversial areas of food security and contamination, having been employed to detect the presence of horse meat in mislabeled beef products.[2]

To their great delight, Fiddyment and Collins discovered that the eraser technique works extraordinarily well as a mode of sampling the animal membrane making up medieval books and documents, a realization that inspired them to seek out scholars working on the parchment record to identify and model research questions that might be addressed through their method. I was lucky enough to be among the first collaborators in the lab's initial parchment project, a wide-scale study of the animal origin of uterine vellum. Our team of twenty (representing seventeen institutions in seven countries) consisted of bioarchaeologists, archaeozoologists, and paleogeneticists; conservationists from libraries, archives, and museums; book historians and paleographers; as well as historians, art historians, and a parchment maker. As of this writing I have met only half of these co-investigators in person, an indication of the expansive yet inevitably fragmented nature of this sort of collaborative international work, not unusual in the so-called hard sciences, of course: a typical physics paper can have as many as thirty or forty co-authors.[3] Our team gathered erdu from over five hundred medieval books, single leaves, and documents from dozens of libraries and archives across the United States, Great Britain, and Europe, sampling all of these parchments with the eraser method and sending the rubbings to York. Several of the samples came from University of Virginia Medieval Manuscript M, from which I took my little pile of erdu that day in Special Collections.

The result of our work together was a paper, "Animal origin of 13th-century uterine vellum revealed using noninvasive peptide fingerprinting" (published in the *Proceedings of the National Academy of Sciences*), that demonstrated the viability of the triboelectric eZooMS approach through the eraser method to the study of membrane books and documents while addressing some long-standing points of controversy in the study of books written on uterine vellum.[4] Figure 13.3 illustrates the relative proportions of quadrupeds (goat, sheep, cow) rendered to make parchment in each of the regions studied from the twelfth through the fourteenth centuries. The lower right quadrant illustrates the more specific distribution of species within the pocket Bibles we sampled, suggesting the important role of geography and animal population in determining the preferences of parchmenters and bookmakers.

This extended account of a sampling protocol and a research collaboration is meant to illustrate both the challenges and affordances of working across paradigms in the study of written artifacts. Our group's analysis of the animal origin of uterine vellum represents just one example of an emerging mode of multidisciplinary inquiry into the complex and heterogeneous nature of written heritage. A convenient shorthand for this type of work is *biocodicology*, a frontier area of research across the sciences-humanities divide that has the potential to reshape in fundamental ways the study of written culture and the history of animals alike.[5] Defined broadly, biocodicology is the extraction, analysis, and interpretation of the molecular substrate

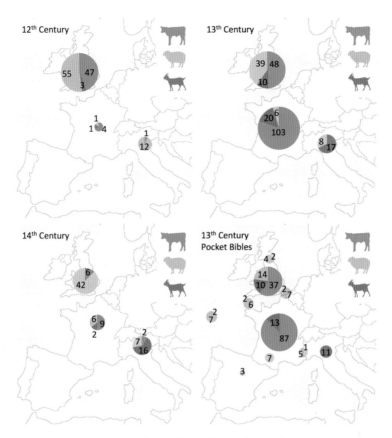

Figure 13.3. Relative proportions of animals used to make parchment in three regions (France, England, and Italy) during the twelfth to fourteenth centuries. The size of the circle indicates the number of samples taken. Except for the figure describing exclusively pocket Bibles, data were obtained from all sources of parchment, including legal documents, secular codices, and Bibles, using the eZooMS method. Circles shown in paler colors indicate inconclusive provenance with respect to location (from Fiddyment, Holsinger, et al., "Animal origin of 13th-century uterine vellum," 2015, fig. 3).

of written artifacts. Biocodicological inquiry studies (1) the history, production, and interrelation of books and documents through scientific methods of analysis and interpretation, such as aDNA testing and peptide mass fingerprinting; as well as (2) the biomolecular composition, interrelationship, and history of the fauna and flora that make up the written record.

Biocodicology: a search for the biome of the book; a codicology of the invisible.

The fields of book and archival conservation have long applied methods of biochemical analysis to written heritage. Parchment alone has been the subject of many hundreds of scientific papers over the years exploring topics from the biological contamination of the Archimedes Palimpsest to the potential role of lipids in maintaining parchment stability to the nature of medieval charters as potential matrixes of microbial hazards.[6] These methods are part of a long tradition of technological analysis that includes multispectral imaging, X-ray fluorescence spectrometry, and many others. What distinguishes the emerging transdisciplinary field of biocodicology is the bi- and even tridirectionality of its aims, methods, and collaborative infrastructure. While our group's work on uterine vellum tackled a few questions that have long provoked medievalists in humanistic fields, it also demonstrated to colleagues in bioarchaeology, zooarchaeology, and paleogenetics the viability of a particular sampling method as well as the significance of the parchment record itself as a reserve of vital yet virtually untapped data at the level of the cell, the molecule, the protein. It offered to conservationists and bibliographers a potential new way of measuring the quality and degradation of parchment. And it asked specialists across numerous fields to think, model, and write between and against the boundaries of our subdisciplines, and to understand the concordant limits of our individual knowledge bases in addressing particular questions.

These limits become quickly apparent for anyone in the humanities disciplines who works with colleagues in the experimental sciences, which rely on certain mathematical and technical knowledges usually lost on those of us in more literary and artistic fields. It can be quite intimidating to talk about sample sizes and probabilities with a microbiologist who works with such concepts on a daily basis—and disorienting to sign on as a co-author of a paper that contains sentences such as these: "The samples were loaded in 0.1% TFA in 1% CH_3CN and eluted with a gradient of 3–35% (vol/vol/vol) CH_3CN in 5% DMSO and 0.1% formic acid for 60 min at a flow rate of 250 nL·min^{-1} . . . Peptides were eluted in a final volume of 50 μL of 50% acetonitrile (ACN)/0.1% TFA (vol/vol) . . . One microliter of eluted peptides was mixed on a ground steel plate with 1 μL of α-cyano-4-hydroxycinnamic acid matrix solution [1% in 50% ACN/0.1% TFA (vol/vol/vol)] and air-dried." I have no earthly idea what most of that means, nor would my scientist colleagues expect me to—just as they would be unable to translate medieval Latin, interpret twelfth-century handwriting, and so on. But such partial ignorance (and therefore trust) is a precondition of meaningful work across the sciences-humanities divide, as it is within disciplines in the sciences.

This interplay of ignorance and good will is one of the more enlivening aspects of biocodicology, which aims to straddle numerous fields while pursuing questions that may have little prestige or play within the fields of individual investigators. Here it may be useful to take a longer view of such transdisciplinary collaborations. Over half a century ago, the English physicist and novelist C. P. Snow famously identified a rift between the "two cultures" of science and the humanities, an institutional divide that had led, in his view, to a fundamental miscomprehension of the methods, aims, and even values of scholarship in scientific disciplines by those in the humanities, and vice versa: "Literary intellectuals at one pole—at the other scientists, and as the most representative, the physical scientists. Between the two a gulf of mutual incomprehension—sometimes (particularly among the young) hostility and dislike, but most of all lack of understanding."[7] For Snow, this mutual incomprehension was the result of bad faith on both sides (though mostly on the humanistic end of the spectrum), informed by long-standing prejudices regarding the supposed shallow optimism of scientists, the anti-intellectualism of literary elites.

Snow's baldly stated views inspired reams of commentary in the succeeding years, including a scathing critique from F. R. Leavis, who objected to Snow's scientistic prejudice against literary types as an elitist cadre with little concern for the well-being of their fellow humans. More recent assessments have been somewhat kinder to Snow's view of the sciences-humanities divide, taking seriously the continuing disparities between the two domains while complicating his view with the "third culture" of the social sciences (at which Snow only glanced).[8] Jerome Kagan, in a wide-ranging study on the present state of disciplinary knowledges in the contemporary university, probes further into the epistemological and institutional distinctions between academic paradigms. Kagan asks us to recognize the "different semantic networks" distinguishing the natural sciences from the social sciences, and each in turn from the humanities—networks that furnish disciplines with their own distinctive (and often incompatible) definitions of terms such as *archive, evidence,* and so on.[9] If Snow recognized that the "process of specialization as such" is the "precondition of intellectual progress," he had little or nothing to say about modes of collaboration that might work against overspecialization within and between disciplines—collaborations that, according to Kagan, would address the "obvious need for greater mutuality of understanding among the members of the three cultures."[10] Biocodicology speaks to a variety of sciences-humanities collaborations in recent years that are rethinking the biohistory of the premodern era, whether a case study of a lapis lazuli fragment found in the denture of a medieval nun or a broad-based inquiry into the archaeoscience of the ancient Mediterranean, including cross-paradigm work on the history of disease and contagion.[11]

As with these other interdisciplinary fields, one of the obvious risks of biocodicological collaborations in this era of expensive equipment and diminishing research funding is the impression they may give of an unthinking scientism, in the same way that scholars in the digital humanities have often been accused of worshipping at the altar of computation and big data. Humanistic enchantment with the methods and machines of the experimental sciences risks succumbing to the view that science will somehow "save" the humanities from institutional ruin—if only we can find scientists to collaborate with, and if only we can get ourselves into their well-funded laboratories.[12]

Yet given its twofold character as a primary record of human culture and an archive of animal life, parchment has inevitably excited a desire for a probing and comprehensive inquiry into its dual nature among those devoted to the medium as an object of study. Biocodicology is emerging during what has been called a "biomolecular revolution" in the discipline of archaeology, an era of breathtaking advances in technology, scale, and efficiency that form part of a broader information explosion shaping scientific inquiry in numerous fields in this Century of Biology.[13] Thus a pre-Conquest English Gospel book can now be imagined and studied as a "1000-year biological palimpsest," to cite the title of another recent study enabled by the eraser method developed by Fiddyment and Collins.[14] For the biomolecular turn in the study of books and documents represents a sweeping epistemological and even ontological shift with respect to our written objects of inquiry: how we know them, the questions we might now or soon be equipped to ask about them, what exactly they are and in what they consist. And it forces us to comprehend in new ways the numberless creatures that populate the parchment record: to sample and see them in their biological specificity, and in a moment when the genetic archives and inheritances of our own species have grown laden with new meaning and unending controversy.

Of all the avenues of biocodicological research emerging in the last several decades, none has inspired the scholarly imagination more than the promise of parchment aDNA. The notion of extracting ancient genetic materials from membrane books and documents and sequencing them to determine the geographical origins and affiliations among manuscripts is irresistible in its potential to answer enduring questions about the production, provenance, and very nature of written artifacts. Timothy Stinson, in the most searching work on the methodology of parchment DNA, has identified its vast potential for the study of written heritage, from broad questions about the localization of herds and the nature of the parchment trade to more particularist inquiries into the construction of codices as well as the origins and provenance of individual manuscripts and their relation to other membrane survivals. As Stinson cautions, however, only by marshaling other types of evidence and learning the right questions to pose of parchment DNA can scholars hope to approach "the fullest possible understanding of the significance and meaning of genetic data found in medieval manuscripts."[15]

No accident that the subject has provoked several generations of scholars, beginning with a team of investigators working in the 1990s with the Dead Sea Scrolls, the assemblages of scrolls and fragments of biblical and other writings found in caves near Qumran in the West Bank. "Decipherers of Dead Sea Scrolls Turn to DNA Analysis for Help," a *New York Times* headline announced as far back as 1995, a sign of the genetic method's potential for major breakthroughs in the study of written heritage.[16] The Qumran texts, dating from the third century BCE through the first century of the Common Era, contain vital evidence attesting to the history, culture, and religious life of Judaism during the Second Temple period, as well as glancing hints about the spread of Christianity in its first centuries. Consider this note of excitement from 1993:

> Cool research will turn into frenzy and delirium if it succeeds in determining the degree of parentage and the genealogical tree of every skin and of the corresponding animal. Especially if identity cards in the form of DNA can be assigned to every sheep and goat, so that the complete Qumran flock is known and sheep and goats can be identified as possible intruders or imports from other herds. This tracking through the caprine genealogy of Qumran will allow one to determine which manuscripts were written in Qumran using skins from native sheep and which manuscripts were written in other places, such as Jerusalem . . . using skins from foreign animals.[17]

The enticing aspirations of such methods ("every skin . . . every sheep and goat . . . the complete Qumran flock") can approach the theological, and it is accordingly difficult not to wax evangelical in touting their promise. "If all the skies were parchment" indeed.

The initial genetic experiments on the Dead Sea Scrolls came about through a series of collaborations among scholars at the Hebrew University of Jerusalem, Brigham Young University, and the Rockefeller Museum in Jerusalem using a polymerase chain reaction (PCR) technique to test and compare DNA sequences extracted from the Qumran membranes. The goal, "to establish a genetic signature unique to each manuscript" in the Qumran assemblages, would potentially allow researchers to identify "three levels of hierarchy" within the specimens: "the species, population, and individual animal from which the parchment was produced."[18] For the longer scrolls made up of multiple skins, the technique could illuminate "the degree of relatedness of the parchments in a single scroll," even as it would allow the investigators to map relations across multiple scrolls within the same assemblages. For those membranes repaired with a patch, it would help answer questions of animal mobility and human migration: "Does the patch represent a herd from a different region, reflecting mobility of either the original scroll or the herd?" Similar questions could then be posed of the entire surviving Qumran corpus: "By comparing DNA fingerprints recovered from the parchments and those obtained from archaeological remains of animals found in ancient sites throughout Israel," the group contended, "the origins or source of the parchment will be determined."[19]

Though the Jerusalem-BYU group published several papers reporting on its initial inquiries, and despite the great promise of the research in enlisting animal DNA to track the course of human culture, the experiments proved inconclusive at best, and sparked some contention within the rarefied world of Dead Sea Scrolls studies from the beginning. One of the controversies long surrounding the Qumran writings has concerned their place of origin and the particular sect or sects of Judaism responsible for their transcription, transmission, and survival. The dominant view over the last several decades has been that the scrolls were the work of the Essenes, a separatist group of ascetic Jews living in Palestine during the Second Temple period. Norman Golb, in *Who Wrote the Dead Sea Scrolls?* (1995), claimed that the early work by Kenneth Woodward and others on the DNA of the Qumran membranes "was based on the unproven assumption that members of an Essenic sect had once lived at Khirbet Qumran," and that the research was not open to the possibility of "a total herd disparity of herd origins among the fifty fragments tested." Golb even claimed that the Antiquities Authority was responsible for "an effort to bend . . . new discoveries to the exigencies of the Qumran-sectarian hypothesis, the rapid tempo of the various harmonious statements contrasting notably with the silence blanketing the aDNA results."[20] Golb's assumption was that the Essenic theory would be contravened if it could be shown that the scrolls parchments came from a widely disparate population of herds and species. There seems to be little basis to Golb's acerbic assumptions about the "secret" results, though the minor controversy suggests the potential of parchment aDNA analysis to overturn long-cherished assumptions about disputed cultural artifacts and their all-too-human makers.

In the decades since the Jerusalem-BYU group's early work on the Qumran assemblages, other teams of researchers have sought to apply aDNA analysis to written heritage toward a variety of ends. One such collaboration, organized from the Cambridge lab of Christopher Howe, resulted in a collaborative essay that identified genetic data from mitochondrial and autosomal loci in a number of eighteenth- and nineteenth-century parchments to raise questions about species use as well as the manufacture, treatment, and storage of the membrane material.[21] An analogous effort by a group of curators, book historians, and scientists working in Crete and Athens sought to address the "phylogeographic relationships of contemporary domestic animals with the stocks bred several hundred years ago" through the analysis of several Greek manuscripts of the thirteenth to sixteenth centuries.[22]

The first two decades of research on parchment aDNA were inevitably hampered by the limitations of the extraction and sampling methods employed by researchers. Available PCR techniques were unable to correct for contamination between species and individuals or elude the "chimeric artifactual sequences" residing in the genetic signature of membrane manuscripts, and the limitations in the effectiveness of the methods made scaling up all but impossible.[23] Only with the widespread adoption of next-generation sequencing in the field of bioarchaeology has the promise of aDNA research on parchment begun to fulfill its potential. In the recent words of Matthew Teasdale and his collaborators, parchment may now finally be regarded by palaeogeneticists as "an excellent substrate for genomic analyses of historical livestock."[24] Indeed, the most recent aDNA findings on the Qumran writings (announced just as I was completing this manuscript) are beginning to suggest a more dispersed origin for the Dead Sea Scrolls, and may push against the theory of Essenic origin (see fig. 13.4).[25]

Such techniques will have wide-ranging and immediate implications for the biomolecular study of written corpori around the world, and they are already bearing remarkable fruit. A case in point is a recent study of a set of nineteenth-century membrane artefacts of great significance to the colonial history of New Zealand. The Treaty of Waitangi is a document signed by British colonial officials and hundreds of Maori chieftains in 1840 and representing the official establishment of New Zealand as a British colony. Originally drafted on paper, the treaty was then transferred onto sheets of ewe parchment by a British missionary writing in Maori, and it was these membranes along with several additional paper sheets that would form the official record of the agreement (see fig. 13.5). Each of the hundreds of chieftains who signed the treaty (both at the original site of the conclave and during subsequent visitations by colonial officials) did so by marking the treaty with replicas of his *moko*, or facial tattoo. As a Ngapuhi chief observed in the 1980s, the treaty "is a sacred taonga, incised with tattoos from the skins of our ancestors [*to moko no o rātou kiri*]. It is their *tapu* (sacred power), the *tapu* of their knowledge, of their priests

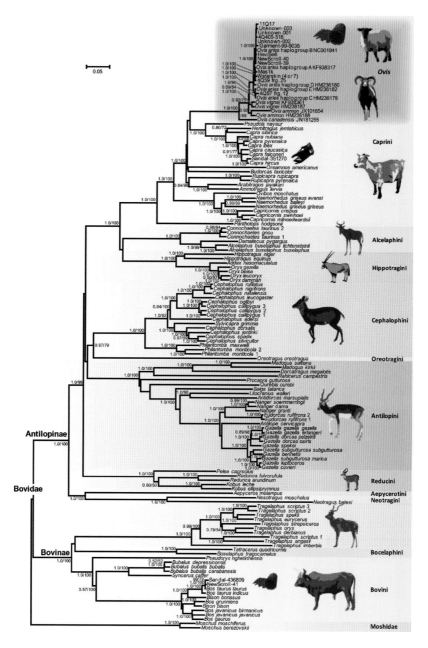

Figure 13.4. Phylogenetic tree of sample fragments from the Dead Sea Scrolls, showing maximal support from the species Ovies aries, with additional specimens assigned to other species (from Anava et al., "Illuminating Genetic Mysteries of the Dead Sea Scrolls," fig. 3).

Figure 13.5. The Waitangi sheet of the Treaty of Waitangi on ewe parchment. Bay of Island, New Zealand, 1840. By courtesy of Auckland, Ministry for Culture and Heritage.

and high chiefs."[26] The afterlife of the treaty has inspired controversies of its own, with some treating it as solely an object of historical knowledge, and others regarding it as a "living document" continually vivified via the inscriptions translated from the skin of aboriginal ancestors onto the sheepskin of the written treaty.[27]

These politically and anthropologically difficult aspects of the treaty's disposition over the last two centuries render its biotic materiality all the more provocative as a subject of biocodicological inquiry. A team of researchers based in Wellington sought to determine whether an archived sheet of blank parchment donated to the Alexander Turnbull Library in 1929 derived from the Waitangi Sheet of the original document. Despite the donor's claims that the fragment represented a "Blank Portion of the Original Skin" of the Treaty of Waitangi, the team was skeptical: while the donated portion is creamy, smooth, and virtually undamaged, the original parchment sheets were for many decades poorly preserved, "damaged by water and . . . partially eaten by rats."[28] The team used several methods to take samples from both parchments: scrapings obtained with a sterile razor blade, small portions cut from the edges, and erdu gathered via the noninvasive eraser technique developed by Fiddyment. The samples obtained were then subjected to various forms of analysis, including Sanger sequencing for species identification, microsatellite genotyping, and illumina dye sequencing. The results were all but conclusive: "The two parchments shared identical mitogenome sequences, including an unusual heteroplasmic site, and both were made from ewes," the team determined. As a result, the blank donor sheet is "highly likely to be a portion cut from the lower membrane of the Waitangi Sheet."[29]

Though this New Zealand study took as its object a relatively recent set of documents, similar research has been initiated on any number of membrane artifacts from the premodern world, work that is genuinely bi-directional in its aims, methods, and openness across paradigms of inquiry—and full of heady surprises.[30] If one is interested in unpacking the literary culture of local reading communities, it may be that the species identification and genetic affiliation of any given leaf or book will prove trivial at best. If, on the other hand, one's aim is to construct a four-dimensional map of the cow metagenome since the beginning of animal domestication in the Neolithic Era some fourteen thousand years ago—a project currently bringing together dozens of scientists around the world—the medieval parchment record may well be a Holy Grail, and medievalist scholars in the humanities may serve as powerful institutional advocates. The microbiology of the parchment record has vast implications for our understanding of the archaeology of human-animal relations, processes of environmental and evolutionary change over the *longue durée*, the genetic histories of both extinct and surviving species and breeds, as well as the manufacture, preservation, and usage of one of the most durable written mediums of the Common Era. It goes without saying that the membrane record is a massive cultural and historical archive. The parchment inheritance is simultaneously a boundless biotic archive, holding countless strands of collagen, DNA, and other molecules that emerged and grew during the lifespans of the discrete animals whose remains make up a good portion of the written record of the premodern world.

Biocodicology, then, might best be understood less as a research method than as a disposition toward the archive—and here, following Lorraine Daston, we must construe what we mean by *archive* in the broadest and most pan-disciplinary of senses, in part by "forging a common way of thinking about these remarkable transgenerational enterprises."[31] Palaeoclimatologists regularly speak of "ice core archives" as evidentiary records for the deep history of climate change; thus Richard B. Alley describes the Greenland ice sheet as "an incomparable, 110,000-year archive" that "provides year-by-year records of how cold and snowy Greenland was, how strong the storms were that blew dust from Asia and salt from the ocean, and even how extensive the wetlands of the world were."[32] Likewise, it is commonplace among paleontologists to describe the fossil record as "an archive of biological information" written in the bones of animals past, both human and non, while the enormous bird taxidermy collections of nineteenth-century Britain formed an "avian imperial archive" avidly supplemented by colonial officers.[33] David Sepkoski writes of "the preserved strata of the earth itself" as the "original archive," the conception of which inspired two centuries of secondary archiving in the history of science.[34]

Both a depthless preserve of biomolecular material and a boundless repository of cultural knowledge, the membrane record ideally embodies this doubled, cross-paradigm implication of the archive. A vellum folio or a parchment charter is a great transhistorical stew of biotic matter, gilded with the gut and skin microbiomes of our human forebears and contemporaries even as it consists in the hide of a singular historical beast, an organism with a genetic signature unique to its lifespan in the past yet enduring through the centuries since its death.[35] A mere thirty years ago the notion of sampling a medieval manuscript for goat collagen or sheep DNA seemed a beguiling dream; now, such technologies have begun to yield concrete data about the sprawling networks of proteomic signatures and genetic relations woven throughout the parchment inheritance. A humble pile of erdu rubbed from a parchment: a scatter of membrane depths and surfaces where the human and the animal converge, their miscroscopic remains gathered in a molecular web of interspecies entanglement.

CHAPTER FOURTEEN

ECOCODICOLOGY

or, Is the Book a Byproduct?

The last word in ignorance is the man who says of an animal or plant,
'What good is it?' If the land mechanism as a whole is good, then every
part is good, whether we understand it or not. If the biota, in the course of
aeons, has built something we like but do not understand, then who but a
fool would discard seemingly useless parts?

—ALDO LEOPOLD, *ROUND RIVER*

In *People of the Book*, a 2008 novel by Pulitzer Prize-winner Geraldine Brooks,
rare books specialist Hanna Heath receives a commission to travel to war-
torn Bosnia to examine the Sarajevo Haggadah, a prayerbook produced in
fourteenth-century Catalonia. In the course of her examination, Hanna investigates
a series of artifacts found on and within the parchment folios of the medieval codex:
an insect's wing, a wine stain, remnants of sea salt, a lone cat's hair. Each piece of biological detritus in the manuscript has its own story to tell, traced through short
historical vignettes set in particular times and places associated with the origin and
survival of the Haggadah. "I know the flesh and fabrics of pages, the bright earths
and lethal toxins of ancient pigments," Hanna avows, echoing the sentiments of
most anyone who works with old books and documents.[1] The innumerable natural
phenomena of written culture are manifest in the smell of leather, parchment, and
paper; the occasional stains made by food, dirt, wine and water, occasionally blood;
visible scars and flaws on the surface of a membrane scroll; the fuzz of parchment
on the thumb; the swirls of pulped and fermented cloth distinguishing certain papers from others.

The book, as object and idea, has multiple histories, the novel suggests, traced
variously across numerous cultures and languages, religious traditions and regions.
The histories of Jewish book cultures look very different at certain moments from
their gentile counterparts; at other times, Malachi Beit-Arié has long reminded us,

the two cultures unfold in parallel, sharing membranes, routes of trade, patterns of transmission.[2] And there are many timelines and scales other than cultural tradition on which to plot the history of writing: technologies, institutions, arts and crafts; the syncretic, the diachronic, the local and the global.

Another is the ecological. Though neither Brooks nor her character Hanna Heath describes their purpose in this way, one of the novel's effects is to plot robust points of intersection between book history and environmental history. The natural and cultural forces that leave sea salt, cat hair, and an insect's wing between the parchment folios of a medieval codex are inseparable from the material history of the book as it travels through human time and passes among human hands and readerships. If one of the principal subjects of environmental history concerns "our encounters and collisions with all the other organisms that make up the Earth's ecosystem," we might understand the mediums of written culture as agents and embodiments of such encounters, places where written culture and environmental forces converge, become indistinguishable.[3] The origin and provenance of a manuscript record ecological relation and environmental change.

What would an environmental history of parchment look like? Where can this history be found, and how might it be recovered? How do our archives and libraries provoke its queries and yield its surprises? The answers to such questions must be both provisional and expansive. The wide unused margins of a luxury vellum codex with a small text block may evoke habits of profligate and careless expenditure; books of hours contain "many folios of blank or wasted parchment," and there is almost a potlatch quality to certain bookish practices that seem to boast a deliberate squandering of membrane.[4] Yet these same volumes may find themselves enlisted in practices of bookish thrift, of squirreling away and reuse. In the Middle Ages, parchment leaves might be sewn into garment linings by nuns, wrapped around the bodily relics of saints, and nailed over windows as protection against foul weather. Any library that holds more than a few dozen early printed books will likely own several volumes in which leaves or bifolia from earlier parchment manuscripts have been employed as binding supports, a form of recycling that is also a hallmark of cultural destruction. Hannah Ryley has written in this regard of the "sustainability of medieval manuscripts," a phrase that helpfully captures the perdurance of membrane books and documents as "endlessly recycled entities that evolve through time."[5]

Such habits remind us that the book (like the charter or the quitclaim) is a thoroughly human invention, a subject of our imagining and a product of our craft and our thought. Yet as the strange history of parchment teaches us, books and documents possess their own agential and material force, shaping us and our human world as much as we shape the written objects we consume and preserve. The book of nature is no fanciful metaphor, but a sustaining and culture-making part of human experience: a cowskin rising up from the earth to receive the *Táin Bó Cúlaigne*, the rendered hide of a sacrificial ram descending from the clouds to preserve the *Zohar*, the inscriptions wrought on the physical world by precipitation, or seismic change, or processes of environmental transformation. Here is Michel Serres, on the sedimented palimpsest of the earth:

> Carried away by torrents and their own weight, halted by obstacles or their own shape, stones descend and break, carve into the talweg the long path of their fall or movement. Masses of sand, driven by the wind, file away at the mountain. Ice cracks and breaks stones and trees, cliffs and the earth on the plain, as does drought. Who is writing? Waters, snow, the return to gentler weather, orphite, granite, equilibrium, density, energy, sun, flora and fauna. This covers, that stains. On what do they write? On snow and water, on fauna or flora, on marble or ice. What the earth displays results from the wrinkles it gives itself. A page.[6]

The book and the earth: a story common to all technologies of text, from stone to skin to screen. Where we might see the forces of environmental change on a parchment folio cockled by moisture or dappled by mold, a medieval theologian might see the furrows of a written field. "He cannot take the plow?" Peter Damian asks. "Then let him take up the pen; it is much more useful. In the furrows he traces on the parchment, he will sow the seeds of divine words."[7] Henry David Thoreau, in *A Week on the Concord and Merrimack Rivers*, casts his gaze across long-cultivated fields with no doubt that those who farmed them were "greater men than Homer, or Chaucer, or Shakespeare, only they never got time to say so; they never took to the way of writing." But just look at their fields, Thoreau implores us, "and imagine what they might write, if ever they should put pen to paper. Or what have they not written on the surface of the earth already, clearing, and burning, and scratching, and harrowing, and plowing, and subsoiling, in and in, and out and out, and over and over, again and again, erasing what they had already written for lack of parchment."[8] Robust metaphors likening agrarian labor to the act of writing, dead bugs long smeared between the folios of a holy book, a sheepskin dappled with follicles and riddled with flaws: all nodes of ecological meaning within the material forms of parchment culture.

Such convergences are the domain of what I will call *ecocodicology*, a term meant to capture a variety of environmental approaches to the archaeology of the text.[9] Ecocodicology: the comprehension and study of books, documents, and other forms of writing for their interrelation over time and space with the flora and fauna that constitute them; the processes of cultivation, husbandry, manufacture, circulation, preservation, destruction, and disposal that govern their making and unmaking; the environmental forces that shape their transmission and are in turn shaped by their nature as material objects; and the modes of animal and human sensation, reaction, emotion, and experience that both embody and represent the complicated relationship between written things and the environmental forces that sustain and surround them. If ecology studies the interaction of organisms within a larger environment, if codicology studies the physical aspects and make-up of manuscripts, ecocodicology studies the environmental histories and formations of written culture, from the clay and stone tablets of the ancient world through the digital effects scrolling across our Kindles and MacBooks.

Seen in this light, the written artifact coheres as an environmental object, its ecological ambitus neither circumscribed nor overdetermined by the material circumstances of its making and use. Thus C. M. Chin has explored the "imaginative ancient biology of the papyrus book" in the cultural and natural environment of the ancient Mediterranean, a world system in which the plant-made book is not simply an instrument but "a collaborator, a colonizer, and an actor, possessing its own natural forces and tendencies."[10] Joshua Calhoun's luminous study of the "ecology of texts" in early modern England shows how a careful attention to the ecopoetics of the material book sheds powerful light on the environmental history of hand-made paper as it was produced, imprinted or inscribed, and circulated.[11] Parchment is one among many textual mediums that manifest often invisible networks of environmental connection, webs of bookish life extending from the deepest past to our own moment. These networks may operate on the smallest of scales—a tiny wormhole in a single folio—and the largest: the sculpting of pastures and forest floors over wide reaches of time and space by the animals whose skins transmit the past to the present.

Ecocodicology must also be alert to the vast differences between cultural systems and civilizations with respect to the ecology of the text, and willing to test cross-cultural generalizations against more particularist readings of written culture's embededness within environmental forces and change. To take the example of parchment, faith traditions outside the Abrahamic creeds have fostered very different moral stances toward the use of animal skin for the transmission and preservation of their written heritages. Over a century ago, Arthur Anthony Macdonell, in his *History of Sanskrit Literature*, contended that "leather or parchment has never been utilised in India for MSS., owing to the ritual impurity of animal materials."[12] Belary Shamanna Kesavan agrees, suggesting that most bookmakers in premodern

Figure 14.1. Signs arranged over a splayed deerskin icon of Xochipilli, prince of flowers, from Codex Borgia. Central Mexico, fifteenth or early sixteenth century. Vatican City, Biblioteca Apostolica Vaticana Codex Borgia, fol. 53r (detail).

South Asia "would have viewed with horror both the slaughtering of young animals for their skin (cf. parchment), and the writing of sacred texts on such material."[13] While there are a number of manuscripts from the premodern era in India, China, and Tibet surviving on animal skin,[14] such artifacts are the rare exceptions that prove the general rule: that unlike their Abrahamic counterparts, these religious traditions are not subtended by a long tradition of animal utility in the transmission of culture.

Yet the Abrahamic creeds were not the only traditions self-conscious about the animality of certain written artifacts. Figure 14.1 reproduces an icon of splayed deerskin from Codex Borgia, a Mixtec screenfold volume produced sometime around 1400 CE in the Mexican highlands near Puebla or Oaxaca. Written on flayed deerskin, "sacred skin" [*ñee ñuhu*] as the medium was known in Dzaha Dzaui, the codex is rife with a complex floral and faunal symbology, self-referential about its creaturely medium in ways that few contemporaneous European codices can match.[15] A deerskin opens itself to view, crossed at midpoint by a sash of deerskin on which yet another deer figures among the symbols displayed. Deerskin on deerskin on deerskin, all produced and circulated on a membrane book that survives by merest chance.[16]

An unfurled scroll of sheepskin parchment, removed from the acid-free paper envelope in which it has been tucked since someone last paged and examined this document. The skin is a rectangle about the height and width of a legal pad, likely one of a handful of sheets cut from a full hide roughly seven centuries ago. The parchment is stiff and rough to the touch, typical of English records from this period, the hair and flesh sides easily distinguishable with a soft brush of the fingertips. The surface shows creases, warps, and wrinkles in abundance. The document is a keeper's description of the holdings of the upper grange of St. Mary's Abbey, Boxley, a Cistercian house near the village of Maidstone in the county of Kent, the great shire stretching southeast from London to the English Channel and the sea.[17] In the early decades of the fourteenth century, the region of woodlands and pasture around Maidstone was becoming a center of the wool trade, with drained marshes and cleared forest making way for flocks that grazed this portion of the Weald just below the North Downs. The herds and flocks in the region suffered frequent adversity, as did their human minders. Though written in the flattening idiom of record-keeping, the account registers the devastating effects of one particular disease afflicting sheep and cattle at Boxley during the years 1334 and 1335. In the Upper Grange alone, the keeper records, out of 264 newborn lambs that year, fully 214 died, while 156 out of the 216 yearlings succumbed.[18] The mass die-offs at Boxley were part of a more general pattern of contagion afflicting livestock throughout the midlands and the south, affecting cows, sheep, goats, pigs, and horses alike, resulting in part from wide-scale crop failures in the preceding years due to excessive rainfall and slow recovery. The surge in animal mortality had particularly dire effects on the manors of Kent and neighboring shires, which saw a drastic plunge in wool production and ewe fertility rates, and, according to multiple reeves' accounts, suffered a corresponding weakness in quadriped milking.[19]

The keeper's account is a written record of pastoral husbandry gone awry, then, part of a micro-history of animals and land in a particular locality afflicted by the forces of disease, deprivation, and climate, with measurable effects on the human population that represented them in various forms while exploiting them for their hair, skin, and flesh—for sustenance, record-keeping, trade, warmth, and other uses. Yet the keeper's account is also part of a much larger assemblage of environmental records of faunal life: the several hundred parchment documents that still survive from Boxley Abbey, all of them likely rendered from the skins of the same animals that once nursed, grazed, and died alongside numerous other members of their flocks and herds nourished among the Kentish hills and plains. For this region of Kent was also emerging as an important hub of the tanning industry, with skinners selling leathers by the bundle to merchants in urban centers. Parchment represented a not insignificant part of the skin trade; roughly ten miles to the west of Boxley, a William Millys, parchment maker, is listed among the debtors to the nunnery at West Malling in the Medway valley.[20]

The environmental history of a written archive is the incalculable sum of its moving parts, an ecological complex of animals and humans, grasslands and woods, hides and documents, as well as the processes that aggregate and disjoin them over decades and centuries. The surviving animal membranes from Boxley—now collected in flattened sheets, neatly tied rolls, small bundles of skins held together with ribbons and cords—include dozens of yearly rentals and surveys of lands and possessions, inventories and descriptions of flocks and built structures by keepers and overseers, records of purchases and sales of commodities and properties. Many of them document specific instances of land use and transfer, such as the abbey's indenture of sale of a woods called "Bereworthesgrof" to one John de Walshe in 1319.[21] These hundreds of human transactions exist by virtue of the zoomorphic form of their inscription and survival, which was inseparable from their enactment, enforcement, and preservation. The membranes are thus both cultural and ecological records of the creaturely habitation and transformation of the Kentish countryside. They archive the generations of animals and humans who gently sculpted the region's hills, forests, and valleys with their patterns of consumption and excretion, which in turn churned and fertilized the grasses and crops on which they fed. Sheep were moved over long distances in this part of England, driven from manor to manor along the Downs, their reproduction even in straitened circumstances ensuring the survival of their breeds and lines, while their shearing, slaughter, and butchery rendered their hides, wool, and flesh into commodities for human consumption and use as meat, leather, cloth, and, of course, parchment.

The material life of an archive, its history of ownership and transfer among individuals and institutions, is also a record of environmental transformation. The passage of time subjects documents to both short- and long-term processes of ecological change. Alterations in temperature and geographical location, decomposition and repair, usage and handling, chemical and biomolecular analysis: these and other processes exert subtle but discernible effects on the environmental state of an archive. This holds especially true for a largely membrane archive such as the written record of St. Mary's, now a small cluster of stone ruins at the edge of Boxley, a village that sits a short and twisty walk south of the North Downs Way. After the Dissolution the abbey's properties came by grant of the crown into the possession of the Wyatt family, and the documents are now stored at the National Archives

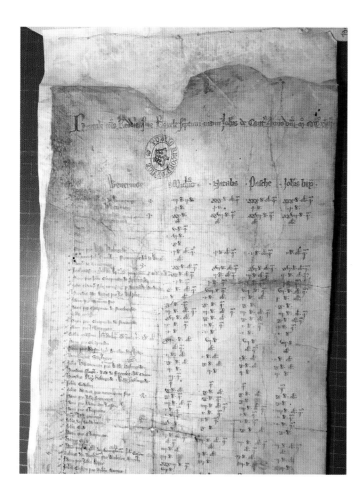

Figure 14.2.
Head of a rental roll. Kent, Boxley Abbey, 1317-18. Kew, National Archives, SC 6/893/24.

in Kew. The creation of this and similar large repositories (such as the numerous county records offices around England) entailed a slow but steady ingathering of animal membrane that took place over several decades of the late nineteenth and early twentieth centuries, as centralized records offices gradually subsumed the local archives of parish, town, manor, and family, in the process disaggregating records that had remained in situ for many centuries while assembling membranes by the thousands and millions and tens of millions into new archival formations. Examined and touched one by one, the Boxley membranes retain little of their ecological intimacy with one another and with the premodern environs of their origin, and it takes a considerable scholarly leap of nostalgic imagination to return them there. We settle instead for glimpses of the singular animals in these archives—as in figure 14.2, which shows the curve of a beast's flayed skin serving as the head of Boxley's yearly rental roll for 1317–18.

We get a later, more distanced perspective on this archival ecology in a series of letters submitted to the *Maidstone Gazette* in 1826 by William Keer Brown, a Kentish diplomat in the royal service. Writing in support of the Corn Laws, Brown included in his correspondence a lengthy argument against the importation of foreign wool as a threat to the native trade. Appended to one of Brown's letters on wool is his transcription of an entry from the *Encyclopædia Brittanica* on the subject of sheep and their material uses to humanity. The entry begins with an arresting image of human dominion and creaturely innocence: "Amongst the various animals with which divine Providence has stored the world for the use of man, none is to be found more innocent, more useful, or more valuable than the sheep." Brown's transcription goes on to document the myriad human needs served by coat, corpse, and hide:

> Besides this, the useful animal after being deprived of his coat, produces another against the next year, and when we are hungry and kill him for food, he gives us his skin to employ the fell-mongers and parchment-makers, who supply us with a durable material for securing our estates, rights and possessions, and if our enemies take the field against us, with a powerful instrument for rousing our courage to repel their attacks. When the parchment-maker has taken as much of the skin as he can use, the glue-maker comes after and picks up every morsel that is left, and therewith supplies a material for the carpenter and cabinet-maker, which they cannot do without, and which is essentially necessary before we can have elegant furniture in our houses.[22]

Parchment is clearly regarded as a byproduct of sheep butchery here, the hides separated from the meat only "when we are hungry," while serving to "employ" the craftsmen involved in the skin trade (in fell and parchment). The innocent sheep, in the form of parchment rendered from its skin, supplies human culture with "a durable material for securing our estates, rights and possessions"—a phrase that recalls Hamlet's rather more bitter vision of membrane indentures and conveyances filling up the grave of a forgotten man. The letter and the entry together demonstrate the continuing indispensability of the parchment trade to England's documentary culture as late as the early nineteenth century.

When Brown transcribed these authoritative passages on sheep, wool, and parchment from the *Encyclopædia Brittanica* and sent them to Maidstone, he could hardly have been thinking of the lambs who died nearby at Boxley Abbey five centuries before. We know about this local die-off only because its extent and particulars were recorded on the skin of one of its victims' fellow creatures, and subsequently preserved among the abbey's records and muniments until transfer to the Public Record Office in the twentieth century. Such circuits of ecological connection define the animal archive, written both in fibers of sheep collagen and in the natural and built environments traversed by creatures human and non alike.

The small story elaborated above is one of many millions that might be told about particular written artifacts in relation to their complex and changing ecologies. One of the thornier questions in the field of ecocriticism as it has developed over the last thirty to forty years (particularly since the so-called Third Wave) has concerned the degree of reciprocity between the written object and the environment, however construed. Literary critics and historians have returned again and again to the problem of the agency of writing with respect to the ecological. How can literature be understood as "environmental," and with what consequences for our habits of writing and reading? Does a poem or a novel relate to the environment on the level of mimesis, imitating and thus somehow internalizing the forces of nature it seeks to reimagine or recast in verse or prose? Is environmental literature's relation to ecology and nature merely thematic, a series of attempts to capture the beings and forces of the earth as subjects of representation? Or does it advocate and promote an ethical orientation toward the natural or nonhuman world, even to the extent of effecting political change in the process?[23]

I want to pause for a moment over a bit of ecocritical snark that may help us address these questions with some directness, and with important bearing on ecocodicological method. The polemic occurs in a book by Dana Philips, *The Truth of Ecology*, a study that aims to reorient ecocriticism "away from the epistemological to the pragmatic" and takes as its primary target a defining work in the field, Lawrence Buell's *The Environmental Imagination* (1995). One of Buell's critical gestures in this influential book was to ponder his own situatedness with respect to the natural world: seated at his desk while looking out on "a grove of second-growth white pines that sway at this moment of writing, with their blue-yellow-green five-needle clusters above spiky circles of atrophied lower limbs, along a brown needle-strewn ridge of shale forty feet from my computer screen." The same grove of trees, Buell writes, "can be found in the pages of American literature, but it is not the woods imagined by American criticism." Thus motivated by the organic specificity of the living things before his eyes, Buell seeks an alternative mode of critical engagement, one that would resist the romantic homogenizations seen so often in nature writing as commonly understood, with its trees and groves "built from chant-like reiterated and generalized images: a forest where treeness matters but the identities and the material properties of trees are inconsequential."[24] This sense of the critic's locatedness is an imperative of environmental criticism; the trees in Buell's sightline function as conceptual anchors of a sort, natural guideposts in any ecologically conscious mode of critique.

For Philips, though, such moments of bonding with nature constitute the "ecocritical epiphany": they are "ecocriticism's moment of origin," entailing a naïve awakening to nature and a statement of "faith in all things green" at the expense of critical thought. This epiphany, Philips argues, is indicative of Buell's desire to find "a relationship between trees in literature and trees in the world closer than a relationship of mere semblance would be, whether that semblance is descriptive, iconic, or metaphorical and symbolic."[25] On this view, Buell is seeking in the history of environmental writing "a literature of presence" that betrays the very notion of imaginative making: "To insist that trees must be present *in literature*, just because they happen to be mentioned and described or even celebrated there, seems hostile to the very possibility of imagination, which pays its dividends in the coin of figuration, not representation." According to Philips, Buell's epiphanic criticism is also an insult to criticism itself, and to the intellectual history that undergirds it: "to persist in thinking that trees might somehow be present in literature after all, despite the strictures of recent literary theory (and at least two thousand years of philosophy), is uncritical and, worse, hostile to criticism." With all this polemic as backdrop, Philips comes to the crux of the matter, dismissing the material medium of environmental writing:

> By the same token, I think it is obvious that trees can never be, as Buell insists they are, *in literature*, and least of all *in a novel*, however much they may be 'in' it figuratively and even if it is true that because books are made from paper, and paper from pulpwood, trees are in our books (and thus make up the sort of content more suited to chemical than literary analysis).[26]

In one rushed clause ("and even if it is true . . ."), Philips dismisses the most palpably material aspect of the literary object: its organic medium, in this case the pulpwood and paper making up the novel or the book. Descriptive bibliography has no place in environmental criticism, then. Fibers, cells, molecules: these are the domain of chemists, not critics.

Yet "trees are in our books," as even Philips acknowledges in the passage above, though what he caricatures as a dogged literalism is for the descriptive bibliographer the very stuff of bookish life. "What would Thoreau say to-day if he returned and saw his beloved forests being ground into pulp?" asks an anonymous writer for *Forest and Stream* in 1916, commenting on the desolation of the Maine forests for lumber and papermills.[27] The question goes to the ecocodicological heart of writing in its immediate organic materiality: for Thoreau, the paper filled with the critical jottings of his hand, that imprints the environmental writings ensuring his fame; for us, perhaps, the cheap global labor and unregulated micro-environments that manufacture the Macs and the iPads on which we write and read and deliver our ecological critiques.

Thoreau himself commented more than once on the nature of paper as a simultaneously indispensable and unsustainable commodity: "Paper is cheap," he writes in *A Week on the Concord and Merrimack Rivers*, "and authors need not now erase one book before they write another. Instead of cultivating the earth for wheat and potatoes, they cultivate literature, and fill a place in the Republic of Letters."[28] A more scathing indictment of contemporary print culture comes in *The Maine Woods*, where Thoreau casts the profligacy of paper waste as an assault on cultural tradition itself:

> The Anglo-American can indeed cut down, and grub up all this waving forest, and make a stump speech, and vote for Buchanan on its ruins, but he cannot converse with the spirit of the tree he fells, he cannot read the poetry and mythology which retire as he advances. He ignorantly erases mythological tablets in order to print his handbills and town-meeting warrants on them. Before he has learned his a b c in the beautiful but mystic lore of the wilderness which Spenser and Dante had just begun to read, he cuts it down, coins a *pine-tree* shilling, (as if to signify the pine's value to him,) puts up a *deestrict* school-house, and introduces Webster's spelling-book.[29]

The ravenous consumption of forests is of a piece with trivial politics and a violent destruction of the "poetry and mythology" of the natural world as written in the trees. Erasure of these "mythological tablets"—the things of the forested earth—is effected through the clear-cutting of trees by the Anglo-American who would "print his handbills and town-meeting warrants on them" once they are pulped and made into paper. The "wilderness" of literary history gives way to a morally compromised coinage, the "*deestrict* school house," and the grade school primer in this vision of a debased society sacrificing its trees on the altar of poor education and cheap print.

Thoreau's sensibilities here speak to a long tradition of self-consciously bookish environmental literature, a certain strain of ecocodicological writing that blurs distinctions between medium and message, a text and its carved, pulped, or flayed ground. We have seen several examples of this tradition already in the Latin and Old English book riddles, a mode of enigmatic poetry that thinks with great imagination about the indissolubility of text and organic medium. A later, no less challenging work is "The Book" by Henry Vaughan, a Welsh metaphysical poet in the school of George Herbert who flourished in the middle decades of the seventeenth century. "The Book," originally published in Vaughan's *Silex Scintillans* (1655), renders the organic elements of the codex as a thoroughgoing conceit, merging ecology and content into a vision of bookish naturalism.[30] The poem has long featured in the study of naturalist and environmental literature, appearing as a centerpiece in Francis T. Palgrave's discussion of landscape poetry in his classic *Landscape in Poetry: From Homer to Tennyson* (1897). "The Book" appears in fifteen couplets divided into five stanzas of unequal length, each of which takes up a physical component of the eponymous book by meditating on its derivation from the things and creatures of the earth:

> Eternal God! Maker of all
> That have lived here since the Man's fall;
> The Rock of Ages! in whose shade
> They live unseen, when here they fade;
>
> Thou knew'st this paper when it was
> Mere seed, and after that but grass;
> Before 'twas dressed or spun, and when
> Made linen, who did wear it then:
> What were their lives, their thoughts, and deeds,
> Whether good corn or fruitless weeds.
>
> Thou knew'st this tree when a green shade
> Covered it, since a cover made,
> And where it flourished, grew, and spread,
> As if it never should be dead.
>
> Thou knew'st this harmless beast when he
> Did live and feed by Thy decree
> On each green thing; then slept (well fed)
> Clothed with this skin which now lies spread
> A covering o'er this aged book;
> Which makes me wisely weep, and look

On my own dust; mere dust it is,
But not so dry and clean as this.
Thou knew'st and saw'st them all, and though
Now scattered thus, dost know them so.

O knowing, glorious Spirit! when
Thou shalt restore trees, beasts, and men,
When Thou shalt make all new again,
Destroying only death and pain,
Give him amongst Thy works a place
Who in them loved and sought Thy face![31]

The poem's hortatory opening embraces its addressee through the expansive idiom of apposition, moving from God to Maker to Rock, from omnipresent being to divine actor to eternal element, while the Rock of Ages casts shade on the dead, those "fade[d]" from earthly life. The second stanza envisions the matter of paper through its organic components—seed becomes grass becomes linen cloth—while pondering with animistic relish the "lives . . . thoughts, and deeds" of the plants that furnished it.

Leah Knight has identified a possible source for this poem in the work of John Gerard, a Renaissance herbalist who wrote vividly of the "provenance, *in* plants, of his book *on* plants," as Knight has characterized his musings on the subject: "this Paper whereon I write . . . first from seed became Flax, then after much vexation thred, then cloth, where it was cut and mangled to serue the Fashions of the time."[32] Moving from plants to animals, Vaughan devotes his fourth and lengthiest stanza to the "harmless beast," an unspecified quadriped (whether pig, deer, cow, goat, or sheep) whose tanned hide now serves as the leathern cover of the "aged book," its words "Clothed with this skin." The beast sacrificed for the bookbinding provokes the speaker's most emotive response, prompting him to "wisely weep" as he looks on his "own dust," not so "dry and clean" as the new cover in the hands. As Palgrave put it, "even the leather sheepkin has its life to this most imaginative poet."[33] The stanza's closing couplet—"Thou knew'st and saw'st them all, and though / Now scattered thus, dost know them so"—could refer either to all of the prior components or to an unspecified panoply of beasts covering myriad volumes in Vaughan's imagined organic library. "The Book" closes with a vision of the resurrection, which promises to "restore trees, beasts, and men"—the book's elements and its readers—to eternal life for those who "sought [God's] face" in its living pages. The poem as a whole encompasses a full circuit of bookish life that imagines the making of the codex from seed to plant to paper, from tree to board, from living animal to the leathern cover rendered from its flayed skin.

A creature, a moth, eats words. How strange, that such a worm could devour written things, while growing none the wiser for the experience. This word-consuming moth is the subject of an anonymous Old English riddle from the Exeter Book:

> A moth ate songs—wolfed words!
> That seemed a weird dish—that a worm
> Should swallow, dumb thief in the dark,
> The songs of a man, his chants of glory,
> Their places of strength. That thief-guest
> Was no wiser for having swallowed words.[34]

A more modest riddle than some of its companion poems in the Exeter Book, perhaps, and less sentimental about the ecology of parchment in scribal culture. Yet the simple solution to this ingenious riddle—bookworm or bookmoth—masks a series of complex puns and self-referential doubles entendres that enrich its subject and the riddle's conceit as a whole. Terms such as *word*, *gied*, and *cwide* suggest that the moth is eating spoken rather than written language, paradoxes augmented by the riddle's celebration of its own cleverness in the fifth and sixth lines.[35] The membrane medium goes unmentioned, yet only with its consumption by the worm can the paradox of eating words be accomplished: as Haruko Momma describes the *wyrm*, "a creature that eats away its own habitat, both the parchment and the ink, without, however, digesting the non-material matter of the codex."[36] By the end of the riddle the moth has fattened itself on the animal skin that supports and contains the eaten words; in Craig Williamson's gloss, the word-eating worm has now "passed from the wordhoard to the delicious *memoria* of the vellum sheet."[37] Here the membrane book is not a transcendent relic of divinity derived from the sacrifice of a beast, as in Riddle 24, but a mundane object of consumption: the manuscript page is unmentionable food for worms, adumbrating the eventual fates of its human readers.

Foodways and bookways run in constant parallel over the course of the parchment epoch, though their divergence and distinctiveness are equally significant to the environmental history of the medium. It is common to characterize the medieval world as defined in part by its economies of scarcity: these were societies of thrift that used or saved everything they could, and would rarely allow portions of a slaughtered animal to go to waste. This perceived sense of scarcity and the resultant avoidance of wastefulness functioned as both a theological virtue and a poetic topos, nowhere more vividly defended than in *The Testament of the Bucke*, a late Middle English poem that elaborates a dying buck's wishes regarding the disposition of his body following his coming death and butchery. His "leniste fleshe" will make "stekis" for maidens, his blood and puddings will go to the "pudying wyffe," his "suette" to the crow, his "small guttes to the harp-strynges that makes mery sondes," and so on. Every part of the buck's body, that is, will be put to some good use.[38] In John Lydgate's "Debate of the Horse, the Goose, and the Sheep," the slaughtered body of a sheep furnishes both "good parchemyn" to "write on books in quaeirs many fold" alongside its "fleesh," the "moton" that serves as "natural restauracion" for the sick.[39]

Such an ethics of efficiency and utility, however satirical in these cases, speaks to a wider understanding of parchment as one among many articles derived from the body of the slaughtered beast. While Daniel Thompson was likely correct to suggest that "any city's preferences in the matter of meat diet were reflected in the local parchment industry,"[40] this does not imply that parchment was merely "a by-product of meat production," as it is often characterized.[41] There is little evidence to suggest that butchers, artisans, or consumers regarded parchment as in any way a secondary product of husbandry and slaughter. When the Persian king Gushtasp orders the slaughter of twelve thousand oxen for the writing and preservation of the *Avesta*, he does not order a corresponding feast for his subjects. When Rabbi Shimon bar Yohai is visited in his cave by the angel Gabriel bearing the sacred parchment from Mount Moriah, the angel says nothing about mutton. And when the anonymous riddler of the Exeter Book speaks in the voice of the animal sacrificed for a holy book, the beast's flesh goes unmentioned (and, as far as the reader knows, unconsumed).

A final perspective on ecocodicology emerges from the vexed and complicated relation between dietary practice and book culture in medieval monasticism, particularly in orders that more radically eschewed the consumption of meat. Some of the foundational dietary precepts of Western monasticism are embodied in a simple sentence from the Rule of St. Benedict, who enjoins his monks, "They should all abstain entirely from the consumption of the meat of quadrupeds [*carnium . . . quadrupedum*], except the gravely ill."[42] The Order of Carthusians was especially strict in this regard, with continual strictures on meat advertised and enforced across centuries and regions despite the treasure and time the order famously invested in membrane books.[43] This investment comes across in a floridly detailed price list commissioned by the Chartreuse of Champmol, the dynastic Carthusian foundation of the

Dukes of Burgundy near Dijon, inventorying books and parchments purchased by the house between the years 1388 and 1399. The list delights in the sheer variety of species, sizes, and qualities of skin: abortives, large abortives, parchment made variously from the skins of sheep, calves, and goats, in varietals that could come from the menu of a discerning chef.[44] The inventory recalls Augustine's polemics a thousand years earlier against the Manichaeans, radically abstaining from animal flesh while taking endless delectation in the words written on their beautiful skin.

Guillaume de Deguileville, a French Cistercian writing in the mid-fourteenth century, devotes a passage of his influential vernacular dream vision *Le Pèlerinage de la Vie Humaine* to the allegorical and material intimacy between membrane and meat. Here, the figure of Estude offers an edible treat resting on a sheet of parchment:

> Une autre vi qui s'en aloit
> par cloistre et, si come me sembloit,
> viande enmielle portoit
> sur parchemin qu'elle tenoit
> et la suioit .i. coulon blanc.

> I saw another walking through the cloister who, as it seemed to me, was carrying honeyed meat on a piece of parchment that she held, and a white dove was following her.[45]

The moralizing character of Grace Dieu glosses the meat and parchment in spiritual terms: Estude "fills the heart, not the belly, with her sweet, good food," thus "sublimating the material parchment support of the word into the ideological nourishment of its contents," as Sarah Kay puts it.[46] Medieval illustrations of this episode mark the connection between meat and parchment with a delightful literalism. In one example (see fig. 14.3), Estude stands behind a column in a covered cloister, slightly bent, as if offering her fleshly wares to the viewer. The portions of honeyed meat she proffers rest atop a length of unfurled parchment extending from her hand and entwined around a second column. The image literalizes the common derivation of *viande* and *parchemin* from the rendered flesh of the beast while evoking the widespread spiritual practice of *ruminatio* derived from various biblical passages on the "eating of the book" (Ezekiel 3; Revelation 10).

Foodways and bookways converge with a practical directness in a brief but telling anecdote found in a grant from Charlemagne to the abbot and monks of St. Denis in the year 774. According to the text of the grant, the monks are permitted to

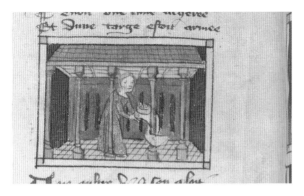

Figure 14.3. The figure of Estude offering a piece of meat on a parchment. From Guillaume de Deguileville, *La Pèlerinage de la Vie Humaine*. Northern France, late fourteenth or early fifteenth century. London, British Library Ms. Harley 4399, fol. 82v (detail).

hunt limitless deer provided they make books of their skins [*ex quorum coriis libros ipsius*] and give the venison to the infirm.[47] Similar linkages appear in a grant to the monks of Sithiu (St. Omer) fourteen years later. The grant gives the right of unlimited hunting of deer in the king's forests, as well as the right to use the rendered skins for the making of bookbindings, gauntlets, and girdles [*ad codices contegendos vel manicas et zonas faciendes*].[48] This is a direct and literal concatenation of meat and skin, animal and book, all in the wider environmental context of game management and forest jurisdiction. Such collocations of meat-eating and bookmaking can be found in any number of medieval sources, with little to no suggestion that the acquisition of flesh was the primary goal of slaughter and rendition. Indeed, where the sources mention specific usages for animal skin, materials for bookmaking are by far the more common destination.

"The historical ecology of any part of the world is always an unfinished manuscript—passed from hand to hand, critiqued, debated, amended, revised." So writes Carole Crumley, an environmental archaeologist who works at the intersection of cultural history, anthropology, and ecology. Crumley is here characterizing recent advances in the field of historical ecology, which brings together "the open-mindedness of scientific inquiry and the phenomenological intensity of human experience" to examine the interconnectedness between human beings and their environments over long stretches of time.[49] Crumley's resonant image of the "unfinished manuscript" nicely captures the sedimented overlays of historical and environmental change as they are comprehended within various disciplines subject to their own epistemological transformations. In the same spirit, we might turn the metaphor to suggest that a membrane manuscript in turn represents an unfinished ecology of any given part of the world: a living record of the animals that traversed the microclimates of their pasturing; the environments through which a codex, charter, or roll travels and that it in turn helps to shape; and those defamiliarizing intimacies with the animal entailed by our continued work with the parchment inheritance. Ecocodicology embraces all of these and more: the environmental histories embodied by the parchment inheritance, the human cultures the medium preserves.

CHAPTER FIFTEEN

PARCHMENT ELEGIES

Here is the flesh side, it understood true dark.
Here is the hair side that met the day's weather,
the long ago rain.
—MICHELLE BOISSEAU, "PARCHMENT"

A polychrome being fills the rough-cut form of a parchment, painted in gouache (fig. 15.1). Six-fingered and with a head shaped in the double curves of a guitar, the being appears flayed like the parchment itself, spread open to the viewer's gaze. Rampant within the being's body: a two-headed centaur-like female figure on a blue field at the center of the membrane, cuddling a dragon splayed in her lap. The being's knees are joined with the conical heads of two faceless robed figures—heads which, on closer inspection, turn out to be heads of garlic. The figures bear totemic staffs topped by the same broomlike thatches of straw that form their feet. Between them reclines a camel, its hump transformed into the grotesque face of a demon. Zoomorphic banners festoon the witchy staffs to either side, inscribed with words and phrases written in reverse and evoking the deep past that inspires the work as a whole.

This astonishing image is *Samhain Skin*, the creation of Leonora Carrington (1907–2011), a Lancashire-born writer and painter known before her death as the last surviving artist of the Surrealist school. Carrington intended the painting to evoke the ancient feast of Samhain, the harvest festival that opened the darker half of the year and was popularized during the Celtic revival around the turn of the twentieth century.[1] The painting speaks as well to Carrington's personal investments in her Irish genealogy, the multiple mythic terms in the inscriptions evoking a maternal Celtic lineage: among others, the *Tuatha dé Danann* (in the upper left banner), the mythical tribe of ancient Ireland driven underground by the coming of Christianity; and the *Sidhe* (written in the blue banner at the top of the

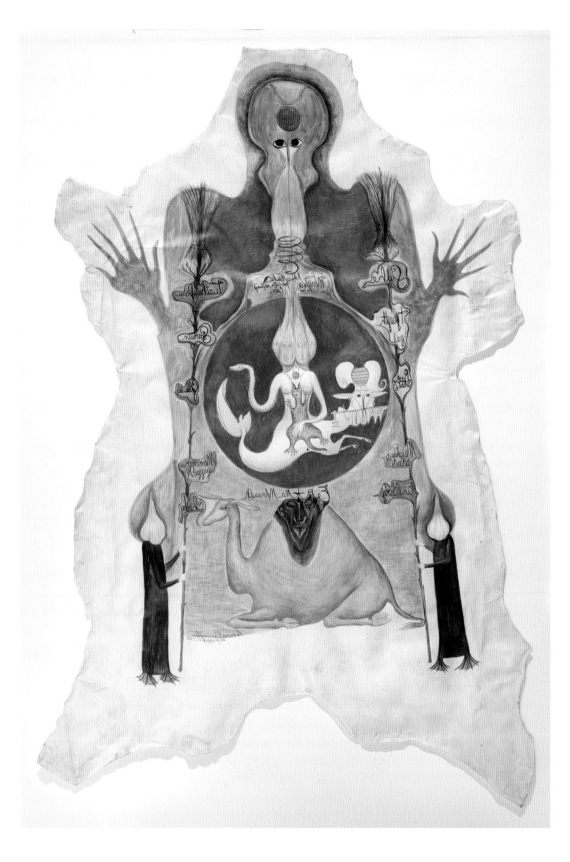

right-hand staff), the fairy peoples from whom Carrington's grandmother claimed direct descent.[2]

Samhain Skin is a fitting object to conjure in gradually bringing this book to a close: a parchment flayed and painted in the latter half of the twentieth century yet reaching back to the dawn of the Common Era to envision the ritual life of a mythical world—and all through the animal medium of premodern writing. Marion Kite and Roy Thomson, writing on conservation practices, note the dimunition of the parchment industry since the Industrial Revolution, and the accordant nostalgia accruing to the medium: "The rapid decline in production of parchment during the twentieth century means that it is now largely a material of the past and this may make it precious to us once more."[3] A work such as *Samhain Skin* embraces this pastness of parchment, its archaic dimensions, as Raymond Williams defines the term: "that which is wholly recognized as an element of the past, to be observed, to be examined, or even on occasion to be consciously 'revived,' in a deliberately specializing way."[4] The trade and craft of parchment remain active forces in certain specialized cultural spheres and in certain religious communities even as its archaism is exemplified in works such as *The Mystique of Vellum*, a volume that celebrates the history of printing on vellum from Gutenberg through the contemporary book arts. The volume includes a tipped-in "parchment specimen" that celebrates its own medium via an epigraph from *Hamlet* (see fig. 15.2). In a similar spirit, Ronald Reed's *Specimens of Parchment* (1976) was a limited-run "album of specimens" released as a companion to his monograph *The Nature and Making of Parchment*, published the preceding year. *Specimens* is extra-illustrated with a selection of medieval and modern fragments of membrane snipped from codices and documents and included in a grangerized portfolio of custom samples.[5] A "portion of a leaf from a very large size antiphonal" of the sixteenth century (fig. 15.3) provides "an example of 'run of the mill' sheepskin parchment widely used in medieval times," while an eighteenth-century indenture comes from "the grain (upper) split of a sheepskin."

An earlier book in the same vein is Karl Jakob Lüthi's *Das Pergament* (1938), of which three hundred copies were printed, the first twenty-five including vellum samples—and the first fifty bound in fragments of parchment choir books, books of hours, and documents, both medieval and modern. The copy owned by my own university's Special Collections library (see fig. 15.4) features fragments of a French book of hours and a nineteenth-century *brevet de libraire*. Lüthi, in an irony surely not lost on fellow enthusiasts at the time, resorted to this premodern binding prac-

Figure 15.1. Leonora Carrington, *Samhain Skin*, 1975. Gouache on vellum.

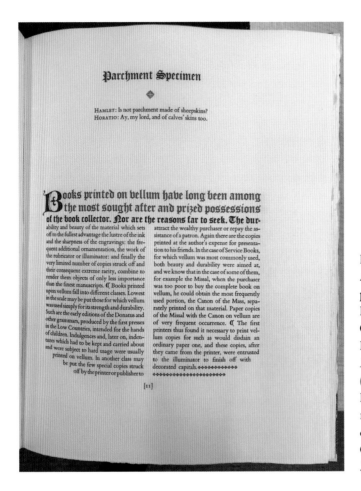

Figure 15.2.
A tipped-in parchment page in Decherd Turner, Colin Franklin, and Richard Bigus, *The Mystique of Vellum* (Boston: Anne and David Bromer, 1984). University of Virginia Special Collections Z1030 .T87 1984, p. 11.

tice to mark the archaism of his own parchment obsessions, which included a full exhibit, "Das Pergament (1000–1900)," at the Schweizerisches Gutenbergmuseum in Bern in 1936.[6]

Such archaisms have long been a feature, not a bug, of the parchment inheritance. Owners and archivists maintain parchments they cannot read, while others discard or reuse membranes whose utility may be long since divorced from the writing they were once intended to preserve. The contemporary life of parchment reflects these elegiac fates: fragments pulled free of their bookish origins to teach or delight, nostalgic homages to this medium of a bygone world, artworks of melancholy beauty that enlist its antiquarian resonance to create startling new perspectives on the skins they transform.

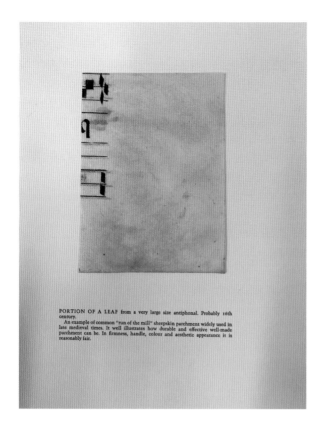

PORTION OF A LEAF from a very large size antiphonal. Probably 16th
century.
    An example of common "run of the mill" sheepskin parchment widely used in
late medieval times. It well illustrates how durable and effective well-made
parchment can be. In firmness, handle, colour and aesthetic appearance it is
reasonably fair.

Figure 15.3. Parchment fragment cut from the leaf of a sixteenth-century antiphonal, from Ronald Reed, *Specimens of Parchment* (1976). Charlottesville, University of Virginia Special Collections TS1165. R44 Suppl. n.p.

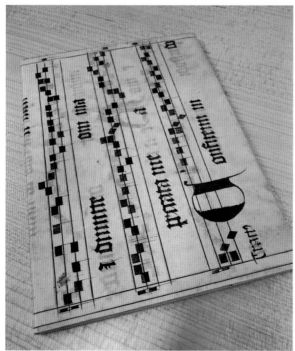

Figure 15.4. A copy of Karl J. Lüthi, *Das Pergament: Seine Geschichte, Seine Andwendung* (1938), binding reinforced with a leaf from a French Gradual. Charlottesville, University of Virginia Special Collections Z112.L9 1938.

➤ ⟵

The news came in the spring of 2017: *Tory fury as historic Brexit Act WON'T be printed for posterity on vellum because the centuries old tradition has been quietly DITCHED*, screamed the *Daily Mail*. The *Telegraph* was more circumspect while placing the blame squarely on the House of Lords: *Anger as MPs bow to peers' pressure and end 500-year old tradition of printing new laws on vellum*.

The tradition invoked in both headlines is the requirement that record copies of public Acts of Parliament be printed on parchment or vellum, a rule originating in a report by the Select Committee on Printing issued in 1848. That rule replaced the previous practice, dating back to the reign of Richard III, that parliamentary acts should be written and preserved ("engrossed and inrolled") on membrane rolls and kept among the official records of the realm.[7] Parliament had occasionally debated the practice on prior occasions, most recently in 1999, when, in the face of fierce opposition from its defenders, the tradition was maintained as an integral part of the governing body's record-keeping practices. In 2016, too, the custom appeared to be on safe ground, at least initially: while the House of Lords moved against the retention of vellum for the recording of Acts, the Commons reversed the decision, in the process apparently saving the fortunes of William Cowley, the Newport Pagnell firm that has furnished vellum sheets to the parliamentary printing office since the nineteenth century. As the company happily proclaimed in an update posted on its webpage that April, "Vellum wins the day!!"

Cowley's optimism, however, proved to be unwarranted. Despite the earlier vote in the full chamber supporting the practice, in March 2017 the House of Commons Administration Committee, by majority vote, ultimately agreed to acquiesce to the Lords and end the venerable tradition. The final and melancholy resolution: "The House of Commons Commission has agreed to provide and pay for vellum front and back sheets for record copies, out of respect for tradition, and hopes to be able to use British vellum from Cowley's."[8] Cold comfort for Cowley and the traditionalists; apparently there is to be no going back.

The parliamentary custom of recording its Acts on vellum represented what may have been the world's last large-scale tradition of official governmental record-keeping on animal skin. The debate transcripts from the House of Commons on the practice, florid with nostalgia, exhibit frequent bursts of Shakespearean eloquence alongside an ersatz environmental consciousness summoned in its defense. "Vellum is almost immortally permanent," David Warburton (C-Somerton and Frome) proclaims, in an echo of Pliny the Elder, "and—from the Domesday Book to the equally wondrous Supply and Appropriation (Anticipation and Adjustments) Act of 2016—has faithfully freighted and defended its contents. If we ditch it for a ream of A4 80 gsm paper, or whatever it might be, our descendants will watch as the laws governing them gradually putrefy, wither and dissolve."[9] Warburton's paean to vellum recalls the "rotten parchment bonds" lamented by Shakespeare's John of Gaunt, playing on the same symbolic association of material ground and written law, though in this case the corruptible medium is acid-free paper rather than animal membrane.

For other defenders of vellum usage, the safeguarding of existing practice goes hand in hand with appeals to technology, craft, and sustainability. Thus Iain Stewart, Conservative MP for Milton Keynes South (where Cowley's is located), argues that in addition to threatening "our heritage and tradition of skilled craftspeople," the abandonment of vellum will be a blow to the local environment in his constituency: "Vellum is eco-friendly. It is, as we have heard, a by-product of the meat and dairy industry. The skins not used for vellum would otherwise have to be incinerated or go to landfill. It avoids tree felling and the use of chemicals to treat the paper." James Gray (C-North Wiltshire) similarly takes on those who would find in the vellum debate "some animal rights or animal welfare matter because of the use of calfskins" in the making of vellum. As Gray points out, "the calfskins are picked up from the abattoir. The calves are killed for the purpose of being eaten, so there is absolutely no animal welfare consideration of any kind at all. Indeed, we could argue that reusing the calfskins is a much more environmentally friendly approach."

Yet for nearly every Member who speaks against this change in documentary practice, it is the tradition and continuity of English culture and its written laws that are most at issue. Thus Ranil Jayawardena (C-North East Hampshire) cites Edmund Burke's vision of society "as a contract between the living, the dead and those who are not yet born" as a justification for maintaining the practice under debate: "I have no wish to deprive future generations of the ability to touch and smell the records of their past. In fact, we have a duty to our descendants to leave behind an abiding physical record of our laws and customs, just as our forebears, in their turn, did for us." The physicality of vellum, its smell and touch: a vital link between past, present, and future, just as the symbolic dimensions of the medium link the contemporary world to medieval polity. This point is made at length in the culminating moment of the debate by Matthew Hancock, Minister for the Cabinet Office and Paymaster General, who rises to defend the retention of membrane:

> Committing our laws to this robust material underlines the point that the law of the land is immutable and that the rule of law is steadfast. We should never take that for granted. To those who say that this is symbolism, I say yes, it is vital symbolism.

What else are laws but symbols on a page? What are these symbols? They are symbols of great importance that make up and underpin the fabric of our society. The vellum record copies of Acts—signed in Norman French, no less, by the Clerk of the Parliaments—are part of the rich character of this House and of our evolving constitution . . . The symbolic power of vellum is undeniable.

Here the robustness of vellum embodies the unchangeability of the law and its rule, the "symbolic power" of the medium inseparable from its material perdurance. As Hancock puts it, "in a world racked by instability, volatility and change, we must safeguard our great traditions . . . this is not a debate that pits tradition against modernity, because a truly modern outlook does not put them up against each other. Novelty is no guarantee of improvement. Traditions matter precisely because they connect us with the collective wisdom of our predecessors." Tradition, heritage, stability, eternity: "I am amazed," Ian Liddell-Grainger (C-Bridgewater and West Somerset) remarks of the proposed change and its implications for the historical record: "The whole point of vellum is that it lasts forever."[10] Pliny the Elder, alive and well and speaking in the House of Commons.

The proponents of the changeover to paper, on the other hand, resist such appeals to tradition as so much outmoded antiquarianism. "Westminster is not a museum," Ronnie Cowan (SNP-Interclyde) avows. "It does not exist to propagate tradition for the sake of tradition. We are here to govern, to pass laws and to do so in a way that reflects the UK's nations as they are today—not as they were in the past. For too long, this Parliament has doggedly refused to enter the 21st century." A more withering objection to the motion comes from Melanie Onn (L-Great Grimsby), who turns the sustainability argument back on itself with an acerbic observation about the hypocrisy of vellum supporters: "I find it particularly surprising that the hon. Member for North East Somerset, who has written an article in *The Daily Telegraph* today, agrees with the argument that it is important for Acts to last 5,000 years. His lack of concern about rising global temperatures had led me to believe that he was not all that bothered about anything still being here in the year 7016." Climate change is not the only contemporary political issue to come in for parliamentary discussion during the vellum debate. As the *Daily Mail* headline suggests, Conservatives seemed particularly concerned that the so-called Article 50 bill, the trigger for Britain's official exit from the European Union, will be one of the first public Acts of Parliament not to be printed on animal skin. Liddell-Grainger insisted that the Brexit bill "should be written on vellum. Because in a thousand years time people will ask, 'what did they do in March 2017?' They will not read it on paper. Ancient man had it right."

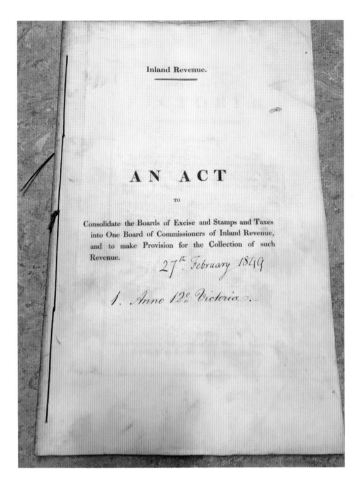

Figure 15.5.
Vellum record copy
of "An Act to Con-
solidate the Boards
of Excise and Stamps
and Taxes [. . .],"
February 27, 1849.
This is the first rec-
ord Act of Parlia-
ment to be printed
rather than writ-
ten on vellum, bound
with silk thread.
Westminster, Victo-
ria Tower.

One of the two repositories that receive the record copies of the public Acts of Parliament is the Parliamentary Archives located in Victoria Tower, Westminster, which I visited less than a month after the final decision to abandon vellum had been made, and just as the archive staff was beginning the initial planning process to prepare this extraordinary collection of membrane rolls and codices for storage, shipping, and eventual relocation to a new records office (the site is still to be determined). For lovers of parchment, the Act Room in Victoria Tower is one of the world's truly wondrous spaces, a low-roofed chamber no larger than a small warehouse filled floor to ceiling with the written and printed membranes carrying the original Acts going back six centuries (see the discussion above in chap. 7). Approximately two-thirds of this animal archive consists of rolls, great tubular bun-

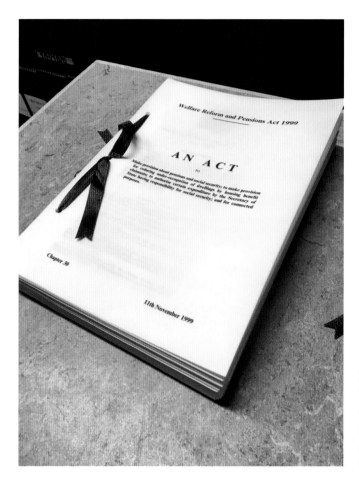

Figure 15.6.
Vellum record copy
of the Welfare Re-
form and Pensions
Act 1999, bound with
red silk ribbon.

dles of parchments sewn or glued together and filled with the labors of generations of clerks who recorded parliamentary law until the middle of the nineteenth century. The other half of the original public Acts, though, consists of loose-bound codices printed on vellum, a practice that began with "An Act to Consolidate the Boards of Excise and Stamps and Taxes into One Board of Commissioners," enacted in February 1849 and apparently the first Act of Parliament recorded in membrane booklet or codex rather than roll form (see fig. 15.5). From this month and for the next century and a half, the original Acts would all be printed in duplicate at the stationers on a creamy vellum and loose-bound in quires with cords and, more recently, broad red ribbons, strung through punched holes. These later documents (see fig. 15.6) are remarkable and quite beautiful objects, some of them brief enough to preserve as single bifolia, others made up of hundreds of vellum sheets gathered in volumes one or two inches thick. Together they must represent one of the largest repositories of printed membrane anywhere in the world.[11] In the English-speaking world, at least, the Parliament Records Office is rivaled in this respect only by the College of Arms, the heraldic authority charged with issuing new coats of arms and maintaining records of past heraldic investitures and grants in the United Kingdom and much of the Commonwealth. The only vellum now used for record copies consists of a single bifold cover used to bind the Acts, which are copied on paper. Membrane in this context represents a fraying and ever more tenuous link to the past.

Though not in others. "Women of the Book" is a global artistic collaborative dedicated to making visible the work of contemporary Jewish women in the interpretation and reenvisioning of the Torah. Launched in 2007 under the direction of Shoshana Gugenheim, the project commissioned fifty-four artists, many of them internationally renowned, each to create an original work on parchment representing and responding to a *parsha* or *parashah*, a weekly portion of the Torah. The pieces were produced over several years by this multidenominational collective, working with a wide variety of media on the skins that serve as their ground. Supported by the Jerusalem Publishing Atelier, an international traveling exhibition has brought these works to an array of audiences in Jerusalem, the United States, and elsewhere, with the goal of jointly creating a reimagined midrashic Torah scroll that foregrounds the interpretive and aesthetic work of women's voices within the long tradition of scriptural commentary.[12]

While the project's diverse contributions explore a panoply of scriptural, political, and theological themes, several of the artists concern themselves with animal sacrifice in relation to the parchment medium that subtends the project as well as the Torah itself. *Acharei Mot*, commissioned from the Jerusalem-based painter and printer Leora Wise, addresses a story from Leviticus 16, in which Aaron selects one goat for a sacrificial offering and a second as "scapegoat," the bearer of the sin and iniquity of the people: "And Aaron shall lay both his hands upon the head of the live goat, and confess over him all the iniquities of the children of Israel, and all their transgressions in all their sins, putting them upon the head of the goat, and shall send him away by the hand of a fit man into the wilderness: And the goat shall bear upon him all their iniquities unto a land not inhabited: and he shall let go the goat in the wilderness" (Leviticus 16:21–22). Wise's Boschean painting (fig. 15.7) features a terrified goat with its hoofs splayed in the air facing the beaked figures

Figure 15.7. Leora Wise, *Acharei mot* (2015). Etching reproduced as glicée print on parchment. Courtesy of Women of the Book.

Figure 15.8. Anne-Françoise Ben-Or, *Vayikra* (2011). Acrylic on parchment. Courtesy of Women of the Book.

who have cast it away. The animal's beseeching companion (the "designated man" of Scripture) embodies a goat-human commonality reinforced through their shared stippled skin on the membrane. Animal sacrifice is also the subject of *Vayikra* by Anne-Françoise Ben-Or, a Belgian-Israeli figurative painter whose works have been exhibited at the National Portrait Gallery and elsewhere. Why are sacrifices imperative? What purposes does sacrifice serve? Ben-Or asks frequently in her work. *Vayikra* (fig. 15.8) takes up an incident of animal sacrifice from Leviticus 3: "You shall lay a hand upon the head of your offering and slaughter it at the entrance of the Tent of Meeting." The chapter goes on to specify the bodily details of the sacrifice, the parts that must be addressed in the course of slaughter: "the fat that covers the entrails . . . the two kidneys and the fat that is on them . . . and the protuberance on the liver, which you shall remove with the kidneys" (Leviticus 3:3–5). Ben-Or, though, set out to capture the episode before the death of the animal, the prescribed laying of a human hand on the head of the sacrificial beast. This interspecies embrace, the "intimate moment" of touch, enacts an overlay of human skin upon animal skin on the surface of the visualized Torah.

Other contributors enlist such conjunctions to explore the textual dimensions of parchment's animality in relation to Jewish scriptural tradition. Thus Sylvia Rubinson's *Yitro* (fig. 15.9) includes etchings from a Torah scroll brought from her family when emigrating from Europe to Argentina in 1928. Below the natural epidermal pigmentation of her parchment portion, left exposed in the course of the work's making, Rubinson has integrated fragmentary poems and commentaries on the Torah while allowing the mixed media to convey the evolution and continuity of written tradition. Myriam Jawerbaum, on the other hand, "cracks" the physical text of the Torah open through a gap painted into the parchment in *Ki tisa* (fig. 15.10). In a reference to the Kabbalistic concept of *tzimtzum*, or the "contraction" of the divine to make space for the earth, the blood-red letter *aleph* emerges through "the crevice of the broken stone" and fragments the scriptural text into frayed and torn remnants of ink, paper, and skin.

The *Shof'tim* portion fell to Judith Serebrin, a painter, sculptor, and calligrapher as well as a book arts instructor at the San Francisco Center for the Book. The Torah portion taken on by Serebrin for the project, from Deuteronomy 16:18–21:9 (see fig. 15.11), includes several passages from Moses's last speech to the Israelites addressing animal sacrifice alongside the production of scrolls, in quick enough succession to suggest to later commentators a vital link between slaughter, sacrifice, and the parchment medium. "You shall not sacrifice to the Lord, your God, an ox or a sheep that has in it a blemish or any bad thing, for that is an abomination to the Lord, your God," reads Deuteronomy 17:1; Moses then enjoins every king to write and

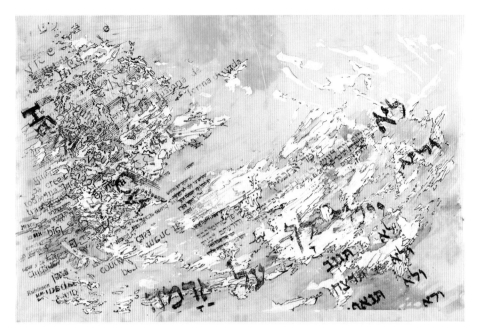

Figure 15.9. Silvia Rubinson, *Yitro* (2012). Mixed media on parchment. Courtesy of Women of the Book.

Figure 15.10. Myriam Jawerbaum, *Ki tisa* (2008). Hand-made paper and oil paints on parchment. Courtesy of Women of the Book.

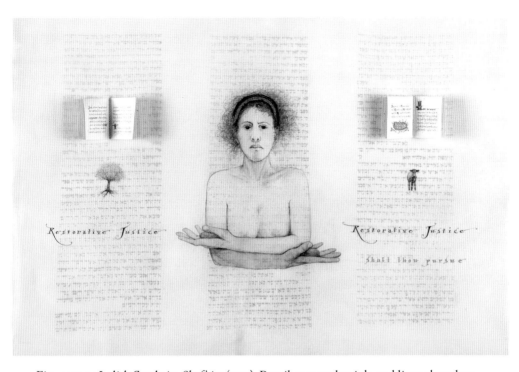

Figure 15.11. Judith Serebrin, *Shof'tim* (2015). Pencil, watercolor, ink, and linen thread on parchment. Courtesy of Women of the Book.

preserve a copy of the Law: "And it shall be, when he sitteth upon the throne of his kingdom, that he shall write him a copy of this law in a book . . . And it shall be with him, and he shall read therein all the days of his life" (Deuteronomy 17:18–19). The "priest's due" from those who "offer a sacrifice, whether it be ox or sheep," includes "the first of the fleece of thy sheep" (Deuteronomy 18:3–4). In Serebrin's painting, these injunctions inspire dense overlays of animal bodies and scriptural production to consider the ethics of restorative justice within the commentary tradition that has sought to understand it. The female figure depicted with crossed arms over the central column holds two stones in her hands, refusing the punitive violence enjoined by the Mosaic text: "Then you shall bring out that man or that woman who has committed this evil thing . . . and you shall pelt them with stones, and they shall die" (Deuteronomy 17:5). The open books in the right and left columns recreate the two Torah copies mandated in the chapter, each casting a shadow onto the membrane. The lamb on the right column, embroidered into the membrane with linen thread, stands below a miniature codex and among the lines of the Torah as an expression of gratitude for parchment, the sacrificial medium of inscription.

If the artists involved in "Women of the Book" draw on parchment's central role in Jewish tradition to reclaim the medium toward revisionist ethical ends, other contemporary illustrators and sculptors enlist parchment into new aesthetic approaches to the natural world at diverse scales. Animal skin has for centuries served illustrators of scientific and naturalistic treatises as an appealing medium for intricate depictions of flora and fauna, a tradition going back well into the early modern period with the work of figures such as Daniel Rabel (1578–1637), who produced hundreds of intricate flower paintings on vellum for Gaston d'Orléans, brother to King Louis XIII of France. These *vélins* initiated a significant royal collection of botanical illustration still maintained today at the Muséum national d'Histoire naturelle.[13] Other renowned illustrators such as Maria Sybilla Merian (1647–1718) and Georgius Dionysius Ehret (1706–1770) continued in the same vein, their robust contributions to botanical art on vellum part of an enduring practice among subcultures of naturalistic illustrators for several centuries.[14]

In the modern era the widespread, almost devotional preference for vellum among certain naturalistic artists can be traced largely to the efforts of one figure, Rory McEwen (1932–1982), a Scottish artist, poet, and musician who worked avidly in the medium in the latter years of his career, after a momentous transition in medium from paper to vellum.[15] Six of McEwen's botanical works on vellum were featured in the Metropolitan Museum of Art's *International Survey of Painting and Sculpture*, an exhibit that marked the reopening of the museum in 1984. At his death, McEwen's family bequeathed a number of vellum sheets remaining in his studio to a select group of illustrators of younger generations through the Hunt Institute for Botanical Documentation. In the years since, certain artists in this tradition have maintained an intimate and often self-reflexive relationship to animal membrane in the making of their naturalistic objects. Yet as I have learned in the course of meeting several of these artists and gaining familiarity with their work, parchment induces compelling innovations that push their aesthetic beyond the illustrative impulse of naturalistic art and illustration.

Arkansas-based Kate Nessler has developed an international reputation for her dazzling works on membrane, which enlist the natural contours of parchment sheets and cuttings as well as the patches and whorls of the membrane's mottled surfaces to limn certain features of the flora and other natural objects she depicts. In

Figure 15.12. Kate Nessler, *Nest with Maple Seeds* (2012). Watercolor and pencil on vellum.

Nest with Maple Seeds (fig. 15.12), a scatter of twigs and seeds wanders along the brindled surface of an oblong contoured parchment, cut at a right angle from a shoulder or haunch. The avian dwelling depicted in *The Nest* (fig. 15.13) rests tenuously on the branch of a tree whose twigs and leaves sprawl across a full and uncut hide. Nessler has incorporated the skin's pigmentation and the holes left by the maker during production into the overall design, while the roughly symmetrical angles along the top edge evoke the wings of a butterfly. *Yellow Rose*, painted vertically on an offcut and shaped to the curves of the animal's skin, rises in thorny parallel to a rose stem affixed to a narrow length of naturally browned parchment (fig. 15.14). The same grubby beauty characterizes *Bluff Dweller*, a rendering of the bristle-leaved sedge common to the eastern and central United States (fig. 15.15). Here the variegated shadings of the membrane accentuate the intricately wrought leaf blades as well as the flask-like sacs (or perigynia) clasping the spires down near the messy tangle by the ground. *Hellebore* (fig. 15.16), like a number of Nessler's vellum creations, combines watercolor with graphite and so-called body-color (a technique already employed in the eighteenth century by Ehret) to reproduce the brownish hues of aged parchment as the painting's earthy ground.[16]

In these and other works, Nessler's technique revels in the organic specificity of the parchment medium, the unique textures, contours, and shape of the skins she brings into her studio. Veiny vellum, she has written, "is deeply expressive even before the companionship with the subject. The skin is not so much a place of light and air but rather a place for grounding—a place for falling and fallen leaves, for old and smooth-worn stumps, a place too where bits of moss and new life might come to life alongside skeletal roots. The skin itself suggests and begins a composition by providing in an individual way a ground for the subject."[17] A statement published in *The Botanical Artist* similarly conveys a strong sense of the empathetic relation between artist and ground that Nessler has cultivated throughout her career, alive as she has always been to the creaturely derivation of her medium: "Working on vellum is not

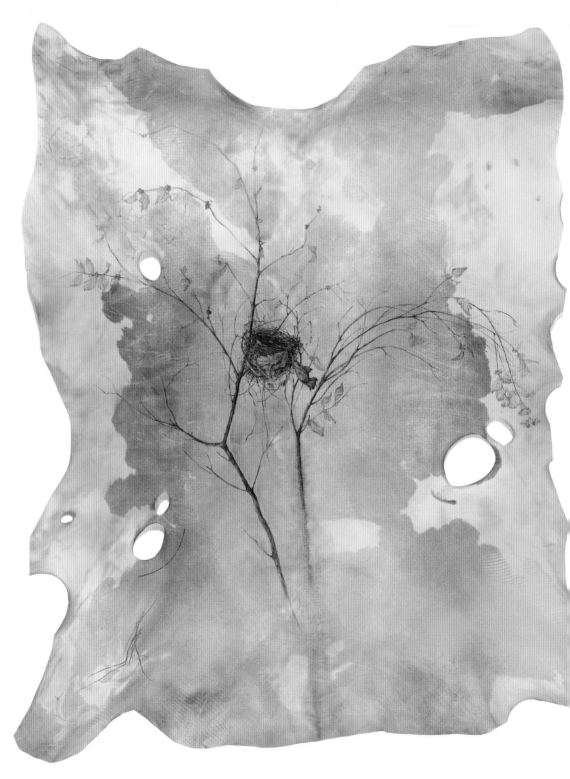

Figure 15.13. Kate Nessler, *The Nest* (2020). Watercolor and pencil on vellum.

Figure 15.14. Kate Nessler, *Yellow Rose* (2011). Watercolor on vellum with rose stem and thorns in transparent vellum box.

Figure 15.15. Kate Nessler, *Bluff Dweller* (2014). Watercolor on vellum.

Figure 15.16. Kate Nessler, *Hellebore* (2012). Watercolor on vellum with dried seeds in transparent vellum envelope, pressed petal and seedling. With vellum maker's inscription at top.

just a technique, it is understanding what vellum is, what it does and developing a partnership with it. Every skin, every piece of vellum is different in some way, requiring adaptability and acceptance."[18] This openness to the internal differences of the medium creates for Nessler a kind of phenomenological circuit at the center of her work, as the vellum shapes her just as she refashions the medium: "you are working together with a background not of your making, but fully present . . . an integral part of the composition"; and elsewhere, "Vellum is best if experienced. Some love it, some fear it (I sure did), and some can't wait to get back to paper. And others can't wait to see what the next skin looks like and what challenges it will bring." Like a number of contemporary artists who work in the medium, Nessler subtly exploits the zoomorphic individuality of skins in her botanical renderings. As she put it in the catalogue for *At the Edge*, a solo show at the Jonathan Cooper gallery in London in 2013, each piece of vellum "holds no expectations, no rules, no dictates from the past. Why not paint what the edge of the vellum requires rather than what a square or rectangle imposes?"[19] Thus *Concord Grapes* (fig. 15.17) splays out along the thickened and darkened edge of the vellum, which contours the vine and forms the meandering course of the painted medium.

Vellum inspires in a different way the botanical renderings of Mali Moir, a Victoria, Australia-based artist who also enlists membrane as a frequent medium in her scientific, anatomical, and botanical work. "Botanic artists make science visible," Moir has said, an aesthetic of visibility in which parchment plays a central yet subtle role. *Falconiformes* (fig. 15.18), titled after the taxonomic order that includes falcons and related birds of prey, renders the foot of a falcon in watercolor on a small square of deer vellum, the central talon fully painted, the others in a progressively

Figure 15.17. Kate Nessler, *Concord Grapes* (2011). Watercolor and pencil on vellum.

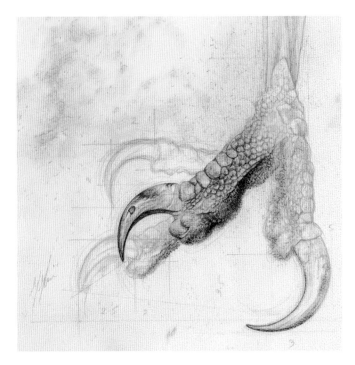

Figure 15.18.
Mali Moir,
Falconiformes (2013).
Watercolor on deer
vellum.

fainter watercolor wash and pencil, the far talon little more than a ghostly sugges-tion on the skin. *Ovuliferous Scale Bunya Pine (Araucaria bidwillii)* (fig. 15.19), a scale rendering of a single cone in watercolor on vellum, was painted during the summer of 2014 during a particularly auspicious year for the Bunya Pine, a sacred tree for ab-original cultures that once inspired yearly pilgrimages to harvest festivals before ex-tensive logging in the nineteenth century decimated the population. Drawn in part by this history and in part by the exquisite, silk-like reflection on the ovuliferous scales, Moir procured specimens from the Royal Botanic Gardens Melbourne and engaged herself and her students in a process of patient observation and depiction. Moir renders the Bunya cone in a dry-brush technique that avoids any washes and enlists what she calls "an 'empirical' approach to seeing" the colors and contours of the cone, captured in their vital particulars on the "reassuringly forgiving" surface of the vellum and its particular tactile and textural effects in arresting overlays of sub-ject and medium.[20] She chose a piece of vellum on which the spread of follicle marks across the skin remains clearly visible, an effect of the medium that helps capture the knotted, bumpy surface of the scale.

Yet Moir's exacting organic realism is often wedded with a tendency toward collage and juxtaposition in her vellum pieces, an environmental aesthetic that comes across clearly in *Hazard Beetles (Anoplophora Horsfieldi)*, a work exhibited at Museum Victoria in 2012 (fig. 15.20). Here Moir has placed three beetles in a triangular pattern, with their carapaces and antennae arranged in a Venn diagram and a fourth circle formed by a yellow ring joining their lower shell casings at the center. The yellow circle has been rendered not in paint, however, but from the sealing ring of a plastic bottle, broken at a point close to midnight in a harbinger of coming apocalypse: the three "hazard beetles" float on the creamy membrane while mimicking a yellow-and-black hazard sign, just as their colors and design warn off potential predators from the consumption of their flesh.

The medium's visual and tactile animality has held a similar attraction for Margaret Fitzpatrick, a calligrapher and heraldic artist who served earlier in her career at the College of Arms and the Inns of Court. There she worked extensively with parchment in producing heraldic emblems and letters patent for a variety of diplomatic, governmental, and commercial functions, working primarily with "the fine

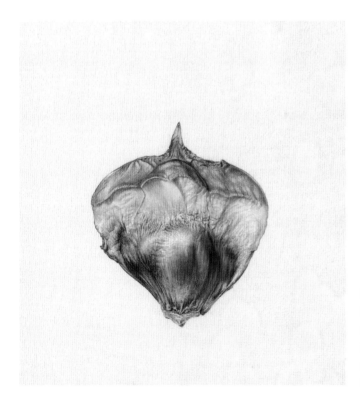

Figure 15.19.
Mali Moir, *Ovuliferous Scale Bunya Pine (Araucaria bidwillii)* (2014). Watercolor on vellum.

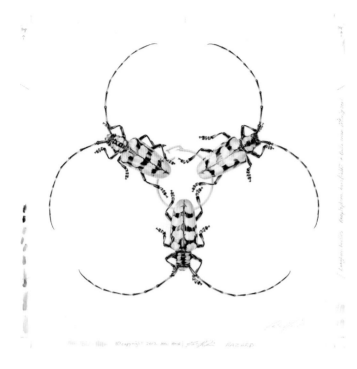

Figure 15.20. Mali Moir, *Hazard Beetles* (*Anoplophora Horsfieldi*) (2011). Watercolor on vellum.

white bleached surface" of calfskin vellum, on which she has produced many hundreds of works over the last thirty years. More recently she has turned to undyed, natural skins for the darker markings and shades that lend the medium distinctive contours and organic designs, choosing each piece she uses from the parchment maker William Cowley. The idiosyncrasies of individual skins play "an integral part in the design and composition" of each work. To create *Bracken and bramble caught in veined calfskin* (fig. 15.21), Fitzpatrick "chose a heavily marked skin and used the veining and markings to continue the stems and bracken so that the plant, skin and markings would become as one," merging subject and medium, plant and animal on the shadowed surface of the membrane.[21]

A very different sense of the creaturely medium's affordances inspires the recent work of Laura Youngson Coll, whose finely detailed sculptural work with vellum highlights "the artifice of our mimicry of nature." Youngson Coll came to parchment and vellum through her years of work in a bookbinder's shop, where she helped craft bespoke books and did traditional leatherwork for wall paneling and furniture. This intricate work with skin led her to appreciate the qualities of membrane as a sculptural medium, always with what she calls "an acute awareness of the 'animality' of vellum," which is "instrinsic to [her] work." As she observes, "Scars, insect bites and hair follicles can all be visible" on the skin's surface, while a "scalpel can knick on a scar or refuse to penetrate a spiny section of skin. There is also a more subtle, empirical reading of the material, slight variations in the rigidity or structure of different parts of the skin, or different skins, which will render it more or less easy to pare or mould. This can be 'read' in a visual and tactile way. Through experience, the resulting translucency, or robustness, of a particular worked piece of skin can also be ascertained through the observation of an unworked skin."[22]

Such complexities emerge in several of Youngson Coll's recent pieces, which explore themes of death and disease through the sculptural refashioning of microbial formations and an awareness of the ethical complexities of vellum itself. The "contrary nature of being vegetarian and working with vellum," even the "hypocrisy," has a surprising bearing on Youngson Coll's sense of her aesthetic, and has pushed her to

Figure 15.21.
Margaret Fitzpatrick, *Bracken and bramble caught in veined calfskin* (2014). Watercolor on heavily veined vellum.

Figure 15.22.
Laura Youngson
Coll, *Haeckel I*
(detail, 2014).
Vellum, supernatural
vellum, hair, sheep
leather, armature.

explore relations between the personal and the biological on a number of levels. Conversations with a scientist helped her understand the ambivalences involved in seeing this microscopic universe of cells, viruses, and their processes "as a fundamental part of ourselves"—a problem of aesthetic visualization as much as scientific empiricism that lends itself to her making.[23] *Haeckel 1* (fig. 15.22) is named for Ernst Haeckel, a biologist whose unprecedented microscopic investigations led to breathtaking visualizations of new molecules in all their detail and finery. The piece creates a similar shock, an amalgam of vellum, "supernatural vellum," and sheep leather that explodes the invisible microcosm of the cell into a tentacular spectacle within the glass vitrine in which it is displayed. *Angiogenesis* (fig. 15.23 and detail, fig. 15.24), a highly personal work inspired by her husband's death from lymphoma, depicts the process by which a tumor grows its own blood vessels. While the work is cellular it is not "visceral," Youngson Coll suggests: rather, it is a study in compartmentalization, the psychological work required to cope with the extremes of grief and loss, just as the work's making requires the animality of vellum to be effaced in the name of artifice.

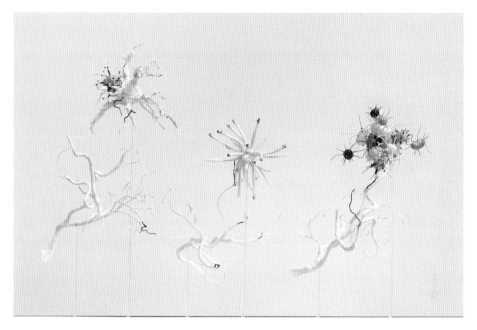

Figure 15.23. Laura Youngson Coll, *Angiogenesis* (2017). Vellum, supernatural vellum, dyed vellum.

Figure 15.24.
Detail of figure 15.23.

In both cases, skin—animal skin, and by association our own—serves to project these cellular creations into the three dimensions that we inhabit in common, even as the biology of this microscopic universe remains invisible to our creaturely eyes.

I turn finally to a collaboration between two artists that addresses parchment in a more distinctly elegiac mode, though with a strong sense of its contemporanaeity as medium and message. In the 1990s, poet Catherine Byron and visual artist and calligrapher Denis Brown together visited the tannery of Joseph Katz, a renowned parchmenter in County Kildare who furnishes drumheads to tympanists in some of the world's leading orchestras.[24] One of the results was Byron's collection *The Getting of Vellum* (1999), discussed briefly in chapter 5 above. The titular poem recounts this visit while mingling in Katz's and Brown's musings about the animals butchered on site and rendered for their skins:

> In the Vellum Works in Celbridge,
> County Kildare,
> in the last years of the twentieth century,
> master calligrapher Denis Brown
> is choosing skins from the fresh stock
> of Joe Katz, Czech vellum maker extraordinaire.
> …
> *Born dead, a proper slink calf.*
> *Never breathed. You get a lot like that.*
> *Born dead—*
>
> *This calf—I probably picked this up*
> *Saturday afternoon. He still looks nice and fresh—*
>
> *When they come out dead*
> *They seem to keep better, y'know.*[25]

The poem goes on to detail the grisly processes of butchery and flaying—"The hide of the calf's belly / ripples and balloons free, / untethering all the membranes / that anchor skin to flesh . . . skinning a calf / a three days dead calf, is another thing altogether"—before turning to Brown in his own scriptorium, "his steel pen . . . moving across fresh vellum."

Figure 15.25. Denis Brown, *Birthday Suit* (2003). Calfskin vellum stretched over prepared plywood, gouache, bronze powders, shell gold, and gold leaf.

Brown's art for the project included a series of vellum-based pieces that he inscribed with Byron's verses as well as Latin texts of poetry and prayer. The polyptych *Birthday Suit* (2003) he describes as "a work about skin," with four panels that combine the materiality of vellum with writing that shows through translucent specimens (fig. 15.25). The top panel, collaged with horsehair, presents the piece's title shining through translucent membrane from a paper surface. The second panel

Figure 15.26. Denis Brown, *The Viking Terror* (2004). Goatskin vellum on wooden frame with painted paper.

from the top displays the pied pigmentation on the calfskin backing a four-square figure showing the anagrammatical relation between *skin* and *inks*. In the third panel Brown has written in calligraphy a number of lines from Byron's poem, un-lineated and presented as a gloss of the piece as a whole: "Who would have thought it needed a winch and a steel hawser to slowly, steadily, undress a calf? . . . So dainty and delicate in its glassy, gleaming pinks and whites, its untried muscles and ten-dons, its organs—lungs, gut, heart—never used ex utero. Uterine vellum. Slunk." Finally, in the lowest pane, the phrase *animal rationale* ("the thinking animal" of the human, as well as our own thinking about interspecies dominion) titles another fleshly collage. Here Brown has positioned an electronic scan of his own hair be-neath a layer of translucent vellum. To the right of the decorative red square, a cut hole in the vellum allows several strands of Brown's stomach hair to protrude above the membrane plane. At the panel's base appear the opening words of the great Old English book riddle, written in one line from Craig Williamson's translation: "A life-thief stole my world-strength, ripped off flesh & left me skin, dipped me in wa-ter & drew me out, stretched me bare in the tight sun."

Brown's medievalist creations often exploit these same conjunctions of the hu-man and the animal, of life and death we have seen so often in more self-conscious moments in the history of parchment. *The Viking Terror* (fig. 15.26) overlays goat-skin and watercolor paper inscribed with Irish verses on the coming of the Northmen, with a burned parchment signifying the destruction of lives and books. *Phoenix* (fig. 15.27) presents Brown's rendition of a glossed page from a Latin psalter that he burned after its completion, splashed with paint, and wrapped in wire, all to foreground themes of textual vulnerability and creative destruction. *The Stroke of Leprosy* (fig. 15.28) displays Levitical verses about leprosy on a piece of untrimmed kangaroo vellum: "The man in whose skin or flesh shall arise a different [. . .] colour, or a blister, or as it were [. . .] something shining, that is the stroke of leprosy." The ellipses correspond to a gristly hole at the center of the membrane that changes the

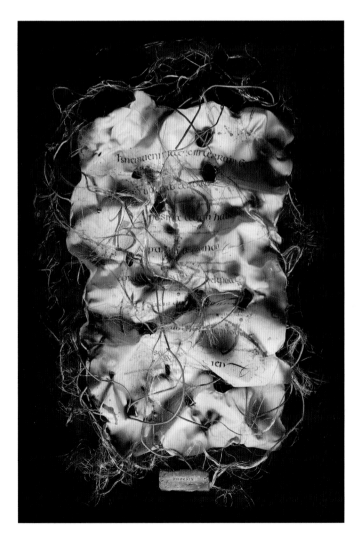

Figure 15.27.
Denis Brown,
Phoenix (1992).
Manuscript page on
calf vellum, burned,
splashed with paint
and wrapped in
copper wire.

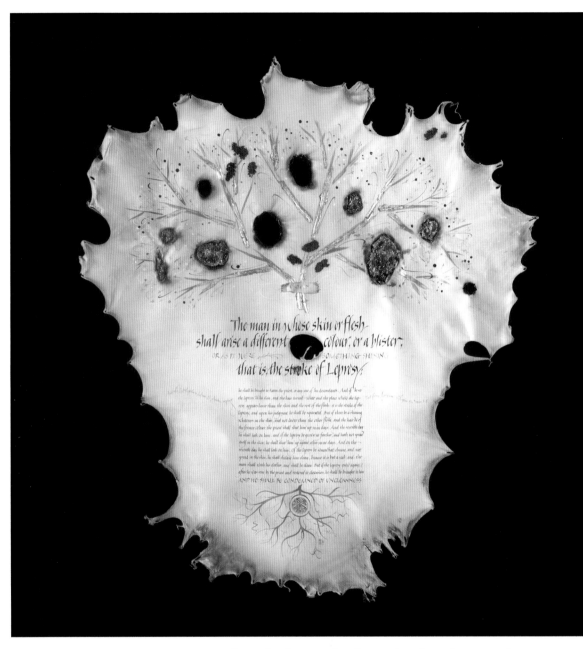

Figure 15.28. Denis Brown, *The Stroke of Leprosy* (1994). Mixed media on kangaroo-skin vellum. Text from Leviticus 13:1–8.

Figure 15.29. Judith Serebrin, *Neither Here Nor There III* (2015), a commission for the Jerusalem Biennale. Stained porcelain and parchment scroll.

texture, color, and contour of the vellum sheet, enlisting the skin into the moral message of the biblical chapter on skin disease (as do the other flaws and elements of mixed media in the larger collage). To reread Byron's collection after encountering Brown's collages is to understand anew the "morbid anatomy" of his making, to enlist the title of one of her poems: the fine lines between tannery and morgue, a corpse's tattoo and a document's script.

Different adjacencies animate *Neither Here Nor There III* (fig. 15.29), an uncanny creation by Judith Serebrin, created for the exhibit *A Sense of Space, A Sense of Place*, put on at the Jerusalem Biennale for Contemporary Jewish Art in 2015. The piece forms part of her "Soul Books" series, which consists of sculpted figures containing unique, hand-made books within the space of their crafted bodies. The books, whether codices or scrolls, are meant to incarnate and reflect on the shifting places of Jewish culture brought on by diaspora, displacement, and expulsion. Serebrin had never worked on parchment prior to this series; as a vegetarian with a commitment to minimizing animal suffering, she was "both excited and ambivalent about working on an animal hide." So she decided "to be intentional" about the medium, she says, "to notice and appreciate the animal on whose back I was writing."[26] *Neither Here Nor There III* displays this animal back as a loosely-rolled scroll filling a cuboid opening in its host's limbless body. With its head at a slight tilt to the viewer's left and its eyes darkened with enigma, the figure is animal and human at once, displaying the talismanic scroll within the earthy medium of fired porcelain, stained to match its parchment hue. Serebrin's piece captures the imaginative charge of parchment in all its strangeness, displaying a membrane record of cultural preservation while putting the medium's sacrificial uncanniness and moral ambivalence on full display.

Here is what we have made while moving from place to place, whispers this haunting confection of earth and skin. Here is what we have made, and here is what we have done.

EPILOGUE
Digital Vellum

Parchment remains with us and around us, as a medium of painting and sculpture and the subject of poets, as an object of ingenious craftsmanship and a tool of documentary repair, as the skins of new Torah scrolls commissioned for temples and tabernacles around the world—let alone as a significant portion of the historical archive, an object of continuing rediscovery, translation, and wonder. Yet for all its vigorous contemporanaeity, and even for its most ardent makers today, there is something about parchment, both earthy and ethereal at the same time, that may always feel archaic, a thing of the past even as it continues to illuminate and reflect our own moment. The parchment record endures in part as a reminder of the entailments and consequences of human dominion, these millennia of written culture that have made, read, destroyed, and yet somehow preserved these things of flayed and flawed beauty that may well survive us all.

After completing the full draft of this book in March 2020, I had intended to spend much of the following six months returning to archives and libraries visited previously: to revisit a number of rolls, codices, documents, and maps in the flesh, to gather some last photographs, to test my prior observations about particular membrane objects. These ambitions inevitably gave way to institutional closures and restrictions on travel necessitated by the COVID-19 pandemic, which forestalled most site-dependent archival research around the world—and, as of this writing, continues to affect much of our relation as scholars to the incarnate objects of our study and delectation. The Special Collections department at my own university remained closed to visitors for many months, and it was only during the spring and summer of 2021 that I would return to a handful of North American libraries to glean a few final kernels. Even these brief forays felt like an immeasurable privilege amid a global health crisis and its uncertain future.

One source of consolation over these long months has been a renewed appreciation for the beguiling surfaces of digitized parchment in all its forms. While scroll-

Figure 16.1. Dozens of thumbnails from the Bury Bible (Cambridge, Parker Library, Corpus Christi College Ms. 2) on the Parker Library on the Web portal.

ing may seem a poor substitute for scrolls, our computers and phones now give us access to a wealth of membrane artifacts on a scale that no amount of archival visitation could replicate. (If you're not familiar with this corner of the online universe, just image-search "book of hours" or "historiated initial" and you'll see what I mean.) For many who work in the early periods, the pandemic has reinforced and may accelerate what has been a paradigm shift in the study, transmission, and preservation of early textual cultures over the last fifteen years facilitated by the large-scale digitization of written artifacts.[1] Earlier in this book I discussed the immensity of the parchment record, an abundance that inspired ancient legends of archives and the jaundiced wit of Charles Dickens alike. The corresponding wealth of digitized animal skin is differently staggering, captured in terabytes of data that comprise the myriad simulacra of parchment on numerous platforms and in a wide variety of formats. A mere thirty years have passed since digitized images of medieval manuscripts first appeared on the internet. Yet by now, I would guess, vastly more people have encountered parchment in digital form than have ever touched a membrane codex or document in the flesh. The digital ecology of parchment makes a universe of its own: a "sea of pixels," in Astrid J. Smith's resonant phrase.[2]

The digital embodiment of cultural heritage has thus become an engrained and essential part of how we now perceive and study the history of the written word, with far-reaching implications for the democratization and accessibility of archives and libraries around the world. We are living in the "age of the digital incunable," Martin Foys has written, when digitized manuscripts (including many millions of parchment artifacts) are increasingly ubiquitous, straddling several technologies and paradigms, even as these bright new avatars of written heritage shape the tools, methods, and ways of knowing we bring to their investigation.[3] Digital manuscript studies has emerged as its own robust field, with sophisticated approaches to the entangled histories of text technologies, and always alive to the distinctions and commonalities between the incarnate book and its digital surrogate. Collaborative digitization projects have opened new portals to the written record now splayed across our screens in numberless thumbnails ripe for clicks and zooms (see fig. 16.1).

A corollary of this revolution in accessibility and proliferation has been the diffusion of parchment artifacts on social media platforms. A pioneer in this effort was the book historian Erik Kwakkel, whose Twitter feed in the early 2010s delighted the internet with its simultaneously learned and irreverent approach to the online presentation of medieval manuscripts. This was back in the good old days of Twitter when users had to click to see the attached photograph, which would pop up in a tab below the original tweet to realize the often elusive meaning of the caption. "Halloween in medieval book culture 1: sliced-open manuscript showing gore and guts," Kwakkel tweeted on October 31, 2012. Clicking on the tweet brought up a shot of a book's cover torn away to reveal a cut-up portion of a membrane folio used as a binding support (see fig. 16.2). Another posted the same day, captioned "Halloween in medieval book culture 5: tortured book, frazzled and with a distorted worldview," opened to reveal a water-damaged codex viewed from above, its pages exploded into spectacular curls. The effects were often sublime, as medieval manuscripts appeared in unusual contexts presented with a mix of scholarly rigor and light irreverence.

Kwakkel's early tweets helped inaugurate a generation of innovation and experiment that brought parchment into the public sphere in voluminous and un-

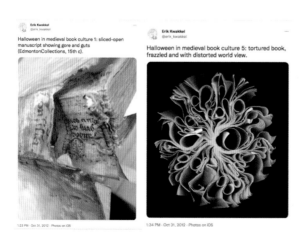

Figure 16.2. Two of Erik Kwakkel's Halloween tweets from 2012, with expanded images.

precedented ways. Feeds proliferated on Tumblr, Pinterest, Twitter, and eventually Instagram devoted to medieval manuscripts and their sensual appeal—as well as their potential for satirical exploitation. The anonymous parody account @MedievalReacts (long suspended) captioned its unattributed images with bits of world-weary drollery that intentionally ripped premodern artifacts and imagery from their contexts. For the most part, though, scholars have drawn on the technologies of digitization and social media to bring parchment objects to life in new and surprisingly multisensory ways, "pushing the boundaries of how we communicate the materiality of medieval manuscripts *digitally*," in Johanna M. E. Green's words.[4] In 2014 *Buzzfeed* featured a piece by Alexis Coe, "8 Book Historians, Curators, Specialists, and Librarians Who Are Killing It Online," complete with thumbnail profiles and visuals illustrating the bookish preoccupations of her subjects: the Getty Museum's Pinterest board of "Monkeys in the Margins," an Iowa librarian's "Miniature Monday" posts featuring some the world's tiniest volumes, and a Harvard curator's delightful punning on bibliographical terminology, among others.[5]

But now the verso, which tells a different, less optimistic story of digitization and its consequences. Fully half of the images included in Coe's piece have disappeared in the years since its initial posting. Scrolling down through the *Buzzfeed* story, the viewer will be greeted with a string of melancholy notifications of visual absence:

> This image is no longer available.
> This image is no longer available.
> This image is no longer available.
> This image is no longer available.
> This image is no longer available.
> This image is no longer available.
> This image is no longer available.
> This image is no longer available.

A number of the corresponding links to the images in their original online contexts are still active, though others remain broken, leaving the article shorn of its visual basis in the work of its subjects. Likewise, the obnoxious, often sacrilegious image-caption pairings posted by @MedievalReacts and other popular parody accounts have vanished, victims of suspension, decay, or self-censorship.

Even Kwakkel's popular early tweets have lost their original aesthetic trappings. Kwakkel created his unique threads of medieval manuscripts before the advent of Twitter's "expanded images" function, introduced in fall of 2013.[6] No longer was the tweeted photo held at bay, awaiting a click before its often jarring revelation. From now on, images and their captions would appear as one (as you see them here), with no affordance for pop-up effects or clever surprises. Tweets originally dependent on click-to-view functionality were now unviewable in this mode. A mere year after Kwakkel's ingenious Halloween series, its rhetorical mechanism had already been rendered inoperable and mostly irrecoverable via a platform innovation engineered in Silicon Valley.

These are just a few small, easily comprehensible examples of the challenges to parchment's digital survival in the twenty-first century and beyond. Questions of sustainability have long been at the center of debates around preservation and access, with bearing on nearly all archives and cultural heritage translated into surrogate digital forms.[7] In the case of premodern membrane artifacts, such questions are inflected with irony given the investment of so many cultures of the past in parchment as a particularly durable support and eternal medium of preservation. In many cases, parchment in its pixelated forms may be more vulnerable to degradation and loss than the inscribed skin it reproduces.

It is this realization that in part explains the concept of "digital vellum," a resonant phrase enlisted by Google vice president and internet pioneer Vint Cerf to connote "a reliable, survivable medium" necessitated by the precarity of data infrastructures and dated software platforms—like "bit rot" and "link rot," to use standard jargon for such phenomena.[8] The concept of digital vellum now suffuses the literature on techno-sustainability as a symbol of how new technologies might remediate the "digital Dark Ages" that lay before us, threatening the survival of colossal data caches that now hold much of our collective history.[9] As Michelle Warren has shown, Cerf's seemingly fanciful notion of digital vellum functions as more than an evangelical metaphor for the age of computation. In fact, the concept emerged in part from Cerf's own hands-on encounters with certain medieval manuscripts (including a well-known palimpsest), and his seeming enchantment with a medium of palpable longevity.[10]

That a Google vice president would formulate such a robust analogy from the animal medium of the premodern world speaks volumes about the perdurance of parchment as an agent of cultural sustainability. We have come a very long way from Herodotus—the "Father of History" who mused twenty-five centuries ago on the Ionians and their eccentric practice of recording their thoughts on animal skin—to Vint Cerf, a "Father of the Internet" promoting digital vellum as a medium indispensable to translating a disappearing past into the unknown. Perhaps this near future of digital vellum will provide solutions to the inexorable decay of the present.

But what more distant future awaits parchment? The question invites an exercise in speculative fiction—about a time, let's say, when we are gone, when the remains of several long-extinct species turn up during an excavation project undertaken by extraplanetary visitors. By happenstance a crew is digging through the ruins of a necropolis, where they come upon the bones of what were clearly important personages intermingled with various artifacts entombed with their remains. At a nearby location in the dig, another crew unearths a large assemblage of organic remains at what was once a great repository of some kind. Sampling ensues: bones, skin, teeth, bits of hair. Some speculate that the bone species was the apex predator, with bodies neatly arrayed in death, buried with objects made of recognizable minerals and gems. Others wonder about the more voluminous remains of these several skin species, close genetic cousins of the bone species but whose well-preserved hides survive by the millions in curious bundles of various shapes and sizes. As it turns out, this planet is the last stop on the voyage, and space on the mother ship is limited. The visitors take some of these skin-bundles along for further study, leaving the less interesting bones behind.

I have placed this imagined alien dig at the site of the Vatican, the necropolis and the Apostolic Library nearby, sites already rich with the remains of mammals intentionally preserved. Humans would represent a small portion of the biological detritus recoverable from this speculative excavation project. Vastly more plentiful would be the remains of the creatures making up the records, books, and scrolls preserved and buried en masse. On these many membranes our DNA would still be entangled with theirs, some odd fragments of our civilization still discernible on fragments of their flesh. And there it will all rest, a great chronicle of human craft and animal existence, made by, for, and of creatures of a shared planet, knowable in its parts and ever elusive in its magnificent whole: this archive of the animal, this inheritance of written skin.

NOTES

Prologue

1. For a sense of the variety of human-inscribed objects and media in the ancient and medieval worlds, see the essays collected in Wagner, Neufeld, and Lieb, *Writing Beyond Pen*; and in Piquette and Whitehouse, *Writing as Material Practice*. On wax tablets and their significance, see Stallybrass et al., "Hamlet's Tables."

2. Bloom, *Paper Before Print*, 46–89; Boyle, *Survey of the Vatican Archives*, 7.

3. See, for example, Cahill, *How the Irish Saved Civilization*.

4. Parchment was "a much more durable material" than papyrus, Reynolds and Wilson write; "its toughness was to prove a vital factor in the survival of classical literature" (Reynolds and Wilson, *Scribes and Scholars*, 35).

5. On parchment currency printed on walrus and seal skin, see the fascinating account in Zander, *The Alaskan Parchment Scrip*.

6. A point made sharply but generously by Turner in "The Materiality of Medieval Parchment," written as a response to work on parchment by several medievalists (including me) inspired in some way by critical animal studies.

7. Haraway, *When Species Meet*, 4.

8. The account appears in the first chapter of Derrida, *Animal That Therefore I Am*.

9. Guerlac, "Derrida and His Cat," 697.

10. Kreiner, "Pigs in the Flesh and Fisc," 4.

11. On the early history of papyrus, see Gaudet's fascinating account, *Pharaoh's Treasure*.

12. See Velasco's discussion in *Dead Voice*, 90.

13. Nongbri, *God's Library*, 24–27; Kurlansky, *Paper*, 66–97; Da Rold, *Paper in Medieval England*, esp. 161–66. For helpful accounts of the implications of paper's emergence in European book production, see Kwakkel, "A New Type of Book"; Lyall, "Materials: The Paper Revolution"; and Gagné, "Paper World."

14. al-Nadīm, *Fihrist*, 1.1, pp. 39–40. On this famous account, see Hirschler, *Medieval Damascus*, 6-7; Blair and Bloom, "The Islamic World," 200-01; and Roxburgh, *Prefacing the Image*, 128.

15. See Prescott, "Tale Tales," 359.

16. Novacich, *Shaping the Archive*, 66.

17. Wright, *Letter of Aristeas*, chap. 176–77. On the significance of the *Letter*, see Stern, *Jewish Bible*, 19.

Chapter 1

1. Stokes, ed. and trans., "Betha Chiaráin Clúana meic Nois," in *Lives of Saints*. On the manuscript's contents and history more generally, see Ó Cuív, "Observations."

2. On the biography and medieval *vitae* of Ciarán, see Kehnel's helpful discussion of the "Dating of St. Ciáran's Lives" in *Clonmacnois*, 16–21.

3. Kemmemer, *Animals and World Religions*, 231; see also the accounts in Waddell, *Beasts and Saints*, 104–6.

4. Stokes, ed. and trans., "Betha Chiaráin Clúana meic Nois," in *Lives of Saints*, 127; translation "Life of Ciarán of Clonmacnois," 272.

5. Joynt, *Tromdámh Guaire*, 40.

6. The manuscript's contents are edited in Best and Bergin, *Lebor na hUidre*; for a description and account of the book's significance, see O'Neill, *Irish Hand*, 26–27.

7. On the technological history of these distinctions, see Marks, *British Library Guide*, 36–45; and Gillespie, "Bookbinding."

8. Frey and Veitch, *Preservation of Leather Bookbindings*, 2.

9. Dreibholz, *Frühe Koranfragmente*.

10. Klack-Eitzen, Haase, and Weißgraf, *Heilige Röcke*.

11. See, among many others, Ommundsen, "A Norwegian—and European—Jigsaw Puzzle," 135: "The widespread reuse of parchment in bindings in accounts for the Dutch administration led to the 'rescue' of an estimated 16,000 fragments from an unknown number of medieval manuscripts for Denmark and Norway combined."

12. Cited and translated in Bamford, *Cultures of the Fragment*, 55.

13. Bale's sentiments about the treatment of medieval parchment codices were well known even in the nineteenth century; the citation here (of Bale's edition of John Leland's *Laborious Journey*) comes from Winters, *Our Parish Registers* (1885), 6. On the attitudes of Bale and his contemporaries toward these bookish remnants of the past, see Reynolds, "'Such Dispersive Scattredness.'"

14. Clanchy, *From Memory to Written Record*, 62, citing Eadmer of Canterbury, *Vita Sancti Anselmi*.

15. Bernard of Clairvaux, *Sermo de conversione ad clericos*, PL 182, col. 849; translated in *Sermons on Conversion*, 64. See the commentary on this passage in Coleman, *Ancient and Medieval Memories*, 185.

16. Caven, "Washington: A Mason," 160.

17. Stetkevych, *Mantle Odes*, 86.

18. On this fresco, see Signori, *Räume, Gesten, Andachtsformen*, 44–46.

19. Kieckhefer, ed., "Edition of the Necromancer's Handbook in Clm 849," chap. 3 in Kieckhefer, *Forbidden Rites*, 199.

20. On the controversies surrounding the phrase see Hamilton, *Veganism, Sex, and Politics*, 127; and Charles Patterson, "This Boundless Slaughterhouse," chap. 7 in *Eternal Treblinka*.

21. Pachirat, *Every Twelve Seconds*, 4.

22. See Steel, *How to Make a Human*, esp. 17.

23. Langeslag, *Seasons in the Literature*, 50; Cooper, *Eat and Be Satisfied*, 108–10.

24. Seetah, *Humans, Animals*, esp. 45–64.

25. See the illuminating discussion in Bloxam, "The Beast, the Book, and the Belt," in Pluskowski, *Breaking and Shaping Beastly Bodies*, chap. 7.

26. Dekker, *Old Russian Birchbark Letters*, 12.

27. Pliny the Elder, *Natural History* 13.21, vol. 4, 140–41.

28. Trithemius, *In Praise of Scribes*, chap. 7, p. 63. Though as Elizabeth Eisenstein once caustically observed, the abbot's avid enlistment of the printing press for the publication of his own writing shows clearly "that as an author he did not favor handwork over presswork"; see Eisenstein, *Printing Press as an Agent*, 15.

29. Hellinga, "Printing," 93–95.

30. Shakespeare, *2 Henry VI*, 4.2, in *Complete Works*, 309.

31. Hoffman and Cole, *Sacred Trash*; on the practice of *genizah*, see also Bamford, *Cultures of the Fragment*, 88–89; and more recently Rustow, *Lost Archive*, 1–2, 413–14.

32. de Hamel, *Scribes and Illuminators*, 8.

33. On the afterlife of the phrase, see Coupland, *Marshall McLuhan*, esp. 12–15.

34. The standard study is Keightley, *Sources of Shang History*. On bovid and turtle slaughter and the preparation of bone and shell for inscription, see pp. 6–14.

35. See the nineteenth-century account in Plongeon, "Mayapan and Maya Inscriptions," 252.

36. Kesavan, *History of Printing and Publishing*, vol. 1:9.

Chapter 2

1. Bischoff, *Latin Palaeography*, 9 (*Paläographie des römischen Alterums*, 23).

2. Bischoff, *Latin Palaeography*, 9. See also de Hamel, *Scribes and Illuminators*, 15; and, on this distinction from an art-historical perspective, Benton, *Materials, Methods*, 3.

3. Kearney, *Incarnate Text*, 3.

4. Camille, "Sensations of the Page," 41.

5. These monikers, first employed by Tormod Torfæus, were already well known in the nineteenth century; see Laing's comments in his translation of *Heimskringla*, vol. 1, p. 23n. On Torfæus's career as historian and bibliophile, see Roggen, "Old Norse Saga."

6. Brown, "Distribution and Significance," in *Palaeographer's View*, 126. One of the great virtues of Brown's work is its humility with respect to knowledge of the medium he studied: "I have been very skeptical about my own ability to tell hair from flesh in Insular membrane" (p. 126).

7. Brown, "Manuscript Thinking," 351; Borland, "Unruly Reading"; Kay, *Animal Skins*, 3.

8. The rise of posthumanist approaches to animals and the material world has cast some suspicion on the sorts of first-person encounters the idiom of phenomenology often entails. As Jane Bennett puts it, phenomenology can often stop short of the "more radical displacement of the human subject" enabled by the more prescriptively post-humanist perspectives advocated in recent years by Bruno Latour, Graham Harman, and others (see Bennett, *Vibrant Matter*, 30). Yet phenomenology seems particularly suited to the comprehension of the parchment inheritance: Elaine Treharne's forthcoming study, *Perceptions of Medieval Manuscripts*, promises to reimagine "the phenomenal book" in rich and salutary ways.

9. De Hamel, *Meetings with Remarkable Manuscripts*, 82.

10. Anonymous of Bern, "De Clarea," 18.

11. The treatise is discussed in detail in the Introduction to Anonymous of Bern, *De Clarea*, ed. Caffaro.

12. Schott, "Footnotes on Life," 39.

13. Dante, *La Commedia*, *Paradiso* II, lines 49–51, ed. Petrocchi, *La commedia*, vol. 3; *Divine Comedy*, trans. Mandelbaum. All citations hereafter will be internal.

14. Moev, *Metaphysics of Dante's Comedy*, 113.

15. Curtius, *European Literature*, 331.

16. See the suggestive readings of these lines by Benfell, "Biblical Truth in the Examination Cantos," esp. p. 96; and Hawkins, *Dante's Testaments*, chap. 2.

17. Montgomery, *Al-Jāḥiẓ: In Praise of Books*, 6.

18. al-Jāḥiẓ, *Rasāʾil al-Jāḥiẓ* vol. 1, pp. 252–53; al-Jāḥiẓ, translated in *Nine Essays of Al-Jahiz*, 105.

19. Bloom, *Paper Before Print*, 44.

20. al-Jāḥiẓ, *Rasāʾil al-Jāḥiẓ* vol. 1, pp. 252–53; al-Jāḥiẓ, translated in *Nine Essays of Al-Jahiz*, 105.

21. al-Jāḥiẓ, *Rasāʾil al-Jāḥiẓ* vol. 1, pp. 252–53; al-Jāḥiẓ, translated in *Nine Essays of Al-Jahiz*, p. 105.

Chapter 3

I have taken the epigraph from Bausi, "Writing, Copying, Translating," 43.

1. Talmud, *Talmud Bavli*, Bava Batra 25a. The Babylonian Talmud will be cited by tractate and folio number from *Talmud Bavli*. All citations hereafter will be internal.

2. See the comments about Moroccan parchment and paper in Ennahid, "Information and Communication," 267–68.

3. Jesse Meyer, interviewed by the author, Montgomery, New York, March 2013.

4. Meyer, in "Parchment Production," describes the process in use at Pergamena. For those wishing to see the makers in action, Pergamena was featured on an episode of the show *Dirty Jobs*, season 4, episode 26, "Vellum Maker," aired November 28, 2008 on the Discovery Channel.

5. On the firm's turbulent and fascinating history, see the reminiscences by Visscher, "Looking Back On a Lifetime," 341–58.

6. "Ethical Sourcing of Raw Materials."

7. Vnouček, "Manufacture of Parchment," 74.

8. Nosnitsin, "Ethiopian Manuscripts," 3; and see Bausi, "La tradizione scrittoria etiopica," 508–9.

9. Nosnitsin, "Ethiopian Manuscripts," 2–3.

10. Selassie, *Bookmaking in Ethiopia*, 4–8.

11. Mellors and Parsons, *Ethiopian Bookmaking*, 7.

12. West, "Congregation Set to Unveil Torah."

13. Danailova, "Prepping Adirondack Deerskins."

14. Gugenheim, "Or Hadash: Sustainable Parchment."

15. Carruthers, *Craft of Thought*, 1.

16. See the thoughtful essay on parchment craft and manuscript culture by Wilcox, "Philology of Smell," which serves as the introduction to a collection, *Scraped, Stroked, and Bound*, on materialist readings of medieval manuscripts.

17. Cooper, *Artisans and Narrative Craft*, 9.

18. Smith, "Craft, Modernity and Postmodernity," 20.

19. Brown, "Theorising the Crafts," 6.

20. See Reed's acerbic comments in *Ancient Skins, Parchments*, 118-19.

21. Helpful discussions of these recipes and instructions include Gottscher, "Ancient Methods of Parchment-Making"; Thompson, "Medieval Parchment-Making"; and Saxl, "Investigation of the Qualities," 1–100.

22. See the comments of Groot, "Die Herstellung von Goldschlägerhaut," 372; as well as Gottscher, "Ancient Methods," who experimented with the eighth-century recipe (more detailed than most) in the *Compositiones variae*. See Burns, "Material Forms of the Past," 210–11 on this recipe.

23. A point made by Reed, *Ancient Skins*, 172. See Gould, "Terms for Book Production," 90–91, on some obscure fifteenth-century English terminology for the tools and techniques for parchment making (including a "rotyng-pot" for the tub used to soak hides in limed water).

24. Edited and translated in Crum, "Coptic Recipe," 169–71.

25. See the discussion in Di Majo, Federici, and Palma, "Die Tierhautbestimmung des Pergaments"; Gullick, "From Parchmenter to Scribe," 146; and Agati, *Il libro manoscritto*, 66.

26. The recipe appears in Conrad of Mure's *De naturis animalium* and has been transcribed by Gall Morel, "Zur Kunde des Schriftwesens," 314; and Saxl, "Investigation of the Qualities," 27–29. On the allegorical aspects of the lines, see Richter, "Die Allegorie der Pergamentbearbeitung"; and Wattenbach, *Das Schriftwesen*, 172–3.

27. From London, British Library MS Sloane 1313, fol. 126v; ed. Wright and Halliwell, *Reliquae Antiquae*, vol. 1, pp. 108–9 (my modernization).

28. On the visual tradition, see Bockwitz, "Die ältesten Abbildungen," 1017–20. A number of the known images of parchment craft from Western Europe are reproduced in Janzen, "Pergament: Herstellung, Bearbeitung."

29. On this image and its manuscript context, see especially Peterson, "Bible as Subject," 209–13; de Hamel, *Scribes and Illuminators*, 13.

30. Alexander, *Medieval Illuminators*, 12.

31. Sachs and Amman, *Das Ständebuch*, 46v, vol. 1, p. 9.

32. Schopper, *Panoplia omnium*.

33. Albrecht Classen has called the Housebook "a memorial and obituary at the same time," a mark of its intricate reverence for the craft of its members past and present; see Classen, "Craftsmanship and the Guilds," 33.

34. Cruse, *Illuminating the "Roman d'Alexandre,"* 184.

35. Maimonides, *Mishneh Torah*, 2.3: "Hilkhot Tephilin."

36. Kohut, ed., *Aruch Completum*, vol. 3, s.v. dukhsustos, p. 60, citing *Mussaf He-arukh* (Amsterdam 1655) 50a s.v. See the commentary in Haran, "Bible Scrolls," 43–45.

37. Diderot, "Alcoran ou Al-Coran (Théol.)," by Abbé Edme Mallet in *Encyclopédie*, vol. 2, pp. 44–45. See Joubin, "Islam and Arabs," on the central role of this entry in defining the encyclopedists' more general view of Islam.

38. For example, Philp, *Dictionary of Useful Knowledge*, 161.

39. Lalande's treatise has recently been translated by Gay McCauley: La Lande [sic], "The Art of Making Parchment." The translation appears in a special issue of *Art in Translation* edited by Caroline Danforth and dedicated to parchment craft. See Hagadorn, "Parchment making in eighteenth-century France," for a wide-ranging discussion of the evidence for European parchment craft on the eve of industrialization.

40. See the observations in Calhoun, *Nature of the Page*, 109–11.

41. Diderot, *Encyclopédie*, vol. 11, pp. 929–31.

42. Diderot, *Encyclopédie*, vol. 11, p. 931.

Chapter 4

The poem excerpted in the epigraph comes from Boker, *Königsmark: The Legend*, 195.

1. See, among many others, Clarkson, "Rediscovering Parchment"; Ryan, "Holes and Flaws"; Clemens and Graham, *Introduction to Manuscript Studies*, 12–13; Kwakkel, *Books Before Print*, esp. chap. 31, "The Skinny on Bad Parchment"; and Kay, "Original Skin," 35–36.

2. Doty, *Art of Description*, 2.

3. See, for example, Adams, Baker, and Zachary, "Sizing in Nineteenth-Century Book"; Haines, "Materials Analysis"; Kowalik, "Decomposition of Parchment"; and Kite, "Gut Membrane." The use of sturgeon glue is discussed in Fuchs, Meinert, and Schrempf, *Pergament*, 91.

4. See the discussion in Wakelin, *Designing English*, 54, of the potential ironies of such scribal maneuvers (referencing MS Junius 85, fig. 25, pp. 52–53).

5. Additional representative examples from the early Middle Ages can be found in *Chartae Latinae Antiquiores*, vol. 2, pp. 55, 62, 95, 111, 115, 120, and 123.

6. The line appears in slightly different form in Vat. Reg. Lat. MS 846, fol. 100r: "Ambrosius: Qui vult Deum possidere, renuntiat mundum, ut sit illi Deus beata possession." See Schmitz, *Miscellanea Tironiana*, 12; and Rochais, "Contribution à l'histoire des florilèges ascétiques du haut moyan âge latin," p. 267.

7. Bennett, *Middle English Literature*, 30. See the illuminating comments on the work's "aesthetic appeal, or appall," in Worley, "Using the *Ormulum*," 19–20. Our understanding of the role and significance of parchment offcuts will be greatly enriched by the forthcoming work of Stephanie Lahey; see "Offcut Zone Parchment" (dissertation cited with permission of the author).

8. See Kwakkel, "Discarded Parchment," for other examples of this codicological practice in insular book production; and the remarks in Kwakkel, "Decoding the Material book," 67–68.

9. Avrin, *Scribes, Script and Books*, 213.

10. On Harley 4431, see Hindman, "Composition of the Manuscript," 105 and 123; on Jesus 37, see Gilbert, "Imperfect Pages."

11. Porter, "Materiality of the Blue Quran," 575.

12. See British Library MSS Additional Ch 76659 and 76660, charters of confirmation by the Patriarch of Constantinople of the rights of the monastery of Theotokos Chrysopodaritissa (olim Nezeron) in the Peloponnese, dating from 1786 and 1798, respectively.

13. On the history and condition of the Hereford membrane, see Harvey, *Mappa Mundi*, 99–105. The map's legends have been transcribed, translated, and annotated in great detail by Westrem, *Hereford Map*.

14. On this image see Berenbeim, *Art of Documentation*, 33–34; Hiatt, "Cartographic Imagination," 859; and Steiner, *Documentary Culture*, 1–4.

15. See Mitchell and Crook, "Pinchbeck Fen Map," 44.

16. Cortesão, *History of Portuguese Cartography*, vol. 1, 215–16; Campbell, "Portolan Charts," 373.

17. Thrower, *Maps and Civilization*, 56.

18. Nikolai, *Enigma of the Origin*, 13.

19. Kieding, *Scuttlebutt: Tales and Experiences*, 303.

20. Whittington, *Body-Worlds*, 26–30.

21. See Salomon on "Tradition und Individualität im Cod. Pal. Lat. 1993," in *Opicinus de Canistris*, 52–129.

22. Whittington, *Body-Worlds*, 3.

23. Dillon, *Medieval Music-Making*, 8; see Rudy, *Rubrics, Images and Indulgences*, 18–19, for discussion of a further example.

24. On embroidered repairs to medieval parchment, see the comprehensive essay by Sciacca, "Stitches, Sutures, and Seams." On Berthold and the piety of the *Rusticanus de Sanctis*, see Francone, "Virgin Mary," esp. 344–51.

25. Durling, "British Library MS Harley 2253."

26. Kay, *Animal Skins*, 85.

27. See, for example, Davis, "London Lands and Liberties," 45.

28. For a codicological description see Leeuw Van Weenen, *Icelandic Homily Book*, 17–18. Terms for loose coverings are explained in Gillespie, "Bookbinding," 151–54.

Chapter 5

The chapter epigraph comes from Mantel, *Wolf Hall*, 44.

1. Boccaccio, *Decameron* 9.5; translated by Rebhorn, 720.

2. On the complex origins and textual tradition of this work across several languages, see Mathiesen, "Key of Solomon."

3. Mathers, *Key of Solomon* 2.17, p. 111.

4. Mathers, *Key of Solomon* 2.17, p. 112.

5. Ruzzier, "Miniaturisation of Bible Manuscripts."

6. Vorst, "Mysterious Vellum," 370.

7. Orcutt, *Author's Desk Book*, 151.

8. Propert, *History of Miniature Art*, 46.

9. Bradley, *Illuminated Manuscripts*, 7; Thompson, *Introduction to Greek and Latin*, 31.

10. *Catalogue of a Portion*, 4.

11. Bischoff, *Latin Palaeography*, 10.

12. Thompson, *Materials and Techniques*, 28.

13. Delorez, *Palaeography of Gothic*, 31.

14. de Hamel, *Scribes and Illuminators*, 15–16; see also the slightly more qualified observation in de Hamel, *Book*, 132.

15. Benton, *Materials, Methods*, 2.

16. Hanna, "Palaeography of the Wycliffite Bibles," 248–49.

17. Hanna, "Palaeography of the Wycliffite Bibles," 249.

18. For Eastern exceptions see Haran, "Bible Scrolls," 45–46.

19. Groot, "Die Herstellung," 379, explains his splitting process.

20. See Haran, "Bible Scrolls," 46, 44.

21. Sirat, *Hebrew Manuscripts*, 106.

22. Hameiri, *Kiryat Sefer*, 28; see Haran, "Bible Scrolls," n50.

23. See also the discussion in Avrin, *Scribes, Script and Books*, 213.

24. Ganzfried, *Keset ha-Sofer*, siman 2, p. 7.

25. Renaud, "Stillborn Calves: Is It a Problem in Your Herd?," 1.

26. Berger, "Lamb Mortality and Causes," 33–34.

27. Holmøy and Waage, "Time Trends."

28. Page, "Technology of Medieval Sheep," 144.

29. Hall, *Pipe Roll of the Bishopric*, 21.

30. Miller, "Southern Countries," 294. See Stephenson, "Productivity of Medieval Sheep."

31. Trow-Smith, *History of British Livestock*, 150–55.

32. Cited and translated in Pouzet, "Book Production," 218.

33. Sorel, *Extravagant Shepherd*, 178.

34. Agrippa von Nettesheim, *Henry cornelius agrippa*, 54.

35. Browne, *Ars Pictoria*, 1.

36. Peacham, *Gentlemans Exercise*, 95.

37. Hilliard, *Art of Limning*, 94–96.

38. Wilkins, *Alphabetical Dictionary*, n.p.

39. Salsitz, *Jewish Boyhood in Poland*, 102.

40. Morrison, *Justification of Johann Gutenberg*, 211.

41. Mantel, *Wolf Hall*, 44.

42. Mantel, *Wolf Hall*, 549.

43. Woodard, *Vellum*, 21.

44. See the interview by Vianu, "Best Critic is the Editor"; and the discussion in chap. 15 below.

45. Byron, *Getting of Vellum*, 32–33.

46. Byron, *Getting of Vellum*, 36–37.

Chapter 6

The chapter epigraph comes from Dickens, *Bleak House*, 635.

1. Dickens, *Bleak House*, 635.

2. Ilerbaig, "Organisms, Skeletons," 21.

3. Assmann, *Cultural Memory*, 369.

4. The definitive study of Amiatinus and its manuscript context is now Chazelle, *Codex Amiatinus*. See pp. 137ff. on the subject of parchment quality and quantity.

5. Browne, *St. Aldhelm*, 65.

6. Bischoff, *Latin Palaeography*, 10.

7. Gameson, "Cost of the Codex Amiatinus," 7; but see Chazelle, *Codex Amiatinus*, 137, whose more conservative estimate suggests that the number "likely exceeded 300."

8. Clanchy, *From Memory to Written Record*, 125.

9. Thomas, "Manuscripts," esp. p. 17.

10. Postan, *Essays on Medieval Agriculture*, 232; Berman, *Medieval Agriculture*, 96.

11. Forsyth, *Horologicon: A Day's Jaunt*, 153.

12. Madden, *List of Additions*, 42.

13. Ásaad, *Descriptive Catalogue*, 1.

14. British Library, *Catalogue of Additions* (1979), 85.

15. "Hand Bookbindings from Special Collections," Princeton University Library, n.p.

16. Amherst and Wilkinson & Hodge Sotheby, *Catalogue of the Magnificent Library*, 167.

17. Davenport, *Cantor Lectures*, 25.

18. Pitamber, "Library Saves Ancient," n.p.

19. *Bibliotheca Butleriana*, 48.

20. From the memorandum book of George III; described in *Bookworm*, 28. On "asses' skin" in such contexts, see Stallybrass et al., "Hamlet's Tables," 387–88.

21. Black, "Ovid in Medieval Italy," 134n.

22. Buringh, *Medieval Manuscript Production*, 19.

23. Buringh, *Medieval Manuscript Production*, 22.

24. Buringh, *Medieval Manuscript Production*, 99.

25. Buringh, *Medieval Manuscript Production*, 17.

26. Prescott, "Tall Tales from the Archives," 360–61.

27. Kerby-Fulton, "Scribe Speaks at Last," in Kerby-Fulton, Hilmo, and Olson, *Opening Up Middle English*, 92; see also Mooney, "Some New Light," 324–25.

28. Mary McKenzi, personal correspondence, March 10, 2016.

29. Bladen, "Report on European Archives," 994.

30. Scargill-Bird, *Guide to the Principal Classes*, iv.

31. Weight and bulk are not typical attributes for bibliographical or diplomatic analysis; for a fascinating perspective on the weight and bulk of medieval codices, see Sawyer, *Reading English Verse*, esp. 107–08.

32. I am grateful to Richard Cassidy for bringing this image and Mills' work to my attention.

33. See Kelly's illuminating account of "scrolls that grow" and the accumulation of (mostly) membranes within individual records, in *Role of the Scroll*, 41–73.

34. *Catalogue of the Collection*, 70.

35. Scargill-Bird, *Guide to the Principal Classes*, xxii.

36. Coke, *Fourth Part of the Institutes*, chap. 11, "Court of Exchequer," 108.

37. Baker, "Why the History of English Law," 70.

38. Baker, "Why the History of English Law," 71.

39. I am deeply grateful to Solange Fitzgerald, Paul Dryburgh, and Sean Cunningham at the National Archives for their thoughts and speculations on the subject.

40. Bouchard, "Monastic Cartularies," 32.

41. Smail, *Imaginary Cartographies*, 23.

42. Nicholas, *Later Medieval City*, 288; citing Waley, *Siena and the Sienese*, 155–6.

43. Bellamy, "Royal and Imperial Libraries," 433.

44. Lewanski, *Guide to Polish Libraries*, 175.

45. Bisson, *Fiscal Accounts of Catalonia*, vii.

46. Baumgarten, "Secret Vatican Archives," 481.

47. *House of Lords Sessional Papers*, vol. 230, p. 319.

48. This distinction is standard in quantitative palaeozoology; see Grayson, *Quantitative Zooarchaeology*, chap. 2, "Basic Counting Units," 16–92.

49. Drucker, "Humanities Approaches," 11.

50. Watkins, *Gold Fame Citrus*, 114.

51. Guldi and Armitage, *History Manifesto*, 85.

52. See Wilkinson, *Rise and Fall*, 365–66.

53. MacCulloch, *Christianity: The First Three Thousand*, 191.

54. Eusebius, *Vita Constantini* iv.36; translated in *Life of Constantine*, 166–67.

55. Grafton and Williams, *Christianity and the Transformation*, 216. The phrase has been construed differently by Knust and Wasserman, who believe that διφθέραις refers to ornamental leather bindings rather than to the biblical pages themselves; see *To Cast the First Stone*, 184.

56. Richard of Bury, *Philobiblon* cap. vii, ed. Thomas, 59.

57. See Camille on Richard of Bury and "the interpenetration of corporeality and codicology"; Camille, "Book as Flesh and Fetish," 35.

58. "Christus miles gloriosus," *Analecta Hymnica* vol. 19, 419; trans. Chambers, *Lauda Syon*, 58–59.

59. Samir and Nwyia, eds., *Une correspondance islamo-chrétienne*, 610; translated and discussed in van Bladel, "Zoroaster's Many Languages," 194.

60. Boyce, *Letter of Tansar*, 1. The letter has an enormously complex transmission and translation history, from a Middle Persian original to a lost Arabic translation to the New Persian redaction that survives; see van Bladel, "Zoroaster's Many Languages," 194.

61. Boyce (*Letter of Tansar*, 37) translates the sum as 1200 rather than 12,000, though as van Bladel explains in his correction ("Zoroaster's Many Languages," 194), the larger sum reflects the entirety of the disaster rather than simply the fire. At the suggestion of Arash Zeini, I have modified Boyce's translation to the more generic skins, as the animal derivation is specified only in the *Ardā Wirāz Nāmag*.

62. Vahman, ed., *Ardā Wirāz Nāmag*, 76; the passage is translated in Bailey, *Zoroastrian Problems*, 151–52.

63. On the resonances of this term see André-Salvini, *Forgotten Empire*, 154.

64. Kant, *Critique of Judgment*, 106.

65. Brady, *Sublime in Modern Philosophy*, 83.

66. Novacich, *Shaping the Archive*, 66.

67. Cross, *Pope Joan*, 45.

68. Metzger, "Gutenberg, Johannes Gensfleisch Zum," 263.

69. New, *Text of the Bible*, 130.

70. Collins, "Flock," in *Trouble with Poetry*, 35.

71. Leopold, *Sand County Almanac*, viii.

Chapter 7

The chapter epigraph is taken from Azzoni and Stolper, "Aramaic epigraph *ns(y)ḥ* on Elamite Persepolis," 49.

1. Pliny the Elder, *Natural History* 13.70.

2. See Johnson, "Ancient and Medieval Accounts," for a helpful overview of later versions of the story, some of which conflict with Pliny's account.

3. Isidore of Seville, *Etymologiae* 6.11.1; translated in *Etymologies of Isidore*, 141.

4. Persius, *Satire* 3.10.; translated by Rudd, 144–45.

5. Winsbury, *Roman Book*, 23–25, discusses this passage from Persius, and what it may indicate about the variety of mediums and their combinations in use at this time.

6. Reed, *Ancient Skins*, 87–94; Ryder, "Sheepskin from Ancient Kerma."

7. On the Dura-Europos membranes, see Teicher, "Ancient Eucharistic Prayers."

8. Gillings, *Mathematics in the Time*, 89–91; and see fig. 9.2, p. 94.

9. Spallinger, "Drama in History," 278–82, examines the palimpsestic character of the membrane and what it suggests about the document's social context.

10. On the Berlin Leather Roll (P. Berlin 3029), see Lichtheim, *Ancient Egyptian Literature*, vol. I, pp. 115–18; and De Buck, "Building Inscription."

11. Translated in Lichtheim, *Ancient Egyptian Literature*, 157–58.

12. Translated in Lichtheim, *Ancient Egyptian Literature*, 158. On this sequence see Eyre, *Use of Documents*, 31–32.

13. These terminological difficulties have been addressed by Sarri, *Material Aspects of Letter Writing*, 85–86.

14. Phillipson, "Parchment Production."

15. Martin, *Corpus of Reliefs of the New Kingdom*, figure 68, plate 23. See Drier-Murphy, "Leatherwork and Skin Products," 303.

16. On this assemblage, see Driver, *Aramaic Documents*; Greenfield, "Some Notes on the Arsham Letters"; and, most recently, Radner, *State Correspondence*, 131–33.

17. Waters, *Ancient Persia*, 189–90.

18. Evison, "Thus Speaks Arshama."

19. See Azzoni and Stolper, "Aramaic Epigraph *nᵓsiḥ*," 44.

20. Azzoni and Stolper, "Aramaich epigraph," 76; see also Driver, *Aramaic Documents*, 1–3.

21. See West, "Papyri of Herodotus," 69–73.

22. Herodotus, *Histories* 5.25. All citations hereafter will be internal.

23. Kurke, *Coins, Bodies, Games*, 83. On the connective logic of these stories in Book V, see Greenwood, "Bridging the Narrative."

24. Aulus Gellius, *Attic Nights* 17.9.22., vol. 3, 238–39.

25. See Mills, *Suspended Animation*, 33–39, on the recasting of the Sisamnes story in the medieval and early modern periods.

26. Emerson, "Civilization," in *Collected Works*, vol. 7, p. 10.

27. McLuhan, *Understanding Me*, 17.

28. The passage has inspired much commentary over the years; see Crostini, "Byzantium," 59.

29. See Josephus, *Jewish Antiquities*, 3.11.270, p. 122.

30. Cited in Silver, *Footprints in Parchment*, 199.

31. The list comes from Martial, *Epigrams* 14.7–192.

32. See the discussion of Martial and the emergence of the codex as literary form in Roberts and Skeat, *Birth of the Codex*, chap. 5.

33. Martial, *Epigrams* 14.188; on these passages, see Winsbury, *Roman Book*, 23–25.

34. On the membranes of the Qumran scrolls, see especially Rabin, "Building a Bridge."

35. The Temple Scroll, 11QTemple Scrollᵃ; see VanderKam and Flint, *Meaning of the Dead Sea*, 57–58.

36. See Young, *Echoes of Two Cultures*, 40–42; and especially McNeal, "On Editing Herodotus," 111–15.

Chapter 8

1. Gamble, *Books and Readers*, 53.

2. Jerome, *De viris illustribus* 113.51, ed. Bernoulli. On this enterprise of librarianship, see Carriker, *Library of Eusebius*, esp. 23–25; on Jerome and this practice of preservation, see Williams, *Monk and the Book*, 185–86, who argues against "sweeping claims for the dominance of parchment over papyrus at the turn of the fifth century."

3. See chap. 6 above.

4. Augustine, *Confessions* 13.15.16, translation by O'Donnell.

5. Curtius, *European Literature*, 319.

6. Stock, *Augustine the Reader*, 294n.

7. Clark, "City of Books," 131–32.

8. Brown, *Augustine of Hippo*, 42.

9. See Spencer, *Heretic's Feast*, which devotes a whole chapter to Gnostic sects and Manichaeism; and Preece, *Sins of the Flesh*, who argues that Augustine "set the stage for the flesh-eating victory within Christendom for centuries to come" (p. 135).

10. On Augustine's struggles with the sexual and ethical failings of the Manichees, see Clark's introduction to Augustine, *St. Augustine on Marriage*, 5–8.

11. On the Manichaean view of Christ and the Trinity current in Augustine's North Africa, see in particular Coyle, "Characteristics of Manichaeism," 108–10.

12. Augustine, *Contra Faustum Manichaeum* 6.3, ed. CSEL 25/1, 171. All citations hereafter will be internal.

13. *Cologne Mani Codex*, 11–13.

14. *Cologne Mani Codex*, 38–39.

15. Klimkeit, *Manichaean Art and Calligraphy*, 20.

16. Augustine, *Enarrationes in Psalmos* 93.6; ed. Dekkers and Fraipont, CCSL 38; trans. Boulding, vol. 2, p. 379. All citations hereafter will be internal.

Chapter 9

The chapter epigraph comes from Cole, ed. and trans., *Dream of the Poem*, 150.

1. See the notes in Gameson, "Origin of the Exeter Book," for an exhaustive summary of the scholarship on the origins, provenance, and codicology of the manuscript.

2. Of the many excellent studies of the Exeter Book riddles published in recent years, see especially Dale, *Natural World*; Bitterli, *Say What I Am Called*; Murphy, *Unriddling the Exeter Riddles*; Cox, "Chaucer's Ethical Palimpsest," 100–107; and the edition and translation by Williamson cited below.

3. On this dimension of Tolkien's medievalism, see Roberts, *Riddles of the Hobbit*; and on its darker resonances, Chism, "Middle-Earth, the Middle Ages," esp. 79 and 86.

4. The Book/Bible riddle is numbered 26 in Krapp and Dobbie, *Anglo-Saxon Poetic Records*; I have followed the revised numbering proposed in Williamson, *Old English Riddles*.

5. Riddle 26, Krapp and Dobbie, eds., *Anglo-Saxon Poetic Records*, vol. 3, translation in Williamson, *Feast of Creatures*, 84 (renumbered as Riddle 24). The poem has also been edited and translated in Orchard, *Old English and Anglo-Latin Riddle*, 332–35.

6. Dale, *Natural World in the Exeter Book*, 95.

7. Holsinger, "Of Pigs and Parchment," 622.

8. Riddle 28, Krapp and Dobbie, eds, *Anglo-Saxon Poetic Records*, vol. 3; translation in Williamson, *Feast of Creatures*, 86 (renumbered as Riddle 24).

9. See Ziegler, "Ein neuer Lösungsversuch." Murphy suggests that such pairings are intended here as part of a deliberate strategy of obfuscation, "chosen as much for their rhyme as for their meaning"; see *Unriddling the Exeter Book*, 41.

10. For well over a century, these Latin aenigmata have been read and considered as likely sources or close analogues of the Exeter Book riddles; see, for example, Wyatt, *Old English Riddles*, 84–86; and more recently Ziegler, "Ein neuer Lösungsversuch"; and Bitterli, *Say What I Am Called*, 182–88.

11. "De membrano," in Tatwine, *Opera Omnia*, 171; trans. Orchard, *Old English and Anglo-Latin Riddle*, 114.

12. See Illich, *In the Vineyard*, esp. 57–58.

13. "De membrano," Berne Riddle 24, in Glorie, *Collectiones Aenigmatum*, 570; trans. Orchard, *Old English and Anglo-Latin Riddle*, 516.

14. "De membrano," in Glorie, *Collectiones Aenigmatum*, CCSL 133a, 242; trans. Orchard, *Old English and Anglo-Latin Riddle*, 160.

15. Kay, "Legible Skins," 23–26.

16. *Ysengrimus*, 2.159–62, in Mann, *Ysengrimus: Text With Translation*, 270–71. All citations hereafter will be to Mann's edition and translation.

17. See Billy, "Hagiographical Parody."

18. Lydgate, "Debate of the Horse," lines 358–64, in *Minor Poems*, 554.

19. Lydgate, "Debate of the Horse," lines 365–78, in *Minor Poems*, 554.

20. See the reading of this passage by Matlock, "Talking Animals, Debating Beasts," 226–27.

21. Brooks, "Death of a Poet."

22. Waterhouse, "Illustrated Calf," in *2nd*, 41.

Chapter 10

The chapter epigraphs come from Stieber, *Haiti's Paper War*, ch. 1, n. 47; and *Teaching of Addai*, ed. and trans. Howard and Philips, 23 and 47.

1. On the historical context of the Declaration, see Gaffield, *Haitian Declaration of Independence*.

2. Quoted in Stieber, *Haiti's Paper War*, ch. 1 n. 47.

3. Fischer, *Modernity Disavowed*, 201.

4. Owenson, *France in 1829–30*, vol. 1, p. 213.

5. See Thompson, "Tanned Human Skin"; and his later survey, "Notes on Corpse Lore." The definition comes from Gordon, "In the Flesh?," 118.

6. See Kerner, "Reliures de livres"; Harrison, "Anthropodermic Bibliopegy"; Marvin, "Body of the Text"; and Rosenbloom, *Dark Archives*.

7. See Gordon, "In the Flesh?" on the implications of these identifications.

8. Hayward, Review of F. Feuillet de Conches, *Causeries*.

9. Carlyle, *French Revolution*, vol. 3, 342. See also the account of the rumors around Meudon in Rosenbloom, *Dark Archives*, 38–42.

10. Crawford, *Doctor Claudius*, 244.

11. Crawford, *Doctor Claudius*, 244n.

12. Mentioned in Brassington's *History of the Art of Bookbinding*, 253.

13. "An Original Edition," 281.

14. Gallé, *Émile Gallé*, 107.

15. Nyong'o, *Amalgamation Waltz*, 33. See also Rosenbloom's discussion in *Dark Archives*, 95–99.

16. Wallis, "Book Bound in Human Skin," 246.

17. Now at the Westcountry Studies Library; see Maxted, "History of the Book."

18. See Curtis, "John Horwood Book"; Bristol Archives ref. no. 35893/36/v_i.

19. Allen, *Narrative of the life*. On this book see Connor, *Book of Skin*, 45.

20. The report was published as Hough, "Two Cases of Trichiniasis." See Rosenbloom, *Dark Archives*, 49–57.

21. Lander, "Skin She Lived In."

22. Cuskelly, *Original Skin*, 170.

23. Compare Striphas in *Late Age of Print*, xii.

24. See Kren, "New Directions," in Kren and McKendrick, *Illuminating the Renaissance*, 417.

25. "Charter of Heaven," in *Middle English Charters*, 100; the passage is cited and discussed in Steiner, *Documentary Culture*, 71.

26. Rudy, "Sewing the Body of Christ," Figure 32.

27. Curtius, *European Literature*, 311.

28. Jager, *Book of the Heart*; Lochrie, *Margery Kempe and Translations*; Frese and O'Keeffe, *Book and the Body*; Camille, "Sensations of the Page."

29. *Teaching of Addai*, ed. and trans. Howard and Philips, 23, 47.

30. I am grateful to Rebecca Stephens Falcasantos for this observation.

31. Krueger, *Writing and Holiness*, 150; see also Peers, *Sacred Shock*, 53–54.

32. Prudentius, "Hymnus in diem Sancte Eolalie," in *Crowns of Martyrdom* 3.136–40, 151; following Leatherbury, *Inscribing Faith*. See Curtius, *European Literature*, 311–12; and Miller, *Corporeal Imagination*, 90–95.

33. "Love that god loveth," lines 182–84, in *Twenty-Six Political*, 78.

34. Suso, *Deutsche Schriften*, vol. 1, pp. 14–15; translated in Suso, *Exemplar*, 70–71.

35. Hamburger, *Nuns as Artists*, 178.

36. Suso, prologue to *Little Book of Eternal Wisdom*; translated in Suso, *Exemplar*, 209.

37. Suso, *Deutsche Schriften*, vol. 1, p. 88; translated in Suso, *Exemplar*, 137.

38. Rudy, *Postcards on Parchment*. See also the discussion in Fuchs, Meinert, and Schrempf, *Pergament*, 82–84.

39. Suso, *Little Book of Eternal Wisdom*, chap. 5, in *Deutsche Schriften*, vol. 2, p. 17; translated in Suso, *Exemplar*, 220.

40. *Fasciculus Morum*, 212 (my more literal translation).

41. Brantley, *Reading in the Wilderness*, 189.

42. "Long Charter B-text," in *Middle English Charters*, 53–54.

43. *Middle English Charters*, 59–61.

44. "Meditation on the Five Wounds," in *Yorkshire Writers* vol. 2, p. 440.

45. "Privity of the Passion," *Yorkshire Writers* vol. 1, p. 206.

46. "Burial of Christ," lines 272–74, in Furnivall, *Digby Plays*, 180.

47. Fisher, "A Sermon verie fruitfull," in *English Works of John Fisher*, vol. 1, 393–94. On this sermon see Kearney, *Incarnate Text*, 19–20.

48. A point I have made elsewhere; see Holsinger, "Of Pigs and Parchments," 621.

49. "Charter of Heaven," in *Middle English Charters*, 100.

50. "Long Charter A-text," in *Middle English Charters*, 27.

51. Stern, *Jewish Bible*, 67.

52. Office of United States Chief of Counsel, vol. 6, p. 791.

53. Nietzsche, *Thus Spake Zarathustra*, 160.

Chapter 11

The chapter epigraph comes from Talmud Bava Metzia 85b, *Talmud Bavli*.

1. Landa, *Jewish Fairy Tales*, 244. The legend in Landa's compilation is a version of the story of Rabbi Judah Loew ben Bezalel, the Maharal of Prague (c. 1520–1609), a kabbalist who forges golems from mud. See the account in Rosen, *Imagining Jewish Art*, 52. The following sentences paraphrase the remainder of the story from Landa's version.

2. On the traditions of the medieval golem, see Schäfer, "Magic of the Golem"; and Donnolo, *Sefer Hakhmoni*, 253, with additional references.

3. Iafrate, *Wandering Throne of Solomon*, 130. The image from the Coburg Pentateuch is briefly discussed by Tahan in *Hebrew Manuscripts*, 42.

4. On the intermingling of parchment and paper in medieval Hebrew and Aramaic manuscripts, see Beit-Arié, "Commissioned and Owner-Produced Manuscripts," esp. 21–25.

5. The history of this topos, widespread in Indo-European religions, is traced in Linn, "If All the Sky," 951–70. On its ascription to Yohanan ben Zakkai, see Neusner, *Life of Rabban Yohanan*, 46; and, in a different context, Tractate Shabbat 11a, where it is attributed to Rav and pertains to the "unquantifiable space of governmental authority."

6. Mroczek, *Literary Imagination*, 41.

7. On the origin and early transmission of *Soferim*, see especially the commentary and extensive notes in Blank, "It's Time to Take," 4–10. For the tract's outsize role in Jewish textual scholarship (both premodern and modern), see Levy, *Fixing God's Torah*, 7–11.

8. For a thorough digest of the material culture of writing in the early centuries, see the discussion and extensive references in Demsky and Bar-Ilan, "Writing in Ancient Israel," esp. 24–28; and, for a far more exhaustive survey, Beit-Arié's encyclopedic work *Hebrew Codicology*.

9. *Soferim* 1.1, in Talmud, *Minor Tractates of the Talmud*, vol. 1, p. 211. All citations hereafter will be internal.

10. On this last point see Jaffeee, *Torah in the Mouth*; Alexander, *Transmitting Mishnah*, and

the helpful summary of Hebrew-language scholarship in chap. 1 of Fishman, *Becoming the People of the Talmud*.

11. Nearly identical language can be found in the opening portions of *Sefer Torah*, likely an even older treatise dealing with the preparation, writing, and handling of Torah scrolls; see *Minor Tractates of the Talmud*, vol. 2, esp. pp. 631–32.

12. Avrin, *Scribes, Script and Books*, 112–13, whose helpful overview presents these distinctions as rather clearer than they are in rabbinic sources, where they are matters of some dispute for centuries. On these terminological controversies, see Beit-Arié, *Hebrew Codicology*, 27–30; and Haran, "Bible Scrolls."

13. In general bodily inscription is prohibited; compare the discussions in Mishnah Makkot 3:6 and Bavli Makkot 21a.

14. *Tefillin* 10; Talmud, *Minor Tractates of the Talmud*, vol. 2, pp. 649–50.

15. Fishman, *Becoming the People*, 199. See also Fishman's compelling discussion of the story of "Samuel the Parchment Maker" and what it suggests about the sacralization of the material text of Torah, p. 202.

16. Sirat, *Hebrew Manuscripts*, 88.

17. Maimonides, *Mishneh Torah, Hilkhot Tefillin* 1.6–8. There are many variations of this rule in medieval commentaries (including Maimonides' own), many of them disputing the literalism of the distinctions.

18. Maimonides, *Mishneh Torah, Hilkhot Tefillin*, 1.10 and 20.

19. Scholem, "Meaning of the Torah," cited from Fine, *Essential Papers on Kabbalah*, 189.

20. Heschel, *Heavenly Torah*, 337; discussed by Idel, *Absorbing Perfections*, 47–48.

21. See Siegal, *Early Christian Monastic Literature*, 194.

22. On this episode in the context of Kabbalistic magic see Wolfson, *Through a Speculum*, 242–44.

23. Ahimaaz ben Paltiel, *Chronicle of Ahimaaz*, 66.

24. Ahimaaz ben Paltiel, *Chronicle of Ahimaaz*, 77–78.

25. The relevant passages are discussed in Greenbaum and Rodrígues-Arribas, *Unveiling the Hidden*, 319, 322.

26. On the significance of this sacrifice within and across Jewish and Christian traditions, see, among many others, Levenson, *Death and Resurrection*.

27. See the discussions in Berman, *Vegetarianism and the Jewish Tradition*, xiv–xv; and Colb, "Linking Judaism and Veganism," 281–82.

28. Cited in Berman, *Akedah: The Binding of Isaac*, 18. On other versions of these legends deriving from the Akedah, see Spiegel, *Last Trial*.

29. Ambrose, Letter VIII, to Justus, *Letters of St. Ambrose*, 28.

30. Play 5, "Abraham and Isaac," in Beadle, *York Plays*, 55. On the play and its relationship to the very active parchment industry in late-medieval York, see Gee, "Printers, Stationers, and Bookbinders," esp. 30–35.

31. Translated in Schwartz, *Leaves from the Garden*, 327–28. The story has many branches, though I have been unable to identify the exact version translated here; see Schwartz's source list on p. 425; and Lachower, *Wisdom of the Zohar*, vol. 3, p. 746. For other early legends around the origins of the Zohar, see Huss, *Zohar: Reception*, chap. 2, "The Zohar as an Imagined Book," 36–66.

32. See Tahan, *Hebrew Manuscripts*, 43–45; Epstein, *Dreams of Subversion*, 58–62, 88–90.

33. On this image, see Gutmann, "Sacrifice of Isaac," 83.

Chapter 12

The chapter epigraph comes from de Certeau, "Tools for Body Writing," 7.

1. Potter, *Life of Shakespeare*, 408–9; Duncan-Jones, *Shakespeare: An Ungentle Life*, 283–85.

2. The documents are discussed in Nelson, "Shakespeare Indentures," 113–14.

3. Transcription in Lewis, *Shakespeare Documents*, 440–43.

4. On the six extant signatures, see the thorough discussion in Purkis, *Shakespeare and Manuscript Drama*, 197–208.

5. Holdsworth, *History of English Law*, vol. 5, p. 157.

6. See the many documents discussed in Lewis, *Shakespeare Documents*; the chapters in Crummé, *Shakespeare on the Record*; and the permanent online exhibit at the Folger Library, *Shakespeare Documented*.

7. James, *English Paleography and Manuscript Culture*, 204.

8. Bosman, "Shakespeare in Leather," 225.

9. See Schoenbaum, *William Shakespeare*, 30.

10. On the symbolic and practical importance of paper to Shakespeare, John Donne, and other early modern writers, see Calhoun, *Nature of the Page*, esp. 126–50.

11. Shakespeare and Anonymous, *Edward III*, scene 3, in *Complete Works*, 501–2. All references to Shakespeare's plays will be to the Oxford edition, by act and scene.

12. On the symbology of Christ's body in *Comedy of Errors*, see Stockton, *Members of His Body*, chap. 1.

13. de Certeau, "Tools for Body Writing," 7.

14. As characterized by Cucu, *Underside of Politics*, 65.

15. Nashe, *Pleasant Comedie*, 252.

16. For example Wilson, "Scribbled Form."

17. Patterson, *Reading Holinshed's Chronicles*, 298n23.

18. Holinshed, "Iohn the youngest sonne," in *Chronicles* (1587), vol. 6, p. 186; subsequent citations by volume and page.

19. Eggert, *Showing Like a Queen*, 78–79; and Herman, "O, 'tis a gallant king'."

20. The phrase has had a fascinating afterlife; see Cash, "Rotten Parchment Bonds," and Black, *Tory World: Deep History*, 362–64.

21. Chartier, "Jack Cade."

22. Justice, *Writing and Rebellion*, 46–47.

23. Yates, *Of Sheep, Oranges, and Yeast*, 2.

24. Chartier, "Jack Cade," 81.

25. Clanchy, *From Memory to Written Record*, 170–71.

26. Eadmer, *Eadmeri Historia Novorum*, 138; discussed in Clanchy, *From Memory to Written Record*, 263.

27. On the parchment references in this passage see most recently Kearney, *Incarnate Text*, 201–2; and Calhoun, *Nature of the Page*, 87–89.

Chapter 13

1. On pocket Bibles of this sort, see most recently Ruzzier, "Miniaturisation of Bible Manuscripts."

2. On the implications of the method, see Collins et al., "ZooMS: The Collagen Barcode."

3. For a comparative statistical analysis of models of collaboration (and non-collaboration) across various fields, see Larivière, Gingras, and Archambault, "Canadian Collaboration Networks"; see also Macfarlane, *Co-authorship in the Humanities.*

4. Fiddyment, Holsinger, et al., "Animal origin of 13th-century uterine vellum."

5. See the helpful overview in Fiddyment et al., "So You Want to Do Biocodicology?"

6. Piñar et al., "Combined Approach"; Ghioni et al., "Evidence of a Distinct Lipid"; and Lech, "Evaluation of a Parchment Document."

7. Snow, *Two Cultures,* 4.

8. See also Jardine, "C.P. Snow's Two Cultures."

9. Kagan, *Three Cultures,* 18.

10. Kagan, *Three Cultures,* 266.

11. Radini et al., "Medieval Women's Early Involvement"; Mordechai et al., "Justinianic Plague"; and Keller et al., "Ancient *Yersinia pestis* genomes."

12. See Claire Hanson's helpful perspective on issues of influence across paradigms, including what she calls "the recent rapprochement between postgenomic and literary perspectives on human nature"; Hanson, *Genetics and the Literary Imagination,* 2.

13. Collins, "Archaeology and the Biomolecular."

14. Teasdale, Fiddyment, et al., "York Gospels."

15. Stinson, "Counting Sheep," 194. See also Stinson, "Knowledge of the Flesh."

16. Hilts, "Decipherers of Dead Sea Scrolls."

17. Barrera, "Qumran Finds," 17.

18. Woodward et al., "Analysis of Parchment Fragments," 216.

19. Woodward et al., "Analysis of Parchment Fragments," 225.

20. Golb, *Who Wrote the Dead Sea Scrolls?,* 398.

21. Campana et al., "A Flock of Sheep, Goats and Cattle."

22. Poulakakis et al., "Ancient DNA and the Genetic Signature."

23. Teasdale et al., "Paging Through History."

24. Teasdale et al., "Paging Through History."

25. Anava et al., "Illuminating Genetic Mysteries."

26. Henare, "Taonga Māori," 52.

27. O'Malley, Stirling, and Penetito, *Treaty of Waitangi Companion,* esp. 366–85.

28. Shepherd, Whitehead, and Whitehead, "Genetic Analysis."

29. Shepherd, Whitehead, and Whitehead, "Genetic Analysis."

30. See, for example, de-Dios et al., "Metagenomic Analysis of a Blood Stain."

31. Daston, preface to *Science in the Archives,* vii.

32. Alley, *Two-Mile Time Machine,* 3–4.

33. Young, *Pet Projects: Animal Fiction*; Greer, "Geopolitics and the Avian."

34. Sepkoski, "Earth as Archive," 55.

35. Piñar, Sterflinger, and Pinzari, "Unmasking the Measles-Like Parchment."

Chapter 14

The chapter epigraph comes from Leopold, *Round River*, 146.

1. Brooks, *People of the Book*, 144.
2. See, among others, Beit-Arié, "Why Comparative Codicology?"
3. The phrase appears in McNeill, *Rise of the West*, xxix.
4. Rudy, *Piety in Pieces*, 50.
5. Ryley, "Waste Not, Want Not," 69.
6. Serres, *Five Senses*, 275.
7. Cited in Leclercq, *Love of Learning*, 155.
8. Thoreau, *Week on the Concord*, 10. See Garber, *Thoreau's Fable of Inscribing*, 97.
9. The term *codicology* is most often construed as the study of the physical form specifically of the codex, in contrast to diplomatics, which deals more narrowly with the study of documents; see, respectively, Beal, *Dictionary of English Manuscript*, 79; and Boyle, "Diplomatics."
10. Chin, "Papyrus Beyond Writing."
11. Calhoun, *Nature of the Page*.
12. Macdonell, *History of Sanskrit Literature*, 19.
13. Kesavan, *History of Printing*, vol. 1, p. 9; cited in chap. 1 above. As Graham Shaw puts it, parchment "found no place in traditional Hindu, Buddhist, or Jain book culture. The Western use of parchment involving the slaughter of young animals for their skin (particularly the holy cow) would have been anathema to them all" (Shaw, "South Asia," 128).
14. Chopra, *Oriental Manuscript Library*, 32.
15. The theology and craft of *ñee ñuhu* is discussed at length in Jansen and Pérez Jiménez, *Mixtec Pictorial Manuscripts*, esp. 12–15 and notes.
16. On this image see Boone, *Cycles of Time and Meaning*; Joyce, "Materiality and Practice," 466–67; and Brotherston, "Contours of Meaning," 18–19.
17. National Archives, Kew, TNA PRO SC 6/886/9.
18. On this die-off, see Mate, "Economy of Kent," 8.
19. See further Stone, *Decision-Making in Medieval*, esp. 76–77.
20. Surrey History Centre 85/12/1; see Mate, *Trade and Economic Developments*, 18.
21. PRO E 210/8936.
22. Brown, "Letters to the Editor," 61.
23. See, among many others, the thoughtful discussion by Oppermann, "Feminist Ecocriticism," 19–20.
24. Buell, *Environmental Imagination*, 10.
25. Philips, *Truth of Ecology*, 6.
26. Philips, *Truth of Ecology*, 9.
27. Langdon, "Up and Down the Caucomgomoc," 1095.
28. Thoreau, *Week on the Concord*, 101.
29. Thoreau, *Maine Woods*, 235.
30. See Calhoun, *Nature of the Page*, 66–69.
31. Vaughan, "To the Holy Bible," in *Silex Scintillans*, 81.
32. Knight, *Reading Green*.
33. Palgrave, *Landscape in Poetry*, 164.

34. Exeter Riddle 47, Krapp and Dobbie, eds., *Anglo-Saxon Poetic Records*, vol. 3; translation in Williamson, *Feast of Creatures*, 107 (renumbered as Riddle 45).

35. See Williamson's gloss, *Old English Riddles*, 286; Robinson, "Artful Ambiguities"; Foys, "Undoing of the Exeter Book"; and Bitterli, *Say What I Am Called*, who reads the riddle as "a self-ironic parable of the vernacular riddle-poet" (p. 193).

36. Momma, "*Worm*: A Lexical Approach," 200. See also Scattergood, "Eating the Book."

37. Williamson, *Old English Riddles*, 286.

38. Lacy, *Wyl bucke his testament*, n.p. On the use of animal parts in this poem, see Holsinger, *Music, Body, and Desire*, 345–46; and Taylor, "Animal Rights, Legal Agency."

39. See chap. 9 above.

40. Thompson, *Materials and Techniques*, 28.

41. Cleaver, *Illuminated History Books*, 39.

42. Benedict, *Regula S. Benedicti*, chap. 39, pp. 321–22.

43. On the order's dietary practices, see Thompson, *Carthusian Order in England*, 103.

44. Printed in Monget, *Chartreuse de Dijon*, 415–19.

45. Cited and translated in Kay, "Flayed Skin," 201.

46. Kay, "Flayed Skin," 201.

47. The text of the grant appears in Mühlbacher, *Die Urkunden Pippins, Karlmanns*, 126. See the observations by Vezin, "Les relations entre Saint-Denis," 18. Paul Lacroix incorrectly identified the source as the "Chronicle of the monk of St. Gall" in *Manners, Customs, and Dress*, 168.

48. Guérard, *Cartulaire de l'Abbaye*, 65.

49. Crumley, "Historical Ecology," 21.

Chapter 15

The chapter epigraph comes from Boisseau, "Parchment," in *Trembling Air*, 21.

1. Castle, *Modernism and the Celtic Revival*, 68–75.

2. The painting has received remarkably little attention in the historiography of Surrealism; see the comments by Schlatter, "Leonora Carrington's Samhain Skin." On Carrington's relationship with Surrealism, see Albert, *Leonora Carrington*.

3. Kite and Thomson, *Conservation of Leather*, 220.

4. Williams, *Marxism and Literature*, 121–22.

5. The term "grangerized" derives from James Granger, whose *Biographical History of England* (1769) encouraged readers to paste in their own illustrations from other sources; a grangerized book is thus "one that has been supplemented with portraits and other images, often cannibalized from other books. (The grangerized book is the enriched one, not the mutilated victim.)"; see Jackson, *Marginalia: Readers Writing*, 186.

6. A brief guide to the exhibit was published as Lüthi, *Kleiner Führer*.

7. For the original language see Thomas, *Handbook to the Public Records*, 61; on the technical history and legal ramifications of the phrasing, see Webley and Samuels, *Complete Public Law*, 204–6.

8. Hope, "Anger as MPs Bow."

9. This and subsequent citations from the 2017 debate are from "Record Copies of Acts."

10. Flood, "Could Brexit Bill VANISH."

11. The collection of printed vellum Acts appears to be considerably larger than those catalogued in Sandars, *Annotated List of Books*; or Alston, *Books Printed on Vellum*. Hellinga ("Printing," 93–95) warns against the view that printing on vellum "invariably indicates archaism," as well into the early modern period the medium was used for printing certain Statues of the Realm, historical chronicles and classic works, and presentation copies.

12. On the collective's artistic vision and the implications of its work, see Margolis, "Torah Scroll," 183–84.

13. Rix, *Golden Age of Botanical Art*, 35, 86. See the spectacular volume compiled by Heurtel and Lenoir, *Vélins du Muséum national*.

14. Rickman, Edmondson, and Le Cornu, "Conservation of Botanical Illustrations," provide a helpful assessment of the tradition and its challenges to conservationists.

15. See the comments by John McEwen, his son, in Rix, *Rory McEwen*, 62.

16. Sherwood, *New Flowering*, 92.

17. Nessler, *Of Two Minds*, n.p.

18. Nessler, "No, Really, That's How," 7.

19. "At the Edge—Kate Nessler," gallery show notice in *The Botanical Artist* 19 (2003): 8.

20. Moir, "Story Behind the Art."

21. Margaret Fitzpatrick, personal correspondence.

22. Laura Youngson Coll, personal correspondence.

23. McNay, "Laura Youngson Coll," interview in *Studio International*, July 31, 2017.

24. The firm has a fascinating history in its own right as "perhaps the oldest manufacturer of calfskin [drum]heads in Europe." The founder, Nathan Elzas, was a Dutch Jew who began the business to provide parchment to record sacred texts in the tradition. See Cook, "Calfskin Heads," in *Encyclopedia of Percussion*, 162.

25. Byron, "Getting of Vellum," in *Getting of Vellum*, 30–31.

26. Serebrin, "Artist Statement."

Epilogue

1. The program for the online symposium on "The Past, Present, and Future of Digital Medieval Studies" (May–June 2021) gestures at the potentially transformational effects of COVID-19 on digital medieval studies, accessed August 18, 2021, https://digitalmedievalist.wordpress.com/the-past-present-and-future-of-digital-medieval-studies-a-global-digital-medievalist-symposium/.

2. Smith, "What it is to be a Digitization Specialist."

3. Foys, "Medieval Manuscripts," esp. 119–20.

4. See the compelling discussion by Green, "Digital Manuscripts," for any number of examples.

5. Coe, "8 Book Historians."

6. See Cooper, "How Twitter's New Expanded."

7. From a medievalist perspective, see especially Warren and Weijer, "Re-Imagining Digital Things."

8. Cerf and Singh, "Internet Predictions," 11.

9. For a variety of usages of this concept in discussions of sustainability, see West, "Digital Dark Ages"; Mihajlovic, Stankovic, and Mihajlovic, "Digital Dark Ages"; and most recently Chew, *Ecology, Artificial Intelligence.*

10. See Warren, introduction to *Holy Digital Grail.*

BIBLIOGRAPHY

Primary Sources

Agrippa von Nettesheim, Heinrich Cornelius. *Henry cornelius agrippa his fourth book of occult philosophy of geomancie, magical elements of peter de aban: Astronomical geomancie; the nature of spirits; arbatel of magick; the species or several kindes of magick.* Translated by Robert Turner. London: J. C. for the Rooks, 1665. Wing A786.

Ahimaaz ben Paltiel. *The Chronicle of Ahimaaz.* Translated by Marcus Salzman. New York: Columbia University Press, 1924.

Al-Jāḥiẓ, Abū ʿUthmān ʿAmr ibn Baḥr. *Nine Essays of Al-Jahiz.* Translated by William Hutchins. Bern: Peter Lang, 1988.

———. *Rasāʾil al-Jāḥiẓ.* Ed. ʿAbd al-Salām Muḥammad Hārūn. 2 vols. Cairo: Maktabat al-Khānjī, 1964.

Allen, James. *Narrative of the life of James Allen: alias George Walton, alias Jonas Pierce, alias James H. York, alias Burley Grove, the highwayman: being his death-bed confession, to the warden of the Massachusetts State Prison.* Boston: Harrington & Co., 1837. [Collection of the Boston Athenæum, Reference number $65 .Al57]

Al-Nadīm [Abū al-Faraj Muḥammad ibn Isḥāq ibn Muḥammad ibn Isḥāq]. *The Fihrist of al-Nadīm: A Tenth-Century Survey of Muslim Culture.* Edited and translated by Bayard Dodge. 2 vols. New York: Columbia University Press, 1970.

Ambrose, Saint. *Letters of St. Ambrose, Bishop of Milan.* Translated by John Parker. Oxford: Oxford University Press, 1881.

Analecta hymnica medii aevi. Edited by G.M. Dreves, C. Blume, and H. M. Bannister. 55 volumes. Leipzig: Riesland, 1886-1922.

Anonymous of Bern. "De Clarea." Edited and translated by D. V. Thompson in "The *De Clarea* of the So-Called Anonymous Bernensis." *Technical Studies in the Field of the Fine Arts* 1, no. 2 (1932): 8–19, 70–81.

———. *De clarea: Manuale medievale di tecnica della miniature (secolo XI).* Edited by Adriano Caffaro. L'Officina dell'Arte. Vol. 2. Salerno: Arci Postiglione, 2004.

"An Original Edition." *Cornhill Magazine* 11 (July 1888): 281–91.

Augustine. *Confessiones.* Edited by Lucas Verheijen. CCSL 27. Turnhout, Belgium: Brepols, 1981.

———. *Confessions.* Translated by James J. O'Donnell. Oxford: Oxford University Press, 1992.

———. *Contra Faustum Manichæum.* Edited by J. Zycha. CSEL 25.1: 351–797. Vienna: Tempsky, 1891.

———. *Enarrationes in Psalmos.* Edited by E. Dekkers and J. Fraipont. 3 vols. CCSL 38, 39, and 40. Turnhout, Belgium: Brepols, 1956

———. *Expositions of the Psalms (Enarrationes in Psalmos).* 3 vols. Translated by Maria Boulding, O.S.B. Hyde Park, New York: New City Press, 2003.

———. "Reply to Faustus the Manichæan." Edited by Marcus Dods, translated by Richard Stothert. *Writings in Connection with the Manichæan Heresy.* Edinburgh: T&T Clark, 1872.

———. *St. Augustine on Marriage and Sexuality.* Edited by Elizabeth Clark. Washington, D.C.: Catholic University of America Press, 1996.

Baum, Paull F. *Anglo-Saxon Riddles of the Exeter Book.* Durham, NC: Duke University Press, 1963.

Beadle, Richard, ed. *The York Plays: A Critical Edition of the York Corpus Christi Play as recorded in British Library Additional MS 35290.* 2 vols. EETS s.s. 23. Oxford: Oxford University Press, 2009–2013.

Benedict of Nursia, St. *Regula S. Benedicti.* In *Benedict's Rule: A Translation and Commentary.* Edited and translated by Terrence G. Kardong. Collegeville, MN: The Liturgical Press, 1996.

Bernard of Clairvaux, St. *S. Bernardi Abbatis Primi Claræ-Vallensis Opera Omnia.* Vol. 1. Edited by John Mabillon. PL 182. Paris: Garnier, 1879.

———. *Sermons on Conversion.* Translated by Marie-Bernard Saïd. Kalamazoo, MI: Cistercian Publications, 1981.

Best, Richard Irvine, and Osborn Bergin, eds. *Lebor na hUidre: Book of the Dun Cow.* Dublin: Hodges, Figgis, 1929.

Boccaccio, Giovanni. *Decameron.* 2 vols. Edited by Vittore Branca. Turin: Einaudi, 1992.

———. *The Decameron.* Translated by Wayne Rebhorn. Norton Critical Editions. New York: W. W. Norton, 2015.

Boisseau, Michelle. *Trembling Air: Poems by Michelle Boisseau.* Fayetteville: University of Arkansas Press, 2003.

Boker, George H. *Königsmark: The Legend of the Hounds and Other Poems.* Philadelphia: Lippincott, 1869.

Bookworm: An Illustrated Treasury of Old-Time Literature, The. London: E. Stock, 1888.

Boyce, Mary, ed. and trans. *The Letter of Tansar.* Rome: Istituto Italiano per il Medio ed Estremo Oriente, 1968.

Brooks, Geraldine. *The People of the Book.* New York: Penguin, 2008.

Brown, William Keer. Letters to the Editor. *Maidstone Gazette,* January 30, February 16, and February 25, 1826.

Browne, Alexander. *Ars Pictoria or, an Academy treating of drawing, painting, limning, and etching.* London: J. Redmayne, 1669.

Byron, Catherine. *The Getting of Vellum.* Ennistymon, Co. Clare, Ireland: Salmon Poetry, 2001.

Carlyle, Thomas. *The French Revolution: A History in Three Volumes.* 3 vols. London: James Fraser, 1837.

Catalogue of the Collection of Animal Products Belonging to Her Majesty's Commissioners for the Exhibition of 1851, Exhibited in the South Kensington Museum. London: Clowes and Sons, 1858.

Caven, John. "Washington: A Mason; Address delivered by Brother John Caven, its First Worshipful Master, Before Mystic Tie Lodge, No. 398." In *Proceedings of the Thirty-Fourth Council of De-*

liberation for the Bodies of the Ancient Accepted Scottish Rite Northern Masonic Jurisdiction, U.S.A. of the State of New York. New York: Order of the Council, 1903.

Chartae Latinae Antiquiores: Facsimile-Edition of the Latin Charters Prior to the Ninth Century. Edited by Albert Bruckner and Robert Marichal. 49 vols. Olten and Lausanne: Urs Graf-Verlag, 1954–1998.

Cole, Peter, ed. and trans. *The Dream of the Poem: Hebrew Poetry from Muslim and Christian Spain 950–1492*. Princeton, NJ: Princeton University Press, 2007.

Collins, Billy. *The Trouble with Poetry: and Other Poems*. New York: Random House, 2005.

Cologne Mani Codex, The (P. Colon. inv. nr. 4780): Concerning the origin of his body. Edited and translated by Ron Cameron and Arthur J. Dewey. Missoula, MT: Scholars Press, 1979.

Conrad of Mure. *De naturis animalium*. Edited by A. P. Orbán. Heidelberg: C. Winter, 1989.

Crawford, Francis Marion. *Doctor Claudius: A True Story*. London and New York: Macmillan, 1883.

Cross, Donna Woolfolk. *Pope Joan: A Novel*. New York: Three Rivers Press, 1996.

Dante Alighieri. *La Commedia secondo l'antica vulgata*. Edited by Giorgio Petrocchi. Milan: Mondadori, 1966–67.

———. *The Divine Comedy of Dante Alighieri*. Translated by Allen Mandelbaum. New York: Bantam Books, 1980–82.

Dickens, Charles. *Bleak House*. New York: Vintage Classics, 2012.

Diderot, Denis, and Jean le Rond d'Alembert, eds. *Encyclopédie, ou Dictionnaire raisonné des sciences, des arts et des métiers, par une Société de Gens de lettres*, 35 vols. Paris: Briasson, 1751–1780. Reprint, Stuttgart/Bad Cannstatt: Frommann, 1966.

Donnolo, Shabbatai. *Sefer Hakhmoni*. Edited and translated by Piergabriele Mancuso. Studies in Jewish History and Culture 27. Leiden: Brill, 2010.

Eadmer of Canterbury. *Eadmeri Historia Novorum in Anglia, et opuscula duo de vita Sancti Anselmi et quibusdam miraculis ejus*. Edited by Martin Rule. Rerum Britannicarum Medii Ævi Scriptores 81. London: Longman & Co., 1884.

Emerson, Ralph Waldo. *Collected Works of Ralph Waldo Emerson*. Volume 7: *Society and Solitude*. Edited by Ronald A. Bosco and Douglas Emory Wilson. Cambridge, MA and London: Belknap Press of Harvard, 2007.

Eusebius of Caesarea. *Vita Constantini*. Edited by F. Winkelmann. Die griechischen christlichen Schriftsteller. Berlin: Akademie-Verlag, 1975.

———. *The Life of Constantine*. Translated by Averil Cameron and Stuart G. Hall. Oxford: Clarendon Press, 1999.

Fasciculus Morum: A Fourteenth-Century Preacher's Handbook. Edited and translated by Siegfried Wenzel. University Park and London: Penn State University Press, 1989.

Fisher, John. *The English Works of John Fisher, Bishop of Rochester*. Edited by John E. B. Mayor. 2 vols. EETS e.s. 26 and 27. London: Early English Text Society, 1876.

Furnivall, F. J., ed. *The Digby Plays with an Incomplete "Morality" of Wisdom, Who is Christ*. EETS e.s. 70. London: Paternoster House, 1896.

Ganzfried, Solomon Ben Josef. *Keset ha-Sofer*. Translated by Jen Taylor Friedman. Accessed July 15, 2021. http://www.hasoferet.com/halakha-for-scribes/keset-ha-sofer/chapter-2/.

Gascoigne, George. *The noble arte of venerie or hunting Wherein is handled and set out the Vertues, Nature, and Properties of fifteen sundry Chaces, together with the order and manner how to Hunt and kill every one of them*. London: Thomas Purfoot, 1611. STC 24329.

Gellius, Aulus. *Attic Nights, Volume III: Books 14-20.* Translated by J. C. Rolfe. Loeb Classical Library 212. Cambridge, MA: Harvard University Press, 1927.

Glorie, Franciscus, ed. *Collectiones Aenigmatum Merovingicae Aetatis.* CCSL 133a. Turnhout, Belgium: Brepols, 1968.

Guérard, Benjamin, ed. *Cartulaire de l'Abbaye de Saint-Bertin.* Collection des Cartulaires de France 3. Paris: Ministre de l'Instruction Publique, 1840.

Hall, Hubert, ed. *Pipe Roll of the Bishopric of Winchester, 1208–09.* London: P. S. King & Son, 1903.

Hameiri, Menahem ben Shlomo. *Kiryat Sefer al Hilkhot Sefer Torah, Tefillin, Umzuzah.* Edited by Moshe Hershler. Jerusalem, 1956.

Herodotus. *The Histories.* Edited and translated by A. D. Godley. 4 vols. Loeb Classical Library. Harvard: Harvard University Press, 1920–1925.

Hilliard, Nicholas. *The Art of Limning.* Edited by R. K. R. Thornton and T. G. S. Cain. Manchester, UK: Mid Northumberland Arts Group, 1981.

Holinshed, Ralph. *Chronicles.* 6 vols. London: Lucas Harrison, 1587.

Horstman, Reginald. *Yorkshire Writers: Richard Rolle of Hampole and His Followers.* 2 vols. London/New York: Swan Sonnenschein/Macmillan, 1896.

House of Lords Sessional Papers, 1801–1833. Vol. 230.

Isidore of Seville. *Etymologiae.* Edited by W. M. Lindsay. Oxford: Oxford University Press, 1911.

———. *The Etymologies of Isidore of Seville.* Translated by Stephen A. Barney, W. J. Lewis, J. A. Beach, and Oliver Berghof. Cambridge: Cambridge University Press, 2006.

Jerome. *De viris illustribus.* Edited by Carl Albrecht Bernoulli. Freiburg and Leipzig: Mohr, 1895.

Johnson, Samuel. *Bred a Bookseller: Samuel Johnson on Vellum Books; A New Essay.* Edited by O. M. Brack. Los Angeles: Samuel Johnson Society of Southern California, 1990.

Josephus, Flavius. *Jewish Antiquities.* Translated by William Whiston. London: Wordsworth Classics, 2006.

Joynt, Maud, ed. *Tromdámh Guaire.* Mediaeval and Modern Irish Series 2. Dublin: Dublin Institute for Advanced Studies, 1931.

Kant, Immanuel. *Critique of Judgment.* Translated by Werner S. Pluhar. Indianapolis, IN: Hackett, 1987.

Kieckhefer, Richard, ed. *Forbidden Rites: A Necromancer's Manual of the Fifteenth Century.* University Park: Penn State University Press, 1998.

Kohut, Alexander, ed. *Aruch Completum sive Lexicon vocabula et res, quae in libris Targumicis, Talmudicis et Midraschicis.* 18 vols. Vienna: Hebräischer Verlag "Menorah," 1926.

Krapp, George Philip, and Elliott Van Kirk Dobbie, eds. *The Anglo-Saxon Poetic Records: A Collective Edition.* 6 vols. New York: Columbia University Press, 1931–1953.

Lachower, Yeruham Fishel, and Isaiah Tishby. *The Wisdom of the Zohar: An Anthology of Texts.* 3 vols. Translated by D. Goldstein. Oxford: Oxford University Press, 1991.

Lacy, John. *Wyl bucke his testament.* London: Wyllam Copland, 1560. STC15118.5.

Laing, Samuel, trans. *The Heimskringla; or, Chronicle of the Kings of Norway.* 3 vols. London: Longman, Brown, Green, and Longmans, 1844.

La Lande, Jérôme de. "The Art of Making Parchment." Translated by Gay MCauley. *Art in Translation* 13 (2021): 326-386.

Langdon, Palmer H. "Up and Down the Caucomgomoc." *Forest and Stream* 86 (1916): 1094–95.

Lewis, B. Roland. *The Shakespeare Documents: Facsimiles, Transliterations, Translations, & Commentary*. Stanford, CA: Stanford University Press, 1940.

Lydgate, John. *The Minor Poems of John Lydgate 2: The Secular Poems*. Edited by Henry Noble Mac-Cracken and Meriam Sherwood. EETS e.s. 192. Oxford: Oxford University Press, 1934.

Maimonides, Moses. *The Code of Maimonides (Mishneh Torah) Book 2, The Book of Love*. Translated by Menachem Kellner. New Haven and London: Yale University Press, 2004.

Mann, Jill, ed. and trans. *Ysengrimus: Text With Translation, Commentary, and Introduction*. Mittellateinische Studien und Texte 12. Leiden: Brill, 1987.

Mantel, Hilary. *Wolf Hall*. New York: Henry Holt and Co., 2009.

Martial. *Epigrams*. 3 vols. Edited and translated by D. R. Shackleton Bailey. Loeb Classical Library 94–95, 480. Cambridge, MA: Harvard University Press, 1993.

Martin, Geoffrey Thorndike. *Corpus of Reliefs of the New Kingdom from the Memphite Necropolis and Lower Egypt*. Vol. 1. London and New York: KPI, 1988.

Mathers, S. L. MacGregor, trans. *The Key of Solomon the King: Clavicula Salomonis*. London: G. Redway, 1889.

Middle English Charters of Christ, The. Edited by M. C. Spalding. Bryn Mawr, PA: Bryn Mawr College, 1914.

Miller, Edward. "The Southern Countries." In *The Agrarian History of England and Wales*. Vol. 3, 1348–1500, edited by Edward Miller, 285–302. Cambridge: Cambridge University Press, 1991.

Morrison, Blake. *The Justification of Johann Gutenberg*. London: Chatto & Windus, 2000.

Mühlbacher, Engelbert, ed. *Die Urkunden Pippins, Karlmanns und Karls des Großen*. MGH Diplomatum Karolinorum. Vol. 1. Hannover: Hahnsche Buchhandlung, 1906.

Nashe, Thomas. *A Pleasant Comedie, Called Summer's Last Will and Testament*. In *The Works of Thomas Nashe*, vol. 3, edited by Ronald B. McKerrow. London: A. H. Bullen, 1905.

Nietzsche, Friedrich. *Thus Spake Zarathustra*. Translated by Adrian Del Caro. Cambridge Texts in the History of Philosophy. Cambridge: Cambridge University Press, 2006.

Office of United States Chief of Counsel for Prosecution of Axis Criminality. *Nazi Conspiracy and Aggression*. Vol. 6. Washington, D.C.: United States Government Printing Office, 1946.

Orchard, Andrew, ed. and trans. *The Old English and Anglo-Latin Riddle Tradition*. Dumbarton Oaks Medieval Library. Cambridge, MA and London: Harvard University Press, 2021.

Owenson, Sydney, Lady Morgan. *France in 1829–30*. 2 vols. New York: J&J Harper, 1830.

Peacham, Henry. *The gentlemans exercise Or, an exquisite practise, as well for drawing all manner of beasts in their true portraitures [. . .]* London: Printed by J. Legat for I. Marriott, 1634. STC 19509.

Persius. *Satires*. Edited by G. G. Ramsay. New York: G. P. Putnam's Sons. 1918.

———. *Satires*. In *Horace. Satires and Epistles. Persius: Satires*. Translated by Niall Rudd. New York and London: Penguin, 2005.

Philp, Robert Kemp. *Dictionary of Useful Knowledge: A Companion to the "Dictionary of Daily Wants."* London: Houlston & Wright, 1858.

Pliny the Elder. *Natural History*. 10 vols. Edited and translated by H. Rackham, W. H. S. Jones, and D. E. Eichholz. Loeb Classical Library. Cambridge, MA: Harvard University Press, 1961–68.

Prudentius. *Crowns of Martyrdom*. Edited and translated by H. J. Thomson. Loeb Classical Library 5. Cambridge, MA: Harvard University Press, 1995.

"Record Copies of Acts." House of Commons Debate. April 20, 2016. Hansard Vol. 608, cols. 1001–1030.

Richard of Bury. *The Philobiblon of Richard De Bury*. Edited and translated by Ernest C. Thomas. London: Kegan Paul, Trench and Co., 1888.

Sachs, Hans, and Jost Amman. *Das Ständebuch*. Edited by Hans Blosen, Per Bærentzen, and Harald Pors. 2 vols. Aarhus, Denmark: Aarhus Universitetsforlag, 2009.

———. *A Sixteenth-Century Book of Trades: Das Ständebuch*. Translated by Theodor Rabb. Palo Alto, CA: Society for the Promotion of Science and Scholarship, 2010.

Salsitz, Norman. *A Jewish Boyhood in Poland: Remembering Kolbuszowa*. As Told to Richard Skolnik. Syracuse, NY: Syracuse University Press, 1999.

Samir, Khalil, and Paul Nwyia, eds. *Une correspondance islamo-chrétienne entre Ibn al-Munaǧǧim, Hunayn ibn Isḥāq et Qusṭā ibn Lūqā*. Patrologia orientalis 40.4. Turnhout, Belgium: Brepols, 1981.

Schopper, Hartmann. *Panoplia omnium illiberalium mechanicarum aut sedentariarum artium*. Frankfurt: Georg Corin and Sigmund Feyerabend, 1568.

Schwartz, Howard, ed. and trans. *Leaves from the Garden of Eden: One Hundred Classic Jewish Tales*. Oxford: Oxford University Press, 2009.

Shakespeare, William. *The Complete Works: Modern Critical Edition*. Edited by Gary Taylor, John Jowett, Terri Bourus, and Gabriel Egan. Oxford: Oxford University Press, 2016.

Sorel, Charles. *The Extravagant Shepherd; or, The History of the Shepherd Lysis: An Anti-Romance*. London: Thomas Heath, 1653.

Stokes, Whitley, ed. and trans. *Lives of Saints from the Book of Lismore*. Anecdota Oxoniensia, Mediaeval and Modern Series 5. Oxford: Clarendon Press, 1890.

Suso, Henry. *The Exemplar, with Two German Sermons*. Translated by Frank Tobin. Classics of Western Spirituality. New York: Paulist Press, 1989.

———. (Heinrich Seuse). *Deutsche Schriften*. 2 vols. Edited by Karl Bihlmeyer. Jena, Germany: Eugen Diederichs, 1907.

Talmud. *Minor Tractates. Massekhet Soferim*. Edited by Michael Higger. New York: Debe Rabanan, 1937.

Talmud. *The Minor Tractates of the Talmud*. 2 vols. Translated by A. Cohen. London: Soncino Press, 1965.

Talmud. *Talmud Bavli. The Schottenstein Edition*. Edited and translated by Hersh Goldwurm, Nosson Scherman, and other Torah scholars. 73 vols. Brooklyn, NY: Mesorah Publications, 1990–2005.

Tatwine. *Tatuini Opera Omnia. Variae Collectiones Aenigmatum Merovingicae Aetatis*. CCSL 133. Edited by Maria de Marco and Franciscus Glorie. Turnhout, Belgium: Brepols, 1968.

Teaching of Addai, The. Edited and translated by George Howard and G. Philips. Chico, CA: Society of Biblical Literature, 1981.

Thoreau, Henry David. *The Maine Woods*. Boston: Houghton, Mifflin, 1884.

———. *A Week on the Concord and Merrimack Rivers*. Boston and Cambridge: James Munroe and Company, 1849.

Trithemius, Johannes. *In Praise of Scribes (De Laude Scriptorum)*. Edited by Klaus Arnold. Lawrence, KS: Coronado Press, 1974.

Twenty-Six Political and Other Poems. Part 1. Edited by J. Kail. EETS o.s. 124. Oxford: Oxford University Press, 1904.

Vahman, Farīdūn, ed. *Ardā Wirāz Nāmag: The Iranian "Divina Commedia."* London: Curzon, 1986.

Vaughan, Henry. *Silex Scintillans: Sacred Poems and Private Ejaculations.* 2nd ed. London: Crips and Lloyd, 1655. Wing V126.

Waterhouse, Andrew. *2nd.* Aylsham: The Rialto, 2002.

Wilkins, John. *An Alphabetical Dictionary Wherein all English Words According to their Various Significations* [. . .] London: Samuel Gellibrand and John Martin, 1668.

———. *Essay Toward a Real Character, and a Philosophical Language.* London: Printed for Gellibrand and Martin, 1668.

Williamson, Craig, ed. and trans. *A Feast of Creatures: Anglo-Saxon Riddle-Songs.* Philadelphia: University of Pennsylvania Press, 2011.

———, ed. *The Old English Riddles of the "Exeter Book."* Chapel Hill: University of North Carolina Press, 1977.

Woodard, Chelsea. *Vellum.* San Jose, CA: Able Muse Press, 2014.

Wright, Benjamin, III, ed. and trans. *The Letter of Aristeas: "Aristeas to Philocrates" or "On the Translation of the Law of the Jews."* Berlin: De Gruyter, 2015.

Wyatt, A. J., ed. *Old English Riddles.* Boston and London: D. C. Heath, 1912.

Secondary Studies

Abt, Jeffrey, and Margaret A. Fusco. "A Byzantine Scholar's Letter on the Preparation of Manuscript Vellum." *Journal of the American Institute for Conservation* 28 (1989): 61–66.

Adams, Morgan Simms, Cathleen A. Baker, and Shannon Zachary. "Sizing in Nineteenth-Century Book Papers." *The Book and Paper Group Annual* 28 (2009): 1–6.

Agati, Maria Luisa. *Il libro manoscritto da Oriente a Occidente: per una codicologia comparata.* Rome: L'Erma di Bretschneider, 2010.

Albert, Susan L. *Leonora Carrington: Surrealism, Alchemy and Art.* London: Lund Humphries, 2010.

Albritton, Benjamin, Georgia Henley, and Elaine Treharne, eds. *Medieval Manuscripts in the Digital Age.* New York and London: Routledge, 2021.

Alexander, Elizabeth Shanks. *Transmitting Mishnah: The Shaping Influence of Oral Tradition.* Cambridge: Cambridge University Press, 2006.

Alexander, Jonathan J. G. *Medieval Illuminators and Their Methods of Work.* New Haven and London: Yale University Press, 1992.

Alley, Richard B. *The Two-Mile Time Machine: Ice Cores, Abrupt Climate Change, and Our Future.* Princeton, NJ: Princeton University Press, 2000.

Alston, R. C. *Books Printed on Vellum in the Collections of the British Library.* London: British Library, 1996.

Amherst, William Amhurst Tyssen-Amherst, Baron, and Wilkinson & Hodge Sotheby. *Catalogue of the Magnificent Library of Choice And Valuable Books & Manuscripts, the Property of the Rt. Hon. Lord Amherst of Hackney: Which Will Be Sold by Auction, by Messers Sotheby, Wilkinson & Hodge. . .the 3rd of December, 1908, And Two Following Days, And. . .the 24th of March, 1909, And Three Following Days.* London: Dryden Press, 1908.

Anava, Sarit, Moran Neuhof, Hila Gingold, Or Sagy, Arielle Munters, Emma M. Svensson, Ebrahim

Afshinnekoo, David Danko, Jonathan Foox, Pnina Shor, Beatriz Riestra, Dorothée Huchon, Christopher E. Mason, Noam Mizrahi, Matthias Jakobsson, and Oded Rechavi. "Illuminating Genetic Mysteries of the Dead Sea Scrolls." *Cell* 181 (2020): 1218–31.

André-Salvini, Béatrice. *Forgotten Empire: The World of Ancient Persia*. Berkeley: University of California Press, 2005.

Ásaad, Máz-Haru-'d-Dîn. *A Descriptive Catalogue of the Oriental Caligraphs, &c., collected by the late Frederick Ayrton, Esq*. Translated by George Percy Badger. London: William Whiteley, 1885.

Assmann, Aleida. *Cultural Memory and Western Civilization: Arts of Memory*. Cambridge: Cambridge University Press, 2011.

Atiyeh, George N., editor. *The Book in the Islamic World. The Written Word and Communication in the Middle East*. Albany: State University of New York Press, 1995.

Avrin, Leila. *Scribes, Script and Books: The Book Arts from Antiquity to the Renaissance*. Chicago: American Library Association, 1991.

Azzoni, Annalisa, and Matthew Stolper. "The Aramaic Epigraph *nᵊsiḥ* ns(y)h on Elamite Persepolis Fortification Documents." *Persepolis Fortification Archive Project 5. Arta/Achemenet* 4 (2015): 1–88.

Bailey, H. W. *Zoroastrian Problems in the Ninth-century Books*. Ratanbai Katrak Lectures. Oxford: The Clarendon Press, 1943.

Baker, J. H. "Why the History of English Law Has Not Been Finished." *Cambridge Law Journal* 59.1 (2000): 62–84.

Bamford, Heather. *Cultures of the Fragment: Uses of the Iberian Manuscript, 1100–1600*. Toronto: University of Toronto Press, 2018.

Barrera, Julio Trebolle. "The Qumran Finds Without a Hint of Scandal." In *The People of the Dead Sea Scrolls*, edited by Florentino García Martínez and Julio Trebolle Barrera and translated by Wilfred G. E. Watson, 17–30. Leiden: Brill 1993.

Baumgarten, Paul Maria. "The Secret Vatican Archives." In *The Vatican: Its History—Its Treasures*, edited by Ernesto Begni, 473–98. New York: Letters and Arts Publishing, 1914.

Bausi, Alessandro. "La tradizione scrittoria etiopica." *Segno e testo* 6 (2008): 507–57.

———. "Writing, Copying, Translating: Ethiopia as a Manuscript Culture." In *Manuscript Cultures: Mapping the Field*, edited by Jörg Quenzer, Dmitry Bondarev, and Jan-Ulrich Sobisch, 37–78. Berlin: De Gruyter, 2014.

Beal, Peter. *A Dictionary of English Manuscript Terminology 1450–2000*. Oxford: Oxford University Press, 2008.

Beit-Arié, Malachi. "Commissioned and Owner-Produced Manuscripts in the Sephardi Zone and Italy in the Thirteenth–Fifteenth Centuries." In *The Late Medieval Hebrew Book in the Western Mediterranean: Hebrew Manuscripts and Incunabula in Context*, edited by Javier del Barco, 15–27. Leiden: Brill, 2015.

———. *Hebrew Codicology: Historical and Comparative Typology of Hebrew Medieval Codices based on the Documentation of the Extant Dated Manuscripts Using a Quantitative Approach*. Preprint English Edition. Jerusalem: Israel Academy of Sciences and Humanities, 2020.

———. "Why Comparative Codicology?" *Gazette du livre médiéval* 23 (1993): 1–5.

Bellamy, C. H. "The Royal and Imperial Libraries of Munich and Vienna." *Papers of the Manchester Library Club* 27 (1901): 432–35.

Benfell, V. Stanley. "Biblical Truth in the Examination Cantos of Dante's *Paradiso.*" *Dante Studies* 115 (1997): 89–109.

Bennett, Jane. *Vibrant Matter: A Political Ecology of Things.* Durham, NC and London: Duke University Press, 2010.

Bennett, J. A. W. *Middle English Literature.* Edited and completed by Douglas Gray. Oxford: Oxford University Press, 1986.

Benton, Janetta Rebold. *Materials, Methods, and Masterpieces of Medieval Art.* Westport, CT: Praeger, 2009.

Berenbeim, Jessica. *Art of Documentation: Documents and Visual Culture in Medieval England.* Toronto: Pontifical Institute of Mediaeval Studies, 2015.

Berger, Y. M. "Lamb Mortality and Causes: A Nine-Year Summary at the Spooner Agricultural Research Station." Proceedings of the 45th Annual Spooner Sheep Day, University of Wisconsin-Madison, USA, August 23, 1997, 33–40. Madison: University of Wisconsin Department of Animal Sciences.

Berman, Constance. *Medieval Agriculture, the Southern French Countryside, and the Early Cistercians: A Study of Forty-three Monasteries.* Philadelphia: The American Philosophical Society, 1986.

Berman, Louis. *Vegetarianism and the Jewish Tradition.* New York: Ktav Publishing House, 1982.

———. *The Akedah: The Binding of Isaac.* Northvale, NJ and Jerusalem: Jason Aronson, 1997.

Bibliotheca Butleriana: A Catalogue of the Library of the Late Right Rev. Samuel Butler, D.D. Lord Bishop of Lichfield. London: Christie & Manson, 1840.

Billy, Dennis. "Hagiographical Parody in the *Ysengrimus.*" *Journal of the Rocky Mountain Medieval and Renaissance Association* 12 (1991): 1–12.

Bischoff, Bernhard. *Latin Palaeography: Antiquity and the Middle Ages.* Translated by Dáibhí ó Cróinín and David Ganz. Cambridge: Cambridge University Press, 1979.

———. *Paläographie des römischen Alterums und des abendländischen Mittelalters.* Berlin: Erich Schmidt Verlag, 1979.

Bisson, Thomas, ed. *Fiscal Accounts of Catalonia under the Early Count-Kings (1151–1213).* 2 vols. Berkeley: University of California Press, 1984.

Bitterli, Dieter. *Say What I Am Called: The Old English Riddles of the Exeter Book and the Anglo-Latin Riddle Tradition.* Toronto: University of Toronto Press, 2009.

Black, Jeremy. *The Tory World: Deep History and the Tory Theme in British Foreign Policy, 1679–2014.* New York and London: Routledge, 2016.

Black, Robert. "Ovid in Medieval Italy." In *Ovid in the Middle Ages,* edited by James G. Clark, Frank T. Coulson, and Kathryn L. McKinley, 123–42. Cambridge: Cambridge University Press, 2011.

Bladen, F. M. "Report on European Archives by Mr. F. M. Bladen, Barrister-at-Law, Presented by Command; ordered by the House of Representatives to be printed, 26th August, 1903." Papers Presented to Parliament: Printed Paper no. 50. In *The Parliament of the Commonwealth of Australia* (Session 1903). Vol. 2, 993–97.

Blair, Sheila S. and Jonathan M. Bloom. "The Islamic World." In *The Oxford Illustrated History of the Book,* edited by James Raven, 195–220. Oxford: Oxford University Press, 2020.

Blank, Debra Reed. "It's Time to Take Another Look at 'Our Little Sister' Soferim: A Bibliographic Essay." *Jewish Quarterly Review* 90 (1999): 1–26.

Bloom, Jonathan M. *Paper Before Print: The History and Impact of Paper in the Islamic World*. New Haven and London: Yale University Press, 2001.

Bockwitz, Hans Heinrich. "Die ältesten Abbildungen zur Geschichte des Pergamenter-Handwerks." *Wochenblatt für Papierfabrikation* 99 (1938): 1017–20.

Boone, Elizabeth Hill. *Cycles of Time and Meaning in the Mexican Books of Fate*. Joe R. and Teresa Lozana Long Series in Latin American and Latino Art and Culture. Austin: University of Texas Press, 2007.

Borland, Jennifer. "Unruly Reading: The Consuming Role of Touch in the Experience of a Medieval Manuscript." In *Scraped, Stroked and Bound: Materially Engaged Readings of Medieval Manuscripts*, edited by Jonathan Wilcox, 97–114.

Bornstein, George, and Teresa Tinkle, eds. *The Iconic Page in Manuscript, Print, and Digital Culture*. Ann Arbor: University of Michigan Press, 1998.

Bosman, Anston. "Shakespeare in Leather." In *The Forms of Renaissance Thought: New Essays in Literature and Culture*, edited by Leonard Barkan, Bradin Cormack, and Sean Keilen, 225–45. New York and London: Palgrave, 2009.

Bouchard, Constance. "Monastic Cartularies: Organizing Eternity." In *Charters, Cartularies, and Archives: The Preservation and Transmission of Documents in the Medieval West*, edited by Adam J. Kosto and Anders Winroth, 22–32. Toronto: Pontifical Institute of Mediaeval Studies, 2002.

Bowden, William H. *Printing on Vellum*. Islip, UK: The Strawberry Press, 1994.

Boyle, Leonard E. "Diplomatics." In *Medieval Studies*, edited by James M. Powell, 69–101. Syracuse, NY: Syracuse University Press, 1976.

———. *A Survey of the Vatican Archives and of Its Medieval Holdings*. Toronto: Pontifical Institute of Mediaeval Studies, 2001.

Bradley, John William. *Illuminated Manuscripts*. Chicago: A. C. McClurg & Co., 1909.

Brady, Emily. *The Sublime in Modern Philosophy: Aesthetics, Ethics, and Nature*. Cambridge: Cambridge University Press, 2013.

Brantley, Jessica. *Reading in the Wilderness: Private Devotion and Public Performance in Late Medieval England*. Chicago: University of Chicago Press, 2008.

Brassington, William Salt. *A History of the Art of Bookbinding with Some Account of the Books of the Ancients*. London: Elliot Stock, 1894.

British Library Department of Manuscripts. *Catalogue of Additions to the Manuscripts, 1946–1950*. 2 vols. London: British Library, 1979.

Brooks, Libby. "Death of a Poet." *The Guardian*, January 2, 2002.

Brotherston, Gordon. "Contours of Meaning in the Scripts of Ancient Mesoamerica: Western Epistemology and the Phonetic Issue." In *Visible Writings: Cultures, Forms, Readings*, edited by Marija Dalbello and Mary Shaw, 15–37. New Brunswick, NJ and London: Rutgers University Press, 2011.

Brown, Catherine. "Manuscript Thinking: Stories By Hand." *postmedieval* 2 (2011): 350–68.

Brown, Julian. *A Palaeographer's View: The Selected Writings of Julian Brown*. Edited by Janet Bately, Michelle Brown, and Jane Roberts. Turnhout, Belgium: Brepols, 1993.

Brown, Michelle. "Continental Symptoms in Insular Codicology: Historical Perspectives." In *Pergament: Geschichte, Struktur, Restaurierung, Herstellung*, edited by Peter Rück, 57–62. Sigmaringen, Germany: Jan Thorbecke Verlag, 1991.

Brown, N. C. M. "Theorising the Crafts: New Tricks of the Trades." In *Craft and Contemporary Theory*, edited by Sue Rowley, 3–17. St. Leonards, AU: Allen & Unwin, 1997.

Brown, Peter. *Augustine of Hippo: A Biography*. 2nd ed. with Epilogue. Berkeley: University of California Press, 2000.

Browne, George Forrest. *St. Aldhelm: His Life and Times*. London: Society for Promoting Christian Knowledge, 1903.

Buell, Laurence. *The Environmental Imagination: Thoreau, Nature Writing, and the Formation of American Culture*. Cambridge, MA: Belknap Press of Harvard, 1996.

Buringh, Eltjo. *Medieval Manuscript Production in the Latin West: Explorations with a Global Database*. Leiden: Brill, 2011.

Burns, Thea. "The Material Forms of the Past and the 'Afterlives' of the *Compositiones variae*: Recovering, Conserving, and Exhibiting the Personal History of an Early Medieval Manuscript." In *The Explicit Material: Inquiries at the Intersection of Curatorial and Conservation Cultures*, edited by Hanna B. Hölling, Francesca G. Bewer, and Katharine Ammann, 209–35. Leiden: Brill, 2019.

Cahill, Thomas. *How the Irish Saved Civilization: The Untold Story of Ireland's Heroic Role from the Fall of Rome to the Rise of Medieval Europe*. New York: Random House, 1995.

Calhoun, Joshua. *The Nature of the Page: Poetry, Papermaking, and the Ecology of the Text in Renaissance England*. Philadelphia: University of Pennsylvania Press, 2020.

Camille, Michael. "The Book as Flesh and Fetish in Richard de Bury's *Philobiblon*." In *The Book and the Body*, edited by Dolores Warwick Frese and Katherine O'Brien O'Keeffe, 34–77. Notre Dame, IN: University of Notre Dame Press, 1997.

———. "Sensations of the Page: Imaging Technologies and Medieval Illuminated Manuscripts." In *The Iconic Page in Manuscript, Print, and Digital Culture*, edited by George Bornstein and Theresa Tinkle, 33–54. Ann Arbor: University of Michigan Press, 1998.

Campana, Michael G., Mim A. Bower, Melanie J. Bailey, Frauke Stock, Tamsin C. O'Connell, Ceiridwen J. Edwards, Caroline Checkley-Scott, Barry Knight, Matthew Spencer, and Christopher J. Howe. "A Flock of Sheep, Goats and Cattle: Ancient DNA Analysis Reveals Complexities of Historical Parchment Manufacture." *Journal of Archaeological Science* 37 (2010): 1317–25.

Campbell, Tony. "Portolan Charts from the Late Thirteenth Century to 1500." In *Cartography in Prehistoric, Ancient, and Medieval Europe and the Mediterranean*, edited by J. B. Harley and David Woodward, 371–463. The History of Cartography. Vol. 1. Chicago: University of Chicago Press, 1987.

Carriker, Andrew James. *The Library of Eusebius of Caesarea*. Leiden and Boston: Brill, 2003.

Carruthers, Mary. *The Craft of Thought: Meditation, Rhetoric, and the Making of Images, 400–1200*. Cambridge: Cambridge University Press, 1998.

Cash, Bill. "Rotten Parchment Bonds." *European Journal* 12 (2005): 2.

Castle, Gregory. *Modernism and the Celtic Revival*. Cambridge: Cambridge University Press, 2001.

Catalogue of a Portion of the Valuable Collection of Manuscripts, Early Printed Books, &c., of the Late William Morris of Kelmscott House, Hammersmith. London: Dryden House, 1898.

Cerf, Vinton G., and Munindar P. Singh. "Internet Predictions." Guest editors' introduction. *IEEE Internet Computing* 14 (2010): 10–11.

Chahine, Claire. "Travaux réalisé en France dans le domaine du parchemin." In *Pergament: Ge-*

schichte, Struktur, Restaurierung, Herstellung, edited by Peter Rück, 195–202. Sigmaringen, Germany: Jan Thorbecke Verlag, 1991.

Chartier, Roger. "Jack Cade, the Skin of a Dead Lamb, and the Hatred for Writing." *Shakespeare Studies* 34 (2006): 77–89.

Chazelle, Celia. *The Codex Amiatinus and its "Sister" Bibles: Scripture, Liturgy, and Art in the Milieu of the Venerable Bede*. Leiden: Brill, 2019.

Chew, Sing C. *Ecology, Artificial Intelligence, and Virtual Reality: Life in the Digital Dark Ages*. Washington, D.C.: Lexington Books, 2021.

Chin, C. M. "Papyrus Beyond Writing: Early Christian Texts and Ancient Natural History." In *Books and Readers in the Premodern World: Essays in Honor of Harry Gamble*, edited by Karl Shuve, 15–32. Atlanta: SBL Press, 2018.

Chism, Christine. "Middle-Earth, the Middle Ages, and the Aryan nation: Myth and History in World War II." In *Tolkien the Medievalist*, edited by Jane Chance, 63–92. New York and London: Routledge, 2003.

Chopra, H. S. *Oriental Manuscript Library: Origin, Development, Management, and Conservation*. New Delhi: National Book Organisation, 1995.

Clanchy, M. T. *From Memory to Written Record: England 1066–1307*. 3rd ed. London: Wiley-Blackwell, 2012.

Clark, Gillian. "City of Books: Augustine and the World as Text." In *The Early Christian Book*, edited by William E. Klingshirn and Linda Safran, 117–39. Washington, D.C.: Catholic University of America Press, 2007.

Clarkson, Christopher. "Rediscovering Parchment: The Nature of the Beast." *Paper Conservator* 16 (1992): 5–26.

Classen, Albrecht. "Craftsmanship and the Guilds in the Late Middle Ages: The Testimony of *Des Teufels Netz* and of the *Mendel Housebooks*." *History Research* 6 (2016): 23–39.

Cleaver, Laura. *Illuminated History Books in the Anglo-Norman World, 1066–1272*. Oxford: Oxford University Press, 2018.

Clemens, Raymond, and Timothy Graham. *Introduction to Manuscript Studies*. Ithaca, NY and London: Cornell University Press, 2007.

Coe, Alexis. "8 Book Historians, Curators, Specialists, and Librarians Who Are Killing It Online." *Buzzfeed*, February 16, 2014. Accessed August 18, 2021. https://www.buzzfeed.com/alexiscoe /book-historians-curators-specialists.

Coke, Sir Edward. *The Fourth Part of the Institutes of the Laws of England Concerning the Jurisdiction of Courts*. London: W. Clarke and Sons, 1817.

Colb, Sherry F. "Linking Judaism and Veganism in Light and Dark." In *Jewish Veganism and Vegetarianism: Studies and New Directions*, edited by Jacob Ari Labendz and Shmuly Yanklowitz, 267–88. Albany: State University of New York Press, 2019.

Coleman, Janet. *Ancient and Medieval Memories: Studies in the Reconstruction of the Past*. Cambridge: Cambridge University Press, 1991.

Collection de livres imprimés sur vélin du début de l'art typographique jusqu'à nos jours. Florence, Italy: Leo S. Olschki, 1930.

Collins, Matthew. "Archaeology and the Biomolecular 'Revolution': Too Much of the Wrong Kind of Data." *Stichting Voor de Nederlandse Archeologie* 18 (2006): 1–18.

Collins, Matthew, Mike Buckley, Helen H. Grundy, Jane Thomas-Oates, Julie Wilson, and Nienke van Doorn. "ZooMS: The Collagen Barcode and Fingerprints." *Spectroscopy Europe* 22 (2010): 6–10.

Connor, Steven. *The Book of Skin*. Ithaca, NY and London: Cornell University Press, 2004.

Cook, Gary. "Calfskin Heads: Their History and Manufacture." In *Encyclopedia of Percussion*, edited by John H. Beck, 161–66. New York and London: Garland Publishing, 1995.

Cooper, Belle Beth. "How Twitter's New Expanded Images Increase Clicks, Retweets and Favorites." *TNW News*, November 16, 2013. Accessed August 18, 2021. https://thenextweb.com/news/twitters-new-expanded-images-increase-clicks-retweets-favorites.

Cooper, John. *Eat and Be Satisfied: A Social History of Jewish Food*. Lanham, MD: Jason Aronson, 1993.

Cooper, Lisa. *Artisans and Narrative Craft in Late Medieval England*. Cambridge: Cambridge University Press, 2011.

Cortesão, Armando. *History of Portuguese Cartography*. 2 vols. Coimbra, Portugal: Juna de Invistagado do Ultramar-Lisboa, 1969–71.

Coupland, Douglas. *Marshall McLuhan: You Know Nothing of My Work!* Fayetteville, NC: Atlas, 2010.

Cox, Catherine. "Chaucer's Ethical Palimpsest: Dermal Reflexivity in the General Prologue." In *Writing on Skin in the Age of Chaucer*, edited by Nicole Nyffenegger and Katrin Rupp, 97–118. Berlin and Boston: De Gruyter, 2018.

Coyle, J. Kevin. "Characteristics of Manichaeism in North Africa." In *New Light on Manichaeism: Papers from the Sixth International Conference on Manichaeism*, edited by Jason David BeDuhn, 101–14. Leiden and Boston: Brill, 2009.

Crane, Susan. *Animal Encounters: Contacts and Concepts in Medieval Britain*. Philadelphia: University of Pennsylvania Press, 2012.

Crostini, Barbara. "Byzantium." In *The Oxford Illustrated History of the Book*, edited by James Raven, 54–83. Oxford: Oxford University Press, 2020.

Crum, W. E. "A Coptic Recipe for the Preparation of Parchment." *Proceedings of the Society of Biblical Archaeology* 27 (1905): 166–70.

Crumley, Caroline. "Historical Ecology: Integrated Thinking at Multiple Temporal and Spatial Scales." In *The World System and the Earth System: Global Socioenvironmental Change and Sustainability since the Neolithic*, edited by Alf Hornborg and Caroline Crumley, 15–28. New York: Routledge, 2006.

Crummé, Hannah Leah. *Shakespeare on the Record: Researching an Early Modern Life*. The Arden Shakespeare. London and New York: Bloomsbury, 2019.

Cruse, Mark. *Illuminating the "Roman d'Alexandre": Oxford, Bodleian Library, MS Bodley 264; The Manuscript as Monument*. Cambridge: D. S. Brewer, 2011.

Cucu, Sorin Radu. *The Underside of Politics: Global Fictions in the Fog of the Cold War*. New York: Fordham University Press, 2013.

Curtis, Fay. "The John Horwood Book." *The Bristol Archives*, April 17, 2014. Accessed August 14, 2020. https://www.bristolmuseums.org.uk/blog/archives/john-horwood-book/.

Curtius, Ernst Robert. *European Literature and the Latin Middle Ages*. Translated by Willard R. Trask. Bollingen Series 36. Princeton, NJ: Princeton University Press, 1953.

Cuskelly, Maryrose. *Original Skin: Exploring the Marvels of the Human Hide*. Berkeley, CA: Counterpoint Press, 2011.

Dale, Corinne. *The Natural World in the Exeter Book Riddles*. Cambridge: D. S. Brewer, 2017.

Danailova, Hilary. "Prepping Adirondack Deerskins for DIY Torah Project." *Hadassah*, May 2020. Accessed July 19, 2020. https://www.hadassahmagazine.org/2020/05/12/preparing-parchment -adirondack-deerskin-diy-torah-scroll/.

Da Rold, Orietta. "Materials." In *The Production of Books in England 1350–1500*, edited by Alexandra Gillespie and Daniel Wakelin, 12–33. Cambridge: Cambridge University Press, 2011.

———. *Paper in Medieval England: From Pulp to Fictions.* Cambridge: Cambridge University Press, 2020.

Daston, Lorraine, ed. *Science in the Archives: Pasts, Presents, Futures.* Chicago and London: University of Chicago Press, 2017.

Davenport, Cyril. *Cantor Lectures on Decorative Bookbinding.* Society for the Encouragement of Arts, Manufactures, & Commerce. London: William Trounce, 1898.

Davis, H. W. C. "London Lands and Liberties of St. Paul's, 1066–1135." In *Essays in Medieval History Presented to Thomas Frederick Tout*, edited by A. G. Little, 45–60. Manchester: Manchester University Press, 1925.

De Buck, Adriaan. "The Building Inscription of the Berlin Leather Roll." In *Studia Aegyptiaca* I. Analecta Orientalia 17, 48–57. Rome: Pontificio Instituto Biblico, 1938.

De Certeau, Michel. "Tools for Body Writing." *Intervention* 21/22 (1988): 7–11.

De-Dios, Toni, Lucy van Dorp, Philippe Charlier, Sofia Morfopoulou, Esther Lizano, Celine Bon, Corinne Le Bitouzé, Marina Alvarez-Estape, Tomas Marquès-Bonet, François Balloux, and Carles Lalueza-Fox. "Metagenomic Analysis of a Blood Stain From the French Revolutionary Jean-Paul Marat (1743–1793)." *Infection, Genetics and Evolution* 80 (June 2020): 104209.

De Hamel, Christopher. *The Book: A History of the Bible.* London and New York: Phaidon Press, 2001.

———. *Making Medieval Manuscripts.* Oxford: Bodleian Library, 2018.

———. *Meetings with Remarkable Manuscripts: Twelve Journeys into the Medieval World.* New York and London: Penguin, 2017.

———. *Scribes and Illuminators.* 2nd ed. Medieval Craftsmen Series. Toronto: University of Toronto Press, 1992.

Dekker, Simeon. *Old Russian Birchbark Letters: A Pragmatic Approach.* Leiden: Brill, 2018.

Del Barco, Javier, ed. *The Late Medieval Book in the Western Mediterranean: Hebrew Manuscripts and Incunabula in Context.* Leiden: Brill, 2015.

Delorez, Albert. *The Palaeography of Gothic Manuscript Books: From the Twelfth to the Early Sixteenth Century.* Cambridge: Cambridge University Press, 2003.

Demsky, Aaron, and Meir Bar-Ilan. "Writing in Ancient Israel and Early Judaism." In *Mikra: Text, Translation, Reading and Interpretation of the Hebrew Bible in Ancient Judaism and Early Christianity*, edited by Martin Jan Mulder, 1–38. Philadelphia: Assen/Maastricht, 1988.

Derrida, Jacques. *The Animal That Therefore I Am.* Translated by David Wills. New York: Fordham University Press, 2008.

Dillon, Emma. *Medieval Music-Making and the Roman de Fauvel.* Cambridge: Cambridge University Press, 2002.

Di Majo, Anna, Carlo Federici, and Marco Palma. "Die Tierhautbestimmung des Pergaments der italienischen 'Chartae Latinae Antiquiores'." In *Pergament: Geschichte, Struktur, Restaurierung, Herstellung*, edited by Peter Rück, 47–55. Sigmaringen, Germany: Jan Thorbecke Verlag, 1991.

Doty, Mark. *The Art of Description*. New York: Macmillan, 2010.

Dreibholz, Ursula. 2003. "Der Fund von Sanaa: Frühislamische Handschriften auf Pergament." In *Pergament: Geschichte, Struktur, Restaurierung, Herstellung*, edited by Peter Rück, 299–314. Sigmaringen, Germany: Jan Thorbecke Verlag, 1991.

———. *Frühe Koranfragmente aus der Grossen Moschee in Sanaa*. Yemen: Deutsches Archäologisches Institut Orient-Abteilung Aussenstelle Sanaa, 2003.

Driel-Murray, Carol van. "Leatherwork and Skin Products." In *Ancient Egyptian Materials and Technology*, edited by P. T. Nicholson and I. Shaw, 299–319. Cambridge: Cambridge University Press, 2000.

Driver, G. R. *Aramaic Documents of the Fifth Century B.C.* Oxford: Clarendon Press, 1965.

Drucker, Johanna. "Humanities Approaches to Graphical Display." *Digital Humanities Quarterly* 4 (2011): 1–51.

Duff, Edward Gordon. *English Printing on Vellum to the End of the Year 1600*. Aberdeen, Scotland: Bibliographical Society of Lancashire, 1902.

Duncan-Jones, Katherine. *Shakespeare: An Ungentle Life*. London: Bloomsbury, 2014.

Durling, Nancy Vine. "British Library MS Harley 2253: A New Reading of the Passion Lyrics in Their Manuscript Context." *Viator* 40 (2009): 271–308.

Eggert, Katherine. *Showing Like A Queen: Female Authority and Literary Experiment in Spenser, Shakespeare, and Milton*. Philadelphia: University of Pennsylvania Press, 2000.

Eisenstein, Elizabeth. *The Printing Press as an Agent of Change*. 2 vols. Cambridge: Cambridge University Press, 1980.

Eisnitz, Gail. *Slaughterhouse: The Shocking Story of Greed, Neglect, and Inhumane Treatment inside the U.S. Meat Industry*. Lanham, MD: Prometheus, 2006.

Eliot, Simon, and Jonathan Rose, eds. *A Companion to the History of the Book*. Oxford: Blackwell, 2009.

Ennahid, Said. "Information and Communication Technologies for the Preservation and Valorization of Manuscript Collections in Morocco." In *The Trans-Saharan Book Trade: Manuscript Culture, Arabic Literacy and Intellectual History in Muslim Africa*, edited by Graziano Krätli and Ghislaine Lydon, 265–89. Boston: Leiden, 2011.

Epstein, Marc Michael. *Dreams of Subversion in Medieval Jewish Art and Literature*. University Park: Penn State University Press, 1997.

"Ethical Sourcing of Raw Materials." Accessed June 12, 2019. http://www.williamcowley.co.uk /ethical/.

Evison, Gillian, et al. "Thus Speaks Arshama: Letters of a Fifth-Century BC Persian Prince." The Arshama Project, Bodleian Library. Accessed August 14, 2017. http://arshama.bodleian.ox.ac .uk/. Website withdrawn April 15, 2020.

Eyre, Christopher. *The Use of Documents in Pharaonic Egypt*. Oxford Studies in Ancient Documents. Oxford: Oxford University Press, 2013.

Febvre, Lucien, and Henri-Jean Martin. *The Coming of the Book*. Translated by David Gerard. London: Verso, 1997.

Fiddyment, Sarah, Bruce Holsinger, Chiara Ruzzier, Alexander Devine, Annelise Binois, Umberto Albarella, Roman Fischer, Emma Nichols, Antoinette Curtis, Edward Cheese, Matthew D. Teasdale, Caroline Checkley-Scott, Stephen J. Milner, Kathryn M. Rudy, Eric J. Johnson, Jiří

Vnouček, Mary Garrison, Simon McGrory, Daniel G. Bradley, and Matthew J. Collins. "Animal origin of 13th-century uterine vellum revealed using noninvasive peptide fingerprinting." *Proceedings of the National Academy of Sciences* 112.49 (2015): 15066–71.

Fiddyment, Sarah, Matthew D. Teasdale, Jiří Vnouček, Élodie Lévêque, Annelise Binois, and Matthew J. Collins. "So You Want to do Biocodicology? A Field Guide to the Biological Analysis of Parchment." *Heritage Science* 7 (2019): 35.

Fine, Lawrence. *Essential Papers on Kabbalah.* New York: NYU Press, 2000.

Fischer, Sibylle. *Modernity Disavowed: Haiti and Cultures of Slavery in the Age of Revolution.* Durham, NC: Duke University Press, 2004.

Fishman, Talya. *Becoming the People of the Talmud: Oral Torah as Written Tradition in Medieval Jewish Cultures.* Philadelphia: University of Pennsylvania Press, 2011.

Flood, Rebecca. "Could Brexit Bill VANISH from history? Outrage as MPs Plan to Print Crucial Act on PAPER." *Express*, March 21, 2017.

Folger Shakespeare Library. *Shakespeare Documented: A Multi-Institutional Resources Documenting Shakespeare in His Own Time.* Online collaborative exhibit. Accessed August 15, 2020. https://shakespearedocumented.folger.edu.

Forsyth, Mark. *The Horologicon: A Day's Jaunt Through the Lost Words of the English Language.* New York: Berkley Books, 2013.

Foscarini, Fiorella, Heather MacNeil, Bonnie Mak, and Gillian Oliver, eds. *Engaging with Records and Archives: Histories and Theories.* London: Facet Publishing, 2016.

Foys, Martin. "Medieval Manuscripts: Media Archaeology and the Digital Incunable." In *The Medieval Manuscript Book: Cultural Approaches,* edited by Michael Johnston and Michael Van Dussen, 119–39. Cambridge: Cambridge University Press, 2015.

———. "The Undoing of the Exeter Book Riddle 47: 'Bookmoth.'" In *Transitional States: Cultural Change, Tradition and Memory in Medieval England,* edited by Graham Caei and Michael D. C. Drout, 101–30. Tempe: Arizona Center for Medieval and Renaissance Studies, 2018.

Francone, Alessia. "The Virgin Mary in Latin and Germon Sermons of Berthold of Regensburg." In *Medieval Franciscan Approaches to the Virgin Mary: Mater Sanctissima, Misericordia, et Dolorosa,* edited by Steven J. McMichael and Katherine Wrisley Shelby, 337–65. Leiden: Brill, 2019.

Frese, Dolores Warwick, and Katherine O'Brien O'Keeffe, eds. *The Book and the Body.* Notre Dame, IN: University of Notre Dame Press, 1997.

Frey, R. W., and F. P. Veitch. *Preservation of Leather Bookbindings.* USDA Leaflet No. 69. Washington, D.C.: United States Department of Agriculture, 1933.

Fuchs, Robert, Christiane Meinert, and Johannes Schrempf. *Pergament: Geschichte, Material, Konservierung, Restaurierung.* Munich: Siegl, 2001.

Gaffield, Julia. *The Haitian Declaration of Independence: Creation, Context, and Legacy.* Charlottesville: University of Virginia Press, 2016.

Gagné, John. "Paper World: The Materiality of Loss in the Pre-Modern Age." In *Approaches to the History of Written Culture: A World Inscribed,* edited by Martyn Lyons and Rita Marquilhas, 57-72. New York: Palgrave Macmillan, 2017.

Gall Morel, P. "Zur Kunde des Schriftwesens im Mittelalter." *Anzeiger für Kunde der Deutschen Vorzeit* 10 (1872): 314.

Gallé, Émile. *Émile Gallé.* New York: Parkstone Press, 2014.

Gamble, Harry. *Books and Readers in the Early Church: A History of Early Christian Texts*. New Haven and London: Yale University Press, 1995.

Gameson, Richard, ed. *The Cambridge History of the Book in Britain: Vol. 1, c. 400–1100*. Cambridge: Cambridge University Press, 2011.

———. "The Cost of the Codex Amiatinus." *Notes & Queries* 39 (March 1992): 2–9.

———, ed. *The Early Medieval Bible: Its Production, Decoration and Use*. Cambridge Studies in Palaeography and Codicology 2. Cambridge: Cambridge University Press, 2009.

———. "The Material Fabric of Early British Books." In *The Cambridge History of the Book in Britain: Vol. 1, c. 400–1100*, edited by Richard Gameson, 13–93.

———. "The Origin of the Exeter Book of Old English Poetry." *Anglo-Saxon England* 25 (1996): 135–85.

———. *The Scribe Speaks? Colophons in Early English Manuscripts*. Cambridge: University of Cambridge Department of Anglo-Saxon, Norse and Celtic, 2002.

Garber, Frederick. *Thoreau's Fable of Inscribing*. Princeton, NJ: Princeton University Press, 2016.

Gaudet, John. *The Pharaoh's Treasure: The Origin of Paper and the Rise of Western Civilization*. Stroud, UK: Amberley Publishing, 2019.

Gee, Stacey. "The Printers, Stationers and Bookbinders of York before 1557." *Transactions of the Cambridge Bibliographical Society* 12 (2000): 27–54.

Ghioni, C., J. C. Hiller, C. J. Kennedy, A. E. Aliev, M. Odlyha, M. Boulton, and T. J. Wess. "Evidence of a Distinct Lipid Fraction in Historical Parchments: A Potential Role in Degradation?" *Journal of Lipid Research* 46, no. 12 (2005): 2726–34.

Gilbert, Sarah. "Imperfect Pages." Bodleian Libraries blog. Accessed July 14, 2019. https://bodleianlibs.tumblr.com/post/160513401375/imperfect-pages.

Gillespie, Alexandra. "Bookbinding." In *The Production of Books in England 1350–1500*, edited by Alexandra Gillespie and Daniel Wakelin, 150–72. Cambridge Studies in Palaeography and Codicology. Cambridge: Cambridge University Press, 2011.

Gillespie, Alexandra, and Daniel Wakelin, eds. *The Production of Books in England 1350–1500*. Cambridge Studies in Palaeography and Codicology. Cambridge: Cambridge University Press, 2011.

Gillings, Richard J. *Mathematics in the Time of the Pharaohs*. New York: Dover, 1982.

Golb, Norman. *Who Wrote the Dead Sea Scrolls? The Search for the Secret of Qumran*. New York: Touchstone, 1995.

Gordon, Jacob. "In the Flesh?: Anthropodermic Bibliopegy Verification and Its Implications." *RBM: A Journal of Rare Books, Manuscripts, and Cultural Heritage* 2 (2016): 118–33.

Gottscher, Leandro. "Ancient Methods of Parchment-Making: Discussion on Recipes and Experimental Essays." In *Ancient and Medieval Book Materials and Techniques, Erice 18-25 September, 1992*, edited by Marilena Maniaci and Paola Munafò, 41–56. Vatican City: Biblioteca Apostolica Vaticana, 1993.

Gould, Karen. "Terms for Book Production in a Fifteenth-Century Latin-English Nominale (Harvard Law School Library MS. 43)." *Papers of the Bibliographical Society of America* 79 (1985): 75–100.

Grafton, Anthony, and Megan Williams. *Christianity and the Transformation of the Book: Origen, Eusebius, and the Library of Caesarea*. Cambridge, MA: Belknap Press of Harvard, 2006.

Grayson, Donald K. *Quantitative Zooarchaeology: Topics in the Analysis of Archaeological Fauna*. Studies in Archaeological Sciences. New York: Academic Press, 1984.

Green, Johanna E. M. "Digital Manuscripts as Sites of Touch: Using Social Media for 'Hands-On' Engagement with Medieval Manuscript Materiality." In "Digital Medieval Manuscript Cultures," edited by Michael Hanrahan and Bridget Whearty. Special issue of *Archive Journal* (September 2018). Accessed August 18, 2021. http://www.archivejournal.net/essays/digital -manuscripts-as-sites-of-touch-using-social-media-for-hands-on-engagement-with-medieval -manuscript-materiality/.

Greenbaum, Dorian Gieseler, and Josefina Rodrígues-Arribas, eds. *Unveiling the Hidden—Anticipating the Future: Divinatory Practices Among Jews Between Qumran and the Modern Period.* Leiden: Brill, 2021.

Greenfield, J. C. "Some Notes on the Arsham Letters." In *Irano-Judaica: Studies Relating to Jewish Contacts with Persian Culture Throughout the Ages,* edited by S. Shaked, 4–11. Jerusalem: Ben-Zvi Institute for the Study of Jewish Communities in the East, 1982.

Greenwood, Emily. "Bridging the Narrative: 5.23–7." In *Reading Herodotus: A Study of the Logoi in Book 5 of Herodotus' Histories,* edited by Elizabeth Irwin and Emily Greenwood, 128–45. Cambridge: Cambridge University Press, 2007.

Greer, Kirsten. "Geopolitics and the Avian Imperial Archive: The Zoogeography of Region-Making in the Nineteenth-Century British Mediterranean." *Annals of the Association of American Geographers* 103 (2013): 1317–31.

Groot, Zeger Hendrik de. "Die Herstellung von Goldschlägerhaut, transparentem und gespaltenem Pergament." In *Pergament: Geschichte, Struktur, Restaurierung, Herstellung,* edited by Peter Rück, 373–80. Sigmaringen, Germany: Jan Thorbecke Verlag, 1991.

Guerlac, Suzanne. "Derrida and His Cat: The Most Important Question." *Contemporary French and Francophone Studies* 16 (2012): 695–702.

Gugenheim, Shoshana. "Or Hadash: Sustainable Parchment." Accessed July 15, 2021. https://www .shoshanagugenheim.com/ethically-sourced-parchment.

Guldi, Jo, and David Armitage. *The History Manifesto.* Cambridge: Cambridge University Press, 2014.

Gullick, Michael. "From Parchmenter to Scribe: Some Observations on the Manufacture and Preparation of Medieval Parchment Based Upon a Review of the Literary Evidence." In *Pergament: Geschichte, Struktur, Restaurierung, Herstellung,* edited by Peter Rück, 145–58. Sigmaringen, Germany: Jan Thorbecke Verlag, 1991.

Gutmann, Joseph. "The Sacrifice of Isaac in Medieval Jewish Art." *Artibus et Historiae* 8 (1987): 67–89.

Hagadorn, Alexis. "Parchment making in eighteenth-century France: historical practices and the written record." *Journal of the Institute of Conservation* 35 (2012): 165-188

Haines, B. "Materials Analysis: The Physical and Chemical Characteristics of Parchment, Casings, Goldbeater's Skin and Gelatin." In *Conservation for the Future: Proceedings of the Annual Instructional Meeting Hosted by Dorset County Archive Service,* edited by C. S. Woods, 26. London: Society of Archivists, Preservation and Conservation Group, 1994.

Hamburger, Jeffrey. *Nuns as Artists: The Visual Culture of a Medieval Convent.* Berkeley: University of California Press, 1997.

Hamilton, C. Lou. *Veganism, Sex, and Politics.* Bristol: Intellect Books, 2019.

"Hand Bookbindings from Special Collections in the Princeton University Library." Princeton University Library, 2004. Accessed August 15, 2020. https://library.princeton.edu/visual_materials /hb/cases/german/index.html.

Hanna, Ralph, III. "Palaeography of the Wycliffite Bibles." In *The Wycliffite Bible: Origin, History and Interpretation*, edited by Elizabeth Solopova, 245–65. Oxford: Oxford University Press, 2017.

Hanson, Clare. *Genetics and the Literary Imagination*. Oxford: Oxford University Press, 2020.

Haran, Menahem. "Bible Scrolls in Eastern and Western Jewish Communities from Qumran to the High Middle Ages." *Hebrew Union College Annual* 56 (1985): 21–62.

———. "Technological Heritage in the Preparation of Skins for Biblical Texts in Medieval Oriental Jewry." In *Pergament: Geschichte, Struktur, Restaurierung, Herstellung*, edited by Peter Rück, 35–44. Sigmaringen, Germany: Jan Thorbecke Verlag, 1991.

Haraway, Donna. *When Species Meet*. Minneapolis: University of Minnesota Press, 2009.

Harrison, Perry Neil. "Anthropodermic Bibliopegy in the Early Modern Period." In *Flaying in the Pre-Modern World: Practice and Representation*, edited by Larissa Tracy, 366–83. Woodbridge, Suffolk, UK: D. S. Brewer, 2017.

Harvey, P. D. A. *Mappa Mundi: The Hereford World Map*. British Library Studies in Medieval Culture. Toronto: University of Toronto Press, 1996.

Hawkins, Peter. *Dante's Testaments: Essays in Scriptural Imagination*. Stanford, CA: Stanford University Press, 1999.

Hayward, Abraham. Review of F. Feuillet de Conches, *Causeries d'un Curieux: Variétes d'Histoire et d'Art*. In *Edinburgh Review*, October 1866.

Hellinga, Lotte, and J. B. Trapp, eds. *The Cambridge History of the Book in Britain: Vol. 3, 1400–1557*. Cambridge: Cambridge University Press, 1999.

———. "Printing." In *The Cambridge History of the Book in Britain: Vol. 3, 1400–1557*, edited by Lotte Hellinga and J. B. Trapp, 65–109. Cambridge: Cambridge University Press, 1999.

Henare, Amiria. "Taonga Māori: Encompassing Right and Property in New Zealand." In *Thinking Through Things: Theorising Artefacts Ethnographically*, edited by Amiria Henare, Martin Holbraad, and Sari Wastell, 47–67. London and New York: Routledge, 2017.

Herman, Peter. "'O, 'tis a gallant king': Shakespeare's *Henry V* and the Crisis of the 1590s." In *Tudor Political Culture*, edited by Dale Hoak, 204–6. Cambridge: Cambridge University Press, 1995.

Heschel, Abraham Joshua. *Heavenly Torah: As Refracted through the Generations*. Edited and translated by Gordon Tucker and Leonard Levin. New York: Continuum, 2006.

Heurtel, Pascale, and Michelle Lenoir. *Les Vélins du Muséum national d'histoire naturelle*. Paris: Citadelles & Mazenod, 2016.

Hiatt, Alfred. "The Cartographic Imagination of Thomas Elmham." *Speculum* 75 (2000): 859–86.

Hilts, Philip J. "Decipherers of Dead Sea Scrolls Turn to DNA Analysis for Help." *New York Times*, Section C, Page 2, March 28, 1995.

Hindman, Sandra. "The Composition of the Manuscript of Christine de Pizan's Collected Works in the British Library: A Reassessment." *British Library Journal* 9 (1983): 93–123.

Hirschler, Konrad. *Medieval Damascus: Plurality and Diversity in an Arabic Library*. Edinburgh: Edinburgh University Press, 2016.

Hobson, Anthony. *Humanists and Bookbinders: The Origins and Diffusion of Humanistic Bookbinding 1459–1559*. Cambridge: Cambridge University Press, 1989.

Hoffman, Adina, and Peter Cole. *Sacred Trash: The Lost and Found World of the Cairo Geniza*. New York: Schocken, 2011.

Holdsworth, William Searle. *A History of English Law*. 17 vols. London: Methuen & Co., 1903–66.

Holmøy, I. H., and S. Waage. "Time Trends and Epidemiological Patterns of Perinatal Lamb Mortality in Norway." *Acta Veterinaria Scandinavica* 57 (2015): 65.

Holsinger, Bruce. "Animality." In *Reactions: Medieval/Modern; An Exhibition at the University of Pennsylvania*, edited by Dot Porter, 7–18. Philadelphia: University of Pennsylvania Libraries, 2016.

———. *Music, Body, and Desire in Medieval Culture: Hildegard of Bingen to Chaucer.* Stanford, CA: Stanford University Press, 2001.

———. "Of Pigs and Parchment: Medieval Studies and the Coming of the Animal." *PMLA* 124 (2009): 616–23.

Hope, Christopher. "Anger as MPs Bow to Peers' Pressure and End 500-year old Tradition of Printing New Laws on Vellum." *The Telegraph*, March 21, 2017.

Hough, J. Stockton. "Two Cases of Trichiniasis Observed at the Philadelphia Hospital, Blockley." *American Journal of the Medical Sciences* 1.57 (1869): 565–66.

Huss, Boaz. *The Zohar: Reception and Impact.* Liverpool: Littman Library of Jewish Civilization and Liverpool University Press, 2016.

Husserl, Edmund. *Logical Investigations.* Vol. 1. Translated by J. N. Findlay. London and New York: Routledge, 1970.

Iafrate, Allegra. *The Wandering Throne of Solomon: Objects and Tales of Kinship in the Medieval Mediterranean.* Leiden: Brill, 2015.

Idel, Moshe. *Absorbing Perfections: Kabbalah and Interpretation.* New Haven and London: Yale University Press, 2008.

Ilerbaig, Juan. "Organisms, Skeletons and the Archivist as Palaeontologist: Metaphors of Archival Order and Reconstruction in Context." In *Engaging with Records and Archives*, edited by Fiorella Foscarini, Heather MacNeil, Bonnie Mak, and Gillian Oliver, 21–40. London: Facet Publishing, 2016.

Illich, Ivan. *In the Vineyard of the Text: A Commentary to Hugh's Didascalicon.* Chicago: University of Chicago Press, 1996.

Jackson, H. J. *Marginalia: Readers Writing in Books.* New Haven and London: Yale University Press, 2001.

Jaffee, Martin S. *Torah in the Mouth: Writing and Oral Tradition in Palestinian Judaism, 200 BCE–400 BCE.* Oxford: Oxford University Press, 2001.

Jager, Eric. *The Book of the Heart.* Chicago: University of Chicago Press, 2000.

James, Kathryn. *English Paleography and Manuscript Culture, 1500–1800.* New Haven and London: Beinecke Library and Yale University Press, 2020.

Jansen, Maarten E. R. G. N., and Gabina Aurora Pérez Jiménez. *The Mixtec Pictorial Manuscripts: Time, Agency and Memory in Ancient Mexico.* Leiden: Brill, 2011.

Janzen, Stefan. "Pergament: Herstellung, Baearbeitung und Handel in Bildern des 10. Bis 18. Jahrhunderts." In *Pergament: Geschichte, Struktur, Restaurierung, Herstellung*, edited by Peter Rück, 391–414. Sigmaringen, Germany: Jan Thorbecke Verlag, 1991.

Janzen, Stefan, and Angelika Manetzki. "Pergamentbibliographie." In *Pergament: Geschichte, Struktur, Restaurierung, Herstellung*, edited by Peter Rück, 415–65. Sigmaringen, Germany: Jan Thorbecke Verlag, 1991.

Jardine, Lisa. "C. P. Snow's Two Cultures Revisited." *Christ's College Magazine* 235 (2010): 49–57.

Jenkins, Penny. "Printing on Parchment or Vellum." *The Paper Conservator* 16 (1992): 31–39.

Johnson, Richard R. "Ancient and Medieval Accounts of the 'Invention' of Parchment." *California Studies in Classical Antiquity* 3 (1970): 115–22.

Johnston, Michael, and Michael Van Dussen, eds. *The Medieval Manuscript Book: Cultural Approaches*. Cambridge: Cambridge University Press, 2015.

Joubin, Rebecca. "Islam and Arabs through the Eyes of the *Encyclopédie*: The 'Other' as a Case of French Cultural Self-Criticism." *International Journal of Middle East Studies* (2000): 197–217.

Joyce, Rosemary. "Materiality and Practice in the Study of Mexican Manuscripts." In *Mesoamerican Manuscripts: New Scientific Approaches and Interpretations*, edited by Maarten E. R. G. N. Jansen, Virginia M. Lladó-Buisán, and Ludo Snijders, 460–73. Leiden: Brill, 2019.

Justice, Steven. *Writing and Rebellion: England in 1381*. Berkeley: University of California Press, 1996.

Kagan, Jerome. *The Three Cultures: Natural Sciences, Social Sciences, and Humanities in the 21st Century*. Cambridge: Cambridge University Press, 2009.

Kay, Sarah. *Animal Skins and the Reading Self in Medieval Latin and French Bestiaries*. Chicago: University of Chicago Press, 2017.

———. "Flayed Skin as *objet a*: Representation and Materiality in Guillaume de Deguileville's *Pèlerinage de vie humaine*." In *Medieval Fabrications: Dress, Textiles, Clothwork, and Other Cultural Imaginings*, edited by E. Jane Burns, 193–205. New York: Palgrave Macmillan, 2004.

———. "Legible Skins: Animals and the Ethics of Medieval Reading." *postmedieval* 2 (2011): 13–32.

———. "Original Skin: Flaying, Reading, and Thinking in the Legend of St. Bartholomew and Other Works." *Journal of Medieval and Early Modern Studies* 36 (2006): 35–74.

Kearney, James. *The Incarnate Text: Imagining in the Book in Reformation England*. Philadelphia: University of Pennsylvania Press, 2009.

Kehnel, Annette. *Clonmacnois: The Church and Lands of St. Ciarán: Change and Continuity in an Irish Monastic Foundation (6th to 16th centuries)*. Münster: LIT, 1997.

Keightley, David N. *Sources of Shang History: The Oracle-Bone Inscriptions of Bronze Age China*. Berkeley: University of California Press, 1985.

Keller, Marcel, Maria A. Spyrou, Christiana L. Scheib, Gunnar U. Neumann, Andreas Kröpelin, Brigitte Haas-Gebhard, Bernd Päffgen, et al. "Ancient *Yersinia pestis* genomes from across Western Europe reveal early diversification during the First Pandemic (541–750)." *Proceedings of the National Academy of Sciences* 116 (2019): 12363–372.

Kelly, Thomas Forrest. *The Role of the Scroll: An Illustrated Introduction to Scrolls in the Middle Ages*. New York and London: W. W. Norton, 2019.

Kemmerer, Lisa. *Animals and World Religions*. Oxford: Oxford University Press, 2012.

Kerby-Fulton, Kathryn, Maidie Hilmo, and Linda Olson. *Opening Up Middle English Manuscripts*. Ithaca, NY and London: Cornell University Press, 2012.

Kerner, Jennifer. "Reliures de livres avec la peau du condamné : hommage et humiliation autour des corps criminels." In *(Re)lecture archéologique de la justice en Europe médiévale et moderne : actes du colloque international tenu à Bordeaux les 8-10 février 2017*, edited by Mathieu Vivas, 195–211. Bordeaux, France: Ausonius, 2019.

Kesavan, Belary Shamanna. *A History of Printing and Publishing in India: A Story of Cultural Awakening*. 3 vols. New Delhi: National Book Trust, 1985.

Kieding, Robert B. *Scuttlebutt: Tales and Experiences of a Life at Sea*. New York: iUniverse, 2011.

Kirby, David. *Animal Factory: The Looming Threat of Industrial Pig, Dairy, and Poultry Farm to Humans and the Environment*. New York: St. Martin's Press, 2010.

Kite, Marion. "Gut Membrane, Parchment and Gelatine Incorporated into Textile Objects." *The Paper Conservator* 16 (1992): 98–105.

Kite, Marion, and Roy Thomson. *Conservation of Leather and Related Materials*. Oxford and Burlington, MA: Butterworth-Heinemann, 2006.

Klack-Eitzen, Charlotte, Wiebke Haase, and Tanja Weißgraf. *Heilige Röcke, Kleider für Skulpturen in Kloster Wienhausen*. Regensburg, Germany: Schnell & Steiner, 2013.

Klimkeit, Hans-Joachim. *Manichaean Art and Calligraphy*. Leiden: Brill, 1982.

Klingshirn, William E., and Linda Safran. *The Early Christian Book*. Washington, D.C.: Catholic University Press, 2007.

Knight, Leah. *Reading Green in Early Modern England*. New York and London: Routledge, 2016.

Knust, Jennifer, and Tommy Wasserman. *To Cast the First Stone: The Transmission of a Gospel Story*. Princeton, NJ: Princeton University Press, 2019.

Kowalik, R. "Decomposition of Parchment by Micro-organisms." *Restaurator* 4 (1980): 200–208.

Krätli, Graziano, and Ghislaine Lydon, eds. *The Trans-Saharan Book Trade: Manuscript Culture, Arabic Literacy and Intellectual History in Muslim Africa*. Leiden: Koninklijke, 2011.

Kreiner, Jamie. "Pigs in the Flesh and Fisc: An Early Medieval Ecology." *Past & Present* 236 (2017): 3–42.

Kren, Thomas, and Scot McKendrick. *Illuminating the Renaissance: The Triumph of Flemish Manuscript Painting in Europe*. Los Angeles: The J. Paul Getty Museum, 2003.

Krueger, Derek. *Writing and Holiness: The Practice of Authorship in the Early Christian East*. Philadelphia: University of Pennsylvania Press, 2013.

Kurke, Leslie. *Coins, Bodies, Games, and Gold: The Politics of Meaning in Archaic Greece*. Princeton, NJ: Princeton University Press, 1999.

Kurlansky, Mark. *Paper: Paging through History*. New York: W. W. Norton, 2016.

Kwakkel, Erik. *Books Before Print*. Leeds, UK: Arc Humanities Press, 2018.

———. "Decoding the Material Book: Cultural Residue in Medieval Manuscripts." In *The Medieval Manuscript Book: Cultural Approaches*, edited by Michael Johnston and Michael van Dussen, 60–76. Cambridge: Cambridge University Press.

———. "Discarded Parchment as Writing Support in English Manuscript Culture." *English Manuscript Studies: 1100–1700* 17 (2012): 239–61.

———. "A New Type of Book for a New Type of Reader: The Emergence of Paper in Vernacular Book Production." *The Library* 4 (2003): 219–48.

Lacroix, Paul. *Manners, Customs, and Dress During the Middle Ages and During the Renaissance Period*. New York: D. Appleton, 1874.

Lahey, Stephanie. "Offcut Zone Parchment in Manuscript Codices from Later Medieval England." 2 vols. Ph.D. dissertation. University of Victoria, 2021.

Landa, Gertrude. *Jewish Fairy Tales and Legends*. New York: Bloch Publishing, 1921.

Lander, Beth. "The Skin She Lived In: Anthropodermic Books in the Historical Medical Library." In "Fugitive Leaves: A Blog from the Historical Medical Library" of the College of Physicians of Philadelphia, October 1, 2015. Accessed August 15, 2020. https://histmed.collegeofphysicians.org/skin-she-lived-in/.

Langeslag, Paul S. *Seasons in the Literature of the Medieval North*. Cambridge: D. S. Brewer, 2019.

Larivière, Vincent, Yves Gingras, and Éric Archambault. "Canadian Collaboration Networks: A

Comparative Analysis of the Natural Sciences, Social Sciences and the Humanities." *Sciento-metrics* 68 (2006): 519–33.

Leatherbury, Sean V. *Inscribing Faith in Late Antiquity: Between Reading and Seeing.* Abingdon: Taylor & Francis, 2019.

Lech, Tomasz. "Evaluation of a Parchment Document, the 13th Century Incorporation Charter for the City of Krakow, Poland, for Microbial Hazards." *Applied and Environmental Microbiology* 82 (2016): 2620–31.

Leclercq, Jean. *The Love of Learning and the Desire for God: A Study of Monastic Culture.* 3rd ed. New York: Fordham University Press, 1961.

Leeuw van Weenen, Andrea de. *The Icelandic Homily Book: Perg. 15 4° in the Royal Library, Stockholm.* Reykjavík: Stofnun Árna Magnússonar á Íslandi, 1993.

Leopold, Aldo. *Round River: From the Journals of Aldo Leopold.* Edited by Luna B. Leopold. Oxford: Oxford University Press, 1993.

———. *A Sand County Almanac, and Sketches Here and There.* Oxford: Oxford University Press, 1989.

Le Plongeon, Augustus. "Mayapan and Maya Inscriptions." *Proceedings of the American Antiquarian Society* 77 (1881): 246–82.

Levenson, Jon Douglas. *The Death and Resurrection of the Beloved Son: The Transformation of Child Sacrifice in Judaism and Christianity.* New Haven: Yale University Press, 1993.

Levy, B. Barry. *Fixing God's Torah: The Accuracy of the Hebrew Bible Text in Jewish Law.* Oxford: Oxford University Press, 2001.

Lewanski, Richard Casimir. *Guide to Polish Libraries and Archives.* East European Monographs 6. New York: Distributed by Columbia University Press, 1975.

Lichtheim, Miriam. *Ancient Egyptian Literature: Vol. 1, The Old and Middle Kingdoms.* Berkeley: University of California Press, 2006.

Linn, Irving. "If All the Sky Were Parchment." *PMLA* 53 (1938): 951–70.

Lochrie, Karma. *Margery Kempe and Translations of the Flesh.* Philadelphia: University of Pennsylvania Press, 1994.

Lokanadam, B., and M. Ray Chaudhury. "Parchment in India: Some Observations." In *Pergament: Geschichte, Struktur, Restaurierung, Herstellung,* edited by Peter Rück, 315–22. Sigmaringen, Germany: Jan Thorbecke Verlag, 1991.

Lüthi, Karl J. *Kleiner Führer in die Sommerausstellung 1936: I. Der Buchdruck von Gutenberg vis Morris (1450–1900); II. Das Pergament (1000–1900).* Bern: Schweizerisches Gutenbergmuseum, 1938.

Lyall, R. J. "Materials: The Paper Revolution." In *Book Production and Publishing in Britain 1375–1475,* edited by Jeremy Griffiths and Derek Pearsall, 11–29. Cambridge: Cambridge University Press, 1989.

MacCaffrey, Wallace T., and Sandra Hindman, eds. *Printing the Written Word: The Social History of Books c. 1450–1520.* Ithaca, NY and London: Cornell University Press, 1991.

MacCulloch, Diarmaid. *Christianity: The First Three Thousand Years.* New York: Penguin, 2010.

Macdonell, Arthur A. *A History of Sanskrit Literature.* New York: D. Appleton and Co., 1900.

Macfarlane, Bruce. *Co-authorship in the Humanities and Social Sciences: A Global View.* A White Paper from Taylor & Francis. London: Taylor & Francis, 2017. Accessed August 15, 2020. https://authorservices.taylorandfrancis.com/wp-content/uploads/2017/09/Coauthorship-white-paper.pdf.

Madden, Frederic. *List of Additions to the Manuscripts in the British Museum in the Years MDCCCXXXVI-MDCCCXL*. London: By Order of the Trustees of the British Museum, 1843.

Margolis, Judith. "A Torah Scroll." *Nashim: A Journal of Jewish Women's Studies and Gender Issues* 21 (2011): 179–84.

Marks, P. J. M. *The British Library Guide to Bookbinding: History and Techniques*. Toronto: University of Toronto Press, 1999.

Martin, Geoffrey Thorndike. *Corpus of Reliefs of the New Kingdom from the Memphite Necropolis and Lower Egypt I*. London: KPI, 1987.

Marvin, Carolyn. "The Body of the Text: Literacy's Corporeal Constant." *Quarterly Journal of Speech* 80 (1994): 129–49.

Mate, Mavis. "The Economy of Kent, 1200–1500: An Age of Expansion, 1200–1340." In *Later Medieval Kent 1220–1540*, edited by Sheila Sweetinburgh, 1–10. Woodbridge: Boydell/Kent County Council, 2010.

———. *Trade and Economic Developments, 1450–1550: The Experience of Kent, Surrey and Sussex*. Woodbridge, UK: Boydell Press, 2006.

Mathiesen, Robert. "The Key of Solomon: Toward a Typology of the Manuscripts." *Societas Magica Newsletter* 17 (2007): 1–9.

Matlock, Wendy A. "Talking Animals, Debating Beasts." In *Rethinking Chaucerian Beasts*, edited by Carolynn Van Dyke, 217–32. New York: Palgrave Macmillan, 2012.

Maxted, Ian. "A History of the Book in Devon." Exeter Working Papers in British Book Trade History 12. Exeter: University of Exeter, 2001. Accessed August 15, 2020. https://bookhistory.blogspot.com/2007/01/devon-book-55.html.

McCracken, Peggy. *In the Skin of a Beast: Sovereignty and Animality in Medieval France*. Chicago: University of Chicago Press, 2017.

McKitterick, Rosamond. *The Carolingians and the Written Word*. Cambridge: Cambridge University Press, 2009.

McLuhan, Herbert Marshall. *Understanding Me: Lectures and Interviews*. Cambridge, MA: MIT Press, 2005.

McNay, Anna. "Laura Youngson Coll." Jerwood Makers Open interview in *Studio International*, July 31, 2017.

McNeal, R. A. "On Editing Herodotus." *L'Antiquité Classique* 52 (1983): 110–29.

McNeill, William H. *The Rise of the West: A History of the Human Community*. Chicago: University of Chicago Press, 1963.

Mellors, John, and Anne Parsons. *Ethiopian Bookmaking: Bookmaking in Rural Ethiopia in the Twenty-First Century*. London: New Cross Books, 2002.

Metzger, Bruce. "Gutenberg, Johannes Gensfleisch Zum." In *The Oxford Companion to the Bible*, edited by Bruce Metzger and Michael David Coogan, 263–64. Oxford: Oxford University Press, 1996.

Meyer, Jesse. "Parchment Production: A Brief Account." In *Scraped, Stroked, and Bound: Materially Engaged Readings of Medieval Manuscripts*, edited by Jonathan Wilcox, 93–96. Turnhout, Belgium: Brepols, 2013.

Mihajlovic, Aleksandar, Ivica Stankovic, and Radomir Mihajlovic. "Digital Dark Ages as a Major Cybersecurity Threat." *International Journal of Economics and Law* 5 (2013): 75–83.

Miller, Patricia Cox. *The Corporeal Imagination: Signifying the Holy in Late Antique Christianity*. Philadelphia: University of Pennsylvania Press, 2012.

Mills, Robert. *Suspended Animation: Pain, Pleasure and Punishment in Medieval Culture*. London: Reaktion Books, 2006.

Mitchell, Rose, and David Crook. "The Pinchbeck Fen Map: A Fifteenth-Century Map of the Lincolnshire Fenland." *Imago Mundi* 51 (1999): 40–50.

Moev, Christian. *The Metaphysics of Dante's Comedy*. Oxford: Oxford University Press, 2008.

Moir, Mali. "The Story Behind the Art of Mali Moir." 18th Annual International American Society of Botanical Artists at The Horticultural Society of New York. Posted on ASBA blog, December 2015. Accessed August 15, 2020. https://www.asba-art.org/article/18th-annual-backstory-mali-moir.

Momma, Haruko. "*Worm*: A Lexical Approach to the *Beowulf* Manuscript." In *Old English Philology: Essays in Honor of R. D. Fulk*, edited by Leonard Neidorf, Rafael J. Pascual, and Tom Shippey, 200–14. Cambridge: D. S. Brewer, 2016.

Monget, Cyprien, ed. *La Chartreuse de Dijon: d'après les documents des archives de Bourgogne*. Vol. 1. Montreil-sur-Mer: Imprimerie Notre-Dames des Prés, 1848.

Montgomery, James E. *Al-Jāḥiẓ: In Praise of Books*. Edinburgh: Edinburgh University Press, 2013.

Moog, Gerhard. "Häute und Felle zur Pergamentherstellung: Eine Betrachtung histologischer Merkmale als Hilfe bei der Zuordnung von Pergamenten zum Ausgangsmaterial." In *Pergament: Geschichte, Struktur, Restaurierung, Herstellung*, edited by Peter Rück, 171–82. Sigmaringen, Germany: Jan Thorbecke Verlag, 1991.

Mooney, Linne. "Some New Light on Thomas Hoccleve." *Studies in the Age of Chaucer* 29 (2007): 293–340.

Mordechai, Lee, Merle Eisenberg, Timothy P. Newfield, Adam Izdebski, Janet E. Kay, and Hendrik Poinar. "The Justinianic Plague: An Inconsequential Pandemic?" *Proceedings of the National Academy of Sciences* 116 (2019): 25546–54.

Morgan, Nigel, and Rodney M. Thompson, eds. *The Cambridge History of the Book in Britain: Vol. 2, 1100–1400*. Cambridge: Cambridge University Press, 2008.

Mroczek, Eva. *The Literary Imagination in Jewish Antiquity*. Oxford: Oxford University Press, 2016.

Murphy, Patrick K. *Unriddling the Exeter Riddles*. University Park: Penn State University Press, 2011.

Mystique of Vellum, The: Containing an Introduction by Decherd Turner and a Historical Essay on Vellum Printed Books by Colin Franklin Along With a Manual to Printing Letterpress on Vellum and Parchment by Richard Bigus that is Edited by Lester Ferriss. Boston: Anne and David Bromer, 1984.

Nelson, Alan H. "Shakespeare Indentures and Chirographs." In *Shakespeare on the Record: Researching an Early Modern Life*, edited by Hannah Leah Crummé, 23–32. The Arden Shakespeare. London: Bloomsbury, 2019.

Nessler, Kate. *At the Edge*. Exhibit catalogue. London: Jonathan Cooper, 2013.

———. "No, Really, That's How I Do It." *The Botanical Artist* 15 (2009): 7–8.

———. *Of Two Minds*. Exhibit catalogue. London: Jonathan Cooper Gallery, 2008.

Neusner, Jacob. *A Life of Rabban Yohanan Ben Zakkai, Ca. 1–80 C.E .* Leiden: E. J. Brill, 1970.

New, David S. *The Text of the Bible: Its Path through History and to the People*. Jefferson, NC: McFarland, 2013.

Nicholas, David. *The Later Medieval City 1300–1500*. London and New York: Routledge, 1997.

Nikolai, Roel. *The Enigma of the Origin of Portolan Charts: A Geodetic Analysis of the Hypothesis of a Medieval Origin.* Leiden: Brill, 2016.

Nongbri, Brent. *God's Library: The Archaeology of the Earliest Christian Manuscripts.* New Haven and London: Yale University Press, 2018.

Nosnitsin, Denis. "Ethiopian Manuscripts and Ethiopian Manuscript Studies: A Brief Overview and Evaluation." *Gazette du livre médiéval* 58 (2002): 1–16.

Novacich, Sarah. *Shaping the Archive in Late Medieval England: History, Poetry, and Performance.* Cambridge Studies in Medieval Literature 97. Cambridge: Cambridge University Press, 2017.

Nyffenegger, Nicole, and Katrin Rupp, eds. *Writing on Skin in the Age of Chaucer.* Berlin and Boston: De Gruyter, 2018.

Nyong'o, Tavia. *The Amalgamation Waltz: Race, Performance, and the Ruses of Memory.* Minneapolis: University of Minnesota Press, 2009.

Ó Cuív, Brian. "Observations on the Book of Lismore." *Proceedings of the Royal Irish Academy* 83 (1983): 269–92.

O'Donoghue, Heather. "Historical and Archaeological: The Poetry of Recovery and Memory." In *The Oxford Handbook of Contemporary British and Irish Poetry,* edited by Peter Robinson, 341–58. Oxford: Oxford University Press, 2013.

O'Malley, Vincent, Bruce Stirling, and Wally Penetito. *The Treaty of Waitangi Companion: Māori and Pākehā from Tasman to Today.* Auckland: Auckland University Press, 2010.

Ommundsen, Åslaug. "A Norwegian—and European—Jigsaw Puzzle of Manuscript Fragments." In *Nordic Latin Manuscript Fragments: The Destruction and Reconstruction of Medieval Books,* edited by Åslaug Ommundsen and Tuomas Heikkilä, 135–62. London: Routledge, 2017.

O'Neill, Timothy. *The Irish Hand: Scribes and Their Manuscripts from the Earliest Times.* Keough Naughton Notre Dame Centre. Cork, Ireland: Cork University Press, 2015.

Oppermann, Serpil. "Feminist Ecocriticism: A Posthumanist Direction in Ecocritical Trajectory." In *International Perspectives in Feminist Ecocriticism,* edited by Greta Gaard, Simon C. Estok, and Serpil Oppermann, 19–36. New York and London: Routledge, 2013.

Orcutt, William Dana. *The Author's Desk Book: Being a Reference Volume Upon Questions of the Relations of the Author to the Publisher, Copyright, the Relation of the Contributor to the Magazine, Mechanics of the Book, Arrangement of the Book, Making of the Index, Etc.* New York: Frederick A. Stokes, 1914.

Pachirat, Timothy. *Every Twelve Seconds: Industrialized Slaughter and the Politics of Sight.* New Haven: Yale University Press, 2014.

Page, Mark. "The Technology of Medieval Sheep Farming: Some Evidence from Crawley, Hampshire, 1208–1349." *Agricultural History Review* 51 (2003): 137–54.

Palgrave, Francis Turner. *Landscape in Poetry: From Homer to Tennyson.* London: Macmillan, 1897.

Patterson, Annabel. *Reading Holinshed's Chronicles.* Chicago: University of Chicago Press, 1994.

Patterson, Charles. *Eternal Treblinka: Our Treatment of Animals and the Holocaust.* New York: Lantern Books, 2002.

Peers, Glenn. *Sacred Shock: Framing Visual Experience in Byzantium.* University Park: Penn State University Press, 2005.

Peterson, Erik. "The Bible as Subject and Object of Illustration: The Making of a Medieval Manuscript; Hamburg 1255." In *The Early Medieval Bible: Its Production, Decoration and Use,* edited by Richard Gameson, 205–22. Cambridge: Cambridge University Press, 1994.

Philips, Dana. *The Truth of Ecology: Nature, Culture, and Literature in America*. Oxford: Oxford University Press, 2003.

Phillipson, Lauren. "Parchment Production in the First Millennium BC at Seglamen, Northern Ethiopia." *African Archaeological Review* 30 (2013): 285–303.

Piñar, Guadalupe, Katja Sterflinger, Jö Ettenauer, Abigail Quandt, and Flavia Pinzari. "A Combined Approach to Assess the Microbial Contamination of the Archimedes Palimpsest." *Microbial Ecology* 69 (2015): 118–34.

Piñar, Guadalupe, Katja Sterflinger, and Flavia Pinzari. "Unmasking the Measles-Like Parchment Discoloration: Molecular and Microanalytical Approach." *Environmental Microbiology* 17 (2015): 427–43.

Piquette, Kathryn, and Ruth Whitehouse, eds. *Writing as Material Practice: Substance, Surface and Medium*. London: Ubiquity Press, 2013.

Pitamber, Priya. "Library Saves Ancient African Manuscripts in Timbuktu." *Media Club South Africa*, May 10, 2016.

Pluskowski, Alexander, ed. *Breaking and Shaping Beastly Bodies: Animals as Material Culture in the Middle Ages*. Oxford: Oxbow, 2007.

Porter, Cheryl. "The Materiality of the Blue Quran: A Physical and Technological Study." In *The Aghlabids and Their Neighbors: Material Culture in Ninth-Century North Africa*, edited by Glaire D. Anderson, Corisande Fenwick, Mariam Rosser-Owen, and Siherne Lamine, 575–86. Leiden: Brill, 2018.

Postan, Michael M. *Essays on Medieval Agriculture and General Problems of the Medieval Economy*. Cambridge: Cambridge University Press, 1973.

Potter, Lois. *The Life of Shakespeare: A Critical Biography*. Hoboken, NJ: Wiley, 2012.

Poulakakis, Nikos, A. Tselikas, I. Bitsakis, M. Mylonas, and P. Lymberakis. "Ancient DNA and the Genetic Signature of Ancient Greek Manuscripts." *Journal of Archaeological Science* 20 (2006): 1–6.

Pouzet, Jean-Pascal. "Book Production Outside Commercial Contexts." In *The Production of Books in England 1350–1500*, edited by Alexandra Gillespie and Daniel Wakelin, 212–38.

Preece, Rod. *Sins of the Flesh: A History of Ethical Vegetarian Thought*. Vancouver: UBC Press, 2014.

Prescott, Andrew. "Tale Tales from the Archives." In *Medieval Historical Writing: Britain and Ireland, 500–1500*, edited by Jennifer Jahner, Emily Steiner, and Elizabeth M. Tyler, 356–69. Cambridge: Cambridge University Press, 2019.

Propert, John Lumsden. *A History of Miniature Art with Notes on Collectors and Collections*. London: MacMillan, 1887.

Purkis, James. *Shakespeare and Manuscript Drama: Canon, Collaboration, and Text*. Cambridge: Cambridge University Press, 2016.

Quandt, Abigail. "Printing on Parchment." In *Prayers in Code: Books of Hours from Renaissance France*, edited by Martina Bagnoli. Baltimore: Walters Art Museum, 2009.

Rabin, Ira. "Building a Bridge from the Dead Sea Scrolls to Mediaeval Hebrew Manuscripts." In *Jewish Manuscript Cultures*, edited by Irina Wandrey, 309–22. Berlin: De Gruyter, 2017.

Radini, A., M. Tromp, A. Beach, E. Tong, C. Speller, M. McCormick, J. V. Dudgeon, et al. "Medieval Women's Early Involvement in Manuscript Production Suggested by Lapis Lazuli Identification in Dental Calculus." *Science Advances* 5 (2019).

Radner, Karen. *State Correspondence in the Ancient World: From New Kingdom Egypt to the Roman Empire*. Oxford: Oxford University Press, 2014.

Razmjou, Shakrokh. "Religion and Burial Customs." In *Forgotten Empire: The World of Ancient Persia*, edited by John Curtis and Nigel Tallis, 150–80. Berkeley: University of California Press, 2005.

Reed, Ronald. *Ancient Skins, Parchments, and Leathers*. London: Seminar Press, 1972.

———. *The Nature and Making of Parchment*. Leeds: Elmete, 1975.

———. *Specimens of Parchment*. Los Angeles: Dawson's Book Shop, 1976.

Renaud, David. "Stillborn Calves: Is It a Problem in Your Herd?" *Progressive Dairy*, July 31, 2019. Accessed July 22, 2020. https://www.progressivedairycanada.com/topics/calves-heifers/stillborn-calves-is-it-a-problem-in-your-herd.

Resl, Brigitte, ed. *A Cultural History of Animals in the Medieval Age*. Oxford: Berg, 2007.

Reynolds, Anna. "'Such Dispersive Scattredness': Early Modern Encounters with Binding Waste." *Journal of the Northern Renaissance* 8 (2017): n.p.

Reynolds, L. D., and N. G. Wilson. *Scribes and Scholars: A Guide to the Transmission of Greek and Latin Literature*. 4th ed. Oxford: Oxford University Press, 2013.

Richter, Dieter. "Die Allegorie der Pergamentbearbeitung: Beziehungen zwischen handwerklichen Vorgängen und der geistlichen Bildersprache des Mittelalters." In *Fahliterature des Mittelalters: Festschrift für Gerhard Eis*, edited by Gundolf Keil, Rainer Rudolf, Wolfram Schmitt, and Hans J. Vermeer, 83–92. Stuttgart, Germany: Metzler, 1968.

Rickman, Catherine, Kate Edmondson, and Emma Le Cornu. "The Conservation of Botanical Illustrations on Vellum: Past, Present, and Future." *Journal of the Institute of Conservation* 35 (2012): 117–36.

Rix, Martyn. *The Golden Age of Botanical Art*. Chicago: University of Chicago Press, 2013.

———. *Rory McEwen: The Colours of Reality*. Richmond, Surrey: Royal Botanical Gardens, Kew, 2013.

Roberts, Adam. *The Riddles of the Hobbit*. New York: Palgrave, 2013.

Roberts, Colin H., and T. C. Skeat. *The Birth of the Codex*. London: Oxford University Press for the British Academy, 1983.

Robinson, Fred C. "Artful Ambiguities in the Old English 'Book-Moth' Riddle." In *Anglo-Saxon Poetry: Essays in Appreciation, for John C. McGalliard*, edited by Lewis E. Nicholson and Dolores Warwick Frese, 355–62. Notre Dame, IN: University of Notre Dame Press, 1975.

Rochais, H.-M. "Contribution à l'histoire des florilèges ascétiques du haut moyen âge latin: Le 'Liber scintillarum'." *Revue Bénédictine* 63 (1953): 246–91.

Roggen, Vibeke. "Old Norse Saga Versus Neo-Latin History Writing: Some Aspects of the Style in Torfæus' *Historia Rerum Norvegicarum* (1711)." *Humanistica Lovaniensia* 55 (2006): 183–94.

Rosen, Aaron. *Imagining Jewish Art: Encounters with the Masters in Chagall, Guston, and Kitaj*. New York and London: Routledge, 2009.

Rosenbloom, Megan. *Dark Archives: A Librarian's Investigation Into the History of Books Bound in Human Skin*. New York: Farrar, Straus and Giroux, 2020.

Rowley, Sue, ed. *Craft and Contemporary Theory*. St. Leonards, AU: Allen and Unwin, 1997.

Roxburgh, David J. *Prefacing the Image: The Writing of Art History in Sixteenth-Century Iran*. Leiden and Boston: Brill, 2014.

Rück, Peter, ed. *Pergament: Geschichte, Struktur, Restaurierung, Herstellung.* Historische Hilfswissen-schaften 2. Sigmaringen, Germany: Jan Thorbecke Verlag, 1991.

Rudy, Kathryn M. *Piety in Pieces: How Medieval Readers Customized their Manuscripts.* Cambridge, UK: Open Book Publishers, 2016.

———. *Postcards on Parchment: The Social Lives of Medieval Books.* New Haven and London: Yale University Press, 2015.

———. *Rubrics, Images and Indulgences in Late Medieval Netherlandish Manuscripts.* Leiden: Brill, 2016.

———. "Sewing the Body of Christ: Eucharist Wafer Souvenirs Stitched into Fifteenth-Century Manuscripts, Primarily in the Netherlands." *Journal of Historians of Netherlandish Art* 8 (2016). https://doi.org.10.5092/jhna.2016.8.1.1.

Rustow, Marina. *The Lost Archive: Traces of a Caliphate in a Cairo Synagogue.* Princeton, NJ: Princeton University Press, 2020.

Ruzzier, Chiara. "The Miniaturisation of Bible Manuscripts in the Thirteenth Century: A Comparative Study." In *Form and Function in the Late Medieval Bible,* edited by Eyal Poleg and Laura Light, 105–25. Leiden: Brill, 2013.

Ryan, Kathleen. "Holes and Flaws in Medieval Irish Manuscripts." *Peritia* 6–7 (1987): 243–64.

———. "Parchment as Faunal Record." *MASCA: University of Pennsylvania Journal* 4 (1987): 124–38.

Ryder, M. "Sheepskin from Ancient Kerma, Northern Sudan." *Oxford Journal of Archaeology* 6.3 (1987): 369–80.

Ryley, Hannah. "Waste Not, Want Not: The Sustainability of Medieval Manuscripts." *Green Letters* 19 (2015): 63–74.

Salomon, Richard. *Opicinus de Canistris: Weltbild und Bekenntnisse eines Avignonesischen Klerikers de 14. Jahrhunderts.* London: Warburg Institute, 1936.

Sandars, Samuel. *An Annotated List of Books Printed on Vellum to be Found in the University and College Libraries at Cambridge.* Cambridge: Cambridge Antiquarian Society, 1878.

Sarri, Antonia. *Material Aspects of Letter Writing in the Graeco-Roman World, 500 BC–AD 300.* Berlin: De Gruyter, 2018.

Sawyer, Daniel. *Reading English Verse in Manuscript c. 1350–1500.* Oxford: Oxford University Press, 2020.

Saxl, H. "An Investigation of the Qualities, the Methods of Manufacture, and the Preservation of Historical Parchment and Vellum with a View to Identifying the Animal Species Used." Master's thesis, University of Leeds, 1954.

Scargill-Bird, S. R. *A Guide to the Principal Classes of Documents Preserved in the Public Record Office.* 2nd ed. London: Her Majesty's Stationery Office, 1896.

Scattergood, John. "Eating the Book: Riddle 47 and Memory." In *Manuscripts and Ghosts: Essays on the Transmission of Medieval and Early Renaissance Literature,* edited by John Scattergood, 83–94. Dublin: Four Courts, 2006.

Schäfer, Peter. "The Magic of the Golem: The Early Development of the Golem Legend." *Journal of Jewish Studies* 46 (1995): 249–61.

Schlatter, N. Elizabeth. "Leonora Carrington's *Samhain Skin.*" In *Women in the Arts,* summer 2006, 22–24. Washington, D.C.: National Museum of Women in the Arts, 2006.

Schmitz, Wilhelm. *Miscellanea Tironiana aus dem Codex Vaticanvs Latinvs Reginae Christinae 846 (fol. 99–114).* Leipzig: B. G. Teubner, 1896.

Schoenbaum, Samuel. *William Shakespeare: A Compact Documentary Life.* Oxford: Oxford University Press, 1987.

Scholem, Gershom. "The Meaning of the Torah in Jewish Mysticism." In *Essential Papers on Kabbalah,* edited by Lawrence Fine, 179–211. New York: New York University Press, 1995.

Schott, Christine. "Footnotes on Life: Marginalia in Three Medieval Icelandic Manuscripts." Master's thesis, University of Iceland. Leiðbeinandi: Svanhildur Óskarsdóttir, 2010.

Sciacca, Christine. "Stitches, Sutures, and Seams: 'Embroidered' Parchment Repairs in Medieval Manuscripts." In *Medieval Clothing and Textiles 6,* edited by Robin Netherton and Gale R. Owen-Crocker, 57–92. Woodbridge, UK: Boydell and Brewer, 2010.

Seetah, Krish. *Humans, Animals, and the Craft of Slaughter in Archaeo-Historic Societies.* Cambridge: Cambridge University Press, 2018.

Selassie, Sergew Hable. *Bookmaking in Ethiopia.* Leiden: Brill, 1981.

Sepkoski, David. "The Earth as Archive: Contingency, Narrative, and the History of Life." In *Science in the Archives: Pasts, Presents, Futures,* edited by Lorraine Daston, 53–84. Chicago: University of Chicago Press, 2017.

Serebrin, Judith. "Artist Statement for *Neither Here Nor There.*" Unpublished typescript. July 2021.

Serres, Michel. *The Five Senses: A Philosophy of Mingled Bodies.* Translated by Margaret Sankey and Peter Cowley. London: Bloomsbury, 2016.

Shaw, Graham. "South Asia." In *A Companion to the History of the Book,* edited by Simon Eliot and Jonathan Rose, 126–37. Malden, MA: Blackwell, 2007.

Shelf List of Hebrew Books Printed on Vellum Held in the British Library. London: British Library, Hebrew Section, Oriental and India Office Collections, 1994.

Shepherd, Lara D., Peter Whitehead, and Anna Whitehead. "Genetic Analysis Identifies the Missing Parchment of New Zealand's Founding Document, the Treaty of Waitangi." PLOS ONE 14 (1): e0210528.

Sherwood, Shirley. *A New Flowering: 1000 Years of Botanical Art.* Oxford: Ashmolean Museum, 2006.

Siegal, Michal Bar-Asher. *Early Christian Monastic Literature and the Babylonian Talmud.* Cambridge: Cambridge University Press, 2016.

Signori, Gabriela. *Räume, Gesten, Andachtsformen: Geschlecht, Konflikt und religiöse Kultur im europäischen Mittelalter.* Ostfildern, Germany: Thorbecke, 2005.

Silver, Sandra. *Footprints in Parchment: Rome versus Christianity, 30–313 AD.* Bloomington, IN: AuthorHouse, 2013.

Sirat, Colette. *Hebrew Manuscripts of the Middle Ages.* Edited and translated by Nicholas de Lange. Cambridge: Cambridge University Press, 2002.

Smail, Daniel Lord. *Imaginary Cartographies: Possession and Identity in Late Medieval Marseille.* Ithaca, NY: Cornell University Press, 2000.

Smith, Astrid J. "What it is to be a Digitization Specialist: Chasing Medieval Materials in a Sea of Pixels." In *Medieval Manuscripts in the Digital Age,* edited by Benjamin Albritton, Georgia Henley, and Elaine Treharne, 17–24. London: Routledge, 2021.

Smith, S. M. "The Design Relationship Between the Manuscript and the Incunable." In *A Millennium of the Book: Production, Design and Illustration in Manuscript and Print, 900–1900,* edited by R. Myers and M. H. Harris, 23–44. New Castle, DE: Oak Knoll Press, 1994.

Smith, Terry. "Craft, Modernity and Postmodernity." In *Craft and Contemporary Theory*, edited by Sue Rowley, 18–28. St. Leonards, AU: Allen & Unwin, 1997.

Snow, C. P. *The Two Cultures*. Cambridge: Cambridge University Press, 1959.

Spallinger, Anthony. "Drama in History: Exemplars From Mid Dynasty XVIII." *Studien zur Altägyptischen Kultur* 24 (1997): 269–300.

Spencer, Colin. *The Heretic's Feast: A History of Vegetarianism*. Hanover, NH: University Press of New England, 1996.

Spiegel, Shalom. *The Last Trial: On the Legends and Lore of the Command to Abraham to Offer Isaac as a Sacrifice*. Translated by Judah Goldin. Woodstock, VT: Jewish Lights, 1993.

Stallybrass, Peter, Roger Chartier, J. Franklin Mowery, and Heather Wolff. "Hamlet's Tables and the Technology of Writing in Renaissance England." *Shakespeare Quarterly* 55, no. 4 (Winter 2004): 379–419.

Steel, Karl. *How To Make a Human: Animals and Violence in the Middle Ages*. Columbus: Ohio State University Press, 2011.

Steiner, Emily. *Documentary Culture and the Making of Medieval English Literature*. Cambridge: Cambridge University Press, 2003.

Stephenson, M. J. "The Productivity of Medieval Sheep on the Great Estates 1100–1500." PhD thesis, University of Cambridge, 1986.

Stern, David. *The Jewish Bible: A Material History*. Seattle and London: University of Washington Press, 2017.

Stetkevych, Suzanne Pinckney. *The Mantle Odes: Arabic Praise Poems to the Prophet Muhammad*. Bloomington: Indiana University Press, 2010.

Stieber, Chelsea. *Haiti's Paper War: Post-Independence Writing, Civil War, and the Making of the Republic, 1804–1954*. America and the Long Nineteenth Century 25. New York: NYU Press, 2020.

Stinson, Timothy D. "Counting Sheep: Potential Applications of DNA Analysis to the Study of Medieval Parchment Production." In *Kodikologie und Paläographie im digitalen Zeitalter 2*, edited by Franz Fischer, Christiane Fritze, and Georg Vogeler, 192–207. Schriften des Instituts für Dokumentologie und Editorik 3. Norderstedt: BoD, 2010.

———. "Knowledge of the Flesh: Using DNA Analysis to Unlock the Secrets of Medieval Parchment." *Papers of the Bibliographical Society of America* 103 (2009): 435–53.

Stock, Brian. *Augustine the Reader: Meditation, Self-Knowledge, and the Ethics of Interpretation*. Cambridge, MA: Belknap Press of Harvard, 1996.

Stockton, Will. *Members of His Body: Shakespeare, Paul, and a Theology of Nonmonogamy*. New York: Fordham University Press, 2017.

Stone, David. *Decision-Making in Medieval Agriculture*. Oxford: Oxford University Press, 2005.

Striphas, Ted. *The Late Age of Print: Everyday Book Culture from Consumerism to Control*. 2nd ed. New York: Columbia University Press, 2009.

Tahan, Ilana. *Hebrew Manuscripts: The Power of Script and Image*. London: The British Library, 2007.

Taylor, Jamie. "Animal Rights, Legal Agency, and Cultural Difference in *The Testament of the Buck*." In *Theorizing Legal Personhood in Late Medieval England*, edited by Andreea D. Boboc, 271–90. Medieval Law and Its Practice 18. Leiden: Brill, 2015.

Teasdale, Matthew, Sarah Fiddyment, Jiří Vnouček, Valeria Mattiangeli, Camilla Speller, Annelise Binois, Martin Carver, et al. "The York Gospels: A 1000-year Biological Palimpsest." *Royal So-*

ciety Open Science 4 (2018): 2–170988. Accessed August 15, 2020. http://dx.doi.org/10.1098/rsos .170988.

Teasdale, Matthew, N. L. van Doorn, Sarah Fiddyment, C. C. Webb, T. O'Connor, M. Hofreiter, Matthew Collins, and Dan G. Bradley. "Paging Through History: Parchment as a Reservoir of Ancient DNA for Next Generation Sequencing." *Philosophical Transactions of the Royal Society of London* 370 (2015): 20130379.

Teicher, J. L. "Ancient Eucharistic Prayers in Hebrew (Dura-Europos Parchment D. Pg. 25)." *Jewish Quarterly Review* New Series 54 (1963): 99–109.

Thomas, F. S. *Handbook to the Public Records.* London: Public Record Office, 1853.

Thomas, Marcel. "Manuscripts." In *The Coming of the Book*, edited by Lucien Febvre and Henri-Jean Martin, 15–28. Translated by David Gerard. London: Verso, 1997.

Thomas, Richard. "Of Books and Bones: The Integration of Historical and Zooarchaeological Evidence in the Study of Medieval Animal Husbandry." In *Integrating Zooarchaeology*, edited by Mark Maltby, 17–26. Oxford: Oxbow Books, 2006.

Thompson, Daniel Varney. "Medieval Parchment-Making." *The Library* 16, no. 1 (1935): 113–17.

———. *The Materials and Techniques of Medieval Painting.* London: Allen & Unwin, 1936.

———. *The Schedula of Theophilus Presbyter.* Cambridge, MA: Medieval Academy of America, 1932.

Thompson, E. Margaret. *The Carthusian Order in England.* Published for the Church Historical Society. London: S.P.C.K., 1930.

Thompson, Sir Edward Maunde. *Introduction to Greek and Latin Palaeography.* Oxford: Clarendon Press, 1912.

Thompson, Lawrence S. "Notes on Corpse Lore in Kentucky." *Kentucky Folklore Record* 23, no. 2 (1977): 38.

———. *Religatum de Pelle Humana.* In *Bibliologia Comica: Or, Humorous Aspects of the Caparisoning and Conservation of Books*, 119–60. Hamden, CT: Archon Books, 1968.

———. "Tanned Human Skin." *Bulletin of the Medical Library Association* 34 (1946): 93–103.

Thrower, Norman J. W. *Maps and Civilization: Cartography in Culture and Society.* 3rd ed. Chicago: University of Chicago Press, 2007.

Tracy, Larissa, ed. *Flaying in the Pre-Modern World: Practice and Representation.* Woodbridge, UK: D. S. Brewer, 2017.

Treharne, Elaine. *Perceptions of Medieval Manuscripts: The Phenomenal Book.* Oxford: Oxford University Press, 2021.

Trow-Smith, Robert. *A History of British Livestock Husbandry, to 1700.* London and New York: Routledge, 2013.

Turner, Decherd. *One Text, Two Results: Printing on Paper and Vellum.* Dallas: The Bridwell Library, 1991.

Turner, Nancy K. "The Materiality of Medieval Parchment: A Response to 'The Animal Turn'." *Revista Hispánica Moderna* 71 (2018): 39-67.

Van Bladel, Kevin. "Zoroaster's Many Languages." In *Arabic Humanities, Islamic Thought: Essays in Honor of Everett K. Rowson*, edited by Joseph Lowry and Shawkat Toorawa, 199–210. Leiden: Brill, 2017.

VanderKam, James, and Peter Flint. *The Meaning of the Dead Sea Scrolls: Their Significance for Understanding the Bible, Judaism, Jesus, and Christianity.* New York: HarperOne, 2004.

Van Dyke, Carolynn, ed. *Rethinking Chaucerian Beasts*. New York: Palgrave Macmillan, 2012.

Van Praet, Joseph. *Catalogue des livres imprimés sur vélin de le Bibliothèque du roi*. Paris: Du Bure frères, 1824.

Velasco, Jesus. *Dead Voice: Law, Philosophy, and Fiction in the Iberian Middle Ages*. Philadelphia: University of Pennsylvania Press, 2019.

Vezin, Jean. "Les relations entre Saint-Denis et d'autres scriptoria pendant le haut moyen âge." In *The Role of the Book in Medieval Culture*, edited by Peter Ganz, 17–39. Vol. 1, Bibliologia 3–4. Turnhout, Belgium: Brepols, 1986.

Vianu, Lidia. "The Best Critic is the Editor Within." Interview with Catherine Byron, *Desperado Essays-Interviews*. Bucharest: Bucharest University Press, 2006.

Visscher, J. "Looking Back On a Lifetime in Parchmentmaking at William Cowley." In *Pergament: Geschichte, Struktur, Restaurierung, Herstellung*, edited by Peter Rück, 341–58. Sigmaringen, Germany: Jan Thorbecke Verlag, 1991.

Vnouček, Jiří. "The Manufacture of Parchment for Writing Purposes and the Observation of the Signs of Manufacture Surviving in Old Manuscripts." In *Care and Conservation of Manuscripts*, Vol. 8, 74–92. Proceedings of the Eighth International Seminar Held at the University of Copenhagen, October 16–17, 2003. Copenhagen: Museum Tusculanum Press, 2005.

Vorst, Benjamin. "Mysterious Vellum." In *Pergament: Geschichte, Struktur, Restaurierung, Herstellung*, edited by Peter Rück, 365–70. Sigmaringen, Germany: Jan Thorbecke Verlag, 1991.

Waddell, Helen, trans. *Beasts and Saints: Stories of Mutual Charities between Saints and Beasts*. New York: Henry Holt, 1934.

Wagner, Ricarda, Christine Neufeld, and Ludger Lieb. *Writing Beyond Pen and Parchment: Inscribed Objects in Medieval European Literature*. Berlin: De Gruyter, 2019.

Wakelin, Daniel. *Designing English: Early Literature on the Page*. Oxford: Bodleian Library, 2018.

Waley, Daniel. *Siena and the Sienese in the Thirteenth Century*. Cambridge: Cambridge University Press, 1991.

Wallis, Alfred. "Book Bound in Human Skin." *Notes & Queries* 7.7 (March 30, 1889): 246.

Wandrey, Irina, ed. *Jewish Manuscript Cultures*. Berlin: De Gruyter, 2017.

Warren, Michelle R. *Holy Digital Grail: A Medieval Book on the Internet*. Stanford, CA: Stanford University Press, 2022.

Warren, Michelle R., and Neil Weijer. "Re-Imagining Digital Things: Sustainable Data in Medieval Manuscript Studies." *Digital Philology: A Journal of Medieval Cultures* 10.1 (2021): 111–34.

Waters, Matt. *Ancient Persia: A Concise History of the Achaemenid Empire, 550–330 BCE*. Cambridge: Cambridge University Press, 2014.

Watkins, Claire Vaye. *Gold Fame Citrus: A Novel*. New York: Riverhead Books, 2015.

Wattenbach, Wilhelm. *Das Schriftwesen im Mittelalter*. Leipzig, Germany: Verlag Von S. Hirzel, 1875.

Webley, Lisa, and Harriet Samuels. *Complete Public Law: Texts, Cases, and Materials*. 3rd ed. Oxford: Oxford University Press, 2015.

West, Brent. "The Digital Dark Ages: Preserving History in the Era of Electronic Records." MWAIS 2014 Proceedings, 12. Accessed August 18, 2021. http://aisel.aisnet.org/mwais2014/12.

West, Melanie Grayce. "Congregation Set to Unveil Torah Transcribed by Woman." *The Wall Street Journal*, September 18, 2017.

West, Stephanie R. "The Papyri of Herodotus." In *Culture in Pieces: Essays on Ancient Texts in Honour of Peter Parsons*, edited by Dirk Obbink and Richard Rutherford, 69–83. Oxford: Oxford University Press, 2011.

Westrem, Scott D. *The Hereford Map: A Transcription and Translation of the Legends with Commentary.* Turnhout, Belgium: Brepols, 2001.

Whittington, Karl. *Body-Worlds: Opicinus de Canistris and the Medieval Cartographic Imagination.* Toronto: Pontifical Institute of Mediaeval Studies, 2014.

Wilcox, Jonathan. "The Philology of Smell." In *Scraped, Stroked, and Bound: Materially Engaged Readings of Medieval Manuscripts*, edited by Jonathan Wilcox, 1–13. Turnhout, Belgium: Brepols, 2013.

———, ed. *Scraped, Stroked, and Bound: Materially Engaged Readings of Medieval Manuscripts.* Turnhout, Belgium: Brepols, 2013.

Wilkinson, Toby A. H. *The Rise and Fall of Ancient Egypt.* New York: Random House, 2011.

Williams, Megan Hale. *The Monk and the Book: Jerome and the Making of Christian Scholarship.* Chicago: University of Chicago Press, 2014.

Williams, Raymond. *Marxism and Literature.* Oxford: Oxford University Press, 1977.

Wilson, Richard. "A Scribbled Form: Shakespeare's Missing Magna Carta." *Shakespeare Quarterly* 67 (2016): 344–70.

Winsbury, Rex. *The Roman Book: Books, Publishing and Performance in Classical Rome.* London: Bloomsbury, 2009.

Winters, W. *Our Parish Registers: Being Three Hundred Years of Curious Local History, as collected from the Original Registers, Churchwardens' Accounts, and Monumental Records of the Parish of Waltham Holy Cross.* Waltham Abbey, Essex: Published by the author, 1885.

Wolff, Heather, and Peter Stallybrass. "The Material Culture of Record-Keeping in Early Modern England." *Archives and Information in the Early Modern World*, edited by Liesbeth Corens, Kate Peters, and Alexandra Walsham, 179–208. Oxford: For the British Academy by Oxford University Press, 2018.

Wolfson, Elliot R. *Through a Speculum That Shines: Vision and Imagination in Medieval Jewish Mysticism.* Princeton, NJ: Princeton University Press, 1997.

Woodward, Scott R., Gila Kahila, Patricia Smith, Charles Greenblatt, Joe Zias, and Magen Broshi. "Analysis of Parchment Fragments from the Judean Desert Using DNA Techniques." In *Current Research and Technological Developments on the Dead Sea Scrolls*, edited by Donald W. Parry and Stephen D. Ricks, 215–38. Studies on the Texts of the Desert of Judah 20. Leiden: Brill, 1996.

Worley, Meg. "Using the *Ormulum* to Redefine Vernacularity." In *The Vulgar Tongue: Medieval and Postmedieval Vernacularity*, edited by Fiona Somerset and Nicholas Watson, 19–30. University Park: Penn State University Press, 2003.

Wright, Thomas, and James Orchard Halliwell, eds. *Reliquiae Antiquae: Scraps from Ancient Manuscripts Illustrating Chiefly Early English Literature and the English Language.* 2 vols. London: John Russell Smith, 1845.

Yates, Julian. *Of Sheep, Oranges, and Yeast: A Multispecies Impression.* Minneapolis: University of Minnesota Press, 2017.

Young, Arthur M. *Echoes of Two Cultures.* Pittsburgh, PA: University of Pittsburgh Press, 1964.

Young, Elizabeth. *Pet Projects: Animal Fiction and Taxidermy in the Nineteenth-Century Archive*. University Park: Penn State University Press, 2019.

Zander, Randolph. *The Alaskan Parchment Script of the Russian American Company, 1816–1867*. Bellingham, WA: The Russian Numismatic Society, 1996.

Zeini, Arash. *Zoroastrian Scholasticism in Late Antiquity: The Pahlavi Version of the Yasna Haptaŋhāiti*. Edinburgh Studies in Ancient Persia. Edinburgh: Edinburgh University Press, 2020.

Ziegler, Waltraud. "Ein neuer Lösungsversuch für das altenglische Rätsen Nr 28." *Arbeiten aus Anglistik und Amerikanistik* 7 (1982): 185–90.

ACKNOWLEDGMENTS

This book has benefited from the generosity of numerous scholars and archivists, artisans and artists, colleagues and friends, and it is a humbling pleasure to acknowledge their help and encouragement over many years.

I owe profound debts to the many dozens of librarians, archivists, and collections care specialists who gave me the gift of their time and attention, granting me access to closed stacks and seldom handled artifacts, indulging my curiosity about shelf mileage and bulk, teaching me the fine points of preservation and repair, and addressing my often idiosyncratic research questions with patience, expertise, and care. I would especially like to thank Liz Ralph and Tom Bower of the Parliamentary Archives in Westminster; Massimo Ceresa of the Vatican Apostolic Library; Antoinette Curtis and Yuki Russell at the Norfolk Record Office; Ilana Tahan at the British Library; Gilian Evison, Matthew Holford, and Oliver House at the Bodleian Libraries in Oxford; Solange Fitzgerald, Paul Dryburgh, and Sean Cunningham at the National Archives at Kew; Mike Buscher and his colleagues at the Geography and Map Division at the Library of Congress; Father Justin at St. Catherine's Monastery, Mount Sinai; and Dot Porter at the Schoenberg Institute for Manuscript Studies at the University of Pennsylvania. Eliza Gilligan, Petrina Jackson, Molly Schwartzburg, David Whitesell, and other colleagues in Special Collections at the University of Virginia have supported this work in numerous ways over the years, whether by arranging manuscripts for student instruction or facilitating the collection of samples from books and documents.

My appreciation for parchment craft past and present has been greatly enhanced through acquaintance with several of its contemporary practitioners, whether through hands-on instruction, workshops, or interviews. Henk de Groot, Shoshana Gugenheim, Jiří Vnouček, and Paul Wright have been generous interlocutors, while Jesse Meyer at Pergamena has been a fount of knowledge and practical wisdom.

A turning point in this project occurred when Matthew Collins and Sarah Fiddyment introduced themselves after a lecture I delivered at the University of Leeds. They invited me to their lab up the road in York, and over the following weeks and months we assembled a larger team of researchers devoted to the biomolecular analysis of parchment and the emerging field of biocodicology. Collaborative research and writing with our group—which also included Annelise Binois, Dan Bradley, Caroline Checkley-Scott, Mary Garrison, Kate Rudy, Chiara Ruzzier, Matthew Teasdale, among others—opened my eyes to the hidden realm of cells, molecules, acids, and proteins common to every artifact making up the parchment inheritance.

A further revelation came in a moment of serendipity when I stumbled upon the work of Kate Nessler years ago at the Jonathan Cooper gallery in London. Her inventive creations at the edges of vellum dazzled me and led me to other contemporary painters and sculptors working in the medium across four continents, including Anne-Françoise Ben-Or, Denis Brown, Laura Youngson Coll, Margaret Fitzpatrick, Shoshana Gugenheim, Myriam Jawerbaum, Mali Moir, Silvia Rubinson, Judy Serebrin, and Leora Wise. I am grateful for the time and attention of these brilliant artists as they answered my queries, opened their studios and shared their work, and taught me more than I thought possible about the object of our mutual obsession.

I have learned a great deal from interactions with colleagues and students at Leeds, York, Oxford, the University of London, SUNY-Binghamton, Wake Forest, Barnard College, Sewanee, Kalamazoo, the Medieval Academy of America, the New Chaucer Society, the University of Oklahoma, Oklahoma State, Stanford, Wisconsin, the University of Washington, Washington University in St. Louis, Harvard, NYU, Princeton, Northwestern, George Washington, Penn, Cornell, Rice, UCLA, the Folger Shakespeare Library, and the many other institutions and conferences where I have presented this work over the years. I am so grateful to the colleagues who invited me for lectures, symposia, workshops, classroom visits, and visiting appointments as this project took shape, as well as to the numerous individuals who asked a challenging question, suggested a helpful reference, or glossed a thorny passage. Many thanks to Sherif Abdelkarim, Elizabeth Alexander, Steve Arata, Asher Bieman, Eltjo Buringh, Catherine Byron, Joshua Calhoun, John Carey, Richard Cassidy, Jeffrey Jerome Cohen, Andrew Cole, Megan Cook, Rita Copeland, Lisa Fagin Davis, Marilynn Desmond, Emmalee Dove, Consuelo Dutschke, Rebecca Falcasantos, Elizabeth Fowler, Martin Foys, Aranye Fradenburg, Fenella France, Camela Franklin, Simon Gaunt, Alexandra Gillespie, Greg Given, Dalia-Ruth Halperin, Martien Halvorson-Taylor, Greg Hayes, Eileen Joy, David Scott Kastan, Sarah Kay, Paul Kershaw, Richard Kieckhefer, Erik Kwakkel, Stephanie Lahey, Jerome McGann, Deborah McGrady, Jeannie Miller, Timothy Morton, Kelsey Nasson, Barbara Newman, Sarah Novacich, John Parker, Sif Ríkharðsdóttir, Megan Rosenbloom, Christine Schott, Avram Schwarz, Myra Seaman, Jim Seitz, Angela Bennett Sigler, Dan Smail, Peter Stallybrass, Andy Stauffer, Karl Steel, Emily Steiner, Brian Stock, Zach Stone, Elaine Treharne, Michelle Warren, Karl Whittington, Neguin Yavari, and Arash Zeini.

Avram Schwarz walked me through numerous rabbinic writings on parchment while explaining key terms and concepts in the Hebrew. Paul Halliday has been a cheerful guide to legal history and its written record. A series of conversations about parchment quantity with the late Michael T. Clanchy confirmed some hunches and gave me additional avenues to pursue. Shamma Boyarin, Ray Clemens, Marisa Galvez, Paul Halliday, Sara Lipton, Tim Stinson, and Michael Suarez read portions of the manuscript with precision and care. I have benefited enormously from the generosity and friendship of Scott Gwara, whose incisive responses showed me dimensions of the project I would otherwise have missed.

A number of the final plates were gathered during a global pandemic, and I am grateful to the many colleagues—including Ben Albritton, Solange Fitzgerald, Matthew Holford, Kristen McDonald, Victoria Perry, Kate Rudy, and Jessica Tubis—who went out of their way to help me secure suitable images in a time of closures and travel restrictions (even to the extent of visiting a closed castle to snap a shot of an old map). Dayanna Knight created the beautifully drawn renderings in chapter 4 and chapter 7 especially for this book, responding to my input with flexibility and speed.

Jennifer Banks, my editor at Yale University Press, responded to my initial query with enthusiasm and imagination, and her vision helped me immensely during final revision. Abbie Storch has been a tireless guide through the slough of permissions, releases, and manuscript preparation. Annie Imbornoni has been an exacting production editor, and Gretchen Otto and her team have handled editing and design with precision and creativity. The two external readers for the press pushed me to sharpen my arguments and clarify their stakes at every turn.

The book has its distant origins in a piece commissioned for a "Theories and Methodologies" cluster in *PMLA*, published in 2009 as "Of Pigs and Parchment: Medieval Studies and the Coming of the Animal," from which a few paragraphs survive here. Several others come from a 2015 essay published in *The New York Review of Books*, "Written on Beasts," and I have taken a few pages and plates from a museum catalog essay, "Animalities," written at the invitation of Dot Porter for the Schoenberg Institute's *Reactions: Medieval/Modern* exhibition in 2016.

Anna Brickhouse has tolerated this book for too long, and I'm more grateful than I can say for the continuing gifts of her intellect, tracked changes, and love. Campbell and Malcolm listened to me complain about the inscrutable "parchment book" through too much of their youth, and I thank them for their blasé humor. Our beloved Daisy sat curled nearby for most of the decade I spent writing this book, and left us just as it went to press. Her eyes, her breath, her tail, her ruff, her bark, her paws, her stride, her hunger, her leaps and bounds, her fear of cats, her head-butts and clawings for attention, her final pain: she curated our animal side, and made us all better humans to boot.

PHOTO CREDITS

Figure 1.1: By permission of the Royal Irish Academy © RIA

Figure 1.2: mauritius images GmbH / Alamy Stock Photo

Figure 1.3: © British Library Board

Figure 2.1: Bruce Holsinger

Figure 2.2: The Árni Magnússon Institute for Icelandic Studies

Figure 3.1 : © Tom Pilston

Figure 3.2 : Courtesy of William Cowley

Figure 3.3: Bruce Holsinger

Figure 3.4: Shoshana Gugenheim

Figure 3.5: © British Library Board

Figure 3.6: Royal Danish Library, Copenhagen

Figure 3.7: Royal Danish Library, Copenhagen

Figure 3.8: Staatsbibliothek Bamberg

Figure 3.9: Staatsbibliothek Bamberg

Figure 3.10: Lebrecht Music & Arts / Alamy Stock Photo

Figure 3.11: Stadtbibliothek im Bildungscampus Nürnberg

Figure 3.12: Courtesy of the British Museum

Figure 3.13: The Bodleian Libraries, University of Oxford

Figure 3.14: The Bodleian Libraries, University of Oxford

Figure 3.15: Courtesy of the ARTFL Encyclopédie Project, University of Chicago

Figure 3.16: Courtesy of the ARTFL Encyclopédie Project, University of Chicago

Figure 4.1 : Columbia University Libraries

Figure 4.2: Irish Script on Screen (Dublin Institute for Advanced Studies)

Figure 4.3: Courtesy of Princeton University Library

Figure 4.4 : Courtesy of the Department of Special Collections, Stanford University Libraries

Figure 4.5 : By permission of Saint Catherine's Monastery, Sinai, Egypt

Figure 4.6: Bruce Holsinger

Figure 4.7: Bruce Holsinger

Figure 4.8: Bruce Holsinger

Figure 4.9 : Irish Script on Screen (Dublin Institute for Advanced Studies)

Figure 4.10: Bruce Holsinger

Figure 4.11: Stiftsarchiv St.Gallen (www.e-chartae.ch)

Figure 4.12: Drawing by Dayanna Knight

Figure 4.13: Kislak Center, University of Pennsylvania

Figure 4.14: By permission of Saint Catherine's Monastery, Sinai, Egypt

Figure 4.15: © British Library Board

Figure 4.16: The Bodleian Libraries, University of Oxford

Figure 4.17: Drawing by Dayanna Knight

Figure 4.18: Drawing by Dayanna Knight

Figure 4.19: © British Library Board

Figure 4.20: © British Library Board

Figure 4.21 : © British Library Board

Figure 4.22 : Scott Gwara

Figure 4.23: © British Library Board

Figure 4.24: © British Library Board

Figure 4.25: National Library of Sweden

Figure 4.26 : The Bodleian Libraries, University of Oxford

Figure 4.27 : © British Library Board

Figure 4.28 : © British Library Board

Figure 4.29 : © Crown copyright (2017). Licensed under the Open Government Licence v3.0

Figure 4.30 : Bruce Holsinger

Figure 4.31 : Bruce Holsinger

Figure 4.32 : Ian Dagnall / Alamy Stock Photo

Figure 4.33: The National Archives, Kew

Figure 4.34: Victoria Perry, By courtesy of the Duke of Rutland/Belvoir Castle

Figure 4.35: The Master and Fellows of Trinity College, Cambridge

Figure 4.36: Library of Congress Geography and Map Division, Washington, D.C.

Figure 4.37: Library of Congress Geography and Map Division, Washington, D.C.

Figure 4.38: Courtesy of the Biblioteca Apostolica Vaticana

Figure 4.39 : Courtesy of the Biblioteca Apostolica Vaticana

Figure 4.40 : Courtesy of the Biblioteca Apostolica Vaticana

Figure 4.41: Bruce Holsinger

Figure 4.42: Courtesy of The Lewis Walpole Library, Yale University

Figure 4.43: Bible, General Collection, Beinecke Rare Book and Manuscript Library, Yale University

Figure 4.44: The Árni Magnússon Institute for Icelandic Studies

Figure 4.45: © British Library Board

Figure 4.46 : Rare Book and Manuscript Library, Columbia University Libraries

Figure 4.47: Uppsala universitetsbibliotek

Figure 4.48: Uppsala universitetsbibliotek

Figure 4.49: Staatsbibliothek Bamberg

Figure 4.50: Staatsbibliothek Bamberg

Figure 4.51: © British Library Board

Figure 4.52: © British Library Board

Figure 4.53: By permission of Saint Catherine's Monastery, Sinai, Egypt

Figure 4.54: The Bodleian Libraries, University of Oxford

Figure 4.55: National Library of Sweden, Stockholm

Figure 4.56: © British Library Board

Figure 4.57: © British Library Board

Figure 4.58: Nationaal Archief, The Hague

Figure 4.59: Folger Shakespeare Library, Washington, D.C.

Figure 5.1: Bruce Holsinger

Figure 5.2 : Courtesy of Chichester, Inc.

Figure 5.3: General Collection, Beinecke Rare Book and Manuscript Library, Yale University

Figure 6.1 : Alicia Canter

Figure 6.2 : National Library of Sweden, Stockholm

Figure 6.3: Norfolk Record Office/Antoinette Curtis

Figure 6.4: Norfolk Record Office/Antoinette Curtis

Figure 6.5: Norfolk Record Office/Antoinette Curtis

Figure 6.6: Norfolk Record Office/Antoinette Curtis

Figure 6.7: Bruce Holsinger

Figure 6.8: Bruce Holsinger

Figure 6.9: Bruce Holsinger

Figure 6.10: Bruce Holsinger

Figure 6.11: Hanna Holborn Gray Special Collections Research Center, University of Chicago Library

Figure 7.1: By courtesy of the British Museum

Figure 7.2: bpk Bildagentur / Staatliche Museen, Berlin / Art Resource, NY

Figure 7.3: Drawing by Dayanna Knight

Figure 7.4: The Bodleian Libraries, University of Oxford

Figure 7.5: The Bodleian Libraries, University of Oxford

Figure 7.6: The Bodleian Libraries, University of Oxford

Figure 7.7: The Bodleian Libraries, University of Oxford

Figure 7.8 : Courtesy of The Israel Museum, Jerusalem

Figure 8.1 : Papyrussammlung Koeln

Figure 10.1: Wellcome Collection. Attribution 4.0 International (CC BY 4.0)

Figure 10.2: Boston Athenæum

Figure 10.3: Historical Medical Library of The College of Physicians of Philadelphia

Figure 10.4 : J. Paul Getty Museum

Figure 10.5 : Free Library of Philadelphia, Rare Book Department

Figure 10.6: The Morgan Library and Museum/Art Resource

Figure 10.7 : The Morgan Library and Museum/Art Resource

Figure 10.8: Bibliothèque nationale de France

Figure 10.9: Prinsenhof Library, Delft

Figure 10.10: Bibliothèque nationale de France

Figure 10.11: Bibliothèque nationale de France

Figure 10.12 : Coll. and photogr. BNU de Strasbourg

Figure 10.13: Coll. and photogr. BNU de Strasbourg

Figure 10.14: Coll. and photogr. BNU de Strasbourg

Figure 10.15: © British Library Board

Figure 11.1 : © British Library Board

Figure 11.2: © British Library Board

Figure 11.3: © British Library Board

Figure 11.4: © British Library Board

Figure 12.1 : Folger Shakespeare Library, Washington, D.C.

Figure 12.2: © Shakespeare Birthplace Trust

Figure 12.3: The National Archives, Kew

Figure 12.4 : The National Archives, Kew

Figure 13.1 : Bruce Holsinger

Figure 13.2 : Bruce Holsinger

Figure 13.3: Proceedings of the National Academy of Sciences

Figure 13.4 : Reprinted from *Cell* 181, Anava et al., "Illuminating Genetic Mysteries of the Dead Sea Scrolls," Copyright 2020, with permission from Elsevier.

Figure 13.5 : Auckland, Ministry for Culture and Heritage

Figure 14.1 : Courtesy of the Biblioteca Apostolica Vaticana

Figure 14.2: Bruce Holsinger

Figure 14.3: © British Library Board

Figure 15.1: © 2021 Estate of Leonora Carrington / Artists Rights Society (ARS), New York; photo courtesy of National Museum of Women in the Arts

Figure 15.2 : Bruce Holsinger

Figure 15.3 : Bruce Holsinger

Figure 15.4: Bruce Holsinger

Figure 15.5: Bruce Holsinger

Figure 15.6: Bruce Holsinger

Figure 15.7: Women of the Book, a project by artist Shoshana Gugenheim, www.womenofthebook.org

Figure 15.8: Women of the Book, a project by artist Shoshana Gugenheim, www.womenofthebook.org

Figure 15.9: Women of the Book, a project by artist Shoshana Gugenheim, www.womenofthebook.org

Figure 15.10: Women of the Book, a project by artist Shoshana Gugenheim, www.womenofthebook.org

Figure 15.11: Women of the Book, a project by artist Shoshana Gugenheim, www.womenofthebook.org

Figure 15.12: Kate Nessler

Figure 15.13: Kate Nessler

Figure 15.14: Kate Nessler

Figure 15.15 : Kate Nessler

Figure 15.16: Kate Nessler

Figure 15.17: Kate Nessler

Figure 15.18: Mali Moir

Figure 15.19: Mali Moir

Figure 15.20: Mali Moir

Figure 15.21: Margaret J. Fitzpatrick
Figure 15.22: Anna Arca
Figure 15.23 : Anna Arca
Figure 15.24: Anna Arca
Figure 15.25: Denis Brown
Figure 15.26: Denis Brown
Figure 15.27: Denis Brown
Figure 15.28: Denis Brown
Figure 15.29: © 2015 Judith Serebrin, *Neither Here Nor There III*
Figure 16.1: Parker Library, Corpus Christi College, Cambridge
Figure 16.2: By permission of Erik Kwakkel

INDEX OF MANUSCRIPTS

Page numbers in *italics* indicate illustrations.

SUBJECT INDEX

Page numbers in *italics* indicate illustrations.

Bennett, J. A. W., 68

Bennett, Jane, 349n8

Ben-Or, Anne-Françoise, *318*, 319

Benton, Janetta, 109

Beowulf manuscript, survival of, 163

Berlin Leather Roll, 150–51

Bernard of Clairvaux, 17, 95–97, *97*

Bernardus de Gordonia, 72–75, *77*, *78*

Berne Riddles (*Ænigmata Bernensia*, 8th century), 184–85

Berthold of Regensburg, 92–94, *95*

bestiaries, 95

Bible: Augustine's *firmamentum* as Scripture, 167; Constantine I and archival scale of Bible production, 137; Exeter Book riddle about, 120, 137–82; Jerome's Vulgate, 123; Paris Bibles/pocket Bibles, 113, 273, *274*, 276, 277. *See also* Hebrew Bible; New Testament

Bigus, Richard, 309, *310*

biocodicology, 2, 273–87; aDNA studies, 277, 280–83, *284*, 286, 287; anthropodermic books, testing of, 195, 200; archive, as disposition toward, 286–87; cow metagenome, mapping, 286; of Dead Sea Scrolls, 281–83, *284*; defined, 276–78; erdu ("eraser doo"), collection of, 273–75, *274*; multidisciplinary and collaborative nature of, 276, 278–80; relative proportions of animals used to make parchment, 12th–14th centuries, 276, 277; scientism and, 279, 280; technologies used in, 275, 278, 283, 286; of Treaty of Waitangi (New Zealand, 1840), 283–86, *285*; of uterine vellum, 273, 276, 278

birchbark, as writing medium, 20

bird skin, 231–32, 236

Birthday Suit (Brown and Byron, 2003), 335, *335*–36

Bischoff, Bernhard, 26–27, 108, 123–24, *142*

Bitterli, Dieter, 366n35

Blackbourne Hundred, England, size of flock maintained at (1283), 124

Blackfriars gatehouse, London, Shakespeare's purchase of, 244–46, *245*, 249, 262

Bladen, F. M., 128–29, 356n61

Bleak House (Dickens, 1852–1853), 122

Bluff Dweller (Nessler, 2014), 323, *325*

Boccaccio, Giovanni, 4, 105–6, 113, 121

body as book, 5, 193–222; animal-human relations and, 194, 195, 196, 203, 207, 210–13, 217, 220–21, 222; anthropodermic bibliopegy (making books from human skin), 6, 195–204, *199*, *202*, *203*, 211, 222; Augustine's theology of parchment and, 162, 169; criminals, use of skin of, 200–201; Herodotus, on written skin, 157–60; John the Baptist and Lamb of God, 204–7, *205*–7; in martyrologies, 212, 237; Nietzsche's *Thus Spake Zarathustra* on, 222; premodern associations between, 193, 195–96, 211–22; resurrection of the body and, 193, 212; revolutionary associations of anthropodermic books, 193–200, *199*, *204*, 222; in Shakespeare's *Comedy of Errors*, 254–56; in Suso's *Exemplar*, 213–16, *214*–16. *See also* Christ, body of, parchment reflections of

body-color, 323

Boisrond-Tonnerre, Louis, 193–94, *195*

Boisseau, Michelle, 307

Boker, George Henry, 64

"The Book" (Vaughan, 1655), 300–302

Book of Lismore, 13, 15

Book of the Dun Cow (*Lebor na hUidhre*, before 1106), 14, *14*–15

The Book of the Queen (France, ca. 1410–1414), *78*

bookbindings: from human skin, 6, 195–204, *199*, *202*; from parchment, 99–103, *100*–*103*

bookworm/bookmoth riddle in Exeter Book, 302

Codex Borgia (late 15th–early 16th century), 292

Borland, Jennifer, 28

Bosman, Anston, 248

Boston Massacre, *199*, 199–200

The Botanical Artist (periodical), 323

Durling, Nancy Vine, 94
Dzaha Dzaui, 292

Eadmer, 266
ecocriticism, literary, 297–302
ecodicology, 288–306; Boxley Abbey rental
     rolls, 293–97, 295; William Keer Brown
     letters (1826) and, 296; byproduct, book
     as, 21, 39, III, 296, 302–5, 313; Codex Bor-
     gia, 292; cultural differences in attitudes
     toward parchment, 291–92, 292; defined,
     290–91; foodways and bookways, conver-
     gence of, 302–5, 305; literary ecocriticism
     and, 297–302; nature and culture, inter-
     relationship of, 2–3, 289–90; repurposing
     and recycling of parchment, 16–17, 36, 289,
     309–10, 311, 348n11 (See also palimpsests);
     Sarajevo Haggadah, in Brooks' People of
     the Book, 288–89; sustainability of medie-
     val manuscript practice, 289, 302–3
edge pieces of hide, pages taken from, 68, 70–73
Edinburgh Review, 196
Edward III (Shakespeare and Anonymous),
     250
Egypt: Alexandria, destruction of library of,
     138, 142; early parchment/leather from, 2,
     6, 8, 150–52, 151, 153; papyrus from, 4, 147
Egyptian mathematical leather roll, 150, 151
Ehrer, Georgius Dionysius, 322, 323
Eisenstein, Elizabeth, 349n28
Eisnitz, Gale, 19
elephant intestines, parchment made from, 149
Elijah (biblical figure), 232, 241
Elizabeth I (queen of England), 260, 262
Elzas, Nathan, 367n24
embroidered repairs, 92–94, 95, 321, 353n24
Emerson, Ralph Waldo, 159
Enarrationes in psalmos (Augustine), 166,
     174–78
Encyclopaedia Brittanica, 296
Encyclopédie (1751–72), on parchment making,
     59–63, 61, 62
Engelbrecht, Martin, 54, 55
England. See Britain

Enigmata ("Eusebius," prob. Hwaetberht, ab-
     bot of Wearmouth, 8th century), 185–86
environmental history of parchment. See
     ecodicology
The Environmental Imagination (Buell, 1995),
     297–98
Epigrams (Martial), 161–62
eraser method for collecting biomolecular
     data, 273–75, 274
erdu ("eraser doo"), 273, 274
Essenic origin theory of Dead Sea Scrolls, 282,
     283
Essex Record Office, England, 127
ethical treatment of animals and use of parch-
     ment, 19–20, 21, 22
Ethiopian Orthodox Church: Ge'ez an-
     tiphonary, 65, 66; Ge'ez colophon, from
     Pistola Octoteuch, 37; parchment mak-
     ing by, 42
Etymologies (Isidore of Seville, 7th century), 65,
     70, 148–49
Eulaila of Barcelona, hymn of Prudentius to
     (4th century), 212
Eumenes (king of Pergamon), 147
Eusebius (prob. Hwaetberht, abbot of Wear-
     mouth), 185–86
Eusebius of Caesaria, 137
Euzoius, 165
Every Twelve Seconds (Pachirat, 2014), 19
Exemplar (Das Buch von dem Diener/The Book
     of the Servant; Henry Suso, 14th cen-
     tury), 213–16, 214–16, 225
Exeter Book (10th century), 120, 179–83, 184,
     302, 303, 359n10

Fagrskinna (Icelandic saga), 28
Falconiformes (Moir, 2013), 326–28, 328
Fasiculus Morum (14th century), 217
The Fat-Hen Field Hospital (Byron, 1985–1992),
     119
Faustus of Mileve, 166, 169–70
Fergus mac Roich (king of Ulster), 14
Fes, Morocco, tanneries of, 37–38
"The Fiddler" (Boker, 1869), 64

Fiddyment, Sarah, 275, 280, 286

Fínghin Mac Carthaigh Riabhach (prince of Carbery), 13

fish skin, 1, 4, 65, 125, 232–33, 236

Fisher, John (bishop of Rochester), 220

Fishman, Talya, 229, 362n15

Fitzpatrick, Margaret, 329–30, *331*

Flaubert, Gustave, 199

flayed/flawed pages, 64–104; assemblage into quires or booklets, 75, *76*, 81; bookbindings, 99–103, *100–103*; conservators, repairs by, 65; drape (malleability/bendability) of membrane, 80–81; drawing attention to/making use of flaws, 92–97, *94–98*; edge pieces of hide, pages taken from, 68, *70–73*; embroidered repairs, 92–94, *95*, 321, 353n24; follicle marks, 80, *232–34*, 236, *248*, *249*; hair/wool, remnants of, 75, *78*; holes, working around, 65–67, *66*, *68*, *69*, 75, *77*, *78*, 92, *93*, *94–97*, *97*, *337*, *337–40*, *338*; modern artists working with, 330–31, *331*, *337*, *337–40*, *338*; molding, cockling, and bulging, 80, *81*; pigmentation signatures, 80, *83*; reader's experience of text affected by, 72–75, *78*, *79*; red, outlining holes with, 92, *94*, *95*; shape of page, irregularities in, 67–72, *70–74*; spine imprints, 81, *83*, 90, *90–92*, *91*; sutured repairs, 65, *67*, 75, *76*, 97–99, *98*, *99*; swan rolls and swan marks, 92, *93*; thick contoured edge membranes, 68, *72*, 75, *77*; veining, 75, *78*, *79*, *248*, *249*, 330, *331*; whole-hide membranes, documents making use of shape of, 81–92, *83–85*, *87*, *88*, *90*, *91*; as "wounds" in parchment, 92

flesh versus hair side of parchment, 27, 28, 31, 33, 58, 111, 230–31, 234–35, 293, 307, 349n6

follicle marks, 80, 232–34, 236, 248, 249

food. *See* diet

Forest and Stream, 299

Forsyth, Mark, 124

fossil record, as archive, 287

Fourth book of occult philosophy (1665, attrib. Nettesheim), 114, *115*

Foys, Martin, 342

France: *The Book of the Queen* (ca. 1410–1414), *78*; Charlemagne, monastic grants by, 304–5; Chartreuse of Champmol, inventory of (1388–1399), 303–4; public records in, 133; relative proportions of animals used to make parchment, 12th–14th centuries, 276, *277*; Rohan Hours (1420–1440), 208–10, *211*; Saint-Médard de Soissons, Gospels of, 207–8, *209*; Valmagne, size of flocks owned by Cistercians of, 124

Franciscans, 24, 92, 217

Franklin, Colin, *310*

French Constitution of 1793 (Montagnard Constitution), 194–95, *196*, 197

French Revolution, 194–200

The French Revolution (Carlyle, 1837), 196–97

Fritz the Parchment-maker, 53–54, *54*

Gabriel (archangel), 60, 240, 303

Gallé, Émile, 199

Gamble, Harry, 165

Gameson, Richard, 124

Gascoigne, George, 102–3, *103*

Gaston d'Orleans (brother of Louis XIII), 322

gazelle skin, 1, 17, 86, 126, 239

Ge'ez antiphonary, 65, *66*

Ge'ez colophon, from Pistola Octoteuch, 37

Gemara, 230–33

gender issues: Eadmer on word of bishop versus words written on skin of castrated ram, 266; love spell written on skin of female dog in heat, 4, 18–19; parchment makers, female, 54, *55*

genizah, ritual deposition of discarded documents in, 22, 163

The Gentlemans Exercise (Peacham, 1661), 114, *116*

Geometria (Sylvester II, 10th–11th century), 67, *69*

George III (king of England), memorandum book of, 125, 355n20

Gerard, John, 301

Hebron Valley, Israel, camel skin parchment from, 150

Heliopolis, temple of Atun at, 150

Hellebore (Nessler), 323, *326*

Henry I (king of England), 266

2 Henry VI (Shakespeare), 22, 264–67, 269, 349n30

Henry VIII (king of England), 255, 261

Herbert, George, 300

Hereford Mappa Mundi (ca. 1300), *83*, 83–84

Herodotus, *Histories*: on origins of parchment use, 156–60; papyrus most likely used by, 156, 157; Shakespeare's *Comedy of Errors* compared, 255–56; survival of, 2, 163–64

Hilliard, Nicholas, 115–16

Hinduism, parchment eschewed in, 24

hinges in folded parchment, 27

Histaeus, 157–58

Histoire d'Haïti (Madious, 1847), 193

Historia adversus paganos, Orosius's Old English translation of (late 9th century), *80*, 97, *98*

Historia Novorum in Anglia (Eadmer, ca. 1123), 266

A History of Miniature Art (Propert, 1887), 108

history of parchment, 147–64; in ancient Near East, 149–56, *153–55*; Christian book culture and adoption of, 136–37, 160, 165–66; Herodotus on, 156–60; origin legends, 147–50; in Roman empire, 160–63; survival of Herodotus's works and, 163–64

History of Sanskrit Literature (Macdonnell, 1900), 291

The Hobbit (Tolkien, 1937), 180

Hoccleve, Thomas, 127

holes in parchment pages, 65–67, *66*, *68*, *69*, 75, *77*, *78*, 92, *93*, 94–97, *97*, 337, *337–40*, *338*

Holinshed, Ralph, *Chronicles* (16th century), 260–61, 264

Holocaust, 222

Homer, 2, 161, 162

Horace, survival of works of, 2

Horwood, John, 201

Hough, John Stockton, 201–2

Howe, Christopher, 283

Hrokkinskinna (Icelandic saga), 28

Hugh of St. Victor, 44

human body as book. *See* body as book

human skin: anthropodermic bibliopegy (making books from human skin), 6, 195–204, *199*, *202*, *203*, 211, 222; Herodotus on writing on, 157–58

human-animal relations. *See* animal-human relations

Rabbi Huna, 232, 233

Hunt Institute for Botanical Documentation, 322

Hwaetberht (abbot of Wearmouth; probably identity of Eusebius, *Enigmata*, 8th century), 185–86

Ibn al-Nadīm, 5–6, 140

Ibrāhīm Al Mursī, 86

Iceland: condition of parchment used, saga manuscripts named for, 28; *Jónsbók* (ca. 1500), 94; *Margrétar saga* (ca. 1500), scribal comments about parchment quality in, *30*, *31*; Old Icelandic Homily Book, sealskin wrapper for (ca. 1200), *100*

Ilerbaig, Juan, 122

Ilich, Ivan, 184

Illuminated Manuscripts (Bradley, 1905), 108

illumination. *See* manuscript illumination

In (Waterhouse, 2000), 191

India and Asia, scarcity of parchment manuscripts in, 24, 291–92, 365n13

indigenous American cultures: Codex Borgia (late 15th–early 16th century), 292; mammal hide documents created by, 24

Instagram, 344

Insular manuscripts. See *specific volumes*

Introduction to Greek and Latin Palaeography (Sir Edward Maunde Thompson, 1912), 108

Ionian Revolt, 157–58

Iphigenia, sacrifice of, 139

Ireland: Carrington's *Samhain Skin* and, 4, 307–9, *308*; St. Ciarán and the Book of the Dun Cow, 13–16, 23, 24, 25, 59, 184,

Katz, Joseph, and drumhead-manufacturing firm, 334, 367n24

Kay, Sarah, 28–29, 94–95, 187, 304

Kent County Archives, England, 127

Kerma, Sudan, parchment fragments from, 150

Kesavan, Belary Shamanna, 24, 291–92

Keset ha-Sofer (1835), 111

Khurasani paper, 35, 36

Ki tisa (Jawerbaum), 319, 320

King John (Shakespeare), 259–62, 269

King Lear (Shakespeare), 263–64

Kingdom, Francis, 200

Kirby, David, *Animal Factory*, 19

Kiryat Sefer (Menahem Hameiri, 13th–14th century), 110–11

Kitāb al-Fihrist (Ibn al-Nadīm, tenth century), 5–6, 140

Kite, Marion, 309

Klaf Bak, Jerusalem, *43*

Knight, Leah, 301

Knust, Jennifer, 356n55

Kreiner, Jamie, 3

Kurke, Leslie, 157

Kwakkel, Erik, 342–45, *343*

Lacroix, Paul, 366n47

Lalande, Joseph Jérôme Le Français de, 60–63, *61*, *62*, 351n39

Land Tax Act (UK, 1821), 128, *130*

Landscape in Poetry (Palgrave, 1897), 300

Latin Palaeography (Bischoff, 1979), 26–27, 123–24

Latour, Bruno, 349n8

Laurence, Thomas, *199*

Leabhar Buidhe Lecain (Yellow Book of Lecan, ca. 1400), *70*

Leabhar Ua Maine (14th century), *66*

Leavis, F. R., 279

Lebor na hUidhre (Book of the Dun Cow; before 1106), 14, *14–15*

lectio divina, 52, 189

Leopold, Aldo, 144, 288

leprosy, 229, 337–40, *338*

Letter of Aristeas (ca. 140–60), 8

Letter of Tansar (2nd century), 140, 356nn60–61

Leviticus, 231–32, 317, 319, 337, *338*

Liber A sive pilosus, 100

liber/codex, conflation of, 168–69

Liddell-Grainger, Ian, 314

Life of Constantine (Eusebius of Caesaria, 4th century), 137

Life of St. Gregory the Great (John the Deacon, 9th century), 75, 79

Lindisfarne Gospels (c. 700), 191–92

literary ecocriticism, 297–302

Livy, 161

Rabbi Loew of Prague and the golem, 223–24, 361n1

Louis XIII (king of France), 322

lunellum, 33, 38, 49, 50, 51, 52, 53, 54, 56

Lunow, Robert, 103

Lüthi, Karl Jakob, 309–10, *311*

Lydgate, John, 190–91, 303

Lynch, Mary, 201–2

MacCullouch, Diarmaid, 136–37

Macdonnell, Arthur Anthony, 291

Madious, Thomas, 193

magical texts on parchment, 4, 17–19, 105–6, 114, 161, 224, 237–39, 362n15

Magna Carta, 260–61

Maidstone Gazette, 296

Maimonides (Moses ben Maimon), 58, 110, 224, 234–36, 362n17

The Maine Woods (Thoreau, 1864), 299

making parchment, 37–63; craft workers involved in, 37–45, *40*, *41*, *43*; curing and removal of hair, 37, 38; on *Dirty Jobs* (TV show), 350n4; drying, stretching, scraping, and finishing, 38–40, *40*, *45*; *Encyclopédie* (1751–72) on, 59–63, *61*, *62*; flesh versus hair side, 27; hinges in folded parchment, 27; medieval recipes and instructions for, 45–49, *47*, 58; postmortem versus perimortem accounts of, 26; premodern visual depictions of, 49–58, *50*, *51*, *53–57*; Saqqara tomb relief, Egypt, depicting, 152, *152*; sourcing and slaughtering of

Pliny the Elder, 20, 147–48, 162, 312, 314

pocket Bibles, 113, 274, 276, 277

Poor Caitiff tracts, 220–21

Pope Joan (Cross, 1996), 142

portolan charts, 86–89, *87, 88*

posthumanist approaches to animal-human relations, 349n8

Practica dicta Lilium medicine (*Practical Sayings:
The Lily of Medicine*; Bernardus de Gordonia, 14th century), 72–75, *77, 78*

Preece, Rod, 358n9

printing, on vellum, 367n11. *See also* Parliamentary records, United Kingdom

Propert, John Lumsden, 108

Prudentius, 212

Prunes, Mateus, and Prunes chart (1559), 86,
88

Psalm 23, 143

Ptolemy (Egyptian ruler), 147

Public Record Office (PRO), National Archives, Kew, England, 128–33, *131, 132,*
246, 294–95

pumice stone, 38, 46, 48–49, 55, *61, 62*

purple parchment, 148, 149

PVC eraser, used to gather biomolecular data,
273–75, *274*

al-Qarawiyyin (university), Fes, Morocco,
37–38

qelaf, 111, 227–28, 230–31, 234–35

quantity of parchment record. *See* archival
scale of parchment record

Qumran texts, 8, *162,* 163, 281–83, *284. See* Dead
Sea Scrolls

Qur'ān: ram sacrificed by Abraham in place of
Isaac, hide of, 240; survival of early texts
of, 2, 9, 16; tradition of original parchment
version of, 59–60

ram sacrificed by Abraham in place of Isaac,
use of hide of, 6, 23, 60, 239–43, *240, 242,*
290

Rashi (Jewish commentator), 234, 240

Rav (Jewish sage), 232–33, 361n5

Ravel, Daniel, 322

Ravina, 232

Read, Ronald, 45

red ink or thread, outlining holes with, 92, *94,
95*

Reed, Ronald, 309

repurposing and recycling of parchment, 16–
17, 36, 289, 309–10, 311, 348n11. *See also*
palimpsests

resurrection of the body as book, 193, 212

revolution: anthropodermic books associated
with, 193–200, *199, 204,* 222; Jack Cade in
Shakespeare's *2 Henry VI* and, 264–67.
See also specific revolutions

Revolutionary War, 200

Richard II (Shakespeare), 250, 262–64, 269, 313

Richard III (king of England), 312

Richard of Bury, 137–39, 141, 142

riddling about parchment, 179–92; Anglo-
Latin riddling tradition, 180, 183, 359n10;
animal voice in, 181, 184, 185, 186–87, 191–
92; Berne Riddles (*Ænigmata Bernensia*), 184–85; Brown's calligraphic use of
Old English book riddle, *335, 336;* ecodicology and, 300; Eusebius (prob. Hwaetberht, abbot of Wearmouth), *Enigmata,*
185–86; Exeter Book, 120, 179–83, *184,*
302, *303,* 359n10; Judah HaLevi, 179; Lydgate's "Debate of the Horse, the Goose,
and the Sheep," 190–91; Tatwine's "De
membrano," 183–84; in Waterhouse's poetry, 191–92; *Ysengrimus,* 187–89

Rievaulx glossed Book of Genesis (12th century), sealskin binding of (before 1600),
100, 101

Rohan Hours (1420–1440), 208–10, *211*

Rolle, Richard, 219

Roman d'Alexandre (14th century), 54–58, *56,
57*

Roman empire: parchment used in, 160–63;
preference for papyrus, 160, 165

Round River (Leopold, 1949), 288

Rousseau, Jean-Jacques, 197–99

Rubinson, Sylvia, 319, *320*

Talmud (*continued*)

33, 361n5; Soferim (tractate), 229; on split parchment, 58–59; Tefillin (tractate), 229; tefillin, on appropriate sources of parchment for, 4, 17, 111, 116, 226, 227, 228–30, 232–35; Torah scrolls, parchment used for, 223, 226, 228, 230, 233–36

Tatwine, 183–84

The Teaching of Addai (ca. 400), 193, 212

Teasdale, Matthew, 283

tefillin, parchment used for, 4, 17, 111, 116, 226, 227, 228–30, 232–35

Tegg, Thomas, 200

Temple Scroll, Dead Sea Scrolls, *162, 163*

Ten Martyrs of Emperor Hadrian, 237

terefot, 227, 230

The Testament of the Bucke (late Middle English), 303

Thackeray, William Makepeace, "An Original Edition" (1888), 197–99

theology of parchment, 4, 162, 165–78. *See also* Augustine of Hippo

Theotokos Chrysopodaritissa, monastery of, Peloponnese, 352n12

Thomas, Marcel, 124

Thomas Aquinas, 125

Thompson, Daniel Varney, 108–9, 303

Thompson, Lawrence, 195

Thompson, Sir Edward Maunde, 108

Thomson, Roy, 309

Thoreau, Henry David, 290, 299

Thus Spake Zarathustra (Nietzsche, 1883), 222

Tibet, animal skin manuscripts from, 292

Tolkien, J. R. R., 180

"Tools for Body Writing" (de Certeau, 1988), 244, 255

Torah scrolls: Rabbi Hanina burnt with, 237; magical/sacred properties of parchment written with name of God/Torah verses, 17, 224, 237–39, 362n15; parchment used for, 23, 43–44, 110–11, 116–17, 223, 226, 228, 230, 233–36; *Sefer Torah*, 229, 362n11; "Women of the Book" project, 317–22, *318, 320, 321*

Torfæus, Tormod, 349n5

trade books, parchment makers in, 52–54, *53–55*

Treaty of Waitangi (New Zealand, 1840), 283–86, *285*

Treharne, Elaine, 349n8

Tristia (Ovid), 125

Trithemius, Johannes (abbot of Sponheim), 20–21, 349n28

Tromdámh Guaire (Middle Irish text), 13–15

The Troublesome Reign of King John (Anonymous), 260

The Truth of Ecology (Philips, 2003), 297–98

Tumblr, 344

Turner, Decherd, *310*

Turner, Robert, 114, 116

Twitter, 342–45, *343*

tzimtzum, 319

unborn skin. *See* uterine vellum

United Kingdom. *See* Britain

U.S. Declaration of Independence, on parchment, 17

uterine vellum, 105–21; biocodicology of, 273, 276, 278; Boccaccio's *Decameron* on, 4, 105–6, 113, 121; Catherine Byron on, 336; defined, 107–8, 115–16; *Encyclopédie* (1751–72) on, 61; fetal animals, use of skins of, 43, 61; Jewish communities' use of, 43, 111, 116–17; medieval/early modern literary and historical accounts of, 105–6, 113–16; medieval/early modern rates of animal miscarriage/stillbirth, 112–13; modern industrial beef production and commercial availability of, 43, 111, 112; modern novelists and poets on, 117–21; modern skepticism about actual origins of, 108–10, 116; physical properties of, *107*; ritual magic, used for, 105–6, 114; split parchment versus, 109–11; virgin parchment and, 106, 113–16, *115*

Valmagne, size of flocks owned by Cistercians of, 124

York play of Abraham and Isaac (14th century), performed by parchment-makers
and bookbinders, 240, 362n30
Youngston Coll, Laura, 330–34, 332, 333
Ysengrimus (12th century), 187–89

Zeini, Arash, 356n61
Rabbi Zera, 232

Ziegler, Waltraud, 183
Ziereis, Franz, 222
Zodiac Man, 89
Zohar (13th century), 60, 241, 290
Zoroaster, 140, 141
Zoroastrian *Avesta*, creation and loss of, 4,
139–41, 303